MW01196897

A History of the
University of Wisconsin
System

A History of the
University of Wisconsin System

Patricia A. Brady

The University of Wisconsin Press

Publication of this book has been made possible, in part,
through support from the Anonymous Fund
of the College of Letters and Science at the University of Wisconsin–Madison.

The University of Wisconsin Press
728 State Street, Suite 443
Madison, Wisconsin 53706
uwpress.wisc.edu

Gray's Inn House, 127 Clerkenwell Road
London EC1R 5DB, United Kingdom
eurospanbookstore.com

Printed in the United States of America

This book may be available in a digital edition.

Library of Congress Cataloging-in-Publication Data

Names: Brady, Patricia A., author.
Title: A history of the University of Wisconsin System / Patricia A. Brady.
Description: Madison, Wisconsin: The University of Wisconsin Press, [2020]
| Includes bibliographical references and index.
Identifiers: LCCN 2019039026 | ISBN 9780299326401 (cloth)
Subjects: LCSH: University of Wisconsin System—History.
| Public universities and colleges—Wisconsin—History.
| Education, Higher—Wisconsin—History.
Classification: LCC LD6096 .B725 2020 | DDC 378.775—dc23
LC record available at https://lccn.loc.gov/2019039026

Contents

Preface

Why write a history of the University of Wisconsin System? It was not a long-term goal or personal ambition or anything I could have imagined doing when I arrived as a freshman at the University of Wisconsin–Madison in 1968. At that time, the UW System did not even exist, and the political battles that would eventually lead to its creation were overshadowed by the campus turmoil from anti–Vietnam War demonstrations and protests over civil rights and related social problems. While I was aware of the proposal to merge UW–Madison and the other state universities, it seemed far less important than the national issues consuming the campus at the time. It was not until years later, in my career as a lawyer, that I became interested in public higher education and the story of the UW System and its institutions. I joined the System's legal office in 1980, later becoming the System's general counsel, and in those roles was both an observer and an occasional actor in many of the events that have affected the System since merger. As my professional involvement grew, my interest in the System's history deepened. Most UW institutions have been the subjects of individual histories, and there is a comprehensive four-volume history of the University of Wisconsin, from its founding in 1848 to 1971 (available online through UW's Digital Collections). These histories are valuable resources in understanding the unique traditions and special concerns of individual UW campuses, but there is no history of the System itself, leaving a gap in the story of statewide, postmerger higher education that this book attempts to address.

The UW System is, in essence, an organization of organizations, and its history contains many narratives. Capturing in a single volume all the key social, economic, and political events that have shaped the System, together with all the remarkable individual achievements of UW institutions and faculty, staff, and students, is simply not possible. Here, I have focused primarily on the System's organizational and administrative development, its support for the growth and success of UW institutions, and its unifying role in Systemwide policy matters, resource allocation, and higher education issues advocacy. As a result, many events and accomplishments of UW institutions—as well as of important divisions within institutions, such as the Law and Medical Schools and major athletics programs—are omitted or not fully detailed in this book. This story is also, inevitably, "Madison-centric," partly because of the sheer size of UW–Madison's operations relative to those of the System as a whole, partly because the System's administrative structure borrowed heavily from the Madison model, but perhaps most importantly because UW–Madison, with its national prominence and distinguished academic reputation, historic traditions, and familiar brand, is critical to the success of the entire System organization. To recognize the important contributions of other UW institutions, I have included a brief appendix describing their unique origins and a sampling of their achievements.

Although the emphasis on the UW System as an entity leaves much individual and institutional accomplishment out of the narrative, there is much to be learned from its successes and struggles in the years since merger. As an organization, despite its roots in the rich historic traditions of the Wisconsin Idea and academic freedom, the System has always had to justify its existence, confronted from the beginning by internal consolidation challenges, budget problems, and political attacks. Despite the remarkable academic, research, and service achievements of UW institutions, state taxpayer support has continued to decline and pleas for reinvestment have been largely unsuccessful. For those who care about the UW System and UW institutions, for those who are interested in public higher education, and for those in state and national government who set policy and provide financial support, this history offers a frame of reference and lessons for those who will lead the System and state public higher education into the future.

*A History of the
University of Wisconsin
System*

Introduction

Provision shall be made by law for the establishment of a state university at or near the seat of government, and for connecting with the same, from time to time, such colleges in different parts of the state as the interests of education may require.

Article X, Section 6, Wisconsin Constitution
(1848)

Whatever may be the limitations which trammel inquiry elsewhere, we believe the great state University of Wisconsin should ever encourage that continual and fearless sifting and winnowing by which alone the truth can be found.

The Board of Regents of the University of Wisconsin,
Decision in the Matter of Professor Richard Ely
(1894)

The boundaries of the university are the boundaries of the state.

The Wisconsin Idea

The legislature finds it in the public interest to provide a system of higher education. . . . Basic to every purpose of the system is the search for truth.

Section 36.01, Wisconsin Statutes

The University of Wisconsin System was established in October 1971, with the passage of legislation merging all of Wisconsin's public colleges and universities into a single, consolidated organization. Although a new entity, the merged System had deep historical roots. The state's 1848 Constitution required the establishment of a state university at the capital and anticipated the addition of colleges at other locations, ensuring that state government would provide higher education opportunities for citizens throughout the state. While not all the constitution's framers were college educated, they saw in higher education the means of preparing individuals to become productive citizens and leaders, along with the civic and economic value of expanding knowledge and sharing it broadly for the benefit of the entire state. The constitutional provision reflecting their vision supported the expansion of higher education in the state from the founding of the University of Wisconsin at Madison, in 1848, through the subsequent addition of teacher-training and specialized professional institutions in the late nineteenth and early twentieth centuries.

As the state's teacher and technical training institutions expanded their curricular offerings and supported thriving local economies and civic life, the original University of Wisconsin at Madison gained national prominence as a leading academic and research institution. Its Board of Regents provided a powerful endorsement of the principles of academic freedom in the 1894 tenure trial of Richard Ely, committing the institution to the fearless and untrammeled search for truth. An early member of the American Association of Universities (AAU), the University pursued both research and its practical applications, offering direct services to state citizens through its extension programs. The constitutional framers' belief in extending the reach and impact of higher education was further elaborated by University president Charles Van Hise, who in 1905 formulated what would evolve into the widely admired Wisconsin Idea, the belief that the benefits of a state university should extend beyond the campus to all citizens, in all parts of the state. Later popularly expressed as the principle that the boundaries of the university are the boundaries of the state and beyond, the Wisconsin Idea was embraced by Van Hise's successors and endorsed by state government leaders.

The state's commitment to providing high-quality, accessible higher education continued through the post–World War II era, as demand increased, enrollments grew, and new campuses and degree programs were added. By 1971, the steady expansion of public higher education had resulted in what were, in effect, two state university "systems": The University of Wisconsin (UW) and the Wisconsin State Universities (WSU). The UW comprised the original Madison campus, UW–Milwaukee, colleges at Green Bay and Parkside, and the UW–Extension, together with ten two-year centers, while the WSU consisted of nine institutions with origins as teacher training and technical institutes and their own two-year satellites. In all, state higher education included thirteen colleges and universities, fourteen two-year campuses, and extension programs in every county. The 1971 merger combined this diverse set of institutions, establishing a new entity, the University of Wisconsin System (UW System or System), which inherited the state's legacy of strong support for public higher education and recognition of its central importance to economic and civic success.

This volume explores the events, conditions, and challenges that have shaped the UW System since the merger, a period that includes not only remarkable individual and institutional achievements but also disruptive organizational change, financial adversity, and weakening political support. Since its creation, the System—through its institutions, faculty, staff, and students—has produced academic, research, and extracurricular achievements too numerous to list. From groundbreaking scientific accomplishments such as the creation of pluripotent stem cells to liberal arts achievements such as the completion of the *Dictionary of American Regional English*, the UW System's flagship Madison campus has burnished its national and international standing as a preeminent academic and research institution. UW–Milwaukee has grown in stature as an urban institution, while developing and enhancing its own research capacity. UW–Extension has continued its successful state outreach activities, while the regional comprehensive campuses have enhanced their program offerings, sharpening their focus on specialized programs and improving the undergraduate experience. Each of the thirteen universities and the thirteen two-year colleges, as well as the statewide UW–Extension service, has promoted local economic growth and provided important community services. Supporting foundations have increased private endowment support, while the Wisconsin Alumni Research Foundation, its subsidiary WiSys, and the UWM Research Foundation have helped make university research advances available to the public through patents, licenses, and new business enterprises. The System as an organization has successfully coordinated budgets and educational programing, operating with exceptional efficiency. These successes reflect the resilience and ingenuity of the institutions and individuals that make up the System, as well as the enduring vitality of state founders' vision for public higher education and the values and principles embodied in the Wisconsin Idea.

From the beginning, however, the System has operated in an increasingly hostile environment for public higher education, both in Wisconsin and nationally. From its initial organizational difficulties through the shifting fiscal, social, and political dynamics of the late twentieth century, the financial stress resulting from the Great Recession of 2007–9, and pressures in the 2010s to restructure and alter its mission, the System has contended with declining governmental financial resources, damaging political conflicts, and challenges to its educational purposes and economic and civic value. While other public universities have confronted similar kinds of difficulties, the UW System's history reflects challenges and struggles unique to public higher education in Wisconsin.

The merger itself was driven not by past successes but by mounting problems. By 1970, the state confronted rapidly increasing higher education costs, the uncoordinated growth of its two older university "systems," a lagging economy and—because of the aging of the baby boom generation—the prospect of declining demand for college. In addition, the violent anti–Vietnam War protests of the 1960s had culminated in the bombing of Sterling Hall on the Madison campus in August. The convergence of these fiscal and demographic problems, national trends, and public pressure to assert control over campus chaos led newly elected governor Patrick Lucey to propose the merger, which became effective on October 12, 1971, within a year of his taking office.

The immediate postmerger period brought organizational instability and internal conflicts stemming from the effort to combine two very different entities. With their distinct historical roots, differences in academic offerings and size, diverse individual missions, and traditional independence, the institutions of the former UW and WSU "systems" did not fit comfortably within a common governance structure. Resistance to changes in their past policies and practices, as well as concerns about loss of identity, dilution of resources, and differential treatment in the combined System, created internal conflicts. Although a solid legal framework for the System was developed during a two-year postmerger implementation period, questions over whether the System should function as a loose federation of independent institutions or a more centralized, unitary organization lingered, feeding ongoing doubts about the wisdom of merger and the viability of the System.

Compounding these organizational challenges were harsh new fiscal realities. The merger effectively marked the end of an era of free-wheeling public higher education growth in the state and the beginning of a long, steady decline in state financial support. Lucey's first budget as governor included a significant reduction in funding for the newly combined System. Later shifts in governmental priorities and a prevailing small government, antitax political climate brought diminishing levels of state taxpayer support for public higher education. The political unwillingness to expand tax revenues or alter spending priorities produced a kind of zero-sum game in which increasing state funds for programs such as health care, prisons, and elementary through high school educational programs translated directly to decreasing taxpayer support for the UW System. Federal expenditures for higher education in the form of research grants and financial aid followed a similar trajectory of uncertainty or decline. The fiscal instability resulting from this long-term erosion of governmental support has made it increasingly difficult for System institutions to preserve academic quality, continue world-class research programs, and maintain broad, affordable access to educational opportunity for state citizens.

Exacerbating these financial problems, relations between political and university leaders have become increasingly strained since the System's creation. The merger was preceded by a major restructuring of all state government agencies in the 1960s that brought them more directly under gubernatorial control and concentrated authority over state budget development in the state's Department of Administration. At the same time, the legislature became a full-time body of career politicians, supported by its own bureaucracy of full-time staff, councils, and research agencies. These changes came with heightened state scrutiny of the operations of the newly merged System, along with more aggressive regulatory efforts, audits, information demands, and state governmental intervention in university affairs. The respect for academic leaders that once characterized the relations between state government and the two older university systems began to erode, replaced by skepticism, criticism, and, often, open hostility from political leaders. Despite some notably successful and constructive collaborative efforts in the late 1990s and early 2000s, the deterioration in relationships between political and university leaders has continued to accelerate, while partisanship in System governance and polarization in the state political climate have grown. In the 2010s, these trends have been reflected in the unsuccessful 2011 attempt to separate UW–Madison from the System, punitive state budget cuts in the 2013–15 and 2015–17 biennia, and related efforts to undermine central System administrative leadership. Adding to these tensions, the decade has also seen attacks on the Wisconsin Idea, academic freedom and faculty governance, and free speech, along with state governmental pressures to tie funding for System institutions to performance in meeting workforce demands, and a major restructuring of the System's two-year UW colleges and Extension organizations.

Paralleling the decline in financial and political backing, public support for higher education has weakened over the course of the UW System's history. Anger over the Vietnam War protests subsided with the end of that conflict, but other campus social issues—from demands by women and minorities for equal opportunity and affirmative action, to complaints about the presence of the ROTC on campus, to efforts to prevent hate speech and sexual assault, to sensitivity training designed to enhance understanding of discriminatory attitudes—have continued to spark public criticism, contributing to campus culture wars, debates about the meaning of free speech and academic freedom, and claims of liberal bias on the part of university leadership and faculty. Confusion about the purposes and goals of higher education has grown, as a college education has increasingly come to be seen as a private benefit rather than a civic, public good. Confidence that a college degree provides the means to a secure middle-class life has also been shaken. In the grim economic times following the Great Recession of 2007–9, rising tuition and mounting student debt have stirred concerns that the benefits of a college education are outweighed by its costs. Questions remain, too, about whether higher education should focus on ensuring the immediate employability of graduates—producing trained workers in areas of need—or on providing a flexible liberal education that gives students the skills to succeed in a wide range of professions and prepares them more broadly for leadership roles.

The UW System—its institutions, staff, students, and leaders— have from the beginning managed in the face of these and other challenges, adapting to changing conditions and seeking solutions to institutional problems, while maintaining a remarkable record of academic and research achievement despite diminishing financial resources, fiscal instability, political hostility, and pressures to fundamentally alter its mission, purposes, and structure. This history reflects the enduring power of the Wisconsin Idea and the institutional resilience and momentum that continue to support great achievements even in an adverse climate. If past is prologue, there is reason for confidence that these strengths will bring continued success. The long-term toll taken by the hostile environment for higher education, however, remains a threat, leaving the UW System vulnerable to erosion in quality and undermining its ongoing ability to fulfill the state constitution's promise of educational opportunity for Wisconsin's citizens. Despite its strong record of accomplishment, the System cannot sustain achievement indefinitely without a renewed commitment on the part of state citizens and leaders to preserving the state's legacy of support for public higher education. In 1848, Wisconsin's founders had the foresight to recognize the pivotal role higher education could play in the success of their young state. Their vision inspired the growth and development of a strong and successful state higher education system that has repeatedly proven its value to the citizens of the state, the nation, and beyond. The constitutional promise remains. Ensuring that the benefits of public higher education remain for future generations will depend on a renewed commitment to fulfulling that promise.

↳ This book is designed to generate that support.

Merger

Establishing
the University of Wisconsin System

Prelude: Madison, 1970

It would become the most violent year in the history of the University of Wisconsin. The Madison campus had already seen several years of turbulent anti–Vietnam War protests. From the Dow Chemical riots of 1967 and continuing throughout 1969, there had been numerous demonstrations against the war, accompanied by rising levels of destructiveness and occasional violence. With the drumbeat of antiwar unrest constantly in the background, there were also protests over other social issues, such as the 1969 "Black Strike," a series of actions in response to demands of black students for the creation of an African American Studies department and other changes. The rhetoric of protest had become more radical, and calls for revolutionary action to stop the war and change society were common. The recurring demonstrations and the resulting disruptions had, by the end of 1969, become norms of campus life. But in 1970, the situation would get much worse.

The year began with a bungled attempt, on January 1, at bombing a campus landmark, the Old Red Gym, located on

11

Langdon Street near the Memorial Student Union. The attack was the work of a small group of radical students and former students led by Madison native Karleton Armstrong, later known as the New Year's Day Gang. A few weeks later, the university's teaching assistants went on strike, effectively shutting down many classes, as students refused—or were afraid—to cross picket lines. In late April, President Richard Nixon ordered the bombing of Cambodia, touching off more—and more violent— antiwar protests, the intensity of which increased with the shooting deaths, on May 4, 1970, of four students at Kent State University in Ohio. For much of the rest of that month, Bascom Hall was visible only through a haze of tear gas, as student demonstrators took their protests to the streets on an almost daily basis, clashing with local police, county sheriffs, and the Wisconsin National Guard, which was called up to help quell the unrest. The confrontations followed a pattern: the students rallied on Bascom Hill to march to the state Capitol a mile away, only to be forced back by tear-gas-wielding law enforcement officers stationed at the base of the hill. Madison's chancellor, H. Edwin Young, managed to keep the campus nominally open, but the disturbances were a constant distraction, bringing normal academic routines to a standstill. So many classes had been canceled or missed by the end of the semester that an ad hoc grading process had to be adopted, allowing students to take pass-fail grades or be graded on whatever work they had actually completed. Facing public ire over the chaos and under pressure from his own Board of Regents, University of Wisconsin president Fred Harvey Harrington announced his resignation at the May 11, 1970, board meeting, to be effective in October.[1] The campus limped to the end of the spring term in a fog of tear gas and academic dysfunction.

The disturbances of spring gave way to relative calm as the campus emptied of students for the summer months. And then, on August 24, Armstrong and his New Year's Day Gang returned to commit one of the worst acts of domestic terrorism in United States history, the bombing of Sterling Hall. The explosion caused the tragic death of researcher Robert Fassnacht and injured several others, while doing extensive damage to the building and surrounding campus area. Shocked by the bombing, university administrators and the Board of Regents struggled to cope with the aftermath. As they worked to deal with the enormous damage to people and property, they focused on the immediate internal problems of the institution, including the need to find a replacement for Harrington—one who could, above all, restore order.

Madison's campus crisis would soon have wider consequences for public higher education in the state, though. A public already angry over years of campus disturbances was outraged by the bombing and demanded action. Politicians were equally impatient with the seeming inability of academic leaders to control an increasingly chaotic situation. With the 1970 midterm elections in progress, the gubernatorial candidates, Democrat Patrick J. Lucey and Republican Jack B. Olson, had early in the campaign made campus unrest an issue. Shortly after announcing his candidacy, in April 1970, Olson made a major speech blaming Democrats for campus disturbances and calling for stricter penalties for rioting and similar disruptions.[2] Lucey immediately responded to Olson by pointing out that the crisis on campus had developed under the Republican administration of Governor Warren Knowles and promising his own plan for dealing with the problem.[3] Beyond measures to punish or control protesters, however, Lucey saw an opportunity for much broader changes to state higher education. Long concerned with uncontrolled growth and the rising costs of operating both of the state's existing university systems, the University of Wisconsin (UW) and the Wisconsin State Universities (WSU), Lucey had already characterized higher education as "the worst run program in the state." In a June press conference, he suggested that consolidation of the two systems might be considered by the next governor, urging that neither Harrington's successor nor a replacement for Eugene McPhee, then planning to retire as leader of the WSU, be appointed until after the election so that structural changes in the state's two university systems could be considered by a new administration.[4]

The August bombing of Sterling Hall gave powerful new urgency to Lucey's calls for higher education reform. Concerned with ending the chaos on campus, in a statement on September 3, 1970, he declared that "the University of Wisconsin [at Madison] as a renowned institution of higher learning is near death. Another semester of violence and disruption will surely kill it as a great public university."[5] Public support for the University at

Madison had been seriously compromised, and he believed dramatic action was needed to stop the disturbances and to shield the state's premier university from what his aide and confidant David Adamany described as the "political hurricane" building up against it.[6] In Lucey's view, combining the UW and the WSU offered a means of protecting Madison. As part of a larger organization, the Madison campus would not stand out as the singular target of public and political anger. Elected governor in November 1970, Lucey moved swiftly to propose consolidating all of state public higher education into a single system. Within a year of taking office, he had achieved this merger, establishing the University of Wisconsin System, effective October 12, 1971.

The End of a Golden Age

The public higher education "program" that Lucey had attacked during the campaign as the state's worst-run activity consisted, in 1970, of a large and diverse group of postsecondary institutions, of widely varying sizes and differing levels of academic reputation and achievement, organized under different authorities, with a variety of missions and with locations dispersed throughout the state. The scope and size of the overall enterprise were a direct and natural outgrowth of Wisconsin's long-standing commitment to its publicly supported colleges and universities. As Lucey came to office, however, public higher education faced not only the immediate crises of student unrest and violence but also longer-term questions about the state's capacity to sustain this continued growth and maintain excellence in the face of changing times.

From its admission to the Union, in 1848, the state had recognized the vital importance of public higher education to its future success, providing in its constitution for the establishment of a university in its capital city and for the addition of branches elsewhere. The state's founders recognized the value of higher education in preparing individuals for citizenship and leadership roles, as well as the potential economic benefits of expanding knowledge through academic research and sharing it broadly for the benefit of the entire state and its citizens. Beginning with the establishment of the University of Wisconsin at Madison in 1848, the state supported a steady expansion of its higher education efforts. The original Madison campus became the state's land-grant institution under the federal Morrill Act of 1862, growing as a center of academic training and research. By the early twentieth century, it had gained a distinguished national academic reputation and was a founding member of the American Association of Universities, a group of the country's elite research institutions. In the second half of the nineteenth century and the early part of the twentieth, the state further added to its higher education programs with the establishment of postsecondary teacher training institutions or "normal" schools and technical training institutions focused on fields such as engineering and mining. These more specialized colleges, located throughout the state, made higher education available to a growing number of state residents.

After World War II, all of Wisconsin's public colleges and universities experienced explosive growth. It was a golden age for higher education, both in the state and nationally.[7] Demand had increased dramatically with the GI Bill and the baby boom generation, and Wisconsin colleges expanded to meet the demand, widening their curricular offerings and adding to their physical facilities to accommodate swelling student enrollments. In the 1960s, the state approved new campuses at Green Bay and Parkside (situated between Racine and Kenosha), and two-year centers were added in other communities. Government financial support for higher education grew at state and federal levels.[8] Tuition for state residents was low, financial aid was generous, and Cold War concerns and the Soviet Union's launch of the Sputnik satellite drove substantial increases in funding for research.

By 1970, the UW had grown from the original University of Wisconsin at Madison to include UW–Milwaukee, added in 1955; the recently built Green Bay and Parkside campuses; a statewide extension enterprise; and ten two-year satellite centers. The WSU, established in 1955 as the Wisconsin State Colleges and renamed the WSU in 1964, provided administrative coordination for the eleven colleges that had their origins as the state's teacher training and technical institutes. The WSU, too, had added smaller, two-year branches at four locations. Together, all of these state higher education institutions were educating 133,088 students at twenty-seven campuses and, through the UW, were operating extension offices in every county.[9]

This rapid postwar growth had occurred, however, with little coordination and few restraints. The UW and the WSU had developed into two large but separate higher education organizations, each pursuing its own ambitious—and frequently competing—goals for more expansion. The architect of the UW's efforts was Harrington, a brilliant academic and dynamic institutional leader. Inspired by Clark Kerr, who as president of the University of California had implemented a statewide higher education plan designed to accommodate continuous growth, Harrington sought to add new campuses connected with and led by the principal campus at Madison and its central administration. When Harrington became president of the UW in 1962, it consisted only of the University of Wisconsin at Madison and the UW–Milwaukee. By the time of his departure, in 1970, he had successfully claimed the Parkside and Green Bay campuses as part of the UW and, through the UW Center System, was leading ten two-year centers. He had also established the UW–Extension as a separate, independent institution to manage statewide extension programs that had historically been provided through the Madison campus. The individual campuses and UW–Extension were each headed by a chancellor, reporting to Harrington as president of the entire system. By 1970, the UW was educating a total of 69,554 undergraduate, graduate, and professional students. Harrington had transformed the University of Wisconsin from its single campus origins into a large, centrally managed system of higher education, the UW.

The WSU under McPhee had also experienced dramatic growth, though on a less centralized basis. In 1948, McPhee was appointed acting director of the Board of Regents of State Normal Schools, a predecessor to the WSU that governed the state's nine teacher training colleges and two technical institutes. When the WSU was established, in 1955, McPhee continued as director of the new organization. In that role, he promoted expanding the operations of all eleven WSU campuses. While he lacked the strong executive authority wielded by Harrington, he was an effective, politically astute advocate for the WSU campuses. He supported their individual efforts to increase enrollments, expand their physical facilities, and offer a more diverse array of programs at the undergraduate level while beginning to plan for the addition of new graduate and even doctoral programs. By 1970, WSU institutions were educating approximately 64,100 students, now constituting a majority of the undergraduate students in the state. Like the UW, the WSU had become a powerful higher education organization in its own right.

Although the expansion of both systems had been supported by generous state and federal funding, it was not without critics. From the late 1940s on, state leaders had raised concerns about cost, lack of coordination, and competition between the UW and the WSU for state resources. Consolidation of all public higher education had often been suggested as a means of addressing these issues. Commissions were appointed, studies were conducted, and various bills aimed at reorganizing the system were introduced, including measures proposed by Governor Walter Kohler in 1953 and 1955 to merge the UW and the WSU into a single entity. These early consolidation efforts, however, failed in the face of opposition from UW and WSU leaders.[10] Kohler's merger bills led only to the creation of the Coordinating Committee for Higher Education (CCHE) in 1955.[11] This agency was meant, as its name suggested, to coordinate the programmatic activities and budgets of the UW and the WSU, but—perennially underfunded, understaffed, and politically outmaneuvered by the UW and the WSU—it proved ineffective in fulfilling its mission. Throughout the post–World War II expansionist era, the leadership and development of the state's public higher education enterprise remained firmly in the hands of its two powerful rival systems, the UW and the WSU.

Winds of Change

By 1970, however, this existing order was threatened by winds of change from many directions. In addition to the rising tide of campus violence and the underlying social unrest it represented, state higher education confronted new economic and demographic challenges. Faltering state and national economies had led to depressed tax revenues, fewer government resources for higher education, and shifting legislative priorities. At the same time, the aging of the baby boom generation pointed to a looming decline in the college-going population and, with it, the prospect of lower demand for postsecondary education. The golden age of higher education was drawing to a close in the face of diminishing public resources and shrinking enrollment growth. Other states had responded to similar problems by combining their public colleges and universities into large, centrally managed systems, an approach also suggested by policy studies in Wisconsin. A shrewd observer of state affairs and politics, Lucey saw that, in this increasingly difficult environment, consolidation of the UW and the WSU—so often proposed as a solution to high costs and inefficiency—could have renewed appeal. His understanding of the broad forces of change affecting state higher education and his confident grasp of the state political situation led him to conclude that merger of the UW and the WSU was not only necessary but also, by the time of his November 1970 election, a realistic possibility.

Lucey brought to the governorship close familiarity with the growth and development of state higher education in the 1950s and 1960s, as well as with the failed efforts to control or coordinate it. A Wisconsin native, a graduate of UW–Madison, and the founder of a successful real estate firm in Madison, he had also served in the legislature from 1948 to 1950, organized state Democratic campaigns during the 1950s, chaired the state Democratic Party from 1957 to 1963, and served as lieutenant governor from 1964 to 1966.[12] In his political roles, he had followed the explosive growth of the UW and the WSU in the post–World War II years. Although he had favored some state higher education expansion, by the time of the 1970 gubernatorial campaign he had come to believe that uncontrolled growth—and particularly the creation of new doctoral programs—was a serious problem.[13] He shared the long-standing concerns of many other state leaders about rising costs, duplicative programming, and overall inefficiency. He was also offended by wasteful competition for resources and frustrated by CCHE's failure to control growth.[14] As a businessman and a self-described fiscal conservative, he had become increasingly skeptical about the real budget needs of the UW and the WSU. Convinced that the state could no longer afford to maintain public higher education in its existing form, he focused on consolidation of the two systems as the solution to these problems.

Although well aware of the history of failed merger proposals, Lucey recognized that a number of new circumstances were creating openings for change. He saw that his own skepticism about state spending on higher education was now more widely shared by legislators and other government leaders. The state legislature had become a full-time body in 1967, a change that brought more staffing support for individual lawmakers and allowed more time for legislative oversight of government activities, including higher education. Lucey observed that an increasingly well-educated, more sophisticated legislature, assisted by its own staffers and research councils, had become less deferential to university leaders and their budget requests and less willing to give the UW and the WSU a blank check for growth. As he would later colorfully put it, state government would no longer "just put the money on a stump and walk away."[15] Lucey sensed that this shift in attitudes might make legislators more willing to consider major structural changes to state higher education.

The failure of the CCHE also provided impetus for change. Never successful at reining in the expansion of the UW or the WSU, the CCHE was near complete collapse by 1970. The previous summer, the agency had been the center of a damaging personnel controversy that further diminished its reputation. Following the retirement of its executive director, Angus Rothwell, the CCHE sought to hire Donald Percy, then a UW associate vice president, for the post. Percy's association with the UW set off a storm of protest from conservative legislators,[16] who claimed that a UW executive could not deal fairly with the WSU institutions. Percy withdrew from consideration, and the agency then selected an outsider, Arthur Browne, of the University of Illinois, as its director, but the episode seemed to confirm the agency's ineptitude. Its credibility continued to suffer when, in late 1970, the group rejected its own staff's recommendations for reducing funds for higher education and instead approved the budget proposals made by the UW and the WSU.[17] CCHE's ineffectiveness rendered it essentially irrelevant to the coordination or control of state higher education. Its elimination appeared inevitable, bolstering Lucey's view that some sort of combination of the two university systems was the only viable alternative for improved coordination of state public higher education.

Leadership transitions at the UW and the WSU systems announced in the course of the 1970 gubernatorial campaign further improved the prospects for achieving reorganization. Shortly after Harrington's ouster from the UW presidency in May 1970,

McPhee announced that he would retire as director of the WSU. The simultaneous departures of these two powerful, experienced leaders not only opened the door to a different vision of the structure of state higher education but also eliminated potentially powerful opposition to change. Early in the summer of 1970, Lucey had urged that neither of their positions be filled until after the gubernatorial election to allow for new leadership in a reconfigured state higher education system. The UW ignored his advice, however, and Harrington was replaced shortly before the election by John Weaver, then the president of the University of Missouri System.[18] While Lucey was initially angered by the UW's decision to hire Weaver, he understood that an inexperienced newcomer posed less of a threat to reorganization than would Harrington. With Weaver in place at the UW and with McPhee's departure imminent, Lucey foresaw weakened resistance to a consolidation proposal.[19]

In addition to understanding these changing conditions within state government and higher education, Lucey recognized the potential popular appeal of a merger plan, especially to the students and alumni of WSU institutions. With the WSU system by 1970 educating most of the state's undergraduates, it could claim an increasing number of state residents as students and alumni. Many of them were convinced that WSU colleges, with their small classes and close student-faculty contact, were providing undergraduate teaching that was as good as or better than that offered at UW campuses, where much of the teaching was done by graduate student teaching assistants. Still, the graduates of UW schools received more prestigious "University of Wisconsin" degrees, while WSU graduates were awarded degrees from the specific WSU campus they attended. Lucey believed that the lack of the University of Wisconsin degree handicapped WSU students as they sought to move into graduate and professional programs and felt it only fair that all students receiving baccalaureate degrees from Wisconsin's public universities should have University of Wisconsin degrees—especially if the quality of education offered by the WSU was now on a par with that of the UW. A merger of the two systems would allow all graduates to receive a University of Wisconsin degree, enhancing their status and improving their career prospects, a result that would also have broad popular appeal.[20]

Consolidation of the UW and the WSU also had the potential for addressing an equity issue involving the WSU. WSU institutions had long resented the higher pay rates, lower teaching loads, and greater program resources available on UW campuses. The creation of the Green Bay and Parkside campuses as part of the UW in the late 1960s had stirred more feelings of unfairness, since these newer institutions enjoyed benefits similar to those at the Madison and Milwaukee campuses,[21] though their graduate offerings were minimal and their undergraduate programs were similar to those of WSU schools. These perceived inequities were a source of ongoing complaints and demands for parity in the allocation of resources between the two systems. Lee Sherman Dreyfus, in 1970 president of the WSU's Stevens Point campus and later to become governor, was an outspoken proponent of the need for equal treatment. Dreyfus had begun his academic career as a professor of communications at the UW in Madison, where he was a neighbor and friend of Lucey's. In his role as Stevens Point's leader, he had often raised with Lucey his concerns about what he saw as unfair differential treatment of the UW and the WSU. As he considered advancing a merger proposal, Lucey saw that the promise of providing parity between the UW and the WSU systems would make merger attractive to the WSU and neutralize a potential source of opposition to the idea.

Further support for consolidation of the UW and the WSU came from broader national trends and more recent state policy studies. Nationally, combining individual state universities into large, centrally managed university systems had become increasingly common in the post–World War II era.[22] Reflecting this trend to centralization, by 1970 a number of states—from California to North Carolina, Arizona to New York—had established or were in the process of establishing these consolidated state university systems.[23] In Wisconsin, the UW–WSU merger proposals of the 1950s, advanced by a Republican governor, Herbert Kohler, had been succeeded by the work of the Governor's Commission on Education. This blue-ribbon panel, appointed by Republican governor Warren Knowles in the late 1960s and led by retired Kimberly-Clark president William Kellett, had studied consolidation at all levels of public education. In its November 1970 report, the panel, popularly known as the Kellett

Commission, proposed the creation of a single state agency to oversee all state public education. Under the plan, public K–12 schools, the state's technical colleges, and the merged UW and WSU systems, each operating under its own board, would be supervised by this single state education agency.[24] While Lucey did not support the single state education agency model, he understood that a UW–WSU merger was consistent not only with the direction taken by other states in managing public higher education but also in line with this state-level proposal prepared— importantly—with Republican leadership and support.[25] The spate of state higher education consolidations, together with the Kellett Commission recommendation, lent further support to the idea of merging the UW and the WSU.

With the winds of change blowing from so many quarters, Lucey, on assuming the governorship, determined to act quickly on his plans for state higher education reorganization. The disaster of the Sterling Hall bombing and the need to protect the Madison campus from public anger, the confluence of the leadership transitions and bureaucratic failures in the existing higher education structure, national trends favoring consolidations, the potential popular appeal of unification, and the long-standing desire of political leaders of both parties to control the costs of higher education had all combined to create momentum for reorganization.

Lucey's assessment of the situation was shared by his close friend and political adviser, David Adamany. Lucey trusted and admired Adamany, describing him as a "brilliant individual." They had worked together on many occasions over the years, including during the 1970 gubernatorial campaign, when Adamany had served as a top adviser. Adamany was also an academic, with an insider's perspective on the operations of both the UW and the WSU. A Harvard graduate, he received a PhD from UW–Madison in 1967, and he had taught at the WSU's Whitewater campus. Like Lucey, he was skeptical about higher education management and concerned about UW–WSU competition, program duplication, and excessive cost. He was also sharply critical of expansion of the UW under Harrington, arguing that Harrington's California-style approach was unrealistic and beyond the means of a small state like Wisconsin. A believer in strengthening undergraduate education at Madison, he also felt that faculty there should be more productive as teachers and less focused on research. Adamany was a proponent of merging the UW and the WSU, and Lucey would later credit him with the idea, calling him the "father of the merged system in Wisconsin." Adamany himself attributed the plan to Lucey, but, in any case, their ideas on the issue dovetailed neatly.[26] With Adamany's encouragement, Lucey decided to make a UW–WSU merger the first major policy initiative of his new administration.

A Budget Proposal and the Reactions

Eager for an early legislative success, Lucey chose his first state biennial budget[27] as the vehicle for the merger proposal. Even before taking office, he began building political and public support for the idea. As governor-elect, in December 1970 he held a public hearing seeking input on the budget. With reports that he was serious about achieving a major reorganization of higher education already in wide circulation, many of those who appeared at the hearing addressed the issue of merger. Among the most vocal of the speakers was Dreyfus, who urged Lucey to "merge and merge now," citing the lack of parity between the two systems, a point he illustrated by comparing the budget of his own WSU–Stevens Point campus with that of the UW's Green Bay campus. Dreyfus would repeatedly press for merger in speeches he gave throughout December 1970 and January 1971.[28]

As the idea claimed increasing public attention, Lucey, once inaugurated, pressed forward with discussions of his proposal. Appearing on a television documentary in early February 1971, he acknowledged that a restructuring of higher education was under active consideration.[29] By the end of the month, he had prepared his executive budget, including a merger plan. Presenting the proposal in his budget address to the legislature on February 25, 1971, Lucey argued that the state could no longer afford to support "an archaic organization of higher education" and urged the reorganization as a key part of his plan to cut costs.

As drafted, it was a relatively simple, straightforward plan, establishing a new public higher education organization similar in its basic structure to the model developed by Harrington for the UW.[30] The legislation established a merged system consisting of all the state's colleges and universities to be known as the

"University of Wisconsin," with each of the individual institutions to be known as "UW-(location)." The bill abolished the CCHE and the WSU and created a single governing board of regents for the new entity. As proposed, the merged system's board membership would be weighted in favor of the UW, with six members to be chosen from the current UW board, four from the WSU board, along with four new members appointed by the governor and two ex officio members, the State Superintendent of Public Instruction and head of the state Vocational, Technical and Adult Education System. The system was to be headed by a president and a central administration, with campuses led by chancellors. Under the bill, the current faculty governance and tenure rules of the two older systems were to be continued. While the bill eliminated the institutional governing boards in place at WSU campuses, it provided for their replacement by local advisory councils at each institution.

Primarily a political proposal, however, the plan was not the product of in-depth policy analysis and offered few details as to how a merged system composed of numerous small institutions with diverse histories and missions, an urban campus, and a large, nationally prominent research institution should be structured administratively or governed internally. Lucey and Adamany were seemingly untroubled by this absence of specificity, assuming that a merged system's administrative structure would resemble the UW's and believing that university leaders and the academic community would simply work out the specifics once the merger was accomplished.[31] While the vagueness of the proposal and the deferral of details to a postmerger period would prove helpful as the bill made its way through the legislature, it would also produce longer-term misunderstandings and future conflicts within the newly merged system.

Although merger drew much of the public attention to Lucey's budget, it was just one element of a much larger legislative package. In addition to the merger provisions, Lucey proposed broad funding cuts to higher education. He targeted especially significant reductions to graduate programs in both the UW and the WSU systems, arguing that senior faculty should devote a larger portion of their effort to undergraduate teaching, and pointing to the existing glut of PhDs in the academic market as evidence that such programs were not needed. Sounding the themes of equity that he believed would appeal to WSU institutions and their graduates, he also emphasized the need to move toward "equality" in taxpayer support among the institutions of the two existing systems.[32]

With his budget message, and the formal introduction of the executive budget as Assembly Bill 414, on March 3,[33] Lucey began an active campaign to gain approval of the UW–WSU merger. Over the course of the next eight months, he would advocate energetically for his proposal, guiding its progress through the legislature, making critical compromises and strategic parliamentary maneuvers, and appealing to the public, the media, and the higher education community for support. The response to his proposal from the UW and the WSU systems and the CCHE was, in contrast, weak and disorganized. Their leaders and boards were slow to react or to develop a coherent position on the merger plan, not only giving Lucey the advantage of momentum as he took his case to the legislature and the public but also causing them to miss the opportunity to provide their own input in shaping the legislation.

The immediate responses of the state's higher education leaders to Lucey's budget were directed to the significant funding cuts, rather than to the merger. They challenged the proposed budget on grounds of the educational damage it would cause but expressed general willingness to consider the merger plan. As the legislature's Joint Finance Committee began deliberations on the budget, in March 1971, the CCHE's Arthur Browne, his agency slated for elimination, testified that while he did not believe merger would solve the coordination problems between the UW and the WSU, he was not necessarily opposed to it.[34] The UW's executive vice president, Donald Percy, was also seemingly receptive to the idea, testifying before the legislature in February that "Anything that reduces three bureaucracies to one can't be all bad."[35] The WSU's McPhee, not yet retired, observed publicly that he believed merger to be inevitable but urged the need for further study. He suggested that a committee of representatives from the UW and the WSU systems be appointed by the governor to consider the idea and develop the key components of a merger plan.[36]

Reaction from the new UW president, John Weaver, was similarly cautious. Named UW president only in October 1970,

Weaver was personally unhappy with the idea of merger but careful to avoid raising objections. Weaver had strong personal connections to the UW, where his father had been a professor. He had grown up in Madison, graduated from the University of Wisconsin High School, and received his AB, AM, and PhD degrees, all in geography, from the University of Wisconsin. He revered the UW and feared merger's potentially negative consequences—especially the possible damage to its reputation and the perceived "leveling effect" of being combined with less prestigious WSU institutions. He did not, however, immediately oppose the plan. Though Weaver had been hired to lead only the UW, in proposing merger Lucey had intimated that, as UW's president, Weaver would become head of the consolidated system. Weaver felt that it would be inappropriate for him to fight a plan that he might be called upon to implement.

Perhaps even more important, Weaver was convinced that the proposed budget cuts posed a larger, more immediate threat to the UW than merger. Given the state's long history of failed consolidation efforts, it seemed to him unlikely this one would succeed,[37] a view encouraged by key members of his board. Led by regent Ody Fish, a former chair of the Wisconsin Republican Party and an experienced politician, the regents advised Weaver that he should not launch an active campaign against a proposal that was sure to be defeated by the Republican-controlled state Senate.[38] As a result, Weaver confined his initial public response to the merger proposal to a statement that he favored any plan that would further the educational opportunities of the state's young people at a reasonable cost.[39]

The careful tone of these early reactions from UW and WSU administrators was echoed in comments by their governing boards. Neither board immediately opposed the plan, both bodies maintaining—at least publicly—a degree of openness to the idea and a willingness to study it further. When the issue came before the UW board at its March 12, 1971, meeting, regent Frank Pelisek argued that the concept of merger had "very substantial merit." While several regents expressed concerns with the plan, regent Fish—somewhat disingenuously—commented that he would be eager to support merger if its educational advantages could be shown and urged his colleagues to remain open-minded on the issue. Board president Bernard Ziegler suggested, as had McPhee, that further study was needed.[40] The meeting concluded with the adoption of a resolution affirming Weaver's endorsement of any plan that would further the educational opportunities of the state's young people, recommending further study of merger, and requesting a joint meeting with the WSU board to discuss the advantages and disadvantages of any consolidation. The WSU board, also meeting in March, took no official position on merger but did adopt a resolution supporting McPhee's idea of a gubernatorial study committee[41] and later agreed to the joint study proposed by the UW Board of Regents.[42]

Among the campus leaders of the UW and the WSU, early responses to the merger were similarly restrained. Madison chancellor H. Edwin Young, a close personal friend of Lucey's, did not openly voice concern with the plan, despite growing worries expressed by members of his Madison faculty.[43] Although many WSU faculty members—for whom Lucey's calls for salary and resource parity between UW and WSU institutions had strong appeal—tended to be supportive of the plan, their campus leaders feared loss of local control at their institutions. Accustomed to having substantial administrative autonomy, the WSU presidents were concerned that a unified system with the kind of governing board, central executive authority, and central administration proposed by Lucey would be dominated by the Madison campus, threatening their independence.[44] While Dreyfus continued to be a strong and outspoken proponent, others, notably Eau Claire's Leonard Haas and River Falls's George Field, were uncomfortable with the prospect of becoming part of a unified system and declined to join Dreyfus.[45] Despite their worries, though, they did not immediately challenge the idea.

Taken together, the initial responses of the state's higher education leaders to the merger were cautious or noncommittal. To the extent there was opposition, it was tepid and largely masked by expressions of willingness to consider the idea or to study it further. Whether these reactions stemmed from the view that more study would either kill the plan or delay it indefinitely or from the complacent expectation of failure based on past experiences and a Republican Senate, the result was that the UW and the WSU did not immediately unite to fight against it. As legislative

deliberations on the governor's budget and merger plan proceeded through the spring of 1971, the two systems had no defini-
tive position on the issue.

Meanwhile, though, Lucey and his staff, along with Democratic
supporters, Dreyfus, and most of the state's leading newspapers,
were actively advocating for merger.[46] Lucey continued to work
hard to promote his plan, emphasizing the reasons he had previously cited in support of merger: the need to eliminate wasteful
competition, to restore public faith in the UW's Madison campus,
and to give all public college graduates the benefits of a UW degree. He gave speeches to constituent groups, argued his case
with faculty and other leaders of the UW and the WSU systems,
and defended merger in an unusual personal appearance before
the legislature. His staff worked to gain editorial endorsements
from state newspapers, and other supporters such as Dreyfus
continued to voice their approval publicly. Lucey also made some
important strategic clarifications and changes to his initial proposal. Confirming publicly what he had previously hinted at,
Lucey stated that he would like Weaver to serve as the first president of the merged system.[47] He restored to his proposed budget
some of the UW funds he had first planned to cut and, responding
to McPhee's suggestion, appointed a small group of representatives from the UW and the WSU to propose amendments to his
bill that would make merger more palatable to both systems.
This so-called wrinkle committee was meant to iron out the major
differences between the UW and the WSU over what an acceptable merger would involve.[48] Lucey's energetic efforts to advance
his proposal overbalanced the measured responses of the UW
and the WSU boards and their executives at both the system and
the campus levels. He was building a broad base of statewide
support for his plan, while the university systems were still organizing to respond to it. As the spring of 1971 progressed, adoption
of Lucey's merger proposal began to seem inevitable, with press
reports as early as April saying that it had the votes to pass.[49]

An Alternative Merger Bill

Although Lucey's plan captured most of the public attention,
there was another merger proposal before the 1971 legislature.
An alternative, stand-alone merger bill had been introduced in

the state Senate in late February by Senator Ray Heinzen, with the encouragement of Senate majority leader Raymond Johnson. Heinzen, a Republican, chaired the Senate Education Committee. He and Johnson were veterans of previous Republican efforts at higher education consolidation. They supported the concept of merger but sought to present a Republican alternative to Lucey's plan, using Heinzen's position as chair of the Education Committee as the platform. Arguing that merger was a policy measure that should be decided separately from the budget and debated on its own merits, Heinzen introduced his bill on February 24, 1971, the day before Lucey's budget speech.[50] Heinzen went on to schedule a series of hearings on his proposal for late February and early March at locations around the state.[51] The Heinzen bill was even simpler than Lucey's and somewhat less oriented to the UW model.[52] It created a single board of regents composed of eight members each from the UW and the WSU boards and named the merged organization the University of Wisconsin System. It abolished the WSU and the CCHE and transferred all the powers, staff, records, and property of the WSU and the UW to the new board of regents but offered few other details as to the organizational structure of the merged entity. While Heinzen's hearings were initially treated as a kind of sideshow to Lucey's campaign for merger, his bill took on increasing importance as Lucey's plan became entangled in legislative wrangling over the larger budget. The introduction of this stand-alone bill would ultimately prove crucial to achieving the merger.

With Heinzen's hearings under way and Lucey continuing to push for his own plan, other interested parties within the two university systems and state government began to analyze more closely the potential effects of merger at their own institutions and to prepare their own responses to the merger bills. During March and April 1971, the Madison faculty's University Committee, the Milwaukee faculty, and the WSU's University Faculty Council each weighed in on the subject, outlining their concerns about the Lucey proposal and identifying items they believed should be included in an acceptable merger bill.[53] The "wrinkle committee" also began meeting during this period. Joseph Nusbaum, secretary of the Department of Administration under Lucey and a member of the group, initiated informal background discussions about merger with faculty at Madison and at some of the WSU schools.[54] The UW's Percy, uncomfortable with relying on the Senate to defeat a merger bill and pressing for a more pro-active approach, began work on various alternative merger plans containing the key elements that he believed would satisfy UW needs.[55]

These efforts brought into sharper focus the areas of significant disagreement between UW and WSU representatives about the structure and governance of a consolidated system. Key conflicts between the two groups emerged over the powers of the system's chief executive and administration, the degree of autonomy of the individual campuses, institutional missions, and the appropriate allocation of resources to support those missions. Not surprisingly, individuals and groups from the UW and the WSU tended to favor retaining their respective, existing operational models in a merged system. UW constituents preferred a Harrington-style, centralized administrative structure, along the lines suggested by Lucey: a single governing board of regents, a central administration led by a president, clear delineation of individual institutional missions, centralized budgets providing mission-based support, unit autonomy for operations, active faculty participation in institutional governance, and a merit-based tenure system. WSU campus groups, however, resisted this kind of highly centralized administrative structure. They urged instead a weaker coordinative role for leadership in the new system, similar to their own traditional structure, which would allow for direct access by individual campus leaders to the governing board; limit central executive authority; provide greater local autonomy and budget authority to local boards or councils; and continue existing policies providing for tenure based on length of service.[56] As the merger proposal made its way through the legislature—and long after its passage—the divisions between UW and WSU representatives over these issues and their competing centripetal and centrifugal visions of the merged system's leadership and governance would bring recurring internal conflicts.

Despite the flurry of study and activity at their campuses, the governing boards of the UW and the WSU proceeded down a slower, more measured path to developing a formal position on merger. Following their joint meeting on March 27, 1971, they appointed a study committee to prepare a report on the question.

This document, issued in early May, recommended that merger be removed from the budget and that it be considered only after further study of a number of specifically identified issues. At their regular monthly meetings on May 20 and 21, the two boards reviewed the report but continued to focus primarily on the larger budget problems and the impact of significant cuts on their institutions. Weaver maintained his neutral posture toward merger as his board discussed the effects of various funding changes, with minimal comment on the merger issue. The two May board meetings led only to the adoption of parallel UW–WSU board resolutions approving their joint study report and formally requesting that the legislature and governor remove the merger plan from the budget and delay considering the issue until more study could be done.

These actions did nothing to slow Lucey and the legislature, however, as they moved forward with their own deliberations on the budget and the merger. On May 21, the same day as the UW board meeting, the legislature's joint finance committee approved Lucey's budget bill and, with it, his merger plan. As a result, the legislation was advanced for consideration by the full Assembly, where debate began on June 8. Although Assembly Republicans introduced a series of amendments designed to strip Lucey's merger proposal from the package, they were easily defeated by the Democratic majority. On June 11, Lucey's budget, including his merger proposal, passed the Assembly and was sent to the Senate for action.

The Path to Passage

Although Lucey had steered his budget, with the merger plan, through the Assembly with relative ease, the Republican-controlled Senate now blocked the path to success. Republican support was needed both for a budget agreement and for the merger plan. In this context, Heinzen's stand-alone merger proposal now took on vital strategic importance to Lucey and his Democratic supporters. Senate Republicans were expected to follow the approach of their Assembly colleagues and move to delete Lucey's merger proposal from the budget. This maneuver, however, would not prevent a UW–WSU merger from being considered, since Heinzen's stand-alone bill would remain before the legislature for action. Recognizing the tactical importance of Heinzen's bill, before the budget reached the Senate the DOA's Nusbaum began quietly exploring amendments to the Heinzen proposal that would be acceptable to the governor. This effort resulted in the introduction of a substitute amendment, offered by Heinzen himself on May 19, that was close enough to the original Lucey plan to meet with the governor's approval. The new bill, Substitute Amendment 1 to SB 213, called for a merger along the lines proposed by the governor but added an important new element. Under the amended plan, the more detailed and complex elements of the governance structure of the new system would be developed by a merger implementation committee—but only *after* the elimination of CCHE and the consolidation of the UW and the WSU under a single board had been accomplished.[57] This approach achieved Lucey's goal of an immediate merger, while postponing decisions on issues and disputes like those that had emerged from the preliminary consideration of Lucey's proposal by UW and WSU groups, effectively avoiding the kinds of conflicts and debates that might prevent passage of a merger bill in the current legislative session.

The Republican opponents of merger, too, saw strategic value in Heinzen's legislation, but of a different kind. They believed the stand-alone bill offered a way to dilute the plan by tacking on amendments to the bill that would effectively neutralize the consolidation effort, paving the way for its defeat. To this end, on June 10, a small group of senators introduced an amendment to Heinzen's bill[58] that became known as the "semi-merger" or Devitt plan, after Senator James Devitt, one of the authors. This amendment effectively avoided meaningful consolidation of the UW and the WSU, simply eliminating the CCHE and transferring its responsibilities to a newly created Board of Governors for Higher Education but continuing the existing governing boards and separate administrative structures of the two systems.

As the focus of the merger debate shifted to the Heinzen bill and the Devitt amendment,[59] the boards of the UW and the WSU finally took a position on the issue at their respective June 1971 meetings. In separate, identical resolutions, they declared their fundamental opposition to merger "at this time" but also resolved, not surprisingly, that of all merger proposals made in the legislature, they favored Devitt's essentially meaningless "semi-merger" plan.[60] At last, the university systems were openly on the record in opposition to merger and engaged in resisting the proposal. Lucey, however, was fully prepared to fight back. He renewed his efforts to persuade the Madison faculty that merger was necessary, asking for an opportunity to speak directly with faculty members on the subject. He was invited to appear at the campus on July 8, 1971, when, in a skillful address, he parried faculty questions and argued effectively for the need for merger. Following this highly publicized performance, both opponents and supporters of merger resumed their efforts to advance their positions. Media coverage intensified, with the bulk of editorial opinion continuing to support merger.[61]

Meanwhile, deliberations on the overall state budget continued in the state Senate. As anticipated, the Republican majority stripped Lucey's merger plan from the bill and passed its own version of the budget, sending the measure as amended back to the Assembly for action. The Assembly rejected the Senate's budget on July 15, requiring the creation of a special joint legislative Conference Committee, composed of representatives from both houses and both parties, to reconcile the differences between the two budget bills. Facing the prospect of getting no merger bill in the current legislative session or no agreement on other important components of his budget, Lucey reached an adroit compromise with the Conference Committee: he agreed to the deletion of his own merger plan from the budget bill, on the condition that the Conference Committee would refer the Heinzen measure to the legislature's Joint Finance Committee for consideration in a special legislative session to be convened following approval of the rest of the budget. The agreement guaranteed that a merger bill would come to the floor for action by both houses of the legislature, rather than being deferred to a later legislative session.[62]

With consideration of merger legislation now ensured, negotiations about the substance of the bill intensified, as interested parties from both the WSU and the UW pressed for further amendments to the Heinzen bill that would satisfy the concerns about the governance and organizational structure of a merged system raised on their campuses during the preliminary discussions of Lucey's proposal. WSU representatives, led by faculty members Marshall Wick and Edward Muzik of Eau Claire, sought changes designed to limit central administrative and executive authority and emphasize instead institutional autonomy and local control. Meanwhile, Percy and others within the UW, sensing that merger would pass, worked on plans and alternative amendments that would preserve a centralized leadership and administrative structure for the merged system that was more closely aligned with the Harrington model.

By the end of July, the various negotiations and amendments to Heinzen's merger bill had evolved into a plan that satisfied the Joint Finance Committee. Under this revised approach, an immediate de facto merger of the UW and the WSU would be achieved by combining their boards and eliminating CCHE. The central staffs of the UW and the WSU would be consolidated over a two-year period, and the older systems would continue to operate under their existing statutory provisions for this same period. The missions of the institutions would also be retained during this time, along with existing system laws and regulations on matters such as tenure. Most details of the legal structure and organization of the new system were left to a committee charged with the implementation of the merger, an approach that eliminated the need for immediate legislative solutions to key conflicts between the two systems.[63] The Joint Finance Committee approved this proposal on July 28.

Lucey immediately announced his support for it, but Weaver, finally inserting himself directly in the debate, attacked the bill in a press conference the following day, outlining a number of specific problems and criticisms of the plan. His reaction prompted Lucey to arrange a meeting with him on August 4, at which time the two discussed amendments to the bill that would make it "workable" from Weaver's perspective. Lucey then maneuvered Weaver into joining him at a press conference on August 5, where Lucey announced his support for Heinzen's bill with the amendments he had discussed with Weaver. Lucey explained that Weaver's concerns could all be addressed, conveying the impression that he and Weaver had reached agreement in principle on the idea of merger. While Weaver had not explicitly endorsed merger and would later dispute that he had ever agreed to it,[64] his appearance at the press conference and his failure to dispute Lucey's assertions created ambiguity about his position.

Lucey seized the opportunity to imply that Weaver was, at a minimum, amenable to the idea.[65]

Weaver's apparent acceptance of the merger plan, with Lucey's aggressive advocacy and strategic parliamentary maneuvering, now made legislative approval more likely, while Ody Fish's confidence that merger would never pass the state Senate began to seem misplaced. Merger had been championed by Republicans in the past; the bill before the legislature had been authored by a Republican and was supported by Republican Senate majority leader Johnson. In addition, in late August, William Kellett, whose commission had recommended the UW–WSU merger as part of its comprehensive plan to combine all state public education under one governing board, also endorsed the Heinzen proposal. Virtually all Senate Democrats[66] supported it, together with a coalition of supportive Republicans that included the bill's co-sponsors, Senators Bidwell, Cirilli, and Lorge. This group, in combination with the Senate Democrats, was just one vote short of the total needed for passage. That swing vote belonged to Senator Clifford Kreuger. Kreuger, who had at times appeared sympathetic to merger, was under heavy pressure from his fellow Republicans to vote against the bill. In the end, however, he voted for it—perhaps persuaded by Dreyfus, who claimed to have won him over in a meeting the weekend before the final vote was taken.[67] Despite more delaying tactics, motions, and amendments, the merger law, Chapter 100, Laws of 1971, passed the state Senate on October 5, 1971. The Assembly quickly added its approval, and on October 8, 1971, Lucey signed it into law. The legislation became effective October 12, 1971.[68]

The UW–WSU merger stands as Lucey's most important accomplishment as governor, a testament to his determination and commitment, as well as to his political acumen. In the immediate aftermath of its passage, however, it created uncertainty, conflict, and more controversy. The product of a tumultuous period that had seen campus tragedy, along with economic and social crises and significant leadership transitions, it had been proposed as the solution to many problems. It was, however, a political plan that had not resulted from thorough study or detailed analysis of the state's higher education needs or in-depth consideration of the practical problems of consolidating ill-matched sets of institutions. The slow reactions of academic leaders to the proposal meant that their own input on the plan was minimal. The complexities of implementation had been left to the future, with little in the way of policy guidance, even as expectations about the benefits of merger had been raised. In this uncertain environment, conflicts—internal and external, political and public—over the mission, size, structure, and budget of the new entity were inevitable. It would fall to the newly created UW System and its leaders to deal with these pressures, along with the significant funding reductions that had been imposed along with the merger. Lucey's brave new era in state higher education began with substantial demands, high expectations, and significant challenges to forging a truly unified organization.

2

A Shotgun Wedding and Its Problems

The merger was—not surprisingly—often compared to a shotgun wedding.[1] Lucey had forced the marriage of less-than-willing, poorly matched participants in a hastily performed ceremony, with little planning and considerable uncertainty about the future of the relationship. The merger bill enacted in October 1971 had legally joined the UW and the WSU as one entity, but key details about the arrangement were left for later development. As it worked to consolidate operations and begin implementing the merger law, the new UW System faced immediate challenges stemming from the lack of specifics in the legislation and the clashing expectations of the UW and the WSU about the purposes and goals of merger. Concerns and conflicts that had emerged as the merger bill moved toward passage quickly reappeared as the parties struggled to control the implementation process and shape the new system. In the aftermath of the merger, it became clear that making a success of the union would be a more complicated and long-term endeavor than conducting the marriage ceremony.

The Complex Challenges of Implementing a Simple Law

Lucey's original merger proposal had been relatively simple and became more so as it moved through the legislature to passage.

The legislation finally approved, Chapter 100, Wisconsin Laws of 1971, effected an immediate consolidation of the UW and the WSU and the elimination of the CCHE. The act combined the WSU and the UW into a single entity, the University of Wisconsin System, under a single governing board, with a single executive head and a consolidated central staff from the two former systems. It assigned to the Board of Regents the primary responsibility for administering state public higher education, planning for its future needs, and enacting policies for the governance of the new System. It also changed the names of the individual UW and WSU institutions to "University of Wisconsin–(location or name)" and of the two-year campuses to "University Center–(location)," while providing for various technical transitional matters.[2] In its broad outlines, this centralized governance structure for the combined UW System resembled that developed by Harrington for the former UW and immediately achieved Lucey's goal of ensuring that all graduates of state four-year institutions would gain the advantages of holding a UW degree.

The act, however, left the most complex organizational details to be developed during a two-year merger implementation period set to follow its passage. As David Adamany would later remark, the legislative debate over merger had been a debate over how to govern state higher education, not about the details of its organization.[3] Under the merger law, the responsibility for merger implementation and the specifics of the administration and governance of the merged system were shifted to the new governing board and the central executive leadership, together with a merger implementation study committee, or MISC, also established under the law. The MISC—composed of representatives from the UW and the WSU, state government, and the public, along with advisers from the UW and the WSU and staff support from the new UW System leader—was assigned to merge the existing statutes governing state higher education and to study a lengthy list of issues and make recommendations to the Board of Regents and the legislature on these subjects for adoption in policy or state law. It was also asked to report on the "practicability, feasibility and wisdom of merger."[4] The MISC report and recommendations were required to be presented to the Board of Regents and the legislature by January 31, 1973. In the interim, the UW and the WSU systems were to continue to operate under their existing statutory charters, in accordance with their existing missions and regulations.

While the merger legislation had established a single, central entity for state higher education administration and governance, the practical challenges of bringing together two very different university systems, with their diverse sets of institutions and competing interests, expectations, and concerns, were left to the Board of Regents and to the leaders of this new UW System and the MISC, subject to confirmation by the legislature. With the law's additional invitation to reconsider the wisdom of merger itself, the stage was set for conflict, not only over the mechanics of making the merger work but also over the very existence of the new organization.

Getting Merger "Done and Done Fast"

The task of initiating the implementation effort fell naturally to Weaver, as Lucey's designee to head the UW System. Weaver had a keen sense of his duty to "make the merger work,"[5] telling his UW board at its final meeting on October 8, 1971, "Only history can assess the wisdom of the merger legislation, but history must carry no doubt about the resolve for success of those who are to assume the burden and challenge of its study and implementation."[6] Despite his commitment, however, Weaver lacked a compelling, overarching vision for the new entity. He was not a dynamic leader in the style of his predecessor, Fred Harvey Harrington, nor was he an active, hands-on manager. As UW–Madison professor and MISC member Clara Penniman observed, Weaver enjoyed the status and ceremonial aspects of the presidency much more than administration.[7] Hired to head only the UW, uncomfortable with the idea of merger in the first place, and bruised by the politics of the merger fight and Lucey's manipulation of his position on the issue, Weaver approached the implementation process without a clear plan for shaping this new, expanded UW System—now one of the largest university systems in the country.[8] As merger implementation got under way, Weaver relied heavily on his executive vice president, Don Percy, to spearhead the effort.

A bright, confident, and decisive manager, Percy was well prepared and not hesitant to lead. His experiences working under

Harrington in the UW administration, as well as his knowledge of the CCHE and his work on the Kellett Commission, had provided him with a solid grasp of the operations and politics of public higher education in Wisconsin. He was also familiar with the long history of events leading to merger. He had been receptive to the idea of merger when it was initially proposed by Lucey and, as the issue was debated in the legislature, had participated in the work of the "wrinkle committee." Never as sanguine as Weaver and Fish about the prospects of defeating the merger bill, he had also worked behind the scenes within the UW to develop various alternative merger plans and organizational structures for a merged system. In addition, unlike Weaver, who didn't care for politics generally and did not get along well with Lucey, Percy was willing to engage with political leaders on matters related to merger implementation.[9] Lucey would later recall that he dealt more directly with Percy than with Weaver on these issues, recounting a meeting of the three at which Percy initially deferred to Weaver's leadership but gradually took over the discussion, leaving Weaver "sitting there almost as an innocent bystander."[10]

Percy was convinced that merger "had to be done, and done fast."[11] Not only did the legal deadlines for administrative consolidations and the completion of the MISC's work need to be met, but also continuity of operations had to be maintained, budgets developed, and new program growth or duplication curtailed. Given the failures of the CCHE and the former two-system state higher education structure, the newly established UW System had to quickly demonstrate its ability to perform and to address the policy concerns that had driven the merger. Even before the merger bill was approved, Percy had prepared preliminary plans for the staff consolidations required by the law.[12] Once the legislation was signed, he immediately wrote UW central administration staff members, urging them to become proactive architects of the new UW System, not merely passive bystanders to merger implementation, and asked them to provide him with their ideas for shaping the new organization.[13] He also began organizing the MISC meetings, working on a unified budget for the new System and helping Weaver arrange for the first meeting of the new Board of Regents. These advance preparations and swift post-merger actions laid the foundation for the efforts of the Board of

Regents, UW System leaders, and the MISC as they began to address the requirements of the merger law. They also cemented a crucial leadership role for the former UW's central administration, with its strong ties to UW–Madison, in shaping the new UW System.

The First Steps:
Board and Administrative Consolidations

The System's newly created, combined Board of Regents held its first meeting on October 19, 1971, just days after Lucey signed the merger bill. The circumstances were awkward as the parties to the forced union came together. The new board was drawn primarily from the former governing boards, with eight members each from the UW and the WSU. In addition, there were three new citizen members appointed by the governor and two ex officio members, the State Superintendent of Public Instruction and the president of the State Board of Vocational, Technical and Adult Education, for a total of twenty-one members.[14] Despite the balanced representation from the UW and the WSU on the combined board, there was considerable uncertainty and tension about which individuals and perspectives would dominate the leadership of the new system. Although the former UW and WSU boards had united to oppose merger, there had been no joint contingency planning for the actual consolidation of the two organizations. In this uncharted territory, the significant differences and competing interests of the former systems created concerns on both sides. The smaller institutions represented by the WSU board members feared loss of their local autonomy and dominance by the UW, and especially by UW–Madison, which—by any measure, from academic distinction, to number of students, to size of budget, to physical area and facilities—dwarfed in reputation, size, and scope any other institution in the new System. The UW members and particularly UW–Madison, however, feared what were generally described as the "leveling effects" of merger: the potential dilution or diversion of resources from their institutions to the former WSU campuses and the diminution in academic stature and reputation from their inclusion in the same system.

Adding to these underlying tensions, the logistical arrangements for this first board meeting were clumsy. The location was the meeting room of the former UW board, on the eighteenth floor of Van Hise Hall at UW–Madison, a space not adequate to easily accommodate the significantly larger UW System board. As the twenty-one members of the merged board crammed into the room, there was a kind of musical-chairs crowding that increased the general discomfort.[15] Making matters worse, the location itself seemed to confirm the UW's dominance in the new System. Van Hise Hall, the tallest building in Madison, was originally designed to house UW–Madison's language departments but had been expanded in the late 1960s with the addition of four floors to house Harrington's central administration and the UW board's offices. With its commanding views of the city and its lakes, the building and its administrative offices were an impressive testament to the success and ambitions of the former UW, heightening the concerns of WSU members about the loss of local institutional identity through merger.

Despite these tensions, however, the meeting produced a smooth transition of leadership from the old boards to the new. A collegial tone prevailed, with many board members—even some who, like Ody Fish, had vigorously opposed merger—expressing at the outset their commitment to the success of the new UW System.[16] The group then took up the business of organizing itself and choosing its new leaders. In advance of the meeting, the presidents of the former UW and WSU boards, Bernard Ziegler and Roy Kopp, had reached a gentleman's agreement that the WSU's Kopp should serve as the first president of the new System board, while Ziegler would assume the vice presidency.[17] Their agreement, confirmed by the board, averted a potentially contentious leadership struggle and set a precedent for maintaining a careful balance of UW and WSU representation in key official positions within the new System.

With the issue of its own leadership settled, the board, over the course of its next several meetings, adopted by-laws, selected other officers, appointed committees, and approved the first major appointments in the UW System's central administration. At the November 5, 1971, meeting, Weaver was formally appointed president of the System, fulfilling Lucey's earlier commitment to choose him for the position. At the same time, in keeping with the principle of UW–WSU balance, Leonard Haas, then serving as head of the Eau Claire campus, was named vice president of the UW System.

Meanwhile, the central administrative staff consolidations of the UW and WSU required by the merger law—described by Percy as the "ritual dance of merger"—got under way.[18] Percy had, prior to merger, outlined possible organizational schemes and titles,[19] with executives from UW and WSU offices assigned to functions and offices matching their previous positions and areas of expertise. With Weaver's agreement, he proposed a combined central administrative structure that included leaders from each of the former systems. Although there some was some concern about the lack of faculty involvement in the selection process for these positions,[20] the initial appointments were approved by the board at its February 11, 1972, meeting.

As recommended by Percy, Haas's position was titled "executive vice president." A total of four vice presidencies were established in the areas of academic affairs, budget, administration, and finance. From the former UW, Percy became the vice president for budget, and Reuben Lorenz was named to lead finance. From the WSU, Robert Winter was appointed vice president for administration. For the academic affairs vice presidency, the board initiated a national search for a permanent appointee, later selecting Donald K. Smith for the position. In the meantime, Robert Polk of UW and Dallas Peterson from WSU were chosen to share the post until the search was completed.[21] The offices of the system president, the executive vice president, and the four vice presidents were all located in Van Hise Hall, where the UW's central administration had formerly been housed. With the board's approval of the location of the central offices and the combined central administrative structure, the melding of the central staffs as required by the merger legislation was substantially complete as of the February 11, 1972, meeting.

The new board also acted early to adopt a title structure for the System's institutional executives and to provide mechanisms for ensuring their participation in the leadership of the System as a whole. At its January 7, 1972, meeting, the board took action giving campus and institutional leaders the title "chancellor," while the System's head was assigned the title "president," in effect establishing a UW–style nomenclature.[22] To include the institutional chief executives in Systemwide affairs, the board built on the past practices of the WSU and the UW. Both UW and WSU system heads had met regularly with their campus leaders, the WSU executive director with the WSU Council of Presidents and the UW president in less formal sessions with the chancellors of UW institutions. At its December 17, 1971, meeting, the board eliminated the Council of Presidents and created a single executive leadership group made up of all UW System chancellors and headed by the System president.[23] Later, an additional council consisting of only the institutional leaders was created to allow them to consult with one another, independent of the president and central administration.[24] The convening of the chancellors on a regular basis afforded institutional leaders the opportunity for contact with one another, the president, and the central administration, and gave them a voice on Systemwide issues.

As the result of these early organizing activities, within the first several months of 1972 the merged board was operational and working to address the requirements of the merger law. The board had adopted a title structure, the System's central executive leadership team was in place, and a means for UW institutional leaders to engage in Systemwide affairs had been provided.

Limiting Growth

In addition to addressing these organizational and staffing matters, the new board moved immediately to confront some of the most important policy concerns that had driven merger. The need to control program growth and prevent program duplication and competition between the UW and WSU—long criticized as too expensive—had been major factors leading to the passage of the merger legislation. Recognizing the importance of addressing these problems, the board acted swiftly to signal its intent to limit growth. At its January 7, 1972, meeting, although it confirmed the approvals of several programs granted by the former UW and WSU boards shortly before the merger bill passed, the board imposed a general moratorium on all new programs. At its next meeting, this action was modified to allow some flexibility for special situations and to clarify that the moratorium applied only to graduate programs. Still, these were early, forceful indications of the board's determination to contain growth and to restrain uncoordinated program proliferation.[25]

These actions were followed in succeeding months by the board's approval of a series of budget policies governing the allocation of financial resources within the new System that allowed for providing different levels of funding to the different types of institutions in the new System, effectively addressing premerger equity concerns about comparable funding for comparable educational programs and resource parity between UW and WSU institutions.[26] Here again, Percy's work was critical to the result. As the vice president responsible for developing a unified System budget, Percy proposed a plan for allocating funds that explicitly recognized that different kinds of System institutions would have different needs requiring different levels of financial support. Under his plan, UW System institutions were grouped into four "clusters" on the basis of the size, scope, and academic level of their program offerings: a doctoral cluster, composed of UW–Madison and UW–Milwaukee; a comprehensive cluster including all the four-year WSU campuses, plus UW–Green Bay and UW–Parkside; a separate cluster made up of the fourteen two-year centers under their own central administration; and the statewide UW–Extension. Percy recommended that funding allocations be based on the kinds of programs and activities offered by the institutions within each cluster, distinguishing between and among the needs of the doctoral cluster, with its complex, high-cost advanced degree and major extramural research programs; the comprehensive cluster, with institutions primarily focused on undergraduate teaching at the baccalaureate level; the two-year centers, offering associate degrees; and the UW–Extension, with its county-based outreach and continuing education programs. Under Percy's cluster scheme, comparable programs were to be funded at comparable levels *within* each cluster, but *between* clusters comparable funding for comparable programs would have to be clearly justified. It was a methodology that adhered to principles of funding comparability and resource parity, while allowing for differential treatment based on the important distinctions between and among groups of System institutions. The budget policies adopted by the board in early 1972 approved this cluster classification methodology, an approach that would continue to shape the System's resource allocations in the years ahead.[27]

In addition to its significance for the issues of parity and comparability in resource allocation, the cluster approach further limited program growth by effectively preventing nondoctoral institutions—including former WSU campuses that had once planned to add graduate or professional schools and the newer UW campuses at Green Bay and Parkside that as part of the UW had nursed similar ambitions—from developing doctoral programs or adding new graduate-level offerings. The cluster model assumed that the new System would allocate funding for only two doctoral institutions, the UW–Madison with its extensive major research programs and the UW–Milwaukee with its urban research emphasis. This approach laid the foundation for later, mission-based program growth limitations to be developed under the leadership of Donald K. Smith, who joined the System as vice president for academic affairs in January 1973. Under Smith, each System institution would prepare an individual mission, subject to board approval, that described the scope of its educational programming. These institutional missions, approved in January 1974, would operate as a further constraint on graduate-level program growth going forward and confirmed the distinctions between categories of UW institutions proposed by Percy.[28] As Smith later observed, the cluster approach was essentially "sanctified" by the mission statements, precluding the flow of research funds to the nondoctoral cluster and preventing institutions in that cluster from competing with the two doctoral institutions. Within the doctoral cluster, UW–Milwaukee's designation as an urban institution would further refine its mission and differentiate it from that of UW–Madison as the System's major research institution.[29]

The Devil(s) in the Details: Merger Implementation Study Committee

Like the board, the MISC, too, began meeting shortly after passage of the merger bill. The complexity of its charge and the diversity of its membership, however, soon proved to be a more volatile combination, exposing the divergent, often conflicting interests of the parties to the merger. The MISC's work was marked by struggles between state government and university leaders on the committee for control of the implementation process and by disagreements among all participants over administrative and organizational details. Contentious issues that had arisen during the push for passage of the merger bill fueled disputes between

UW and WSU representatives. While consensus eventually emerged on many subjects, sharp differences and dissatisfaction remained on others.

The MISC had been given a daunting assignment. Its charge, under the law, was to make recommendations to the board and legislature on how to merge the statutes that had governed the UW and the WSU,[30] while at the same time studying and making proposals on an extensive list of sensitive issues: faculty tenure and retirement; faculty governance and campus autonomy; student participation in governance; undergraduate credit transfer; admissions and tuition policies; comparable funding for comparable programs; comparable teaching loads and salaries for faculty based on comparable experience and qualifications; the savings and efficiencies to be achieved by merger; and the highly charged question of "the practicability, feasibility and wisdom of merger."[31]

The committee's membership, also established by law, maintained the same careful balance among UW, WSU, and state government interests that characterized the new Board of Regents. The MISC was composed of equal numbers of regents, faculty, and students from the UW and WSU, together with legislative representatives and public members appointed by the governor. Under the law, staff support was to be provided by the new System head, with further help from two advisers, one each to represent the UW and the WSU.[32] Individual committee members, however, held sharply differing perspectives on merger and had conflicting agendas and goals for the organization of the new System.[33] The group included both merger advocates, including the bill's sponsor, Senator Ray Heinzen, and merger opponents, such as former UW regents Ody Fish and Walter F. Renk, who were still unconvinced that the new System was viable. Student appointees Robert Brabham and Randy Nilsestuen came to the work intent on gaining a stronger student voice in the governance of the new System. Opposing faculty perspectives were represented by Clara Penniman, a member of the Madison faculty senate and a proponent of traditional UW governance and organization, and UW–Eau Claire's Marshall Wick, a leader in The Association of University of Wisconsin Faculties (TAUWF), a nascent faculty union committed to achieving resource and salary parity between the institutions of the former UW and WSU systems. Joseph Nusbaum, secretary of the Department of Administration (DOA), appointed to the committee by the governor, favored ensuring a strong role for state government in the control and policy leadership of the new UW System.

James G. Solberg, an attorney from Menomonie, Wisconsin, and a member of the former WSU board, was named to chair the MISC and to lead this diverse group in fulfilling its complex assignment. He faced immediate challenges as, even before the MISC's first meeting, scheduled for December 3, 1971, state government and university leaders began jockeying to control the committee's work. The first dispute arose in mid-November, over who should provide the necessary staff services and advice to the committee. The merger law clearly stated that the UW System's chief executive, Weaver, was to act as the secretary to the MISC and furnish its staff.[34] Signaling state government's intent to be actively involved in directing the committee's work, however, Heinzen, supported by the DOA's Nusbaum, circulated a plan that called for state agencies such as the Legislative Council, the Legislative Reference Bureau, and the Department of Administration to staff and advise the committee.

Resistance to the Heinzen plan from university leaders was immediate. By letter of November 19, 1971, MISC member and UW regent Frank Pelisek wrote Solberg, complaining that the provision of advice and staffing from nonuniversity agencies would concentrate too much power over the work of the MISC in DOA and would represent a "serious departure from Wisconsin's past educational traditions" of deference to university independence and self-governance. Pelisek, also a lawyer, urged Solberg to follow the plain language of the legislation mandating that Weaver and his staff provide the necessary expertise to the MISC, warning that "it would be a very serious mistake if one of the members of the [MISC] Committee, i.e., Mr. Nusbaum or another, would be designated as Executive Secretary of this Committee and would be directed to provide staff services. . . . I believe it would be a serious mistake to allow the DOA to provide staff services."[35]

This preliminary disagreement led to a contentious debate at the MISC's initial meeting, on December 3. The group's first order of business was the appointment of Weaver as executive secretary, but before a vote on this item could be taken, Heinzen moved to implement the technical advisory committee plan he had previously circulated. His motion—technically out of order—triggered a lengthy discussion and parliamentary maneuvering that occupied much of the meeting. Although the motion was eventually tabled and Weaver was appointed executive secretary, it was an inauspicious start. The wrangling exposed the divisions among MISC members and highlighted state government's distrust of allowing the higher education representatives and the leaders of the new System to manage the merger implementation process.[36]

As the meeting continued, further divisions emerged. The MISC's mission was debated. There was a disagreement over whether, as Weaver had proposed, to create new task forces to study each of the specific subject areas enumerated in the legislation or to rely on the reports of existing faculty-led task forces that had already been working independently on these issues. There was dissension over how best to obtain input on the MISC's work, including the global question "what should the UW System be," from all interested parties. After extended, often frustrating debate on these and related matters, Weaver's task force proposal was defeated, and the group agreed to seek the opinions of any interested parties on the question what the UW System should be. Fulfilling the merger legislation's requirement that one member each from the central staffs of the UW and the WSU be selected to serve the MISC as advisers, the group managed to agree on selecting Percy and McPhee to serve in those roles.[37] Overall, however, little progress was made on the committee's assignments.

A New Direction:
Drafting the Governing Statute

In the wake of this initial session, it was apparent to Solberg—and to most of the other participants—that a different approach would be needed if the MISC was to complete its work by the January 1973 deadline. Again taking the initiative, Percy suggested, with Pelisek's support, that the MISC focus its efforts on drafting the System's governing statute. Under the merger law, the MISC was assigned to recommend a new statute that combined and replaced Chapters 36 and 37, Wisconsin Statutes (1969), the charters applicable to the former UW and WSU systems. Percy and Pelisek agreed that work on the new statute should become the committee's top priority, and Solberg concurred. In preparation for the January 24, 1972, MISC meeting, Solberg sent a memorandum to committee members emphasizing that their principal mission was to "recommend a single, model [statutory] chapter for the UW system."[38] At this meeting, Percy presented a detailed comparison of the existing statutes, and the committee agreed to concentrate its efforts on drafting the new governing legislation, appointing an ad hoc committee to draft the new law. Chaired by Pelisek, the group included Percy and McPhee; MISC members Nusbaum, Penniman, and Wick; and the two student representatives, along with staff from legislative agencies and the UW's legal counsel office.[39] Although the MISC continued to encourage the submission of position papers from any interested persons on the study areas enumerated in the merger bill, as well as on the overarching question "what the UW System should be," drafting and deliberations on the new governing statute became the principal focus of the MISC's activities.

Consensus

This change in direction proved crucial to organizing the committee's work. While it did not eliminate all disagreements or conflicts among committee members, it provided a more orderly framework for deliberations. With the focus on statutory drafting, consensus developed around a number of issues. The MISC quickly reached agreement on consolidating various technical provisions from the former governing statutes. Chapters 36 and 37 both contained language dealing with such matters as corporate titles and status, authority to manage property, and police powers on university lands. These sections were easily harmonized and incorporated into the new draft law without dissent.

Consensus also emerged on three important policy matters: the mission of the new System; faculty governance; and faculty tenure. For the System's mission statement, the MISC drew on the text of the merger law itself, provisions in Chapters 36 and 37, and language reflecting historic commitments to academic freedom and the widely admired Wisconsin Idea articulated by Charles R. Van Hise, the UW's president from 1903 to 1918.

The state's support for the principles of academic freedom had deep roots. In 1894, Professor Richard T. Ely, a distinguished member of the UW faculty, was tried before the Board of Regents on charges that he had encouraged labor unrest and violence through his academic writings. In its report exonerating him, the Board of Regents eloquently affirmed the university's dedication to encouraging the free pursuit of truth in academic inquiry, stating:

> In all lines of academic investigation it is of the utmost importance that the investigator should be absolutely free to follow the indications of truth wherever they may lead. Whatever may be the limitations which trammel inquiry elsewhere we believe the great state University of Wisconsin should ever encourage that continual and fearless sifting and winnowing by which alone the truth can be found.

The last sentence, later memorialized on a plaque in Bascom Hall, reflected the UW's steadfast commitment to academic freedom.

The Wisconsin Idea, that the boundaries of the university are the boundaries of the state and beyond, had also long been a guiding principle for the UW.[40] The idea was a natural outgrowth of the expectations of the state's founders when they included in the state's constitution a requirement for the establishment of a state university. These early state leaders saw in public higher education not only the means of teaching and training individuals for professions and civic leadership but also a vehicle for expanding knowledge through research and applying it broadly to support the state's economic growth. Early in the twentieth century, President Van Hise had elaborated on this vision, emphasizing that the "beneficent influences" of the university should reach all citizens, making the boundaries of the campus coextensive with those of the state. By the time of merger, the UW, through its outreach and extension programs, had for many years been actively engaged in sharing its knowledge and expertise widely, for the benefit of the public, well beyond the confines of the campus.

The legislature, in the merger law, had declared it to be in the public interest to foster diversity in educational opportunity and to promote quality undergraduate programs, while preserving the strength of graduate training and research. It also supported the continuation of the traditional policies and practices of the former UW and WSU systems.[41] The mission statement approved by the MISC for the new UW System incorporated these ideas, together with expressions of commitment to academic freedom and the Wisconsin Idea. The MISC proposed a statement that it was in the public's interest to provide a higher education system that, among other things, enables students of all ages, backgrounds, and levels of income to participate in the search for knowledge, fosters diversity of educational opportunity, and promotes service to the public. The MISC proposed further defining the mission of the new System as follows:

> to develop human resources, to discover and disseminate knowledge, to extend knowledge and its application beyond the boundaries of its campuses, and to serve and stimulate society by developing in students heightened intellectual, cultural and humane sensitivities, scientific, professional and technological expertise and a sense of purpose. Inherent in this broad mission are methods of instruction, research, extended training and public service designed to educate people and improve the human condition. Basic to every purpose of the system is the search for truth.[42]

This reaffirmation of the historical purposes and principles of Wisconsin public higher education was approved by the committee without dissent.

MISC members also reached agreement on issues of faculty governance and faculty tenure. Nationally, the prominent role of faculty in university governance had developed in the late nineteenth and early twentieth centuries with the growing curricular emphasis on science and research.[43] During this period, the American Association of Universities (AAU), composed of the country's elite research universities, and the related American Association of University Professors (AAUP) were formed to support the crucial role of faculty in preserving rigorous academic standards and protecting academic freedom. As a leading research institution and a founding member of the AAU, the UW had a well-established tradition of faculty governance. At the time of merger, the UW's governing statutes specifically provided that the immediate governance of the university was to be vested in the faculty,[44] and the MISC agreed that this concept should be preserved in its draft law for the new System. While noting that faculty governance historically was limited to academic policy and decision making—not the business management of an institution—the MISC approved retention of the faculty's primary responsibility for governance in academic matters and academic personnel decisions, including decisions on which individual faculty members should be granted tenure.

On a closely related issue, the MISC proposed that tenure protections be described and codified in the governing statutes for the new System. While it was unusual to include such provisions in state law—most universities address these matters in university policies, rather than by statute—the tenure rules for WSU faculty were already incorporated in Chapter 37 of the Wisconsin Statutes.[45] WSU representatives on the MISC favored maintaining these rules and including them in the new System's governing statutes. The WSU statute, however, allowed for the achievement of tenure after six years of service at an institution, without any evaluation of performance or qualifications. UW representatives were concerned about this kind of time-in-grade promotional system, not only worried about the lack of quality control but also fearful that tenure granted anywhere in the new System might be transferable to other institutions. From the UW perspective, it was crucial to establish that tenure could be granted only on the basis of merit as determined by peer review, that it could be terminated only for cause after the faculty member had had an opportunity to be heard, and that tenure would be limited to the institution where it was granted. On the MISC, the UW's Penniman persuaded the group that tenure should be granted only to ranked instructional faculty, only upon the approval and recommendation of the individual's academic department and chancellor, and that it should apply only at the institution where it was granted—in essence, the model followed by the former UW. The committee also agreed with the fundamental principle established in the Ely case that dismissal of tenured faculty could occur only for just cause, after the faculty member had had an opportunity to be heard.[46] Despite rejecting the automatic tenure

provisions of Chapter 37 in favor of this UW–style tenure system, MISC members did agree on the importance of codifying
their proposed structure in the statutes. As a result, faculty tenure provisions were included in the proposed statutory charter
for the new UW System, along with similar contract-based job
protections for nonfaculty instructional academic staff members
and academic administrators.[47]

The Unreconciled Differences

The MISC's work on other issues, however, failed to achieve the
wide support reflected in these consensus-based proposals,
leaving many participants in the implementation process disappointed, dissatisfied, and unreconciled to the results. The clashing
interests of UW, WSU, and state government produced sharp
differences among MISC members in three key areas central to
the organizational framework of the new UW System: institutional autonomy; parity in resource allocation; and state government involvement in the direct management of the new System.
The treatment of these matters in the MISC's proposed governing
statute, as well as by intervening board and administrative actions, tended generally to favor the positions taken by UW representatives, leaving dissatisfaction and fueling future conflicts
among the participants in the MISC process.

Institutional Autonomy versus Central Leadership

An important source of WSU opposition to merger had been the
fear that WSU institutions would lose their independence in a
consolidated system dominated by the UW campuses, especially
UW–Madison. The WSU had traditionally operated with minimal
central control. The WSU board was supported by a central administration consisting of a director and a small staff that exercised little management authority over WSU campuses, giving
campus leaders considerable autonomy and broad latitude to
develop their own budgets, determine their own missions, and
decide what programs, both undergraduate and graduate, they
would offer. WSU presidents[48] had direct access to the WSU
board, allowing them to lobby directly for their special local interests. WSU regents represented individual campuses and were

often actively engaged in managing and advocating for "their" institutions. Loss of this kind of local control had fed WSU anxiety about merger.

To address this concern, language had been included in the merger legislation that called for promotion of the "widest degree of individual campus autonomy" in the new System.[49] At the same time, however, the legislation established a strongly centralized leadership structure for the merged organization. It provided for a single governing board supported by a chief executive and central administration and expressly provided that institutional autonomy was subject to the control of the board.[50] It was a governance structure patterned generally after that of the former UW, in effect sweeping the former WSU institutions into a more tightly unified, centrally led and controlled organization. Unhappy with this approach and hoping to preserve as much of their old independence as possible, the WSU representatives on the MISC offered a series of proposals designed to codify a weak, essentially coordinative role for the system president and system administration. They suggested allowing campus executives to report directly to the Board of Regents and to develop and submit their individual campus budgets directly to the board for approval, bypassing the System president. They also proposed allowing institutions to define their individual campus missions without the approval of the System president or central administration. To address their concerns about UW—and particularly UW–Madison—dominance, they advocated requiring intrastate, geographically balanced representation on the Board of Regents and a statutory prohibition on locating the UW System's central administration on any campus.

Strongly opposed by UW representatives on the committee as inconsistent with both the language and the purposes of the legislation, these proposals were ultimately rejected by the MISC. An administrative structure for the merged System that undermined central control by allowing individual institutions direct access to the governing board to advocate for their own programs and budgets threatened to produce the very kind of competition, program duplication, and uncoordinated growth that had driven the push for merger in the first instance. Central leadership was also important from the UW perspective to ensure mission- and program-based allocation of resources through a unified budget and to prevent the dilution or diversion of re-sources generated by and for individual institutions—particularly UW–Madison, with its substantial research grants and outside supporting foundations—to other campuses. The UW represen-tatives on the MISC successfully pressed for a statutory model in which new programs would be added only on the recommenda-tion of the president, consistent with board-approved institu-tional missions, while budgets would be developed and funds distributed at the System level, pursuant to centrally approved policies and principles.[51]

The draft statute that emerged from the MISC deliberations largely followed the UW suggestions. It provided that the System president and central administration would be responsible for administering and developing board policies, coordinating edu-cational program development, preparing System budgets, and overseeing building programs. Chancellors, as executive heads of their institutions, were assigned responsibility for administering board policies and the funds allocated for their institutions, but under the direction of the System president and with account-ability to both the president and the Board of Regents. Under the MISC's proposal, the board was responsible for the governance of the System, charged with promoting institutional autonomy but only "within the controlling limits of systemwide policies and priorities established by the board."[52]

Parity versus Comparability

While WSU concerns about loss of campus autonomy had sparked opposition to merger, the hope that merger would increase WSU resources had had the countervailing effect of generating some WSU support, especially among faculty. Early proponents of merger such as Stevens Point's Dreyfus had argued for parity between the UW and the WSU in institutional funding, as well as in faculty salaries and teaching loads, and Lucey's emphasis on the equitable treatment of the two former systems in the course of the merger debate had seemed to promise it. Although both Lucey and Dreyfus would later deny that this was their intention, many WSU faculty members believed these premerger statements were firm commitments and expected them to be fulfilled.[53] As a result, when the MISC began to study issues of comparable funding for comparable programs and comparable teaching loads and salaries for faculty based on comparable experience and qualifications,[54] WSU representatives argued for equality between the two former systems in these areas. Led by UW–Eau Claire's Marshall Wick, they proposed the inclusion of statutory provisions requiring equal salaries for faculty of equal experience and training at all campuses in the new System, as well as equivalent funding support for comparable academic programs at all System institutions.

UW representatives, however, saw in Wick's proposals the threat of the leveling effect that had been a major factor in their own concerns about merger. They feared that equal distribution of resources across institutions would, in effect, dilute UW—and particularly UW–Madison—resources, bringing a decline in quality at UW institutions and damaging the Madison campus's national stature and reputation.[55] They argued that the idea of "comparable" support provided under the merger law allowed the merged system to recognize the different resource needs of fundamentally different types of institutions, justifying differential treatment of the institutions with regard to program support and faculty salaries and workloads based on the different missions, types of degrees offered, and specific program offerings of individual institutions.

On these issues, too, the UW position prevailed. Wick's proposals for across-the-board equity not only were rebuffed by the MISC but also were effectively rendered moot during the course of the committee's deliberations as a result of the Board of Regents approval of the budget and cluster model developed by Percy to guide institutional funding and program decisions. The approach adopted by the board addressed the comparability issue, confirmed the need for differential treatment of the different institutional clusters, and supported related distinctions in salary and workload comparability for faculty in the different clusters.

State Government versus UW System

Whatever their differences on these matters, however, the UW and WSU members of the MISC were firmly united in their opposition to efforts to codify a role for state government representatives in the new UW System's governing statute. The DOA's

Nusbaum advocated for expanding legislative and gubernatorial power over the activities of state agencies generally[56] and offered a series of proposals to the MISC to provide by statute direct administrative roles for the governor and legislature in university management and operations. He also recommended a requirement that the mission statements of System institutions be approved by the legislature—not by the Board of Regents—and codified in the statutes. And, in a move to gain state and DOA control over university employees, he further proposed that the university's academic staff—nontenure-track instructional staff and academic administrators—be transferred to the state civil service under the direction of the State Bureau of Personnel and his own DOA.[57]

Both UW and WSU members of the MISC resisted these proposals, seeing them as unwarranted and unnecessary intrusions into academic governance. In the context of the MISC's work, UW and WSU representatives on the committee joined forces to oppose Nusbaum's suggestions about defining roles for the legislature and governor in the System's governing statute and transferring university personnel to the state civil service. Both proposals failed to make their way into the MISC's proposed statute. A related proposal that institutional missions be codified in the law likewise failed, the MISC instead recommending that the board establish institutional missions through a nonstatutory process that would ensure the board's authority to decide what types of programs each UW institution could offer and what degrees they would be allowed to grant. Like other contentious topics dealt with at the MISC, though, state government's involvement in the details of university management would remain a source of ongoing conflict and tension. Struggles over the nature of the partnership between the state and the UW System, including the appropriate level and extent of state control over academic administration and issues related to oversight and regulation of university affairs, would recur regularly in the years to come.

As the MISC's work drew to a close, these unreconciled differences on the issues of institutional autonomy, parity in resource allocation, and the degree of state government's involvement in higher education management left lingering dissatisfaction both within the new UW System and externally, in relations between the System and the state. These matters would be revisited when the MISC's proposed governing statute was considered by the legislature and would remain an ongoing source of tension in the UW–WSU union, even after legislative and gubernatorial action on the new statute.

Preempting the MISC:
Board and Executive Policy Actions Affecting MISC Studies

While the committee focused on preparing the draft statute and worked to meet the January 1973 deadline for completion of its report, the board and the Weaver administration continued to deal with the pressing challenges of maintaining continuity of operations for the new System and addressing the problems of program duplication, competition, and cost that had led Lucey to propose merger. Critical management decisions on these matters could not await the outcome of the MISC's studies or the enactment of a new governing law for the System, and the board had moved forward on a number of matters that preempted or mooted the MISC's work on its assigned study areas. Well aware of the situation and with the deadline for the submission of the MISC report approaching, Solberg asked Weaver to provide a description of board and administrative work affecting the MISC's assignments.

Weaver responded with a summary of the most significant of these actions.[58] Pointing out that the board and administration had acted out of necessity in the performance of their duties, Weaver described the new board's early efforts to curtail program growth, citing the moratorium on new programs imposed at its January 7, 1972, meeting and refined at subsequent meetings throughout the year. He also pointed to the approval of the cluster campus organizational structure and related policy papers, which not only affirmed the System's commitment to limited program growth but also responded to the MISC study area of comparability in funding for comparable programs by providing for comparable program funding within clusters but allowing differential funding of clusters.

With regard to comparability in faculty salaries and workloads, Weaver noted that Percy's office had by the end of 1972 begun developing a management information system to collect data on faculty workloads and effort. On Percy's recommendation, policymaking in these areas was to be delayed until analysis of the data was complete and the board could undertake longer-term studies. These studies would, however, take place in the context of the board-approved cluster structure, opening the door to differential pay for faculty based on the type of institutions in which they served, the level and type of their program offerings, and the institutional missions to be developed with Smith's leadership.

Listing other MISC study areas affected by board action, Weaver pointed to the board's decision to combine the two-year campuses into a single institution with its own central administration. He also noted the board had initiated a study of UW–Extension and its various functions and relationships with all the campuses in the combined System. UW–Extension had been classified as a separate institution during Harrington's administration. The move had been controversial at the time because it separated UW–Madison from a critical outreach function that had not only helped to advance the Wisconsin Idea but also generated popular and political support for the flagship campus.[59] The board's study was intended to assess the appropriate role of Extension in the combined UW System, obviating the need for MISC consideration of this issue. Affecting other major MISC study areas, the board had also approved tuition and admissions policies, credit transfer requirements, and affirmative action guidelines for women and minorities.

Together, these board and administrative actions addressed a substantial number of the study areas assigned to the MISC, pre-empting additional study or obviating the need for further action on the part of the committee. As Weaver also noted, however, further work was needed on many of these complex policy issues, especially those academic matters that would become the responsibility of Donald K. Smith, the recently appointed vice president for academic affairs. The challenges of merging "two former systems having substantial differences in regard to many of the [MISC] 'study areas'" would, he noted, be ongoing.[60]

The MISC Report: A Governing Statute and the Feasibility of Merger

The MISC finished its work on the draft statute in the fall of 1972, and the report was discussed in detail at meetings from November 1972 through January 1973. As recommended by the committee, the proposed law reaffirmed the Wisconsin Idea and dedication to academic freedom as essential elements of the System's mission. It established a strong central leadership model, vesting primary authority for the operation of the System in its Board of Regents and president. The duties and responsibilities of the System president, central administration, chancellors, faculty, staff, and students were specifically defined. A merit-based tenure system was adopted. Long-standing faculty tenure protections and an expanded opportunity for student participation in campus affairs were codified.

The completion of the proposed governing statute, together with Weaver's report on the activities of the Board of Regents and administration affecting the MISC study areas, fulfilled nearly all of the MISC's assignments under the merger law. There remained only the question of the practicability, feasibility, and wisdom of merger, which MISC took up at its final meeting on January 19, 1973. After much debate, the committee determined that "no group was in a position at this point of time to determine the practicability and wisdom of merger." Characterizing these as "long-term" questions, the MISC confined itself to considering only whether merger was "feasible." On this issue, over the dissents of regents Renk and Fish, the group concluded that merger was, indeed, feasible. With this action and with the combination of provisions in the draft statute and existing or pending action of the Board of Regents, the MISC concluded its work on January 19, 1973, and authorized the submission of its final report.

By letter of January 29, 1973, Solberg transmitted the report to the Board of Regents and the legislature. The report contained the draft statute recommended by the MISC for approval by the legislature, together with appendices describing the board and administrative actions that responded to the MISC study areas and a summary of other subjects that the committee determined to be more appropriate for ongoing administrative action than for treatment by the committee. Although the report included a unanimous endorsement of the draft statute, it was a compromise document that did not satisfy all participants in the process and reflected ongoing doubts about the merged system's viability. As Solberg noted, "no document conceived and developed by any committee could hope to meet all the varied and often conflicting wishes of the parties to merger, the constituencies affected by it and the many participants and observers involved in our discussions."[61] Many issues addressed in the report and by the proposed statute would continue to be subjects of disagreement and dissension as the MISC-proposed statute moved through the legislature, and later. The emphasis on codifying the new System's governance structure in state law—rather than leaving it for internal policy development by the board and institutional leaders—left it open to amendments by future legislatures and vulnerable to political manipulation. Nevertheless, the organizational framework developed by the MISC and the policy work of the board and administration offered a coherent legal and policy foundation for the new System. The MISC report was approved by the board at its March 9, 1973, meeting and transmitted to the legislature on March 16, 1973. The parties to the shotgun marriage had achieved a postnuptial agreement. It now required approval by the rest of the family—state government.

A New Governing Statute:
Chapter 335, Laws of 1973

Legislative consideration of the MISC's proposed governing statute, introduced as Assembly Bill (AB) 930, began in the state Assembly in March 1973. The merger law had called for the enactment of implementing legislation by July 1, 1973. Progress to final action, however, would be much slower. Those unhappy with the various aspects of the MISC proposal began lobbying for amendments to the implementation bill, while the old opponents of merger seized the opportunity to stall implementation in hopes of killing the consolidation altogether. The legislative process eventually dragged on into the summer of 1974.

An initial obstacle to passage involved a dispute over limitations on graduate and specialty programs. Soon after its introduction, Representative James Azim of Muscoda introduced an amendment to AB 930 that would have prohibited discontinuance of any graduate program in the UW System without legislative approval. The Azim amendment was supported by WSU institutions interested in preserving or expanding their graduate offerings but was opposed by the board, which had approved policies limiting all graduate program growth, effectively restricting doctoral programs to UW–Madison and UW–Milwaukee. Azim's amendment was eventually withdrawn, but, because of other amendments, negotiations, and public hearings that occurred over the course of the summer of 1973, the Assembly was unable to pass the implementation bill until February 27, 1974. As approved, the Assembly bill contained only minor changes from the MISC's draft statute, conforming to the MISC proposal on all substantive issues. The delay in its passage, however, precluded Senate consideration of the measure within the regular legislative session, forcing Lucey to call a special session in the spring of 1974 to complete action on the matter.

As had been the case with the merger bill itself, the Republican-controlled Senate now offered an opportunity for merger opponents to substantially amend the bill or even to completely undo the merger. TAUWF took advantage of the situation to prepare and lobby for a substitute amendment to the Senate bill that would have adopted many of the provisions unsuccessfully advanced by the WSU representatives on MISC. The TAUWF amendments weakened the powers of the president and system administration officers, emphasizing local autonomy and shifting greater authority to the chancellors. Consistent with Wick's proposals during the MISC's deliberations, the TAUWF amendments prohibited establishment of the central administration office on any campus, reduced the president's responsibilities to those of a coordinator, and allowed chancellors to develop and present their own budgets directly to the Board of Regents. The TAUWF bill also called for appointment of regents on a regional basis and provided specifically for across-the-board parity in funding for programs and resources. A different amendment, offered by a group of merger opponents, would have simply "de-merged" the System.

Despite intense lobbying and additional parliamentary maneuvering, however, neither the TAUWF-proposed amendments nor the de-merger proposal succeeded. The Senate adopted relatively minor changes to the Assembly bill, and—to avoid further delays in moving the legislation forward—the Assembly quickly voted to concur in the Senate amendments. The Assembly action sent the bill to the governor, who used his veto powers to restore language changed in the Senate, leaving the completed legislation essentially in the form recommended by the MISC. Lucey signed the measure on July 3, 1974, and the UW System's new governing statute, Chapter 335 of Wisconsin Laws of 1973, became effective July 8, 1974.

The Postnuptial Agreement

The merger implementation statute, in combination with the staff consolidations and Systemwide policies developed by the board, established an administrative and governance framework for the UW System that was widely admired. Praising the merger implementation work and Weaver's fine staff, higher education experts Eugene C. Lee and Frank M. Bowen noted that the UW System's structure "integrates campus objectives, academic program review, evaluation, and sophisticated and informed central policy direction with an ongoing budgetary process," while remaining sensitive to institutional values.[62]

The implementation work had also achieved most of the goals of merger identified by Lucey. Program growth had been brought under the control of the Board of Regents and would be effectively limited, particularly at the graduate level. A centralized administrative structure with centralized budgeting and resource allocation also subject to board control had been established, limiting competition for resources. The adoption of the cluster campus organizational scheme allowed for differentiation between groups of institutions to recognize their distinct missions and programs but provided for parity within groups.

Clouding these achievements, however, were internal problems that would fuel future disputes and struggles. By shaping the new law to reflect the MISC recommendations, Lucey and the legislature had, in effect, adopted a UW–style governance structure for the UW System. As many observers, including such UW advocates as Penniman, Young, and Percy, would later agree, the former UW and UW–Madison could not have asked for a better statute.[63] The approval of this structure, however, caused resentment among the WSU campuses over the loss of local autonomy and the dominant influence of UW–Madison and Weaver's central administration within the new organization. These concerns were heightened by disappointment over the failure of the implementation process to produce the kind of across-the-board salary and resource equality that many in the WSU believed had been promised by Lucey and others during the fight for merger. Dissatisfaction over these issues would spur continuing efforts on the part of TAUWF and its WSU constituents to gain collective bargaining rights for faculty. At the same time, though many of their policies and practices had been adopted for the new System and though the cluster system effectively preserved the distinctions among institutions and recognized the special status of the doctoral campuses at UW–Madison and UW–Milwaukee, UW institutions continued to fear the leveling effect of inclusion in the larger UW System and worried that their resources would be diluted or diverted to support the operations of other UW System institutions.

Externally, there were also problems. The new System faced deepening skepticism and distrust of university management on the part of state government. As Lucey had recognized, traditional legislative deference to academic leadership was rapidly being replaced by increased cost consciousness and heightened interest in actively directing university affairs. While the merger implementation statute did not include a formal role for state government in university management, legislative interest in greater oversight was growing. With newly full-time status,[64] along with support from their research bureaus and councils and growing numbers of staff assistants, in the years following merger legislators would step up their monitoring of university activities, imposing numerous and often onerous new auditing and reporting requirements. As a result, while still dealing with the challenges of merger implementation, the new System was forced to contend with more scrutiny and new regulatory demands from state government. As Adamany would later put it, the days of government by "hand-shake"—personal trust between and among the legislature, governor, and university leaders—had changed, replaced by legislative leaders and governors seeking to manage the System themselves.[65]

While the shotgun marriage had produced an effective and workable postnuptial arrangement, conflicts involving the centralized System leadership structure, institutional autonomy, equitable resource distribution, and the role of state government in university affairs were regularly recurring, destabilizing influences that—together with ever-deepening financial troubles—posed ongoing threats to the success of the union.

3

Welcome to Hard Times

The completion of the MISC's work and the enactment of the UW System's governing statute in 1974 occurred in the midst of difficult economic times and harsh state budget realities, as throughout the country the expansionist post–World War II "golden age" of higher education drew to a close.[1] In Wisconsin, merger and the merger implementation process came with significant funding cuts and pressures to downsize the new UW System, presaging a sustained period of financial uncertainty and declining state support for public higher education.

Adding to the fiscal challenges, in 1976 the UW System faced its first leadership transition when Weaver announced that he would retire at the end of the following year. His departure set off a struggle for control of the process for choosing a successor and a heated debate over the qualifications for the position. UW–Madison chancellor H. Edwin Young would emerge as a compromise choice for the presidency, but because of his age and the mandatory retirement rules then in force, he would serve for less than three years. Philosophically opposed to strong centralized System leadership and primarily focused on UW–Madison affairs, Young did not actively advance Systemwide organizational unity or pursue a statewide higher education agenda. At the end of his term, in 1979, the UW System's internal cohesion, already damaged by the downsizing activities and declining financial support, remained fragile.

Fiscal Austerity:
Retrenchment and Downsizing

The UW–WSU merger was approved at a time when the economy, both nationally and in Wisconsin, was faltering. As the Vietnam War continued to take its toll, the nation was in a period of "stagflation"—recession with high inflation—which led President Richard M. Nixon to impose controls on wages, rents, prices, and interest and dividend rates in 1971.[2] In Wisconsin, state government felt the pinch in losses of real revenues, which in turn put pressure on the state's budgets and added to concerns about the expense of operating its extensive higher education enterprise. The economic constraints, preferences for new and different state priorities such as Lucey's own tax reform proposals,[3] and hardening resistance to tax increases of any kind left fewer dollars in the state budget for higher education. Compounding these problems, the aging of the baby boom generation led some to conclude that the demand for college education would decline and, along with it, UW System enrollments. Lucey had proposed the UW–WSU merger in part as a cost-saving measure, including major funding reductions for higher education along with his original merger plan in 1971. Although he later restored some of these funds, significant reductions remained, and these were followed by deeper cuts in the two succeeding biennial budgets. The glory days of free-wheeling growth and generous state spending on higher education in Wisconsin had effectively come to an end. Irving Shain, later to become UW–Madison's chancellor, would say that 1972 marked the beginning of "the slide" in budget support for the System.[4] Long-standing responsiveness to state university funding requests gave way to skeptical questions about actual needs for higher education in the state, and the newly created UW System, struggling to come together as a functional organization, confronted a harsh, destabilizing reality: the steady withdrawal of state taxpayer support and regularly recurring budget crises. As Weaver put it, Lucey could hardly have given the System a more difficult task than the one he produced by "forcing merger and creating such fiscal austerity as would create the very tensions that merger was meant to overcome . . . making holes in the garment we were trying to sew together."[5]

1973: Retrenchment

In the wake of the 1971 merger legislation, pressure to reduce higher education costs intensified, as the Lucey administration demanded new cuts in the UW System's budget for the 1973–75 biennium. Development of this budget had begun in early 1972, while the merger-required board and staffing consolidations and the MISC work were in progress. In May, DOA secretary Nusbaum informed the Board of Regents and Weaver that the governor planned to implement a 2.5 percent budget reduction in the coming biennium, which he expected would be absorbed through what were euphemistically designated as "productivity" savings. In this context, "productivity" meant increasing faculty teaching loads and closing redundant programs[6]—essentially demanding more work with less financial support, reducing staff and programs, or some combination of such measures. The governor and his team assumed that, with productivity efforts, System institutions would be able to maintain existing access and quality levels, even with a reduced budget. It was an assumption that infuriated faculty and made little sense from a management perspective, failing to recognize the effort faculty devoted to research at the doctoral institutions, the already high teaching loads of faculty in the former WSU institutions, or the commitments to students enrolled in existing programs. Nevertheless, the 1973–75 budget, as approved by the legislature, not only imposed the governor's proposed productivity cuts but increased them, resulting in an even larger 7 percent reduction ($21.5 million) in the UW System's 1973–75 budget.[7] Adding to the pain of these reductions, the budget included an additional decrease of $8.4 million, the result of projected enrollment declines, which translated to lower institutional income from tuition.

The magnitude of these cuts forced drastic action on the part of the UW System, including plans to eliminate staff. Even tenured faculty members were at risk, as it became clear that several of the former WSU campuses could not meet the required cuts through normal attrition or by terminating nontenured employees. Under the rules of the former WSU, which allowed tenure to be achieved after six years of continuous satisfactory service, substantial majorities of their faculty members had been tenured and continued to hold that status in the new System.[8] As a result, the extensive reductions in programs and instructional staffing imposed at many institutions affected tenured faculty along with nontenured, probationary faculty and academic staff members. By memorandum of April 4, 1973, Weaver provided guidance to UW System institutions on managing the funding reductions and advice regarding staff layoffs and terminations. Although at the time there were no specific, formal policies providing for the layoff of tenured faculty, the board, relying on its implied authority to address a fiscal emergency, adopted interim policies establishing a process for laying off tenured faculty in such circumstances, which was communicated to System institutions in May 1973. The situation was serious enough that several campuses proceeded to declare states of fiscal emergency and some eighty-eight tenured faculty members around the System received layoff notices, set to become effective in the spring of 1974. By the 1974–75 academic year, six campuses—the former WSU institutions at Eau Claire, Oshkosh, Platteville, Stevens Point, Stout, and Whitewater—faced the loss of a total of 302 positions, while other institutions faced smaller but still significant cuts.[9]

The actual number of job losses was eventually trimmed, as many of the affected individuals were reassigned or relocated to positions at other institutions within the System. In an early demonstration of the benefits of a unified System, the availability of positions at System institutions having vacancies—including UW–Madison—helped mitigate the pain of the layoffs for those individuals employed at institutions forced to make cuts. Still, while the damage was minimized and layoffs of tenured faculty ultimately occurred only at UW–Oshkosh, the situation brought plummeting morale throughout the System. The invocation of fiscal exigency as a basis for the initiation of layoff procedures led to litigation over tenure rights and due process of law. Faulting Lucey's productivity cuts for the layoffs, TAUWF leader Edward Muzik pressed for legal action to reinstate any tenured faculty members subject to layoff.[10] Although the System's authority to lay off staff and the process it followed in doing so were upheld in the courts,[11] concerns about job security heightened pressure from TAUWF and other unions for collective bargaining rights for faculty members as a means of improving job security. And, because the WSU and two-year schools bore the brunt of the

cutbacks and layoffs, their resentment of the System Administration, which was forced to manage the cuts, along with their
frustrations over perceived salary and workload inequities between the former UW campuses and WSU institutions, also grew.
Reflecting the animosity, Representative Richard Flintrop blamed
the layoffs at Oshkosh on the System administration's neglect of
that campus in favor of Madison and Milwaukee, saying, "They
run around in their red Bucky Badger jackets and seldom think
about the other campuses."[12] The successful completion of the
MISC work and passage of the System's new governing law in
July 1974 were cold comfort in the face of the pain of layoffs and
did nothing to improve the grim financial outlook for the UW
System.

1975: Shrinking the System

The next year brought worse news. On January 8, 1975, Lucey
wrote to the Board of Regents, advising that the System could
expect no budget increase for the coming 1975–77 biennium and
would likely face additional productivity cuts. Stating that state
taxpayers had generously funded higher education in the past
but could not afford to continue current levels of support going
forward and predicting that enrollments would decline in the
coming decade, Lucey asked the board to prepare, by mid-April,
"a plan for phasing out, phasing down, or consolidating institutions and programs, including a statement of language to be in-
serted into the 1975–77 biennial budget which would authorize
implementation of the plan."[13] Coming as it did while the pain of
the 1973–75 cutbacks and layoffs was still raw, this demand to
downsize cast doubt on the viability of many of the System's
institutions, further undermining morale and heightening pre-
existing tensions over merger.

   Reluctantly, the board, now headed by regent president Frank
Pelisek,[14] directed Weaver to comply with the governor's request,
"even though we may not believe that phasing out or phasing
down centers and campuses is necessarily in the best interest of
the University System and the State of Wisconsin." Over the
course of the next few months, Weaver and his team, led by
Percy and Smith, prepared *The President's Report on Reducing the
Scope of the University of Wisconsin System*,[15] presenting it to the
board on April 18, 1975.

Defending the value of the UW System to the state, Weaver began the report with a reminder of Wisconsin's historic commitment to the propositions that (1) the state's citizens should have ready access to quality higher educational opportunity, and (2) a public university education is a public good, from which society benefits in numerous ways. Emphasizing that the state's investment is repaid through the lives and taxes of citizens, the power of vibrant communities, the cultural and economic vitality of society, and the overall quality of life, he urged the state to continue its commitment to support higher education and to maintain its "longstanding traditions of intellectual pioneering for the public good."

The report went on to challenge Lucey's central assumption that enrollments would decline, citing several studies and projections indicating that, to the contrary, enrollments would increase until at least 1983 and stabilize at that point. The document continued by warning that, in the zero-increase or declining budget environment proposed by Lucey, the System could not maintain educational quality if enrollments continued to grow as predicted by the System's own demographic data and studies. Without adequate funding, the System would be forced to limit access— that is, actively reduce enrollments—to ensure educational quality. But limiting access, the report argued, would be a dramatic departure from the state's long-standing commitment to providing generous educational opportunities for its citizens. As to the idea of shuttering campuses and programs, the report pointed out that these measures would not yield savings unless students, too, were dismissed from the System. As Pelisek put it in transmitting the report to the legislature, "a decision to close down a particular campus will *not* produce major dollar savings for use elsewhere in the System *unless* that decision operates to release us from the responsibility of accommodating the students and faculty involved at locations elsewhere in the System."[16]

Pressed, though, to respond to the governor's request, Weaver's report did offer options to scale back the System. Compounding existing anxiety, the report laid out a series of bleak choices: closing or consolidating two-year centers, considering a merger of UW–Superior with the University of Minnesota-Duluth, phasing out several of the comprehensive campuses, and further restricting program growth or eliminating programs at the doctoral institutions and UW–Extension. These were all painful steps that the Report advised the board not to take on its own. Instead, the report pushed the downsizing decision back to the legislature and governor. Emphasizing that a directive to reduce the System's size is a directive to reduce access to educational opportunity, the report called upon the legislature—not the System—to approve any of the options it had outlined for reducing the scope of the System.[17]

In the end, not surprisingly, the legislature proved itself no more willing to take such draconian steps than the Board of Regents or the Weaver administration. The scope of the System was not reduced, effectively confirming its existing size and composition. As Lucey later acknowledged, "once [the campuses] are there, it is hard to eliminate them."[18] The reduction exercise itself, however, had longer-term negative consequences. Lucey's insistence that the state could no longer afford to support the large public higher education system it had developed would continue to resonate with state elected officials and the public, spurring recurrent questions about the appropriate size, mission, and needs of the UW System. Within the System, the report's identification of specific targets for downsizing stoked already high anxieties about the continued viability of some System institutions. The two-year centers and the former WSU campuses that had been identified as possible targets for closure felt unfairly treated and were understandably worried about their futures. Many faculty members at those institutions demanded the development of stronger procedural protections against campus and program closures and—encouraged by TAUWF—stepped up efforts to obtain passage of collective bargaining legislation. The struggle over collective bargaining would remain a source of division and controversy within the System until the late 1980s, while the threat of campus and program closures would persist into the next century, as the System faced ongoing questions about its size and structure in light of changing demographic, economic and social conditions. Overall, the downsizing exercise left the System, as an organization, on the defensive, seeking to justify not only basic budgetary needs but its value to the state and the very existence of some of its institutions.

Further exacerbating these problems, while it was unwilling to opt for any of the closures or other downsizing possibilities outlined in the report, the legislature did impose more reductions in the university budget for the 1975–77 biennium. This round of cuts, following on the heels of the 1973–74 retrenchment, stoked still more uncertainty and fear about the System's future. The program reductions and faculty layoffs left a legacy of bitterness at the affected institutions, while giving rise to a divisive turf-protection mentality elsewhere. The doctoral campuses, though less vulnerable to closure than the other institutions, shared the general pain of the cuts, while premerger worries—particularly at the flagship—about the dilution or diversion of gift, grant, and foundation resources intended or generated for the use of their campuses to support other System units intensified. The general uneasiness fostered the continuation of premerger suspicions and distrust between and among System institutions, destabilizing the new System even as its organizational structure was being approved and implemented.

Summarizing the work of his five years in office in his 1975 end-of-year report, *Retrospect and Prospect Revisited*,[19] Weaver outlined the successes as well as the challenges left by the retrenchment and downsizing efforts. The conclusion of the merger implementation period with the approval of a structurally and organizationally combined state system of higher education was a widely admired accomplishment, but it had been accompanied by damaging funding reductions and financial uncertainty. While other public university systems had undergone reorganizations in the same period, few had faced issues as complex as those in Wisconsin. As Lee and Bowen noted in praising the UW System's merger effort, few other state systems had been forced to deal with major restructuring amid such severe fiscal constraints. Commenting on the "unprecedented series of difficulties" faced by the UW System in the immediate postmerger years, they said, "We know of no other state system of higher education which has progressed as far along this difficult road or any which has had to do this under more demanding circumstances."[20]

In his retrospective, Weaver warned of the ongoing hazards posed by the state's withdrawal of financial support, emphasizing that the state's retrenchment efforts threatened access and quality in the UW System and, further, that, by contributing to internal resentments and fueling lingering opposition to merger, the severe budget cuts threatened the long-term effectiveness of the System. He also noted that the issue of collective bargaining rights for faculty would become a growing source of contention in the wake of the layoff exercises. While the System had achieved a legal and organizational merger, the stability of this union was jeopardized by diminishing state resources and other serious problems.

Leadership Transitions:
Turnover and Turmoil

The anxieties stoked by Lucey's pressure to shrink the System were heightened by a series of leadership transitions in the UW System and state government that began in 1976. On July 25, 1975, Weaver suffered a heart attack that limited his ability to participate fully in System affairs until October of that year. In March 1976, he underwent open heart surgery, returning to work in May.[21] With his health concerns in the background and the applicable employment rules effectively mandating retirement at age sixty-two, Weaver announced in July 1976 that he would leave the presidency as of June 30, 1977.[22]

Meanwhile, in November of that year, Jimmy Carter was elected president of the United States and appointed Lucey to serve as Ambassador to Mexico. Lucey, in the middle of his second term as governor, left office on July 1, 1977, and was succeeded by Lieutenant Governor Martin Schreiber. At UW System, Weaver was followed as president by UW–Madison chancellor H. Edwin Young, also in July 1977, and soon after Young became president, Percy resigned from the System to become secretary of the state Department of Health and Social Services. In 1978, Schreiber would lose the gubernatorial election to Lucey's old friend, UW–Stevens Point chancellor Lee Dreyfus, who took office in January 1979. Within a relatively brief eighteen-month period, many of the key figures in the merger and its implementation had either departed or taken on new roles. For the UW System, the turnovers brought more fiscal uncertainty and new budget problems, as internal divisions, state government regulatory pressures, and recurring efforts to enact collective bargaining legislation continued.

The Search for a System President

Weaver's planned retirement triggered a bitter struggle over the selection of his successor, becoming a flashpoint for conflict among board members. Weaver had been hired only to serve as the former UW's president and had been appointed to lead the merged UW System at Lucey's urging, without a formal selection process. The search for his successor required the board to develop a new protocol specifically for choosing a System president. The effort quickly became mired in struggles for control of the process and the final decision. At the same time, signs of a fundamental disagreement over the qualifications for the presidency emerged, suggesting deepening divisions between those who believed scholarly credentials and experience leading an academic institution were essential and those who emphasized the importance of political skills and connections that strengthen relations with state government leaders. Both the process issues and the divide over academic versus political skills would be revisited in future System presidential searches.

Bertram McNamara, Pelisek's successor as board president, initiated the search process promptly after Weaver announced his retirement in the summer of 1976, seeking guidance on selection procedures from past executive searches at UW and WSU campuses and input from current and past board members. He also solicited advice from experts on academic search processes nationally, including UW–Madison professor and former dean of students Joseph Kauffman,[23] who helped him prepare a draft protocol for the new System presidential search.

McNamara's proposal followed, in most respects, standard academic practice for filling campus leadership positions, involving consultation with faculty, staff, and students and a two-tier process consisting of a search committee to evaluate candidates and develop a list of finalists and a selection committee composed of governing board members to make the final hiring decision.[24] Consistent with models used at other institutions nationally and that were also used to select campus leaders within the UW System, McNamara proposed establishing a search committee composed primarily of System faculty and staff to prepare a short list of finalists and a board selection subcommittee to recommend a final candidate to the full board for its approval. In an effort to adapt campus-level procedures to a System leadership search process, however, McNamara deviated from traditional practice by suggesting that three chancellors and three board members also be included on the first-tier search committee.

With these additions, McNamara's proposed search committee would total twenty-one members, representing faculty and university constituencies, chancellors, and regents. For the board selection subcommittee, McNamara proposed a total of nine members: the six members of the board's executive committee, plus the three regent members serving on the first-tier search committee. This group would evaluate the finalists identified by the search committee and recommend a candidate to the full sixteen-member board for final approval.

This seemingly conventional protocol, however, drew immediate criticism, setting off a heated argument at the board's executive committee meeting on September 8, 1976, about participation in and control of the selection decision. The debate began with expressions of concern by several board members that the first-level search committee was simply too large and questions by others about the inclusion of chancellors and board members at this level. On the latter point, Herbert Grover, a Democrat recently appointed to the board after having served in the state Assembly and as Lucey's floor leader on the merger bill, was especially outspoken. A large, burly man, with an aggressive, often intimidating debate style, he brought what Smith and Kauffman characterized as a new kind of "activist" attitude[25] to the board, demanding greater involvement in the details of System management and administration. Grover first challenged McNamara's addition of chancellors to the first-tier search committee, arguing that they should not have so much influence in choosing the person to whom they would report, and then attacked McNamara's plan to appoint the same three regents to both the first-tier search committee and the board's selection subcommittee. Grover pointed out that the inclusion of the same three regents on both committees would allow them to form a voting bloc with the six members of the board's executive committee that could dictate the board's final choice—and unfairly prevent those, like him, who were not members of either group from having a "piece of the action" on the final decision.[26]

Grover's bald demand for personal involvement and his confrontational tone, at variance with the generally polite tenor of most board meetings, triggered an angry exchange with McNamara, who responded that all board members would have a vote on the final selection. McNamara went on to remind Grover that the Board of Regents is a collegial, nonpolitical body—unlike the highly partisan state legislature where Grover had recently served. Grover retorted that the board is, in fact, politically partisan, citing the past political activities of fellow board members and specifically naming regent Ody Fish, the former chair of the state Republican Party, who, as a member of the former UW board, had been an active merger opponent. These comments sparked more accusations, as board members charged one another with playing politics with the UW System. Regent William Gerrard finally ended the debate, saying that "this kind of conversation has gone far enough." On that sour note, the executive committee voted to recommend McNamara's search protocol to the full board, and the meeting adjourned.[27]

When the full board took up the question of the search process the following week, tempers had cooled, and McNamara's plan for the composition of both the first-tier search committee and the board's selection subcommittee was approved. On the issues of presidential qualifications, however, the board discussion exposed the emerging division between those insisting on an established academic leader with a background similar to Weaver's and those who argued that academic credentials and experience were less important than political skills and the ability to work effectively with the state legislature and governor. Precedent at System campuses and in the former UW favored seeking an experienced educator-administrator, with strong scholarly credentials and credibility with faculty members and the national higher education community. The position description as originally presented to the board reflected this traditionalist view. More activist board members like Grover, however, tended to see the president's job in political terms, requiring a politically savvy, well-connected president who could work closely with the governor and state political leaders on higher education issues and serve as the UW System's chief political spokesperson.

The activist view was aligned with Lucey's understanding of the university presidency as an inherently political, partisan office. Public university systems are by their nature closely tied to state government, making the governor and other state leaders key partners in university affairs and infusing a powerful political element into the state-university relationship that makes it challenging for university leaders to maintain a nonpartisan approach to the position.[28] Familiar with this dynamic, Lucey had made it clear during his first campaign for the governorship that, if elected, he intended to play a significant role in state university affairs. He had urged the UW regents to delay choosing Harrington's successor to allow for possible changes in state higher education under a new governor and was angered when the Republican-dominated UW board[29] ignored his request and proceeded to appoint Weaver. Although Lucey ultimately agreed to name Weaver as president of the merged UW System as a means of gaining support for his merger bill,[30] he believed that Weaver was a Republican and consistently maintained that hiring Weaver before the election and without consulting the incoming governor was "stupid"—a mistake that he felt left Weaver, as the appointee of a board dominated by Republicans, at a political disadvantage in dealing with him as a Democrat.[31]

Agreeing with Lucey that political skills and relationships— and not just scholarly and academic credentials—were of primary importance for a UW System president, board activists advocated for a position description that would allow for consideration of candidates with less higher education administrative experience but other leadership and political credentials. In contrast, the traditionalists, while not naïve about the obvious political aspects of a System president's position or the relationship of a public university to state government, felt that the System president should possess an academic résumé strong enough to command the respect of the faculty and the ability to serve as a nonpartisan voice for higher education needs without being identified solely or too closely with a governor or his party. In the search for Weaver's successor, a kind of compromise was reached as the board amended the position description to indicate that academic credentials similar to Weaver's were preferred, although administrative experience in higher education "would be desirable but not mandatory."[32] The differences of opinion on the underlying issue, however, would remain unresolved, to be debated again in later presidential searches.

Meanwhile, although the board's agreement on qualifications theoretically opened the presidency to nontraditional candidates, the search process itself was unlikely to lead to the selection of such individuals. The first-level search committee, dominated by faculty members, tilted heavily in favor of the view that strong scholarly and academic qualifications were more important than other leadership experiences or partisan political connections, and Weaver confidently predicted that his successor would be a nonpolitical, experienced academic. As he told the media, "The faculty, especially the Madison faculty, won't have it any other way."[33] He dismissed from serious consideration several prominently mentioned nontraditional candidates, including his own vice president for budget, Percy; Adamany, Lucey's secretary of the Department of Revenue; and David Carley, a leading state Democrat, former regent, and president of the Medical College of Wisconsin. While each of them possessed the kind of political skills and experiences that would have made them attractive to those seeking a university leader able to forge strong connections with state government—as well as with Lucey—they lacked the kind of scholarly credentials and academic leadership experiences likely to survive the initial faculty-dominated screening process.

Weaver's prediction proved completely accurate. The first-level search committee met eleven times between September 27, 1976, and February 11, 1977, eventually choosing nine finalists from universities in the Big Ten and California, who were all experienced higher education leaders with credentials similar to Weaver's own. Missing from the list were nontraditional candidates who had political and executive abilities, including Percy, Adamany, and Carley,[34] effectively precluding the board from considering candidates with such alternative backgrounds. Meeting on March 7, 1977, the board, having had one finalist withdraw,[35] was unable to agree on the remaining choices, leaving it apparently deadlocked.[36] Faced with this impasse and hoping to avoid launching a new search, McNamara suggested approaching Young, who had been nominated as a candidate earlier in the process but had declined further consideration.

Young was an attractive compromise candidate. He had the appeal of being both an experienced academic leader and a close friend of Lucey's who was also familiar with the state legislature. He was a tenured professor at UW–Madison, where he had chaired the Department of Economics, served as dean of the College of Letters and Science, and was currently serving as chancellor, having returned to the flagship from a brief stint as president of the University of Maine. He would have been Lucey's first choice to head the UW in 1970 and to continue as president of the merged system if Weaver had not been appointed.[37] He would also have been acceptable to the first-tier search committee as a finalist for Weaver's position if he had not initially declined to be considered. In addition, as a practical matter, his term in office would be brief. Young was nearing age sixty-two, then the mandatory retirement age, and would be able to serve for less than three years. While the interim nature of the appointment was of some concern, it also offered the board time and opportunity to improve on its presidential selection processes. If not all were enthusiastic about the situation, board members agreed that McNamara should approach Young. As regent Ben Lawton put it, "We had, however, reached an impasse in our selection process and I went along with it."[38]

Although Young himself had serious reservations about accepting the position,[39] he agreed, believing that the presidency would give him an opportunity to protect the institution he had long served, UW–Madison. As the flagship's chancellor, he had feared the leveling effects of merger, worried not only about the reputational damage to Madison from being included in an organization with less prestigious institutions but also about having its financial resources either diverted for the support of other System institutions or diluted by the diminution of state funds available for the System as a whole. Young was also deeply suspicious of the kind of strong central administrative authority that Harrington had established as head of the former UW and worried about similar "overcentralization" in the merged UW System. Believing that the System presidency would allow him to shield Madison from these dangers, at McNamara's request he agreed to serve. He was appointed UW System president on March 11, 1977, and took office on July 1. McNamara had successfully averted an embarrassing succession crisis with the appointment, but it left the fundamental differences of opinion about the selection process and qualifications for the System presidency unresolved, while Young's brief term as president would further weaken internal cohesion.

A Governor Departs

Just as Young took office as System president, Lucey left the governorship to be the US ambassador to Mexico, taking with him the potential political benefits to the UW System that might have flowed from the close relationship between the two and leaving Young without a close ally in the governor's office. Lucey's immediate successor, his lieutenant governor and fellow Democrat Martin Schreiber, had inherited the 1977–79 biennial budget developed by the Lucey administration and so had no real opportunity to work with Young to improve the System's budget picture for the next biennium. Schreiber's loss in the 1978 gubernatorial contest meant that Dreyfus would develop the 1979–81 biennial budget, but Young had a troubled relationship with Dreyfus.

Dreyfus, also Lucey's friend and as UW–Stevens Point's chancellor an outspoken advocate for merger, had run successfully as a Republican.[40] With his signature red vest—a device he had first used to make himself easily recognizable on the Stevens Point campus—his folksy demeanor, and his promises to cut taxes, he drew wide popular support. Young, however, had clashed with Dreyfus during the gubernatorial campaign. As the UW–Stevens Point chancellor, Dreyfus had asked for Young's approval to remain on the UW payroll in that capacity while conducting his gubernatorial campaign, but Young denied his request and instead required him to take an unpaid leave of absence. The resulting tension between the two soured their working relationship once Dreyfus assumed office. It was apparent, said Kauffman, that Young "could not just go down to talk with Dreyfus."[41] The rift created another barrier to improving relations between the System and state government and exposed the potential pitfalls of overreliance on partisan political connections for the success of the System. The turmoil of the presidential search and the turnover in state leadership added to the problems facing a system still suffering the destabilizing effects of the retrenchment and downsizing exercises.

The Anti-System President:
The UW System as a "Loose Federation"

Internal System cohesion was further undermined during Young's tenure as he focused on protection of UW–Madison interests and related flagship matters. On becoming System president, Young quickly discovered that he disliked the job.[42] Believing that the

chancellorship at the Madison campus, with its national reputation for academic excellence, extensive research presence, distinguished alumni, and major athletics programs, was a more
prestigious and important job, he preferred to concentrate on
flagship affairs, giving little attention to uniting or leading Wisconsin's statewide higher education system.

Weaver had been a dutiful, if reluctant, leader of merger implementation and the new UW System. The postmerger statutes,[43]
together with the administrative policies approved by the board,
had maintained the highly centralized "flagship" type of organizational structure[44] established for the former UW under Harrington and used by Lucey as the model for the merged UW System.
This framework—providing for a strong System executive and
central administration, a unified UW System budget process,
and differentiated institutional missions based on level and scope
of program offerings—had been preferred by the Madison faculty
during the merger implementation period over the weak, coordinative role for the System sought by the former WSU campuses.
Weaver, with support from Percy and Smith, had worked to unite
the newly merged System within this structure.

Young, however, came to the presidency with a very different perspective on System leadership. Despite his friendship with
Lucey, his service on the premerger "wrinkle committee," and
his claimed acceptance of the merger with the WSU campuses,[45]
Young remained uncomfortable with the idea. Concerned about
its possible harmful consequences for UW–Madison, he was vigi-
lant in protecting its interests against those of the System as a
whole. While he acknowledged that UW–Madison had gained
the kind of administrative structure it had advocated during the
merger implementation work,[46] he was deeply suspicious of
centralized System authority and its potential for diluting or re-
distributing flagship resources. As Madison's chancellor, he had
also distrusted Harrington,[47] chafing at strong central leadership
in the former UW, as well as in the merged System. As System
president he remained hostile to "centralizers"[48] and became a
proponent of weak central System leadership, emphasizing the
importance of institutional autonomy and championing the notion that the System was a "loose federation" of largely independent institutions operating with minimal central direction or
control.

The source of the idea of the System as a federation is not clear. Although the governing statutes recognize the importance of "promoting the widest degree of institutional autonomy," they do not describe the System as a federation and state that local autonomy is limited by controlling board policies and priorities.[49] While both Young[50] and Kauffman[51] would later take credit for it, the idea seems to have originated in a report on UW System Faculty-Administration Relations approved by the Board of Regents. The report recommended against creating a Systemwide faculty senate, saying, "It should be emphasized that the System is a *federation* of institutions, each of which enjoys the maximum autonomy consistent with the statutory responsibilities of the regents and president for statewide planning and coordination of Wisconsin higher education (emphasis added)."[52] In any event, however, it was Young who embraced the idea of the System as a federation—and who further described it as a "loose" federation—to promote a weakened leadership role for the System president and System administration.

While this philosophy overlooked the broad governance responsibilities and powers assigned to the System president and regents under the merger statutes, it had some significant appeal—and generated little controversy—within the System. Young's emphasis on institutional autonomy coupled with a weak central executive authority was attractive to many from the former WSU system, whose campuses had enjoyed greater independence and whose faculties had advocated for greater local autonomy during the merger implementation process. The idea was also popular with those at the Madison campus who were still unhappy about merger and seeking to distance the flagship from the System. Chancellors and campus administrators, natural adversaries of strongly centralized System authority, also tended to like the idea, promising as it did enhanced local control of their individual institutions at the expense of a central administration that was often blamed for overregulation by the state, and insensitivity to institutional needs.

In practice, however, the loose-federation approach to governance stalled progress on Systemwide consolidation and the development of a strategic approach to managing Systemwide problems. In Young's brief tenure, efforts to build on the merger implementation work begun under Weaver or to develop a coherent Systemwide policy agenda slowed, leaving UW institutions to pursue independent, uncoordinated courses of action on these and other matters. Meanwhile, as board president Ben Lawton observed, Young remained "very much a 'Madison person,'"[53] focused on protecting UW–Madison's reputation and preserving its resources from diversion elsewhere in the UW System.[54] He enforced board policies—adopted at his urging while Madison's chancellor—providing that all research funds from the Wisconsin Alumni Research Foundation (WARF) be directed to UW–Madison[55] and that gifts, grants, and bequests designated generally for the "UW" by their donors be directed not to the UW System Board of Regents but to the particular institution with which the donor had been associated—a provision that would, in most instances, benefit UW–Madison.[56] And, in a maneuver that would prove to have painful consequences, late in his term he attempted to transfer the UW System's representation at the American Association of Universities (AAU), the preeminent association of national research universities, from the System president to the UW–Madison chancellor.[57]

Weaver had served in the role as System president, and Young became the representative on succeeding Weaver. Young, however, was convinced that AAU representation properly belonged to the flagship's leader, on the basis of Madison's status as a founding member of the organization and a leading national research institution. In 1977, hoping to recruit his former vice chancellor, Irving Shain, to the UW–Madison chancellorship he had just vacated, Young promised that he would transfer the AAU representative role from the System president to the flagship chancellor. Shain, who was then serving as provost at the University of Washington, was an attractive candidate to succeed Young. He had enjoyed a long and distinguished career at UW–Madison[58] and shared many of Young's views about merger, centralized System authority, and the need to protect UW–Madison's resources from possible diversion to smaller System institutions ambitious for their own growth. He also agreed with Young's position on AAU representation.[59] In the recruitment process, Shain asked that the representative role be made a condition of his employment and Young agreed. His attempt to make this change just before he left the presidency in 1979, however, would set the stage for a bruising struggle between Shain and Robert M. O'Neil, the next UW System president, over who should represent the UW System at the AAU. The clash would badly damage relations between the flagship and the System, further undermining System unity. The "loose federation" approach, Young's hypervigilance for Madison's welfare, and the AAU representation conflict contributed to ongoing fears of flagship dominance at the other System campuses, while encouraging lingering opposition to merger and resentment of System administration at the flagship.

The Ongoing State Issues:
Budgets, Audits and Oversight,
Collective Bargaining

Despite his principal concentration on flagship issues, as System president Young was forced to contend with many of the same ongoing Systemwide problems that had confronted Weaver. The state budget remained relatively flat during his term; state government was increasingly active in its efforts to oversee and regulate UW System affairs, and—as Weaver had predicted—pressure to authorize collective bargaining rights for UW faculty and staff accelerated.

Given the timing of his appointment as System president, Young had not led the development of the System's 1977-79 biennial budget request nor had he worked with the governor on the state budget. This last Lucey budget, continued under Schreiber, provided relatively stable ongoing funding for the UW System. Initial preparations for the 1979-81 budget—begun in June 1978—suggested that ongoing state support would likely remain the same or decrease.[60] Dreyfus's election as governor in November of that year, however, gave his new administration the opportunity to shape the 1979-81 budget. Dreyfus—with his background as a UW–Madison faculty member, UW–Stevens Point's chancellor, and a proponent of merger—was expected to be sympathetic to the UW System's needs, and, despite cool relations with Young, he initially proposed a significant increase in the higher education budget.[61] Although a promising start, this initial budget increase failed to materialize when the state's actual tax revenues proved inadequate to support the proposed additional funding. State fiscal support for the System, declining or flat through the Lucey-Schreiber years, would become increasingly uncertain under Dreyfus.

The System's continued financial difficulties did not, however, slow a steady increase in state regulatory and oversight interventions in university affairs. The Legislative Audit Bureau (LAB), led by state auditor Robert Ringwood, pursued aggressive investigations of UW System operations during Young's term. In early 1976, the LAB had proposed a series of audits designed to review the UW System's academic programs and the performance of its faculty and staff. The Board of Regents vehemently opposed the audits, on grounds that Ringwood lacked statutory authority to conduct such reviews and that they would usurp the board's— and the faculty's—own statutory responsibilities for the management of the System's academic mission and the development of curricula. At its February 6, 1976, meeting, the board adopted a resolution declining to permit the proposed audits and directed staff not to participate in them.[62] This standoff was followed by various meetings and communications between and among regents and other UW leaders, the legislature's Joint Audit Committee and its chair, Senator Dale McKenna, and Ringwood and other LAB representatives, during 1976 and continuing into 1977.

As System president, Young inherited this situation. Shortly after taking office, on October 5, 1977, he appeared at a hearing before the Joint Audit Committee to highlight the UW System's concerns about the LAB's activities. He testified—along with board members, Smith, chancellors, and faculty—to the problems created by state government's escalating requirements for reports and audits. Citing a fifty-page list of audits, reviews, studies, and evaluations that had been required over the previous two years, Young and the other UW representatives emphasized the high costs of responding and the impact on UW System institutions' ability to carry out their teaching, research, and public service missions. They also pointed out the importance of the board's statutory governance role and responsibilities, emphasizing the fundamental differences between universities and other state agencies. While acknowledging the LAB's authority to conduct traditional financial audits, they argued that the educational enterprise was the responsibility of the board and that any management or program audits of the System or its institutions should be reviewed by the regents.[63] These arguments, however, were only marginally successful, and the hearing and other contacts with state officials produced only a modest relaxation in the LAB's aggressive assertion of its authority. After a series of informal discussions, the System agreed to allow management audits, and the LAB agreed to accept more input from the System and its institutions on the details of the work. It was a kind of détente, but it legitimized the LAB's oversight role and left the Young administration in ongoing—and energy-consuming—arguments and negotiations with the LAB over the proper scope and subjects of audits. It also had the less direct but also damaging effect of creating more internal hostility toward the System's central administrators. Forced to pass along burdensome LAB requests for information to UW System institutions, the president and the central administration often found themselves the target of blame for the audits.

In addition to struggling with these state government demands, the System also faced renewed efforts to pass legislation allowing the unionization of faculty and academic staff. Weaver had warned in his 1975 report, *Retrospect and Prospect Revisited*, that collective bargaining would pose a continuing challenge for the System, and Young inherited this problem when he became president. The issue was complex and politically sensitive. Although not widespread, unionization of faculty had been implemented at public universities in New York and was under consideration elsewhere.[64] TAUWF, its membership drawn primarily from the former WSU institutions, advocated the idea as a means of securing improved job security, compensation and benefits—issues that had taken on heightened urgency at the WSU campuses in the wake of the 1974 retrenchment measures. Democrats in the legislature, generally supportive of unions, were also sympathetic, and in late 1974, TAUWF, led by its president, Edward Muzik, succeeded in having its own draft of a collective bargaining bill for UW faculty and academic staff introduced in the legislature.

For the board, however, collective bargaining posed a danger both to traditional shared governance and to university control of personnel policies and practices. Bargaining between labor and management over the terms and conditions of employment exposed traditional employment rights like tenure and faculty participation in university governance to negotiation, while the adversarial nature of the bargaining process threatened to damage institutional collegiality. Further, a "management" bargaining agent designated by law might be an outside state agency—not the Board of Regents—poorly attuned to faculty concerns and needs. Although TAUWF's 1974 bill failed because of its introduction late in the legislative session, it was clear, as Weaver had warned, that TAUWF and others would continue their efforts to secure collective bargaining legislation. The board responded by appointing a task force to study the issue, and in April 1975 it adopted a resolution declining to support collective bargaining legislation "as it presently operates in industry and in public employment" on the grounds that it would not be compatible with traditional faculty shared governance as practiced in the UW System. The board's action, however, stopped short of outright opposition to the concept,[65] and, as Weaver had predicted, the push for faculty unionization continued into succeeding legislative sessions and into Young's presidency.

Young was an expert on labor relations, a veteran of efforts by the UW–Madison Teaching Assistants Association (TAA) to unionize, and an advocate for UW–Madison, where there was strong faculty opposition to collective bargaining. One of his worries about the UW–WSU merger had been the possibility of collective bargaining for faculty, which in his view threatened not only faculty governance but also the transfer of control of all UW personnel matters "downtown"—that is, into the hands of non-UW state government agencies.[66] In addition, he saw TAUWF and its leaders as naïve about the potentially damaging consequences of unionization. As new bills authorizing collective bargaining were offered in the 1977 legislative session, Young and the board reviewed the board's 1975 stance on the issue and adopted a stronger statement of position, declining to support the enactment "at this time" of legislation enabling the faculty and the academic staff of the System to bargain collectively. In a comprehensive report approved at the November 11, 1977, meeting, the board enumerated the negative results of collective bargaining experienced at other higher education institutions and concluded that, although it would continue to monitor the situation, it could not support unionization.[67] On the basis of this report, the Young administration lobbied successfully against the various collective bargaining bills then being proposed in Wisconsin, but the pressure for collective bargaining continued and would confront Young's successors for the next ten years.

Together with these external problems, Young faced some challenges from his own Board of Regents. The new activism reflected in Grover's efforts to intervene in the presidential selection process continued in other areas, as Grover and board members such as Edward Hales and James Lavine pressed for more board involvement in management decisions traditionally left to the university's executives. Impatient with the "hands-off" practices of earlier boards and more concerned with state politics and state government relations, they sought to control Young's appointment to a key vice presidency, leading to a painful conflict between Young and his board.

The situation involved Young's choice of an executive vice president for the System. This position had been held immediately after merger by Leonard Haas, the UW–Eau Claire chancellor. When Haas returned to Eau Claire, Weaver eliminated the executive vice president position, instead organizing his executive team under two senior vice presidents, Smith and Percy. With Percy's departure and at Kauffman's urging, Young decided to return to the previous structure. He conducted a traditional academic search for an executive vice president, and a faculty search committee prepared a list of finalists for his consideration and selection. The list, however, did not include one candidate: David Adamany, Lucey's friend and a leading proponent of merger. Grover, supported by regents Hales and Lavine, insisted that Adamany be added to the list, despite his failure to gain the support of a faculty search committee. Young refused their demand, and the search failed. Young left the position unfilled for the duration of his tenure, with Smith effectively functioning in the role but without the title. Young would later say that that this failure was one of the things that bothered him most about being the UW System president;[68] the bad feelings it left may have hastened Young's departure.[69]

On March 24, 1979, two years after his appointment, Young announced that he would retire at the end of the year. He had resisted some regulatory incursions by state government in university affairs, fended off collective bargaining efforts, and stood up to board micromanagement and political pressure in university hiring processes. His focus on UW–Madison interests, his opposition to strong central leadership for the System, and his promotion of the "loose federation" approach to governance, however, had stalled progress on merger implementation and perpetuated internal conflicts between and among the flagship, other System institutions, and the System's central leadership, undermining System effectiveness.

A Decade of Change

With Young's retirement, the decade of dramatic change for higher education in Wisconsin that had begun with the Sterling Hall bombing and the merger legislation approached its close. Many of Lucey's original goals in proposing the merger had been achieved. The shock of the Sterling Hall bombing, followed by the conclusion of the Vietnam War, had effectively brought violent campus protests to an end. With merger and the policy and legal structure established through merger implementation, the uncoordinated expansion of state higher education programs had been largely brought under control within a workable governance framework. As noted by Weaver, some savings had been realized from the consolidation itself, while curtailing growth promised to yield future savings. More ominously, however, the merger and merger implementation marked the beginning of the state's retreat from its traditionally generous commitment to funding higher education, while internally the System faced conflicts and divisions that weakened System leadership and organizational cohesion, making it difficult to develop a comprehensive agenda for public higher education or a strategy for responding to persistently hard times.

4

Family Dysfunction

Young's departure gave the Board of Regents an opportunity to choose a new leader to take on the UW System's fiscal problems and operational challenges. The search for his successor, though, was marred by a renewal of the old disputes over presidential qualifications and struggles for control of the selection process, while the choice of Robert M. O'Neil as president brought new internal conflicts. Although O'Neil arrived hoping to complete the work of merger by fully consolidating the System, during his term intra-System tensions grew, straining relations among and between System institutions and System administrative leadership. As the internal discord deepened, the System's credibility with state government eroded, and its effectiveness in responding to its fiscal, political, and social problems was further undermined.

Déjà Vu:
The 1979 Presidential Search

The search for a new System president began promptly after the March 24, 1979, announcement of Young's retirement. Edward Hales, now the board's president, invited board members to come to their April 6, 1979, meeting prepared to discuss the process for choosing Young's successor. In a reprise of the dissension that had tarnished the 1977 search, however, the board again divided sharply over the protocol in a contentious debate at this meeting.

The architect of the 1976–77 procedure, former board president Bertram McNamara, opened the discussion. Regretting that he had deviated from standard practice in the previous search by adding regents to the first-level search-and-screen committee, McNamara made a motion recommending that the board limit membership on this committee to faculty, administrators, and students, with no regent representation. His motion further proposed that that the second-level selection committee include the full Board of Regents, sitting as a committee of the whole, and that it choose the System president from the list of finalists developed by the first-level search-and-screen committee.[1]

McNamara's motion immediately reignited the 1976–77 debate between traditionalist board members favoring a two-tier, faculty-dominated academic search model and those demanding greater regent participation in all phases of the process, including as members of both the first-level search-and-screen committee and the board selection committee. The McNamara proposal was, in effect, an endorsement of the traditional approach, likely to limit the finalists to those with strong scholarly and academic leadership credentials. The board, however, now included a growing and influential activist group whose members sought a more direct role in the choice of the next System president. As a group, these activists also believed that scholarly credibility matters less for a System head than political and public relations skills, and they chafed at having their choice of final candidates limited to traditional academic leaders. Among them were some who—like regents Lavine, Hales, and Grover—had also participated in the 1977 search process[2] and who were eager to ensure a strong voice for board members at the first level of the selection effort. Echoing Grover's arguments from 1977, Lavine opposed McNamara's motion, arguing that the choice of finalists should not be left to a group of academics that included no regents. He then offered an amendment that would add four board members to the first-level search-and-screen committee.

The ensuing debate on Lavine's motion to amend sparked a series of angry charges and countercharges about the problems with the 1976–77 search. Speaking against Lavine's amendment, regent Arthur DeBardeleben argued that the addition of regents to the first-level committee in 1977 had been a mistake. Regent

Gerrard responded by asking him "why he had served on the [first-tier search-and-screen] committee a previous time [1977] if it was such a bad idea." DeBardeleben shot back that he had been concerned that if he himself did not agree to serve, Gerrard would be appointed in his stead. Grover reiterated his position that active board involvement in choosing the System president is needed at every step in the process. Referring to his 1977 demand that he get a "piece of the action" in the presidential selection process, he contended that the board should not give away its control over such a key decision by allowing academics to dominate the search-and-screen committee and control the choice of finalists. Dismissing the traditional selection process as inappropriate in the presidential context, he urged the importance of nonacademic skills:

> the argument that picking a Madison chancellor is in any way comparable in terms of the procedure and the involvement of faculty as opposed to picking a president of the System is just a lot of balderdash. . . . The president of the System has to be more than a scholar, and if you get yourself as the next president of this university a pure scholar with no social, political, societal, and public skills, . . . this University is going to suffer massively. . . . We need massive public leadership that transcends a Rhodes scholar mentality.

Regent Lawton retorted that "any Regent who goes on the committee with the attitude described by Regent Grover is really a detriment to our selection process."

Put to the vote, Lavine's amendment failed on an 8–8 tie, leading to a vote on McNamara's main motion, which failed by the same 8–8 margin. Facing the embarrassing prospect of an impasse that would leave the board with no agreed-upon search process, Hales called a strategic recess in the meeting. When the board reconvened, Grover offered conciliatory remarks urging that the discussion be resumed and then moved for a reconsideration of McNamara's main motion, which was unanimously approved by the board.[3]

Having agreed on McNamara's basic approach, the board again turned to Kauffman for professional guidance on other details of the process, asking him to serve as executive secretary to the search. He agreed, but warily, given the evident tensions and divisions on the board. He conditioned his participation on the assurance that the board would not interfere with the approved search protocol or—importantly—seek to add names to the list of finalists produced by the first-level search-and-screen committee. If the board was not satisfied with the list of finalists, he insisted, it could reject all of them and start a new search, but it would not be allowed to add new names to the list submitted by the committee. The board accepted Kauffman's conditions, and he developed the details of the procedure and prepared a position description, which, consistent with Young's view, he crafted to emphasize that the System was a federation of institutions that should be allowed maximum autonomy.[4] At its May 11, 1979, meeting, the board finalized the search process, as refined by Kauffman. The activists gained one concession, though: with little debate, the board declined to include a requirement in the position description that the president have "academic qualifications comparable to those required for tenure at UW–Madison."[5]

Neither agreement on the protocol nor agreement on Kauffman's conditions proved enough to yield a smoother search process. The assurances given by the board to Kauffman about not interfering were honored mainly in the breach. Board members, politicians, and others were not deterred from advancing their own candidates for the job outside the formal process, and Kauffman was faced with recurring demands to add names to the list of final candidates developed by the search-and-screen committee. Grover was elected board president in June 1979 and stepped up the pressure on Kauffman for the selection of a "regular guy" System president who could improve legislative relations—that is, not an academic.[6] Legislators and board members who shared this view publicly expressed their strong preference for a state "insider" already familiar with Wisconsin's problems and politics, rather than a scholar. Percy and Carley were once again promoted as possible candidates in this category, along with UW–Madison chancellor Irving Shain, who, although also a well-regarded academician, was a Wisconsin insider, well known to lawmakers.[7] Shain declined to be considered,[8] however, and the other prominent insiders failed to emerge as final candidates. Instead, the finalists recommended by the search-and-screen committee were all outsiders with solid academic experiences and/or government

credentials.[9] At this point, Grover again made it clear to Kauffman that he was upset that neither Carley nor Percy had made
the list, while Gerrard demanded that Kauffman include Carley
as a finalist, regardless of the recommendations of the search-
and-screen committee.[10]

In the end, Kauffman held firm, enforcing adherence to the
board's agreed-upon search protocol. Following interviews in
the fall of 1979, Robert M. O'Neil was chosen from the search-
and-screen committee's recommended list of finalists and was
officially appointed System president at the December 14, 1979,
meeting of the board.[11] The board members and politicians who
had urged the selection of a nonacademic, politically adept state
insider were frustrated, leaving the disagreement over the qualifications most important in a UW System president unresolved—
and open to future debate.

An Outsider President and an Insider Clash

O'Neil took office on February 1, 1980, as the first real "outsider"
to lead the merged UW System. A Harvard-educated lawyer,
O'Neil was a scholar's scholar, bringing a keen intellect[12] and
an enduring interest in legal issues to his new position. He had
clerked for the United States Supreme Court and had taught law
at Tufts University, San Francisco State University, and the University of California-Berkeley. Even as System president, he made
it a point to stay abreast of current legal developments and could
often be seen carrying a briefcase bulging with the advance reports of the latest federal court decisions. In addition to his legal
background, O'Neil had extensive higher education administrative experience, having held leadership posts at SUNY Buffalo
and the University of Cincinnati. When chosen for the Wisconsin
position, he was serving as chancellor and vice president of the
University of Indiana at Bloomington, that state's flagship campus. With no previous connections to any individual UW System
institutions, O'Neil arrived as a president for the System as a
whole—which, as Senator Fred Risser would later say, made
him, in a sense, the first "true UW System president." His predecessors, Weaver and Young, had both been associated with UW–
Madison, and, as Risser noted, Weaver had only inherited the
System, while Young was a "stand-in" and short-timer.[13] O'Neil

would be the first president selected specifically as a leader for
the merged System, an outsider unencumbered by old prejudices
or allegiances and unscarred by the merger fight.

O'Neil came to his new position with the primary goal of completing the work of merger implementation and fully unifying
the UW System and its diverse institutions.[14] Despite the potential benefits of his outsider perspective, however, he confronted
significant obstacles to achieving his aims. He had inherited a
fractious Board of Regents and an organization still coping with
painful postmerger fiscal troubles and the unhealed internal divisions left by the downsizing exercise and related budget cuts
and layoffs of the Weaver administration. Budgets under Dreyfus
had been uncertain, and relations with state government were
strained. The larger national economic picture also remained
bleak. Young's focus on protecting UW–Madison and antipathy
to strong central management had weakened the office of the
presidency, undermining internal System cohesion and encouraging continued opposition to the merger. Like Weaver, O'Neil
brought to the presidency a sincere commitment to the full implementation of merger, but the System's problems had deepened
with hard times, and the goal of achieving System unity remained
elusive.

Adding to these underlying troubles, O'Neil's term began
with a rocky transition and an early conflict with Shain that caused
long-term damage to the relationship between the System administration and the flagship Madison campus. Young left office
exactly as announced, on December 31, 1979, but O'Neil's appointment was not effective until February 1, 1980, and he did not
actually arrive in Madison until March. For the first two months of
his term, from February through March 1980, O'Neil was winding
down his work at Indiana and commuting between Indiana and
Madison, attempting to do two jobs at once. Young's abrupt departure, the one-month gap before O'Neil officially assumed the
presidency, and the further delay in the move to Madison afforded
little opportunity for a smooth transfer of responsibilities. The
absence of senior vice president Don Smith during this period
was a further complication. Smith, the System's second-ranking
administrator, a veteran of both the Weaver and the Young administrations, and, with Percy, a principal architect of merger
implementation, was recovering from a heart attack at the time
and was not available to assist with the transition. As a result,

O'Neil lacked the support of an experienced System leader and well-regarded insider in the earliest days of his presidency.[15]

Compounding these challenges was the brewing crisis with Shain stemming from Young's late-term effort to transfer the role of representative of the UW System to the American Association of Universities (AAU) from the System president to the UW–Madison chancellor. The AAU, originally founded in 1900 by a small group of elite US higher education institutions that included the University of Wisconsin, is among the most prestigious of American higher education associations, its membership limited to a select group of research universities. Under AAU policies in effect at the time, the head of a state university system was presumptively the representative of the entire state to the AAU, and, as System presidents, both Young and Weaver had served as Wisconsin's representatives.

Young considered the AAU to be "*the* club," the most exclusive group of national higher education leaders, and, true to his Madison roots, he believed that membership in this "club" more appropriately belonged to UW–Madison than to the UW System.[16] It was a view shared by Shain, who, while being recruited by his old colleague for the chancellor post, had asked to be named the AAU representative as a condition of accepting the position.[17] Young agreed, but he made no immediate change. He continued to serve as the AAU representative even after Shain took office as Madison's chancellor, and Shain apparently did not force the issue with him. With his term as System president drawing to a close, however, and the search for the new System president in progress, Young moved to fulfill his commitment to Shain. In July 1979, he wrote to AAU president Thomas A. Bartlett asking him to name Shain the AAU representative. Bartlett immediately responded by reminding Young that AAU policy made the head of a state university system the presumptive representative. He added, though, that the head of a state system could designate the head of an individual campus to serve as the system's representative. In that case, he noted, the individual so designated would represent the entire system, not any single campus. Young promptly advised Bartlett that he was designating Shain to serve as the UW System's representative.[18]

Meanwhile, O'Neil, who had previously served as legal counsel to the AAU and was familiar with the organization's policy on representation, came to the UW System expecting that as System president he, like Weaver and Young before him, would become the AAU representative. O'Neil was unaware of Young's action designating Shain until December of 1979, when he was in the process of finalizing his own employment contract with the Board of Regents. When he discovered that Young had named Shain as the AAU representative, he was deeply offended. O'Neil demanded, as a condition of his acceptance of the presidency, that the board name him to be the AAU representative. The board agreed, but, not surprisingly, Shain was furious.[19] Although O'Neil later asked the AAU to allow Wisconsin two representatives so that both he and Shain could serve, Bartlett denied his request. Responding to Bartlett by letter of May 29, 1980, O'Neil wrote that if no such accommodation was possible, he would "simply assume the Wisconsin seat next fall in the confidence that Irv will understand."[20] His confidence was misplaced. Shain remained angry at O'Neil and resentful of this assertion of authority, describing the situation as a "festering wound" and saying that it marked the beginning of seven years of "incredible stress" between Madison and System.[21]

It was an ominous beginning for the critical relationship between the chief executive of the System and the leader of its flagship campus, and the situation was made worse by O'Neil's efforts to become involved in academic, social, and extracurricular activities at UW–Madison. Based on his experiences at the University of Indiana, where the system president was an active participant in flagship affairs, O'Neil came to Wisconsin expecting to take a similar leadership role at UW–Madison. As his wife, Karen, later put it, the O'Neils arrived thinking that the UW System and its institutions would be a "big happy family."[22] In fact, however, the UW System "family" was not very happy generally, and Shain had a very different view of the appropriate relationship between the flagship and System administrative leadership than did the O'Neils. Suspicious, like Young, of System authority and stung by the AAU representation dispute, he regarded involvement of the System president in the affairs of his campus as an unwarranted intrusion.

Kauffman and others had foreseen the potential for just such a clash. Young had sensed that O'Neil might see himself as president of Madison, not the System, and Smith had early on advised O'Neil that he should not make an issue of the AAU representation.[23] Kauffman, knowing both Shain and O'Neil and sensitive to their differing views and expectations, attempted to warn O'Neil before his first Wisconsin press conference that the flagship relations he had experienced at Indiana might be different at Wisconsin, emphasizing that O'Neil would be president of the UW *System*, not UW–Madison. As Kauffmann feared, however, O'Neil did not fully grasp the situation and ignored the advice.[24] Settling into the presidency, O'Neil assumed the AAU position, accepted a teaching appointment at the UW Law School, began hosting social and athletic events at the campus, and became actively engaged with the academic community in Madison, while Shain became increasingly resentful of what he saw as O'Neil's attempt to act as the president of *his* institution. Although Weaver and Young had maintained close academic and social ties to UW–Madison after assuming the System presidency, they had avoided open conflicts with the campus's leaders. With Shain and O'Neil, however, the situation soon degenerated into turf battles and bickering over guest lists for events, anger at refusal to coordinate party planning, and general ill will on both sides.[25]

If much of this discord involved seemingly trivial matters, the conflict between O'Neil and Shain had significantly broader consequences for the UW System. As the relations between the two continued to deteriorate through 1980 and 1981, the hostility became increasingly open, generating widespread resentment of O'Neil among Shain's deans and other flagship administrators and Vice Chancellor Bryant Kearl. The growing animosity fed renewed opposition to merger and to Madison's inclusion in the UW System,[26] along with thinly veiled contempt for the System as an organization and disregard for System leadership and the System administration. Smith, forced to retire for health reasons in the summer of 1980, was succeeded by Kauffman as the System's executive vice president, but Kauffman, despite his ties to UW–Madison, was unable to mediate the situation. The antagonism to all things System-related was deep enough that when former UW president E. B. Fred died, in January 1981, UW–Madison declined to fly its flag at half-staff, because Fred—having overseen the addition of UW–Milwaukee to the UW in 1955—was viewed as a "system" leader."[27] Any thought on O'Neil's part of holding a celebration of the tenth anniversary of merger

in the fall of 1981 was quickly set aside—on Kauffman's advice—
in favor of a more modest decennial report given to the Board of
Regents at its October 9, 1981, meeting.[28]

In December of that year, matters reached a crisis point when
Shain failed to submit an annual report to O'Neil when due and
did not respond to a request from O'Neil for his input on various
other System issues. O'Neil sent him a curt letter outlining his
expectations for the relationship between the UW System and
UW–Madison. Emphasizing the need for improved communication and collaboration, O'Neil insisted on timely filing of reports,
better coordination of legislative efforts, prior discussion of major
policy statements, and improved cooperation on System and
campus social events. In reply, Shain cast the problem in starker
terms that reflected his embrace of Young's view of the System
as a loose federation and his own hostility to central leadership.
He asserted that O'Neil's expectations reflected disagreement
over "a much more fundamental question—that is, whether public higher education in Wisconsin consists of a federation of strong,
distinctive universities or a single 'university' with branch campuses,"[29] adding that O'Neil's demands jeopardized the stature
of UW–Madison, along with its ability to fulfill its mission. Shain
continued with a lengthy list of his own concerns about System-
flagship relations, ranging from the submission of budgets and
reports to the System administration, to attendance at football
bowl games, to joint social events, to the issues of representation
at the AAU and other higher education organizations. In conclusion, he demanded that O'Neil either reconsider his expectations
or seek clarification of the appropriate relationship between the
System administration and System institutions from the Board of
Regents.

Although O'Neil had previously acknowledged that System
and board policies reflected the view of the System as a federation,
he had also emphasized his own position that the System is not
merely a "conduit through which papers pass from universities
to state government and between institutions" but has broader
responsibilities to "shape and apply policies, enhance relations
among institutions, facilitate contact between the institutions
and state government, and represent to the citizens and the state
needs of higher education in Wisconsin."[30] Unable to reconcile
their divergent understandings of the roles and responsibilities

of the System and System leadership, in February 1982 O'Neil asked board president Joyce Erdman to intervene in the dispute. The board avoided entering the philosophical fray over the federation issue, and uneasy peace was restored, but the personal tensions between the two men remained.

Their inability to establish an effective working relationship had damaging consequences for the entire UW System. The development of close, cooperative relations between a flagship campus and the larger system of which it is a part is a key element in the success of both. Representing the best of the entire organization, the flagship sets the standard for academic excellence and, as Lucey had recognized before merger, provides the larger reputational recognition—the "brand"—that enhances the stature of all other universities within the system and the value of the degrees received by their graduates.[31] In the UW System, the flagship Madison campus plays an especially important role by virtue of its distinguished national and international reputation, the scope of its operations, and its size relative to the other UW institutions. Its success is vital to the success of the entire system. But if the flagship establishes the mark of excellence for the System, the System provides benefits for the flagship, too, shielding it from political pressures and public attacks, as well as preserving its distinctive institutional mission and protecting it from intrastate competition for resources. Without the protective cover afforded by the UW System's central policy and program planning and the unified Systemwide budget allocation process, the UW–Madison flagship's small legislative delegation would always be outnumbered by representatives from other parts of the state and exposed to direct legislative lobbying efforts on behalf of other state institutions that would divert state resources from the flagship to other state higher education institutions and purposes. As later System president Katharine C. Lyall put it, Madison had been advantaged by merger, "just count the votes."[32]

Lucey had understood this, pursuing merger in part to extend the benefits of the UW–Madison brand to all the state's public universities and their students but also to protect the flagship from public outrage over campus protests and from the competition for resources resulting from pressures to expand programs elsewhere in state higher education. Merger, he saw, would make UW–Madison less vulnerable to program competition and

expansion at other state campuses and a less visible single target
for public and political attacks. Maintaining close ties between
the Madison campus and the System and its leaders is key to preserving the reciprocal benefits of reputation and protection. Both
Lyall and another later System president, Kevin Reilly, agreed
that their relations with UW–Madison, its chancellors, academic
leaders, and faculty were the most important of all campus connections for ensuring the success of both the System and its flagship.[33] Young's handling of the AAU issue, the squabbling over
O'Neil's participation in UW–Madison affairs, Shain's insistence
on viewing the System as a loose federation in which his campus should be independent of the System, along with his disdain
for O'Neil's authority as president all prevented the development of this crucial relationship, with harmful consequences. As
the quarrel between O'Neil and Shain became more widely
known, it had ripple effects throughout the System and even in
state government. O'Neil's credibility, already badly damaged
among the flagship's leaders,[34] began to erode elsewhere, undermining his leadership throughout the System and reviving opposition to merger. His chances of bringing unity and complete
integration to the UW System became vanishingly remote, while
the System's ability to manage other important issues—including
what would become O'Neil's most significant legislative initiative, the effort to gain pay increases for UW System faculty and
staff—was impaired.

New Challenges, Old Fiscal Problems, and
the Battle for Catch-Up Pay

Challenges

While their personal conflicts roiled in the background, O'Neil
and Shain—along with the System's other campus and institutional leaders—confronted a growing array of challenges, both
nationally and in Wisconsin. The landscape of higher education
was changing rapidly. As the baby-boomer-dominated protest era
of the 1960s and 1970s gradually came to an end, higher education
leaders throughout the country faced new social and demographic
problems that required new policy responses. Efforts to comply
with equal opportunity requirements, to expand affirmative
action programs for women and minorities, to prohibit sexual

harassment in the workplace and in the classroom, and to provide women equal access to participation in athletic programs brought new legal and policy challenges. Programs designed to improve equity and diversity, however, often generated backlash and complaints about reverse discrimination and political correctness. Defying predictions, the demand for college continued to increase, despite a smaller cohort of traditional-age college students. With growing enrollments came new pressures on admissions—particularly at flagship state institutions—along with changes in the composition of the student body, as more women and minorities entered undergraduate, graduate, and professional programs. Attitudes toward higher education also began to shift, with increasingly career-oriented students seeking degrees as a necessary credential for economic security and choosing majors likely to lead to jobs. At the same time, there were new calls for higher education reform, as the effectiveness of education at all levels came under attack in "A Nation at Risk," a 1983 report of the US Department of Education.

Along with these widely shared national problems, the UW System and its leaders faced difficult in-state and intra-System issues. During O'Neil's tenure as president, state government continued its active efforts to intervene in UW System affairs, while the System dealt with challenging policy and academic program decisions. A request from the legislature's Joint Committee for Review of Administrative Rules (JCRAR) in May 1982 was representative of the expanding legislative interest in controlling the System's internal educational policy decisions. JCRAR proposed that the board undertake administrative rulemaking in several policy areas at the heart of the System's educational mission, including curricula and degree requirements and faculty and student governance. JCRAR asserted that existing System policies on these subjects had to be adopted as administrative rules, which would make them subject to JCRAR review and legislative approval. In a carefully worded report responding to JCRAR, a special committee of the board argued persuasively against subjecting these matters to the rule-making process on both legal and policy grounds. Although JCRAR did not seek any further action on the part of the board, the situation signaled legislators' intent to insert themselves into the details of System policy development.[35]

The legislative impulse to micromanage System operations was also demonstrated vividly in the context of proposed amendments to the System's conflict-of-interest policies governing the outside activities of faculty members. Under rules similar to those governing state civil service employees, System faculty members were permitted to engage in paid consulting and other work outside their regular duties, so long as these activities were disclosed internally and did not interfere with the performance of their UW responsibilities. These reports of outside activities had traditionally been treated as confidential personnel matters, but the university faced media pressure to disclose them. When Madison's *Capital Times* filed a public records request with UW–Madison seeking to obtain copies of the reports, the university's denial of its request led to litigation, and, ultimately, a decision by a Dane County Circuit judge held that these reports had to be publicly disclosed.[36] The litigation sparked publicity and criticism of the policy of allowing outside consulting, along with demands for public disclosure of more information about the outside activities of individual faculty members. Responding to these external pressures for disclosure, in late 1980 the UW System initiated amendments to its existing policies and by September 1981 had forwarded its proposed changes to the Legislative Council for review and comment.[37]

The System's proposed rules soon encountered opposition in the legislature from those demanding more extensive disclosures than had been recommended by the System. The board held public hearings and conducted a series of reviews and revisions to address these complaints, beginning in 1982 and continuing to October 1984, but Senator Lynn Adelman remained dissatisfied with the results. Adelman insisted on the addition of provisions requiring public disclosure of both the sources and the dollar amounts of faculty outside income. His demands led to more protracted negotiations among System administration staff, Adelman and his staff, and other legislators over the appropriate scope of disclosure and the minutiae of the policy language itself. A compromise was not reached until late in 1985, when new rules were finally approved that provided for public disclosure of the amounts earned from outside consulting, within broad dollar ranges. The process, however, confirmed the eagerness of state leaders to intervene in the details of UW System policy decisions and the time-consuming administrative burdens of responding to such intrusions.[38]

Legislative activity in O'Neil's term also reached beyond micromanaging to larger and more complex academic programming issues, including those involving the creation of a school of veterinary medicine. Responding to political pressure from the state's agriculture industry, the legislature in 1979 approved the establishment of a school of veterinary medicine at UW–Madison, but the action drew board leaders O'Neil and Shain into a protracted argument with legislators over how to fund it. The question whether the state even needed a veterinary school had long been controversial. As early as 1947, the UW Board of Regents had voted in favor of establishing such a school,[39] but only when adequate financing became available. Nothing was done for many years, and Wisconsin residents were able to pursue veterinary medicine studies under cooperative agreements with neighboring states. In 1976, however, the legislature voted to finance one-half the cost of building a veterinary school in Wisconsin, with the remaining half to be provided by the System. Weaver, with board support, declined to proceed until all the necessary state resources were provided.[40] In 1977, the legislature reiterated its position, directing the board to establish the school at the Madison campus, with a satellite at UW–River Falls, but again without providing the necessary funding. The board responded by affirming its earlier position that it would not build unless the state funds were in place.[41]

Finally, in 1979 Governor Dreyfus signed the legislatively approved state budget bill providing state bonding and operational funds for the school,[42] but even that did not immediately produce action, and the funding standoff continued into O'Neil's first year in office. Still concerned with adequacy of financial support for the school, especially in light of a fiscal picture that threatened other academic programs, in late 1980 and early 1981 the board adopted a series of resolutions asking the legislature to reconsider its action. The board stressed the importance of its own role in making academic program decisions and its worries about the fiscal impact building the school could have on other System institutions.[43] As UW–Madison's chancellor, however, Shain faced the immediate need to comply with the legislative mandate to begin planning and construction of the school, which was scheduled to admit its first class in 1983. The matter was resolved until March 1981, when last-minute efforts by some legislators to deny essential funding were defeated,[44] and the school was finally established.

In addition to these legislatively driven issues, the System in O'Neil's tenure faced internal problems related to academic programming. Proposals to establish doctoral programs in nursing at both UW–Madison and UW–Milwaukee renewed old concerns about program needs and unnecessary duplication. In early 1984, the two campuses each requested board approval to add new PhD nursing programs to their curricula. Katharine C. Lyall, who had joined the System in early 1982 as vice president for academic affairs and then succeeded Kauffman as executive vice president, reviewed these requests on behalf of the O'Neil administration. Lyall concluded that neither request should be granted, prompting protests from both campuses.[45] With nurses and other supporters of the programs picketing in the corridors of Van Hise Hall and complaining vociferously and publicly about Lyall's decision, the board—in what O'Neil would later describe as a serious mistake—voted to authorize both programs.[46]

The complexities of integrating UW–Extension functions and activities into work at the System's four-year institutions also produced internal study and debate. Harrington's premerger establishment of UW–Extension as a separate institution had been controversial, but its independent institutional status had been confirmed following merger and merger implementation. At the time, it was understood that, postmerger, some Extension functions would be integrated into programs at all of the four-year institutions of the newly combined System. By the 1980s, however, the process of integrating programs had become mired in interinstitutional management and budget problems, particularly at the former WSU campuses. Some in the System believed that Extension should be dissolved and its budget and functions reassigned to individual campuses, while others supported maintaining it as an independent institution with its own budget and functions under the leadership of a chancellor. The differences of opinion led to the creation of a Special Regent Study Committee on UW–Extension. The group's report, issued in April 1982, confirmed the stand-alone structure of the institution and went on to offer a plan for going forward with integration. It was a complex process, however, and the integration work progressed slowly, continuing through July 1985.

The Fiscal Picture

While it shared the problems facing higher education institutions nationally and coped with its own peculiarly Wisconsin challenges, the UW System's difficulties were compounded by the long years of state funding shortfalls and uncertainties. The hard times that had started with merger showed no signs of easing, and it was becoming increasingly clear that the fiscal situation was damaging educational quality and undermining the System's ability to compete with national peers. Managing fiscal instability and budget crises had always been a top priority of the System and its leaders. As concerns about the quality of education grew, however, the focus on the funding crisis intensified, and in that context the need to improve faculty and staff salaries emerged as a critical first step in maintaining the academic excellence of System institutions. The effort to gain pay increases would become the major legislative initiative of O'Neil's administration.

As O'Neil assumed the presidency, state budgets remained unstable. The effects of Lucey's pressure to reduce the size of the System were still being felt, and under Dreyfus the state's biennial budgeting process had been unpredictable, even—as Smith characterized it—chaotic.[47] As Risser would later say, Dreyfus believed in "brinksmanship," or government by crisis,[48] and the state revenue situation reflected this leadership style. The 1970s faculty layoffs at UW–Oshkosh continued to be a source of unrest at that campus and the subject of various internal grievance proceedings and litigation. In December 1980, the board was forced to close the tiny UW Center at Medford, while UW–Superior, although it remained a four-year institution, continued to operate under a state of fiscal emergency that would last until 1983. National and state economic troubles resulting from the 1978 energy crisis and the Iranian revolution continued unabated, causing ruinous inflation rates that stifled growth and depressed the real incomes of individuals. UW System faculty and academic staff salaries lagged relative to those of their peers, and the specter of layoffs like those at Oshkosh spurred the ongoing efforts of TAUWF and other unions to lobby for collective bargaining rights for faculty and academic staff members, despite the board's firm opposition to unionization.

O'Neil was immediately thrust into these financial problems. Within months of his arrival in Madison, Dreyfus's 1979–81 biennial budget collapsed at its midpoint. Relying on a large predicted tax revenue surplus, Dreyfus had proposed increases in state spending, along with massive tax cuts. When the surplus did not materialize and tax revenues actually declined, the state was left with a significant budget shortfall halfway through the biennium. By September 1980, the month of O'Neil's presidential inauguration, Dreyfus had imposed stringent cuts to all state agencies, including a 4.4 percent midcycle budget reduction for the UW System. This action was followed in March 1981 by an additional 1.4 percent cut for the same fiscal year. Compounding the pain, Dreyfus's 1981–83 budget, proposed in early 1981, called for further reductions to the UW System's funding of approximately 2 percent in each year of the upcoming 1983–85 biennium. Although it was never implemented, Dreyfus had even proposed, as a part of this budget, a freeze on pay for all state or university employees earning more than $30,000 per year—a plan that would have had a disproportionate impact on faculty and academic staff members and that drew a predictably angry reaction.[49]

At the federal level, Ronald Reagan's election to the presidency in 1980 brought not only significant cuts in federal funding for higher education but also powerful antitax attitudes and tax cuts in accordance with the "trickle-down" economic theory positing that benefits in the form of tax cuts to businesses and wealthy individuals eventually trickle down to all. Federal financial aid, long the primary source of student grant support, was sharply reduced, along with research funding from the National Science Foundation (NSF).[50] Reacting to these mounting problems, the Board of Regents, at its March 6, 1981, meeting, expressed frustration with the state's treatment of the UW System in the ten years since merger. Regent Tom Fox observed that cuts to higher education were becoming a long-term trend, while regent Russell O'Harrow suggested that the System should receive more—not less—funding to help bring its expertise to bear on the underlying state problems of inflation and lack of job growth. Others questioned whether the state's traditional commitment to broad access to UW institutions could be maintained in the face of rising enrollments and reduced financial support. As for the federal budget, DeBardeleben commented that the Reagan administration's method of dealing with the problem of inflation was "a transfer from the needy in the form of budget cuts to the greedy in the form of tax cuts."[51]

The deteriorating state fiscal forecast and the revenue short-falls resulting from Dreyfus's midcycle cuts forced the Board of Regents to impose a tuition surcharge in November 1981. The situation did not improve in 1982, as another unreliable Dreyfus budget produced another round of midcycle budget adjustments and cuts to the System's funding, along with restrictions on salary increases for faculty and academic staff.[52] Although some of these adjustments were later mitigated by the legislature, the cuts and the resulting uncertainties were a continual source of concern.

The cumulative effects of the state's budget turmoil under Dreyfus, together with the Reagan administration's cuts in federal funding and ever-diminishing postmerger state tax support, by 1982 posed a serious threat to the UW System's ability to fulfill its education, research, and service missions. Early in his term, in his report to the Board of Regents on the first ten years of the UW System, O'Neil described the alarming decrease in state support per full-time equivalent student. He noted that Wisconsin's rank had fallen from sixth among all states in 1971 to thirty-first in 1981[53] and appointed a committee to study the level and adequacy of funding for the System's instructional mission. The committee's report, presented at the July 1982 meeting of the Board of Regents, demonstrated that the System had suffered a "decade of decline" in state support, leaving the organization and each of its institutions underfunded compared to 1972 levels, as well as to their national peer groups. The report concluded that

> Wisconsin has not, in the past decade, maintained its position in respect to other states in support of higher education; it has instead fallen markedly behind at a time when rejuvenation is most needed. The historic ability of the state's public universities to offer qualified applicants an education of respectable quality, and to provide services critical to the state's cultural well-being and economic development, has been seriously compromised.[54]

Discussing these findings with the Board of Regents, O'Neil emphasized that the UW System should not settle for being merely average relative to its peers. Outlining themes and arguments that would be used consistently to support System efforts to improve state support, he urged the state to recognize the System's potential value to the state as an economic driver and a source of solutions to state problems and to relax state regulations that constrained its ability to meet fiscal challenges.[55]

At the same time, O'Neil pointed to a serious related problem. While the 1982 "decade of decline" report did not directly address compensation issues, O'Neil observed that any modifications to instructional funding formulas needed to take into account the impact of inflation on faculty and academic staff salaries.[56] It was clear that in the 1972–82 period their pay had declined, along with the other elements of UW System instructional support. A previous System report on compensation, prepared in 1981, had described the serious decline in real salaries and the resulting competitive difficulties faced by UW institutions. Years of minimal raises, combined with rampant inflation, had lowered purchasing power and driven down real incomes. Salaries for UW System professors were no longer competitive with those offered by other higher education institutions, directly threatening the ability of UW System institutions to retain current faculty and academic staff or to compete for qualified new hires and indirectly jeopardizing educational quality. The 1981 compensation report had recommended naming a System committee to negotiate for improved salaries with state government representatives, an approach endorsed at that time by the Board of Regents.[57] In the wake of the turmoil of the 1981–83 budget cycle, with inflationary pressures continuing to mount and competitive difficulties growing, the need to improve compensation together with overall instructional funding support was becoming urgent.

The Battle for Catch-Up Pay

A change in state leadership seemed to offer the opportunity to address the problem. In the spring of 1982, Dreyfus announced, to O'Neil's surprise, that he would not seek election to a second term. Although O'Neil—aware of the tense relationship between

Dreyfus and Young—had had some success in mending fences with the governor,[58] friendlier relations had not been enough to mitigate the instability in the state's revenue situation or to produce better support for the UW System. The election of Anthony Earl in November 1982 brought hopes for more reliable budgeting and improved funding in the next administration.

Earl, a Democrat from Wausau, came with extensive state government experience and familiarity with the UW System. First elected to the state Assembly in 1969 to fill the seat vacated when David Obey was elected to Congress, Earl quickly became a state legislative leader, serving on the Assembly's education committee and as the Democrats' floor leader. Lucey later chose him to replace Nusbaum at the DOA, where he developed a solid grasp of the state budget and, through his involvement in the 1975 retrenchment exercise, an understanding of the fiscal problems facing the UW System. Like Dreyfus, Earl expressed sympathy for System needs. His first budget, for the 1983–85 biennium, proposed funding for an increased proportion of UW System requests for operations and for a faculty recognition fund to be used to retain and recruit "star" faculty.[59] The budget provided little relief, however, for other compensation problems. O'Neil and the Board of Regents had sought across-the-board salary increases of 4 percent and 7 percent for academic staff and faculty, respectively, together with enhancements to the proposed "star fund." Faced with the revenue problems left over from the Dreyfus administration, Earl proposed a 0 percent across-the-board increase in the first year of the biennium, with a 3.84 percent increase—subject to availability of funds—in the second year. The "star fund" proposal was limited to a modest $1 million over two years. Despite general public support for the system's requested compensation increases, UW's hopes for immediate or meaningful salary improvements under Earl were dashed.

The situation became a source of tension between the UW System and the Earl administration. O'Neil had apparently misread Earl's commitment to the "star fund" increases, believing these would become a permanent $2.5 million addition to the System's base budget, rather than the one-time, $1 million increase that was ultimately approved by Earl.[60] Faculty members throughout the System were angry at receiving no increase and also offended at the "star fund" concept and its meager funding. At UW–Stevens Point, where Chancellor Philip Marshall had been an outspoken advocate for pay improvement, a group of twenty-one faculty members went so far as to advertise for jobs in the *Wall Street Journal*, stating that many professors were available to work "for an honest wage at universities with commitments to quality higher education." This faculty strategy ultimately backfired, irritating lawmakers and the governor, but it reflected the depth of the frustration with salaries that were not competitive with those at other institutions and that had not kept up with high inflation.[61] Acknowledging that the compensation problems were real, Earl, pressed by the Board of Regents and O'Neil, agreed to appoint a state commission to study the issue and identify sources of funding, including tuition increases, that might be used to boost pay.

The work of this commission, appointed in October 1983 and cochaired by DOA secretary Doris Hanson and the UW System's Lyall, laid the foundation for a significant faculty "catch-up pay" proposal in the 1985–87 budget. Lyall, since her arrival at the System in early 1982, had emerged as an effective, well-regarded leader. An economist, she had been a faculty member at Syracuse University and the Johns Hopkins Center for Public Policy and had served in the federal government in the Department of Housing and Urban Development in the Carter administration.[62] At the UW System, she proved to be a confident, capable decision maker. In contrast to O'Neil, who was regarded as indecisive[63] and who often seemed to struggle with policy choices and the politics involved in the governance of the System, Lyall had a common-sense ability to address problems. System chancellors and campus leaders looked to her for direction on important administrative and management issues, pressing her to make necessary decisions when O'Neil did not or could not do so.[64] She had quickly earned wide internal respect and was named the System's executive vice president on Kauffman's retirement in July 1983.

On the salary committee, Lyall and Hanson forged a solid partnership, producing a well-reasoned and well-documented report. Presented in March 1984, the Report of the Governor's Faculty Compensation Study Committee analyzed salary conditions within the UW System and compared System compensation levels with those of national peer groups. The report identified national peer groups for each of the System's doctoral campuses, the comprehensive institutions, and the two-year centers. Analyzing pay within these groups, the report concluded that significant increases for all UW System faculty were needed for the System to become competitive with peer institutions nationally and recommended that the legislature take action to raise salaries at UW institutions to at least the median of their peer groups beginning in the next budget cycle. On the basis of this report, as well as similar studies of the salaries of academic staff members, the board, at its meeting on November 9, 1984, approved a budget request asking the legislature for funds to raise faculty salaries by 15 percent at UW–Madison, 11 percent at UW–Milwaukee, 9 percent at the comprehensive institutions, and 15 percent at the two-year center campuses. For academic staff members, the recommended increases were slightly lower, at 13.9 percent, 10.2 percent, 6.0 percent and 17.6 percent, respectively. The board's proposal was forwarded to the legislature as part of its biennial operating budget request for the 1985–87 biennium.

The recommended increases were supported by the governor, legislators, and the Board of Regents as a means of maintaining educational quality.[65] Within the System, however, the proposal was strongly criticized. TAUWF and some chancellors at the comprehensive institutions complained that the lower percentage increases proposed for them were unfair. Renewing the old arguments about salary parity that had dominated much of the merger implementation debate, they pressed for percentage increases equal to those recommended for the doctoral institutions and university centers. There was even unhappiness at the doctoral institutions. UW–Madison argued that its national reputation and unique stature within the System required that the campus be compared to high-paying private institutions, resulting in the need for even higher percentage pay increases for faculty to achieve true "catch-up" with their peers. The internal bickering soon spilled over into the public arena. UW–Stevens Point's chancellor, Philip Marshall, actively lobbied against the System's position on the proposed increases, seeking larger raises for his faculty and opposing the catch-up plan. And, in what Earl would later characterize as one of the most impolitic statements ever made, TAUWF leaders went so far as to suggest that *no* raise for the comprehensives would be preferable to having a lower increase than Madison's proposed 15 percent, saying, "You won't cram a 10 percent raise down our throats."[66]

At the December 1984 regent meeting, board president Ben Lawton warned that the squabbling was undermining legislative and gubernatorial support for the entire proposal, saying, "If we continue taking irresponsible, wild shots at each other, the whole idea of catch-up pay may just evaporate in a cloud of rhetoric." O'Neil, however, proved unable to put an end to the infighting, frustrating both state leaders and regents. Earl blamed O'Neil for failing to stop chancellors and other insiders from pursuing their independent agendas and lobbying for pay increases that differed from the System's recommendation.[67] Lawton agreed, believing O'Neil should have been more assertive and should have fired Marshall for his activities.[68] O'Neil's inability to control the situation and the System's failure to coalesce around a unified position effectively left it to the legislature and governor to decide the issue.

While a catch-up pay plan similar in its key elements to that recommended by the board was eventually approved in the state's 1985–87 budget, the internal System dissension and discord, together with the failure to stop the political end runs by campus leaders, were further blows to O'Neil's credibility and confirmed the external view that the UW System was incapable of managing its own affairs. The result was more—not less— scrutiny of UW affairs on the part of state government. As Earl later put it, quoting his friend and then Assembly Speaker Tom Loftus, if they can't solve these kinds of issues internally, "they should expect to find us messing in their briar patch on a lot of other things as well."[69] Consistent with this view, in early 1985 Loftus formed the Assembly Select Committee on the Future of the UW System, which he chaired along with Assembly minority leader and colleague Tommy Thompson, to review UW System operations. Earl, too, proposed further study of UW System management practices, in the wake of the catch-up struggle, and later in 1985, still responding to the problems revealed by the catch-up battle, the board would initiate its own study of the System's future.[70]

The catch-up pay effort left internal damage, as well. Those who had demanded across-the-board salary equity at all campuses remained dissatisfied with the results, and many continued to advocate for collective bargaining rights as a better means to achieve their goal of higher salaries. Others were unhappy, even with their more generous increases, believing that different peer comparisons would have yielded better pay. The positive benefits of gaining salary increases were largely lost in the furor, and O'Neil received little credit for advancing the catch-up pay effort.[71] The success of the pay battle proved to be a Pyrrhic victory, achieved at the price of more internal dissension and further damage to relations between the System and state government.

A Presidential Transition

In January 1985, with the catch-up pay proposal slated for incorporation into the 1985–87 state budget, O'Neil announced his resignation to become president of the University of Virginia. In the end, he had been unable to play the kind of unifying role he had sought with the UW System. The discord from the conflicts with Shain left ill will toward the UW System at UW–Madison, encouraging many at the campus to continue waging the old war against merger.[72] Meanwhile, the infighting on the salary catch-up question gave credence to external criticisms that the System was unable to manage its own affairs, leading to renewed scrutiny by state government and undermining O'Neil's leadership. O'Neil left office with his goal of fully integrating the System unmet and his role in winning catch-up pay unappreciated.

Following O'Neil's departure, Lyall was named acting System president, and it fell to her to continue with the implementation of the catch-up pay plan and to begin to address the damage left from the pay debate. At the September 1985 board meeting, she acknowledged the harm done by the internal divisions and emphasized the need to heal those wounds and to counter the public impression that System self-governance had failed—that, "faced with the first really tough policy decision since merger, we had to invite the Legislature in to resolve a family feud." She urged the board and the System to work to "restore the belief of the people of Wisconsin that we can govern ourselves with restraint and in a manner that produces just treatment for all segments of the university community."[73] The family dysfunction, however, had been costly. After nearly fifteen years, Lucey's shotgun marriage of state higher education was troubled by internal discord, vulnerable to hard economic times, and increasingly forced to defend itself from external criticism.

5

Forward Momentum, Changing Conditions

Despite the organizational challenges of merger implementation, cascading budget problems, downsizing pressures, and internal dysfunction that characterized the early years following merger, UW System institutions continued to fulfill their essential teaching, research, and service missions. Building on the solid foundation of past successes, System faculty, staff and students added new academic and research achievements throughout the period. UW institutions also began to explore new commercial opportunities and partnerships based on university research and to engage more actively with private businesses to improve the state's economy. At the same time, however, ongoing financial problems forced UW institutions to turn to nonstate sources of funding for critical instructional support, bringing new concerns about conflicts of interest, independence of university research, and new fundraising roles for university leaders. Meanwhile, shifting student attitudes toward higher education and pressures to expand educational access for women, minorities, and other groups formerly excluded brought new social and legal controversies that would draw the System and its institutions into widening culture wars and divisive political conflicts. These trends, emerging during the early postmerger period, would persist, posing ongoing challenges for the System and its institutions. The capacity of System faculty, staff, and students to maintain achievement in the face of difficult and changing conditions reflected core institutional strength and resilience, but the System continued to struggle to respond to emerging problems and to justify its value to the state.

Maintaining Achievement

As President O'Neil would later remark, whatever the System's postmerger external challenges and internal conflicts, at the institutional level "much of the time, life just went on."[1] UW–Madison, its achievements and brand central to the reputation of the entire UW System, maintained its national and international standing as a major research institution, earning recognition for significant scientific and medical advances. In 1975, Professor Howard Temin, a virologist and oncologist at Madison's McArdle Laboratory for Cancer Research, was awarded the Nobel Prize in Physiology or Medicine for his work on cancer research. Professor Hector DeLuca continued the critical work on the uses of vitamins D and A begun by Professor Harry Steenbock, developing drugs to treat bone, kidney, and other diseases.[2] Professor Paul Moran's magnetic resonance imaging (MRI) innovations improved clinicians' ability to diagnosis injury and disease, while UW scientists Folkert Belzer and James Southard developed organ preservation techniques essential to support life-saving organ transplants. UW–Madison faculty members Joseph Hirschfelder and Robert Burris won the National Medal of Science in 1975 and 1979, respectively,[3] and UW–Madison consistently ranked among the top ten university recipients of federal grants in the country. The flagship also produced Rhodes Scholars in 1973, 1975, and 1976.

At other System institutions, there were new developments in research programs and achievements in other areas. Research activity continued to grow at UW–Milwaukee, where funding more than doubled between 1973 and 1980, rising from $2.2 to $4.6 million, while the number of students enrolled in graduate programs increased from 4,207 to 4,468.[4] Although merger implementation restrained program growth in the newly combined System and limited the development of new graduate programs at the former WSU campuses, graduate programs continued to be added at the two doctoral institutions in the early postmerger years. At UW–Milwaukee, new PhD programs were approved in the areas of Management Science, Urban Social Institutions, Biosciences, and Geosciences, while UW–Madison established the School of Veterinary Medicine in 1981. These new programs enhanced research capacity at the System's doctoral institutions, while complementing the baccalaureate focus of the smaller UW institutions and two-year colleges and their critical role as the principal feeder institutions for the graduate programs at UW–Madison and UW–Milwaukee.

The Quest for Additional Revenue Sources and Cost Savings

The System's research programs gained new importance in the early postmerger period as a source of nonstate financial support. The battle over catch-up pay had exposed the System's troubling internal discord, but it also demonstrated the external obstacles to securing adequate state taxpayer funding, even for such critical, well-documented university needs as competitive faculty salaries. As the decline in state taxpayer support continued, UW institutions began to seek alternative sources of nongovernmental revenue and to focus on internal cost saving measures to maximize resources. The early postmerger period would see more aggressive efforts to capitalize on university research, increasing activity to expand support from private foundations, and a growing emphasis on efficiency and freedom from state regulation as a means of cutting costs.

Recognizing the potential for deriving additional revenues from institutional research and outreach efforts, in the late 1970s and early 1980s UW System institutions stepped up efforts to develop university–industry partnerships and commercialize university research. In contrast to the contentious catch-up pay issues, these efforts to develop extramural funding sources enjoyed general Systemwide support and were encouraged by O'Neil, with strong leadership from Shain and UW–Madison.

In his response to a 1982 task force report on instructional funding, O'Neil emphasized the importance of demonstrating the UW System's economic value to the state and urged UW institutions to build better relationships with the private sector. Noting that university–industry partnerships were consistent with the Wisconsin Idea that knowledge should be shared to benefit state citizens and the economy, he pointed out they could also lead to corporate sponsorship of research and financial support for other university activities.[5] To bolster university-business collaborations, O'Neil promoted the work of a System-wide committee chaired by UW–Stout chancellor Robert Swanson to create an inventory of services available to state businesses at UW institutions and the designation of a university–industry relations liaison officer at each UW institution. O'Neil also encouraged the efforts of UW campuses—including UW–Milwaukee, UW–Parkside, UW–Stout, and UW–Whitewater—to establish industry-supported centers or institutes to strengthen their ties to businesses. O'Neil himself served on the Wisconsin higher education–business roundtable and participated in the Wisconsin Technology Development Council created in 1983.

At UW–Madison, Chancellor Shain led key initiatives to take advantage of the university's research successes and to cultivate university–business connections. The flagship consistently ranked among the nation's top recipients of federal research grants, and its research not only advanced scientific knowledge but also generated valuable intellectual property that could be commercialized for the benefit of the campus and the inventor. UW–Madison had long received significant research funding support from the Wisconsin Alumni Research Foundation (WARF), which had been established in 1925 to provide a mechanism for returning the profits from Professor Harry Steenbock's Vitamin D patents to the campus to support more research.[6] The early 1980s, however, brought two new developments that would significantly enhance the university's ability to capitalize on its research efforts: the passage of the federal Bayh-Dole Act, in 1980, and the establishment of a UW–Madison research park, in 1983. The enactment of the federal legislation and the growth of the research park provided new revenue streams to support university research and develop research-related inventions, while strengthening university–business relationships through collaborative efforts.

The Bayh-Dole Act was a powerful stimulus for commercializing federally funded university research, and WARF played a key role in securing its passage. WARF had been a pioneering national leader with extensive experience in patenting, licensing and developing university research-derived inventions. Before the enactment of Bayh-Dole, however, relatively little had been done to commercialize university inventions produced under federally funded research grants. The federal government, as the granting agency, held ownership rights in these inventions but did not independently pursue their development. Although in the late 1960s WARF had begun the practice of negotiating agreements with federal agencies that permitted WARF and individual faculty members to pursue technology transfer arrangements on a case-by-case basis, the process was cumbersome and inefficient. Chafing at the federal government's inaction and seeking to ensure that research-derived inventions could be commercialized for the benefit of the universities where the inventions originated, WARF's patent counsel, Howard Bremer, and other WARF leaders championed the passage of legislation to achieve that goal. The passage of the Bayh-Dole Act in 1980,[7] with active lobbying support from WARF, allowed universities to own, patent, and license the inventions they developed under federal research grants and to retain the profits from commercialization. Bayh-Dole opened the door to a significant expansion of technology transfer efforts by all universities, and UW–Madison, with WARF as its designated patenting and licensing agent, would see lasting benefits from the change.[8] The funding generated by WARF's activities provided critical new research revenue and infrastructure for the flagship,[9] while helping support new business development in Madison and the state.[10]

Further encouraging technology transfer efforts and university–business partnerships was Shain's work to establish a university research park. The success of North Carolina's Research Triangle Park—a joint effort of the University of North Carolina, North Carolina State University, and Duke University located between Raleigh, Durham, and Chapel Hill, North Carolina—and similar developments at other major research universities demonstrated the value of providing a venue for university–industry partnerships. Shain believed that UW–Madison, too, could benefit from a park that would provide incubator space for its research-derived businesses and a physical base for university–business collaborations. Shain had already expanded UW–Madison's University-Industry Relations Office, and in 1983, with the support of O'Neil, he gained approval from the Board of Regents to establish a research park on university lands on Madison's west side. Originally a farm devoted to agricultural research, the property had gradually been surrounded by the growing city. Shain was able to relocate the agricultural programs and develop the tract for business purposes. By 1984, the research park had its first tenant, the Warzyn Engineering Company, a civil engineering consulting firm. By 1999 the park had grown to include some 72 companies and 2,100 employees, and by 2013 the number had increased to 126 companies and 3,600 employees.

The expansion of technology transfer efforts and university-business relationships that began in the early postmerger period substantially broadened the scope of traditional university activities. No longer simply offering services and ideas in support of private enterprises, the UW–Madison, its faculty members, and WARF were now actively engaging with the private sector to generate income and resources used to sustain core teaching and research missions. While smaller UW institutions initially lacked UW–Madison's resources and research infrastructure, the activities at the flagship would eventually become a blueprint for similar efforts throughout the System. As the System matured, other UW institutions, too, would develop their research initiatives and the capacity to support technology transfer efforts and university–industry partnerships. In 2000, WARF created a subsidiary technology transfer organization, WiSys, to provide technical expertise and legal support for research commercialization at UW institutions other than UW–Madison, and in 2006, UW–Milwaukee established its own independent technology transfer foundation, the UWM Research Foundation.

The successes of these commercial and business enterprises added valuable financial resources and research support, helping to offset declines in government funding and—consistent with the Wisconsin Idea—strengthening important ties to the business community for the benefit of state citizens and the economy. The System's expanding involvement in such activities, however, came with some new concerns. Despite the importance of university research as an important economic driver, the increasingly close connections between universities and businesses generated ethical questions about undue corporate influence on academic research and financial conflicts of interest on the part of individual faculty inventors. These and other related ethical pitfalls were widely examined and discussed by commentators nationally, as

Bayh-Dole, research park development, and similar efforts stimulated more business activity.[11]

In Wisconsin, as UW System institutions increased their own efforts to enhance revenues through business partnerships and commercialization of research, similar issues arose. The controversies over the UW System's conflict-of-interest regulations for faculty and academic staff members that arose during O'Neil's term were driven not only by legislative interest and questions about transparency in reporting employee outside activities but also by concerns about potential conflicts between the private financial interests of individual employees and the university's interests in ownership and control of institution-supported research efforts and in ensuring the independence of its research efforts. The amendments to the UW System's conflict-of-interests policies finally approved in 1985 affirmed limits on the use of an employee's university position for private financial gain, required more detailed reporting of outside activities, and established a procedure for reviewing and resolving conflicts of interest.[12] Over the years, as increasingly sophisticated activities raised new ethical questions and federal agencies established their own conflict-of-interest requirements applicable in the context of university research and related activities, System regulations and campus policies would undergo further review and revision.[13]

As direct engagement in revenue-generating commercial activities grew, UW System institutions also turned to their supporting charitable foundations for financial assistance, becoming increasingly reliant on gift support for academic needs. At the time of merger, the UW Foundation, a nonprofit corporation established in 1945, maintained an endowment providing funds for enhanced academic programming and for capital improvements at UW–Madison and the former UW institutions. The smaller former WSU campuses also received gift income from their own supporting nonprofit foundations, but these organizations generally did not maintain endowments, simply "passing through" donations for specified purposes directly to the institution. In the premerger and early postmerger days, when the state taxpayer share of university budgets was expected to provide full support for instructional costs, gifts from foundations were generally seen as a resource for program enhancements offering margins of academic excellence. As state taxpayer support continued to diminish, however, the importance of private giving to support basic instructional needs grew substantially, generating new efforts on the part of all foundations to build endowments. The UW Foundation launched more sophisticated and ambitious campaigns to attract major gifts to the flagship, while the smaller pass-through foundations supporting other UW institutions began to undertake more extensive fundraising efforts of their own, adding on-campus development offices and beginning to establish endowed funds. Chancellors and other institutional officers assumed more prominent roles in fundraising and donor cultivation—activities that would by the early 2000s become standard expectations for leaders in such positions and that reflected the growing dependence of public institutions on private support to replace state funds for basic operational costs.

Along with the new emphasis on efforts to generate revenues from nonstate sources, the System and its institutions pursued cost-saving strategies to help manage through hard financial times. From merger forward, the System had been highly regulated by state government. These burdens came with high costs. In his 1982 report on instructional funding,[14] O'Neil made a case for deregulation and greater management flexibility as a means of controlling System expenses and maximizing available resources. The pursuit of deregulation and management flexibility would become recurring themes of System budget and policy requests to the state, taking on greater urgency in the hard times of the 2010s. By then, management flexibility had emerged as a critical—to some, the most critical—factor in ensuring the ongoing success of System institutions, and it would become a principal justification for later efforts to radically restructure the System as a whole. The erosion of state government support for the UW System that began in the early postmerger years led directly to the growing emphasis on gaining alternative, private sources of institutional support and the ongoing quest for management flexibilities.

Student Life:
New Attitudes

Student life, too, was changing in the years after merger, as students turned from protests and demonstrations to less confrontational means of engaging in campus activities. Despite the dip

in the birth rate that had occurred with the aging of the baby-
boom generation, major enrollment declines failed to materialize
due to increased demand for college, greater participation by
women, and relatively inexpensive access to higher education.
The increased demand and changing demographics brought
new attitudes and new expectations of higher education from
students.

Protest and Participation

In the years immediately following merger, the period of violent
campus unrest that had culminated in the Sterling Hall bombing
gradually drew to a close. The shock of the bombing itself and
the slow winding down of the Vietnam War had cooled student
enthusiasm for further demonstrations, not only at UW–Madison,
a major hotbed of activity in the late 1960s and early 1970s, but at
other UW System campuses such as UW–Milwaukee and UW–
Oshkosh,[15] which had also seen disturbances. The days of constant demonstrations,[16] arrests, strikes,[17] and violence on System
campuses that had dominated national and local media attention
ended, and relative calm was restored. Addressing UW–Madison
administrators and faculty at the beginning of the 1972–73 academic year, Chancellor Young noted that a major shift had taken
place in the mood on campus, reporting that the hostility and neg-
ativism of recent times had given way to an increasing positivism
that could support long-lasting progress toward addressing the
institution's problems.[18] Although painful reminders of the Sterling Hall bombing continued to haunt the campus,[19] protest activity declined throughout the 1970s as students resumed more
traditional academic and extracurricular activities[20] and former
activists took on civic roles, as did Paul Soglin—a leader of the
Dow Chemical protests of 1967—who by 1973 was serving as the
mayor of Madison.

The return of calm to UW campuses also brought changes in
the nature of student engagement in campus affairs. While the
protest era had damaging consequences, student activism and
demands had also helped produce policy changes that gave students a stronger, more formal voice in campus affairs. The merger
legislation recognized the importance of student participation
in university affairs by requiring the inclusion of two student

representatives, one from the former UW and the other from the WSU, on the merger implementation committee (MISC) charged with developing the governing statute for the new System. The students selected, Randy Nilsestuen (WSU) and Robert Brabham (UW), successfully advocated before MISC for statutory provisions giving students the right to be "active participants" in campus decisions affecting student life and interests and to have a voice in determining how some portions of their student fees[21] were used. On the recommendation of MISC and with the approval of the legislature and governor, these provisions were later incorporated in Chapter 36 of the Wisconsin Statutes, giving students a legal right to participate in university governance unique in the United States.[22]

The codification of student rights in state law reflected a shift in the direction of student activism away from protest and toward participation, but it did not end disputes between students and university administrators, instead bringing a more formal, legalistic—and often litigious—approach to disagreements. In the years following merger, the Board of Regents and UW institutions adopted policies on student governance to implement the statute,[23] but disputes over its proper interpretation led to litigation. An early case involved whether UW chancellors or students themselves had the authority to choose the student representatives who would serve on campus governance committees. In 1976, UW–Milwaukee students sued Chancellor Werner Baum, asserting that he had sought to control the selection process, contrary to the new law. Construing §36.09(5) of Wisconsin Statutes for the first time, the Wisconsin Supreme Court ruled for the students, holding that the statute clearly gives students the right to organize student government as they see fit and to appoint their own representatives to campus governance committees.[24] In a similar case several years later, *UW–Oshkosh Student Association v. Board of Regents*, the Wisconsin District IV Court of Appeals held that students also had the right to choose their representatives to serve on a Systemwide search-and-screen committee appointed by the Board of Regents to advise on the selection of the UW–Oshkosh chancellor.[25] The use of litigation to protect student rights marked another change in strategies by student leaders intent on gaining a voice in campus decision making. Lawsuits would become a regular tool used by students in subsequent struggles with administrators over the appropriate uses of mandatory student activities fees and other policy issues.

In addition to asserting their campus-specific governance rights, students in the early postmerger years sought a voice in UW governance Systemwide. Although under the statutes the right of student participation was at the institutional level, student government representatives from around the System formed an umbrella group, the United Council of Student Governments, to provide input on Systemwide policies affecting students. The UW–Madison's Wisconsin Student Association (WSA) was particularly active in the formation of the United Council, which in the early postmerger period included almost all UW campuses. The United Council and the WSA appeared regularly at meetings of the Board of Regents, representing student opinion on a range of policy and social issues, from tuition levels to the divestiture of UW System holdings in South African businesses to the use of financial aid to enforce draft registration requirements. Seeking a more influential and direct role in UW System affairs, in 1985 the United Council and the WSA successfully lobbied for the addition of a student member to the Board of Regents. The statutes were amended in that year to provide a seat on the board for a student, to be appointed by the governor, to serve a two-year term. John Schenian, a UW Law School student appointed by Governor Earl, became the first student regent. A subsequent change in the statutes added a second student seat, this one to be filled by a "nontraditional" student, defined as a student over the age of twenty-four who was either employed or a parent, further strengthening the student voice in System policymaking.[26]

Apathy and Antics

Although the postmerger expansion of student rights gave students new opportunities to have formal, legal engagement in campus and Systemwide affairs, the number of students actively involved in governance remained very small. Even as the United Council, WSA, and other campus student organizations pressed for a stronger role in governance, the actual participation rates in student government remained low at all UW System campuses. With so few students voting in student government elections, administrators questioned the fairness of the results and whether those elected could claim to represent all students. In August 1974, UW–Milwaukee student services staff, responding to a United Council proposal defining student responsibilities under the merger legislation, noted that only about 2 percent of the student body had voted in the last election and suggested that a more significant percentage of students should be required to vote before the administration would recognize any group as the exclusive representative of all students.[27] Although no such requirement was imposed, the widespread apathy was a concern. Lack of participation meant that student governance rights were effectively left in the hands of a very small group of students, operating with little accountability to their constituents and subject to few controls on their policy decisions or the process through which they exercised the authority to expend the funds raised by student fees.

These underlying weaknesses of student governance were exposed when, in 1978, UW–Madison students elected Jim Mallon and Leon Varjian as president and vice president of the WSA. Mallon and Varjian ran as leaders of the newly created Pail and Shovel Party, winning the WSA elections with 1,500 of the 4,500 votes cast.[28] In contrast to the earnest arguments of Nilsestuen and Brabham for giving students the right to participate in campus governance, Mallon and Varjian had no interest in representing student views to institutional leaders or state government, instead casting themselves as class clowns with no serious platform. As Varjian said in the 1979 UW–Madison Badger Yearbook, "Students can relate. They say 'Those people are as crazy as I am.'" He went on to add, "Goals? Well, we have no goals. All we have is a touch of insanity." Mallon agreed, saying, "We don't take ourselves so seriously. We're just trying to loosen up a little bit and make WSA more of a student organization."[29]

The two proceeded to use student fees[30] for several memorably over-the-top activities, including toga parties in 1978 and 1979 that attracted thousands of students and drew the attention of *60 Minutes*,[31] a marijuana rally at the state Capitol, and the installation of 1,008 plastic pink flamingos on Bascom Hill. Following through on a campaign promise to bring the Statue of Liberty to Madison, on February 22, 1979, they placed a massive papier-mâché replica of the top of Lady Liberty's head and torch on the snowy surface of frozen Lake Mendota, making it appear that the statue had sunk up to the bridge of her nose.[32]

These pranks injected an element of humor into student life that amused both the campus and the community. The Madison city council adopted the pink flamingo as the city's official bird in 2009 and following Varjian's death in late 2015 declared an official day of recognition in his honor, memorializing his legacy of lighthearted fun to the community. The campus, too, embraced the pink flamingo as another university symbol, often displayed on Bascom Hill in connection with fundraising efforts and special occasions. The antics, though, were a distinct departure from the merger implementation work to gain governance rights for students, and the Pail and Shovel group's neglect of shared governance responsibilities contributed to a steady decline in respect for student governance on campus that eventually produced the dissolution of the WSA in 1993.[33] Although student government was reconstituted the following year as the Associated Students of Madison (ASM) and more serious student leadership returned, student participation would remain low at UW–Madison and throughout the System, and concerns about the activities and functions of student government—particularly its role in the disposition of student fees—would grow, setting the stage for future disputes and litigation.

Demographic Changes and Consumerism

With the postmerger changes in student attitudes, the composition of the student body itself was gradually changing, bringing a more diverse group of students to UW System institutions. There had been an influx of young people into colleges and universities in the post–World War II "golden age"; higher education nationally had expanded college participation beyond social elites, and it was increasingly seen as an opportunity that should be affordable and accessible to a majority of high school graduates. Making higher education widely available to this broader group of Americans, however, created new challenges for colleges and universities, including UW System institutions. As participation in higher education continued to expand in the years after merger, a new consumer-oriented attitude about college developed, requiring universities to became more sensitive to the expressed needs and desires of students and their parents on matters ranging from curricular choices to physical facilities. Universities began to see the recruitment and admissions process as an opportunity to sell themselves to students and parents. Students became more career oriented, choosing majors likely to lead to jobs, and more generally cost-conscious, particularly as federal funding for financial aid shifted from tuition grants to loans during the 1980s. These dynamics all contributed to a rethinking on the part of both administrators and students of the meaning and purposes of a university education and the college experience.[34]

Concerns about enrollment declines and reduced demand for college resulting from the aging of the baby boom generation had provided some of the impetus for merger, and these concerns seemed to be borne out when, in 1975–76, "higher education enrollment declined by 175,000—the first drop since the tapering off attributed to the waning of GI Bill participation in 1951."[35] This drop, however, was short-term, and enrollments at UW grew steadily in the postmerger period as greater numbers of state high school students sought entry, attendance by women surged, and campuses began to attract a new cohort of students: part-time or "nontraditional" students, generally older people with employment and/or family responsibilities.[36] With growing enrollments came new pressures on admissions, particularly at the popular Madison flagship, and new concerns about the System's continued capacity to grow while maintaining quality.

Civil Rights, Affirmative Action, and Backlash

As these changes in student life rippled through UW institutions in the early postmerger years, new demands for equal treatment of women and minorities and pressures to expand affirmative action programs intensified—together with backlash and resistance. Civil rights, equal opportunity, and affirmative action had been major issues at Wisconsin's public colleges and universities well before merger. The enactment of the Equal Pay Act of 1963 and the Civil Rights Act of 1964 had opened the doors to full participation in employment and education by those who had previously faced barriers or been excluded completely, and pressures to end discrimination and discriminatory practices at Wisconsin's public colleges and universities continued in the years leading up to the merger. At both UW–Madison and UW–Milwaukee, anger over race discrimination had fueled demands for curricular changes to focus on the history of minority groups and to expand extracurricular support to meet the needs of minorities. Responding to a student group called the United Black Student Front, UW–Milwaukee established one of the nation's first Afro-American Studies programs in 1968.[37] At UW–Madison, the "Black Strike" of 1969 led to the creation, in 1970, of the Department of Afro-American Studies. In October 1971, UW–Madison established a new Equal Educational Opportunity Council to deal with the "admission and recruiting of minority students, academic programming and problems students face on campus." In the same month, UW–Oshkosh established a Task Force on Minority Rights. And, in response to claims of sex-based pay inequities, in December 1971 the new UW System provided pay increases for six hundred women in the former UW, in order to make their pay equal to that of their male counterparts.[38]

By the time the UW System merger implementation was fully under way, the impact of civil rights legislation and these kinds of demands for action to redress past inequities were having profound effects on the System's efforts to comply with new legal requirements and to respond to new expectations about the treatment of women and minorities. Nationally, the Newman Report, a 1971 study by the Department of Health, Education, and Welfare, urged changes in higher education that would support "achieving equality for women, expanding minority access and promoting diverse structures and funding mechanisms."[39] Within the new System, the UW–Oshkosh Task Force declared in 1972 that the school had "not served the legitimate needs of racial minorities" and recommended increasing the number of minority employees at the institution.[40] The May 1972 meeting of the Board of Regents was disrupted by three women protesting rampant sex discrimination within the system who had to be ejected from the meeting by UW Protection and Security.[41] Later that year, a group of female faculty members threatened to sue the UW System when they learned that the university had no plans to budget for salary equity increases needed to "directly attack discrimination against women."[42] In March 1973, the Latin Council of Wisconsin discussed taking legal action against the System on grounds that it had not adequately complied with national affirmative action laws,[43] while in September students confronted the Board of Regents about the closure of two Madison-campus ethnic centers: the Afro-American Center and the Native American

Center.[44] The passage of Title IX of the Education Amendments of 1972, prohibiting sex discrimination in federally funded education programs, including athletics, further expanded equal opportunities for women, spurring additional demands to address inequality and lack of opportunity in the new UW System.

The UW System and its institutions responded to the expansion of civil rights protections and the pressures for equal opportunity by adopting new policies and practices that reflected their own commitment to ensuring equity and diversity. To obtain accurate data to support affirmative action efforts, the UW System began tracking minority populations, asking students in the fall of 1972—for the first time—to indicate their racial heritage on their registration forms.[45] President Weaver appointed special assistants to advise on minority and women's affairs and, in 1972, created a new office to focus specifically on issues of women's equality, believed to be the first in the nation with such an area of responsibility.[46] Equity and affirmative action for students became official policy of the UW System in 1973 with the regents' approval of regulations prohibiting discrimination based on sex or race and committing to affirmative action to ensure access to higher education for women, minorities, and disabled populations. Policies on equal opportunity and affirmative action in employment were approved in 1975 and amended in 1982, as during O'Neil's tenure the System undertook further comprehensive efforts to address race and gender discrimination. In addition, responding to the problem of sexual harassment, the Board of Regents approved a separate policy addressing that issue in 1981.[47]

Progress in achieving equal opportunity goals was, however, painfully slow, and affirmative action efforts often met with backlash and legal challenges. The ongoing disparities in pay between men and women were vividly demonstrated when it was revealed that Marian Swoboda, Weaver's assistant for women's issues, was paid $12,500 per year less than her male counterpart, Joseph Wiley, the assistant to the president for equal opportunities for minorities.[48] Although this problem was remedied with a raise for Swoboda,[49] progress on the broader issues of hiring and improving pay for women around the System continued to be slow. In 1974, Swoboda's office reported that there had not been substantial quantifiable improvement in the areas of hiring female employees and that only six of thirteen campuses had affirmative action programs that satisfied System requirements. Her report also showed "minimal increases in the percentage of women employed at Madison, Milwaukee, Parkside, and the UW Extension system since 1970."[50] Claims of race- and gender-based employment discrimination against UW System institutions rose continuously throughout the 1970s, and UW institutions were regularly criticized for their failure to improve hiring rates of minorities[51] and women.[52]

Women fared better in gaining access to higher education, as their representation in the student body grew steadily. Nationally, their undergraduate participation rates rose from 32 percent in 1950 to 42 percent in 1970. The same period saw an increase in women in graduate education from 27 percent to 39 percent. By 1984–85, women were receiving 37 percent of PhDs, up from 10 percent in 1950.[53] The UW System participation rates followed a similar pattern, with the percentage of women on all campuses growing during this time and rising to over 50 percent of all undergraduates by 2018.[54] There were also dramatic changes in the number of women attending UW professional schools in the early postmerger years. The UW Law School, founded in 1868, had been open to women from the beginning, graduating its first woman, Belle Case LaFollette, in 1885. Until the 1970s, however, the school had typically enrolled only three to four women per class. In 1970–71, the number of women grew to 8.5 percent of all law students, and this percentage increased by approximately 10 percent every three academic years until 1979–80, when women made up 40 percent of the student body.[55] UW Medical School enrollments of women saw the same kind of growth and a parallel increase in participation. In both cases, the percentages of women enrolled would approach the 50 percent mark and stabilize there going forward.[56]

Efforts to improve the representation of minority students on UW campuses, however, seemed frustratingly ineffective. Although in 1971 the Board of Regents had set an ambitious goal of admitting 15 percent of nonresident undergraduates and 3 percent of resident undergraduates from underrepresented minority groups, funding for the effort was not adequate, and, despite some small successes,[57] this goal was not achieved. The recruitment and retention of minority students continued to be a problem throughout the early postmerger years and beyond. Those expecting immediate and dramatic changes to the status quo following the enactment of the civil rights laws of the 1960s and 1970s were inevitably disappointed and dissatisfied at the slow pace of change.

At the same time, though their success was limited, affirmative action programs in higher education drew opposition from those claiming that special efforts to recruit and enroll minorities and women discriminated against nonminorities and men. President John F. Kennedy's 1961 executive order mandating "affirmative action" to ensure equal opportunity in federal employment[58] had, by the early 1970s, inspired similar affirmative action efforts under the later civil rights legislation of the 1960s and 1970s. Some of these early affirmative action programs, however, relied on relatively unsophisticated, quota-based approaches to improving participation by underrepresented groups, leading to complaints of "reverse discrimination"—the illegal exclusion of nonminorities and men on the basis of *their* race and/or sex. Affirmative action in the context of higher education was challenged in 1978 in *University of California Regents v. Bakke*,[59] a case involving a modified quota plan used at the University of California–Davis in its medical school admissions decisions. In the *Bakke* case, the US Supreme Court held that the university's quota plan was unconstitutional but also found that achieving student body diversity was a constitutionally permissible goal that allowed for consideration of race as a factor in admissions decisions. It was, in effect, a split decision that allowed colleges and universities to continue to use race as a factor in admissions but left the door open for further legal attacks on specific affirmative action plans and their application in particular cases.[60] While the UW System remained committed to achieving diversity and continued to pursue its own affirmative action efforts, the *Bakke* case underscored the need for caution in designing and implementing its plans to ensure compliance with developing legal precedents. *Bakke* and the reaction against affirmative action also reflected the broader social conflicts often described as the culture wars—clashes pitting so-called conservative, traditionalist values against those thought to be liberal or progressive.[61] The UW System, with its commitment to equal opportunity and its affirmative efforts to improve campus diversity, would increasingly and inevitably find itself drawn into these larger conflicts.

In addition to the problems of race and sex discrimination, the civil rights era called attention to other forms of unfair treatment, leading to legislation to address these inequities. Federal laws enacted in the 1970s and the 1990s expanded support services and discrimination protections for disabled children and adults in both education and employment.[62] Not only did these laws prohibit discrimination; they also required that disabilities be accommodated in educational environments and in work settings. UW institutions responded with new policies to ensure compliance with these new requirements and supported the establishment of facilities such as the McBurney Disability Resource Center for UW–Madison students in 1977, while building on existing efforts, such as UW–Whitewater's long-successful vocational rehabilitation programs.[63]

By the early 1980s, discrimination based on sexual orientation had emerged as another source of equity concerns. In 1982, Wisconsin became the first state in the nation to prohibit sexual orientation discrimination in housing, employment, and public accommodations and this change in state law led to the inclusion of sexual orientation as a protected status in UW System polices on employment discrimination, as well as in policies prohibiting discrimination in education programs. The prohibition on discrimination based on sexual orientation, however, called into question the legality of continuing certain military programs and activities on UW campuses because of the military's policy of barring homosexuals from service. Various branches of the United States armed forces regularly conducted recruitment efforts at UW institutions, and the Reserve Officer Training Corps (ROTC) was an official academic department at several UW campuses,[64] but these activities appeared to conflict with the state's and the System's general prohibitions on discrimination based on sexual orientation. The Wisconsin attorney general had issued an opinion concluding that ROTC programs were not subject to state discrimination laws or policies, and as ROTC continued to be offered at UW campuses the Board of Regents, reviewing the issue in 1987,[65] adopted a resolution affirming its commitment to eliminating discrimination based on sexual preference and urging Congress to change federal policies on the subject. This compromise position failed to satisfy students and others opposed to the military's ban on homosexuals, but when the board revisited the question in 1990, it adopted a similar position.[66] The unresolved issue followed by President Bill Clinton's "don't ask-don't tell" policy of the 1990s would continue to stoke campus protests, including demonstrations and a sit-in at the UW–Madison chancellor's office in April 1990.[67]

University investment policies were another subject of social concern and protest in the late 1970s. At the time, the government of South Africa maintained a policy of apartheid, strictly segregating the population on racial lines and restricting the civil rights of nonwhites. Opposition to apartheid was strong at UW–Madison,[68] leading students and staff members to demand that the UW System stop investing its trust funds in companies doing business in South Africa. Responding to these concerns, the Board of Regents in 1978 acted to divest its South African–related holdings, becoming one of the few major US universities to do so.[69] Although later political changes in South Africa rendered this action moot, the Board of Regents continued to encourage socially responsible investing in its investment policies, as amended.[70]

Resilience

The rapidly changing social, cultural, and legal conditions of the early postmerger years brought wide-ranging and complex new challenges for the System. Many of the issues and problems that emerged would confront the System well into the future. While the core institutional resilience and momentum from past achievements allowed UW System institutions, faculty, staff, and students to continue their academic and research successes, and to develop new strategies for responding to ongoing financial troubles and difficult social issues, the System continued to face the ongoing pressures and conflicts associated with the shifting landscape for state higher education.

6

Merger 2.0

Toward a More Perfect Union

July 1985 brought another presidential transition. With the family dysfunction and ongoing work on the UW System's catch-up pay proposal in the background, the Board of Regents initiated the search for O'Neil's successor. The now predictable struggles for control of the process and disagreements over the qualifications for the job were renewed, and the board again turned to Kauffman for assistance. Following another contentious search, Kenneth A. "Buzz" Shaw, then president of the Southern Illinois University System, was named president. Although the choice was initially criticized by both political and academic leaders, Shaw overcame early skepticism to prove himself an effective System leader. His success in unifying the System and his focus on strategic, long-term planning would lay the foundation for a period of sustained stability for UW institutions that continued through the term of his successor, Katharine C. Lyall.

Déjà Vu All Over Again

Approached by the board to assist with another presidential search, Kauffman agreed, but he cautioned that recruitment would be difficult. Wisconsin had a tradition of low pay for university executives, and this was still an obstacle. Not only was the salary low relative to that of the System's national peers, but also the lack of unity within the System and the conflict between O'Neil and Shain had become well known among top national university leaders, making the position unattractive to many outside the state.[1] In addition, the old conflicts over presidential qualifications resurfaced, pitting those in favor of a politically adept, nonacademic System head against those who insisted on a seasoned academic administrator acceptable to faculty leaders and holding academic credentials appropriate for tenure at UW–Madison. Further complicating the situation, state political leaders were actively and openly seeking to influence the selection process. Former governor and former UW–Stevens Point chancellor Lee Dreyfus was himself a candidate for the position, while Governor Earl made it clear that he supported David Carley, who, despite pressure from some regents at that time, had not been a finalist in the 1979 search. Still, Carley, a prominent Madison Democrat and real estate developer, former candidate for governor, past member of the Board of Regents, and president of the Medical College of Wisconsin, remained a favorite of the governor and other political leaders, who publicly campaigned for his appointment.[2]

As the search progressed through the summer of 1985, it was plagued by frequent leaks to the media, sparking ongoing speculation about who was in contention for the position. Shain, despite his antipathy to the System and his commitment to its "dismemberment" if he were to be named president, had been nominated, and he remained in the applicant pool, along with another insider, UW–Milwaukee chancellor Frank Horton. Meanwhile, Lyall, another logical "insider" candidate, declined to be considered, concerned that she was a relative newcomer and that her role in the divisive catch-up pay battle would be problematic.[3] Horton subsequently withdrew to accept the presidency of the University of Oklahoma, and it soon became clear that neither Carley nor any in-state candidate would be among the group of finalists.[4] Instead, the board selected Shaw from a group of outsiders, all academic leaders recommended by a faculty-dominated search and screen committee. He was named UW System president in October 1985.

At first, Shaw's selection seemed to make neither politicians nor academics very happy. There were immediate criticisms from the governor and legislators about the search and protests from Carley about unfair treatment by Kauffman. State Senate majority leader Tim Cullen said he and others were offended that a candidate of Carley's caliber was not a finalist, Representative Marlin Schneider accused the regents of hiring "another academic wimp," and Earl said he was disappointed that the process did not include either Carley or Dreyfus. In a vituperative public outburst, Carley went so far as to claim that regent president Lawton and Kauffman had subverted the search process, accusing Kauffman of reducing Lawton to a "diminished bewildered patsy, with little or no power to act in what has always been in the past a leadership role."[5] The uproar prompted complaints of secrecy in the search and calls for a legislative inquiry into the process.[6]

In addition to the public and political furor, Shaw's selection prompted internal concerns about his academic credentials. Although he held a doctoral degree from Purdue and had experience in leading a state university and a university system, some UW–Madison faculty members questioned whether Shaw's academic record was worthy of tenure at their institution, casting doubt on his academic credibility. Shaw himself, however, managed to remain above the fray, and, as the negative publicity about the search process subsided and the calls for legislative action were dropped, he began work on his own presidential agenda.

Ending the Family Feud

Projecting an affable self-confidence and genuine willingness to work with state politicians, Shaw quickly demonstrated his strengths as a leader. Unperturbed by the political sniping, he neatly sidestepped the issue of his academic rank at UW–Madison by deciding not to pursue tenure there. He focused instead on addressing what he saw as the three-fold job before him: bringing the System together, getting the campuses to support a shared legislative agenda, and implementing a Systemwide plan for improving all institutions.[7]

It was an ambitious plan, given the circumstances. The System was still suffering from its internal conflicts, while continuing to

face not only the familiar external headwinds of eroding financial support and heightened legislative scrutiny but also newly
active hostility from state business interests. The System's
lengthy history of budget crises and funding reductions had by
the time Shaw arrived resulted in dramatically diminished levels
of per-student support that posed ever more serious threats to
educational quality. Library resources were inadequate, physical
facilities were deteriorating, and overcrowded classes and course
sequences were making it increasingly difficult for students to
complete a degree in four years. Still, opposition to increasing
state financial support persisted, fueled by a steady barrage of
legislative audits, predictions of falling enrollments, and skepticism about the System's funding needs.

As Shaw assumed office, the System was dealing with the
fallout from a 1985 LAB audit that had sparked legislative anger
over the size and proposed uses of the System's auxiliary reserve
balances. These monies, generated from student user fees for self-
supporting enterprises such as residence halls, student unions,
and dining services, had been set aside to pay for future expenses
for new dormitory construction, student union upgrades, and
maintenance of similar auxiliary facilities. The LAB audit, however, concluded that, because of the absence of strong management controls by System administration, some $22.5 million in
excess of what was required for these purposes had been accumulated in the reserves and that these funds could legally be
made available for other UW System purposes.[8] Legislators were
quick to agree. They acted to move the $22.5 million from the re-
serves to the System's general operating budget and prohibited
the System from replacing the reserves with other student fees.
This shift effectively reduced the state's contribution to the System budget, replacing state tax support with fees paid by students
and intended for other purposes. It also left the System as a whole
with no auxiliary reserves. System institutions were not permitted
to build future reserves unless they had gained prior approval of
specific plans for their uses, while the Board of Regents was forced
to implement a process for drawing down individual, institutional
reserve accounts to satisfy the legislative action transferring the
reserves.[9]

In addition to this "raid" on auxiliary funds, the legislature in
1986 had also requested that the LAB conduct a management

audit of System administration.[10] This audit got under way just as Shaw began his term and continued through most of his first year as president. When completed, in November 1986, the report harshly criticized System administration for not achieving the goals of merger due to inadequate central leadership and management control in three key areas: enrollment management, academic program development, and allocation of funds. Despite his own short time in office, Shaw found himself forced to defend the entire fifteen years of UW System operations since merger and to promise more aggressive leadership and management control in future.[11]

Making matters still more complicated, 1986 was a gubernatorial election year. Seeking election to a second term, Governor Earl was opposed by Assembly minority leader Tommy Thompson. Although higher education was not a major issue in the campaign, as the election season began, two state business groups launched their own targeted attacks opposing state spending in general and support for the UW System in particular. The Council of Small Business Executives and the Wisconsin Manufacturers and Commerce (WMC), an organization composed of prominent state business leaders, prepared publicity materials suggesting that the System was too large and tuition too low. Both Shaw and Laurence Weinstein, a Madison businessman and WMC member who had succeeded Lawton as board president, vigorously challenged these views, arguing that they contravened long-standing state and national traditions of support for broad access to quality public higher education. In a separate letter to WMC president James Haney, Weinstein further attacked the WMC's position as being based on faulty data.[12] Nevertheless, both groups maintained their opposition to UW funding increases, marking a newly hostile attitude to higher education and the UW System on the part of the state's major business organizations.

Despite these and other attacks, Shaw felt the three major goals he had set for himself were reasonable and could be accomplished.[13] He set the tone at his first regent meeting, in February 1986, outlining his position on relations with state government. Aware that governors and legislators disliked what they considered to be "whining" on the part of UW leaders, he promised that the System would abandon the old "sky is falling" approach[14] in favor of legislative initiatives based on System priorities, presented with honesty and forthrightness. He went on to emphasize that, as a System, "we will speak clearly with one voice."[15] Following up on these commitments, Shaw sought out state political leaders, making himself personally available to meet with them to discuss their concerns. As Assembly Speaker Tom Loftus would later recall, Shaw, unlike his predecessors, was an active, accessible presence in the legislature.[16]

Within the System administration, he built an effective working relationship with Katharine Lyall, who, after serving as acting president following O'Neil's departure, had returned to her role as executive vice president under Shaw. Lyall, a stalwart presence in the System administration, provided internal management continuity as Shaw concentrated on his major priorities. In his relations with the System's chancellors and institutional leaders, Shaw made it clear that "end runs" to the legislature to gain special benefits for their institutions would not be tolerated. Early on, he informed them that any special "gifts" they received as the result of individual, backdoor lobbying of the legislature or governor would result in proportionate cuts to the funds they received under the System's budget.[17] Not surprisingly, chancellors did not always like this approach.[18] Nevertheless, it was an effective *in terrorem* mechanism for enforcing System cohesion and avoiding the kind of disunity that had undermined the campaign for catch-up pay.

Shaw also managed to calm relations between System administration and UW–Madison. In contrast to O'Neil, Shaw did not see active involvement in flagship affairs as a part of his role, and he generally deferred to Shain in the management of campus affairs. He liked Shain and, for the relatively brief period when their terms overlapped,[19] he believed they worked well together. For his part, Shain, though remaining suspicious of and resistant to central authority, conceded that Shaw's personal popularity and leadership philosophy commanded respect.[20] Shaw, believing the AAU position was an important way to make the System president's office more visible, continued to serve as the representative, but Shain did not renew the AAU dispute with him.[21] Shaw, in return, did not interfere with Shain's administration of UW–Madison. The result was a less antagonistic relationship between the System and the flagship that freed Shaw to focus on unifying the System around a cohesive approach to working with the state's political leadership and addressing Systemwide problems.

A Strategic Plan for Preserving Quality

As he went about the business of healing internal divisions and improving external relations, Shaw also began to work on his overarching goal of improving all UW institutions. His platform was the board's effort, begun shortly before he took office, to prepare and implement a long-range strategic plan for the System. In November 1985, under fire because of the discord over catch-up pay and facing the prospect of a gubernatorial inquiry into the System's ongoing needs, priorities, and funding, then board president Ben Lawton had established a Board of Regents study group on the future of the UW System. Earlier in 1985, the Governor's Strategic Development Commission had called for a study of structural and management improvements in the System, along with better long-term planning. In addition, the Assembly Select Committee on the Future of the UW System, led by Assembly Speaker Tom Loftus and minority leader Tommy Thompson, had conducted its own hearings on the System's future. After criss-crossing the state, visiting UW campuses, and meeting with citizens and members of the university community, the two legislative leaders had come away impressed with the value of all the UW campuses and the importance of their individual missions. Thompson said the two had begun their work believing that the System was too large but returned convinced that it was not and that no campuses should be closed.[22] Thompson, however, still wondered about the System's future, asking, as O'Neil reported to the board in June 1985, "Where is the System going in the next decade?"[23] Faced with these external pressures, Lawton had established the board's future study group, in effect charging it with answering Thompson's question and with creating a blueprint for the future that would ensure the continued quality of education in the UW System. Composed of all regents, executive vice president Lyall, UW–Madison's Shain, and Chancellor Robert S. Swanson of UW–Stout, the future study group was chaired by regent Ody Fish, with Swanson serving as vice chair. On becoming System president, Shaw built on the work of this group to develop what would become the System's first comprehensive strategic plan.

Working through 1986, with the support of Shaw's staff and institutional leaders from around the System, the study group issued its report, *Planning the Future*, in December 1986. The plan contained recommendations for revitalizing the System by more effective management of resources, better control of enrollments, and mission- and program-based allocation of funding to System institutions.[24] The most important priority under the plan, however, was addressing the System's chronic fiscal problems. From its creation, in 1971, the UW System had faced repeated budget cuts and unstable or inadequate state government support. Describing in detail the extent and depth of the System's underfunding problem, *Planning the Future* concluded that it posed a growing threat to educational quality and access to higher education in the state and that finding solutions to the lack of adequate, reliable state support was now critical to the System's ability to fulfill its teaching, research, and service missions.

Solving the Underfunding Problem

Planning the Future identified the System's low levels of per-student support as a key threat to educational quality and recommended addressing that problem as a first step in solving the underfunding problem. O'Neil had warned in 1983 that persistently diminishing state taxpayer support, combined with low tuition rates, had caused System institutions to fall dramatically behind their peers in the level of per-student instructional support. While state financial support had continued to erode, the dire demographic predictions of shrinking student populations and waning demand for college had proved wrong. Demand for college had increased in the years since merger, enrollments had grown, and by 1983–84 there were fifteen thousand more students attending System institutions than there had been at the time of merger. Taxpayer funding was far below what was needed to educate this growing student body, and tuition revenues were insufficient to offset shrinking state support. Tuition rates for resident undergraduates, the largest group of System students, are effectively, if indirectly, controlled by the state legislature and governor[25] and had historically been held at low levels to ensure wide access to System institutions. Without adequate state funds or the flexibility to raise tuition revenues on its own, however, the System's ability to provide quality educational opportunities for these additional students was threatened.

Planning the Future confirmed that per-student funding in the UW System had fallen to more than $600 per student below the national average and $800 per student below that of peer institutions. While in the 1972–73 academic year the UW System had ranked fourth in the nation in the level of per-student support, it had fallen to thirty-first by 1983–84. Undergraduate tuition at the UW System's doctoral institutions remained significantly below that at Big Ten public universities, and the System's comprehensive campuses and two-year colleges also lagged their peer institutions.[26] Enrollment growth combined with inadequate state funding and low tuition translated to larger class sizes, lack of access to necessary courses, obsolete laboratory equipment, insufficient library resources, and more teaching by instructional academic staff and teaching assistants rather than professors— all threatening educational quality. *Planning the Future* urged the state and the System to work to return the System to at least national averages of per-student support, through a combination of enrollment limits, tuition increases, and efforts to gain new state funding.[27]

Shaw used these findings and recommendations as the basis for the System's 1987–89 budget proposals. At the December 1986 board meeting, Shaw outlined the kinds of practical choices involved in bringing System per-student support to national averages. Per-student support is calculated by dividing the total funds received from state tax revenues and tuition for instructional support by the number of students enrolled, he explained. As a result, the level of per-student support can be improved by adjustments to any of those three components: enrollment, tuition and taxpayer support. With the UW System's 1986 state and tuition funds and enrollments as a base, the UW System would require an additional $88 million from a combination of these elements to reach national averages. This goal could be achieved in a variety of ways, Shaw explained. A direct $88 million increase in state funding, for example, would be one approach. The goal could also be reached by a substantial tuition increase tied to the rate of inflation plus $640 per student per year. Or, it might be achieved in savings from a drastic enrollment cut of some twenty-two thousand students. More realistically, however, reaching the national average for per-student support would require some combination of these three elements. Reviewing possible combinations—or "triangles"—of increased taxpayer funding, higher tuition, and lower enrollments that would yield the desired result, Shaw offered several possible scenarios. In one, the national averages could be reached if the state increased funding by $58 million, tuition was raised by 6.6 percent, and enrollments were cut by 3,500 students. While there were many possible permutations on this theme, the message behind Shaw's triangles was straightforward: if the state is unable or unwilling to provide the funds needed to maintain educational quality for students, then enrollments must be cut, tuition raised, or both.

Shaw's triangle concept had the support of the board and strong institutional backing from campus leaders, including Shain and Swanson, and a group of talented new chancellors who, like Terence MacTaggert at UW–Superior and Steven Portch at UW Colleges, were also committed to the overall strategic goals of *Planning the Future*. Preparing for the 1987–89 budget proposal, the System and its institutions worked internally to develop enrollment management policies and to adopt stricter academic standards to control the numbers of students admitted, while developing biennial budget requests based on a combination of improved taxpayer support and modest tuition increases.

Shaw's triangulated approach was immediately tested in the 1987–89 state budget cycle. Not only was this Shaw's first biennial budget as System president, but it was also Tommy Thompson's first gubernatorial budget. Thompson had defeated Earl in the November election, and while it was not immediately clear what the new governor's budget proposal would include,[28] Thompson had written to all regents following his victory, assuring them that the state's strong tradition of bipartisan support for the UW System would continue. Referring to his own support for faculty catch-up pay and his work on the Assembly Select Committee on the Future of the UW System, he reaffirmed his belief that no System campus should be closed and promised there would be no reduction in the System's funding during his term.[29] As Thompson's first gubernatorial budget was developed and progressed through the legislative process, Shaw and the board set enrollment management targets meant to reduce the System by some seven thousand students over the next four years. To address the other components of instructional support, the System requested a modest tuition increase and state budget funding for more than three hundred new positions, library materials, and basic and applied research, as well as specific management flexibilities in areas such as purchasing, personnel, and expenditure authority, all designed to improve efficiency and save money. The System's institutional leaders unified around Shaw's budget advocacy in the legislature, speaking, as Shaw had promised, with one voice in favor of these Systemwide goals. With further legislative support from his own university relations team, led by System vice president Ronald Bornstein, Judith Ward and David Martin, and UW–Madison's Harry Peterson, Shaw gained a generally favorable 1987–89 biennial budget, in which the UW System received additional state financial support for many of its requests, including 341 new positions, funding for libraries and research, some management flexibilities, and approval of a small tuition increase. Shaw and his efforts to unify System leaders and improve government relations were credited for the budget success and also won the praise of the Board of Regents.[30]

This early budget effort would continue in the 1989–91 biennium, as Shaw maintained internal cohesion and solidified internal support from System institutions for budget and other legislative priorities. Over time, as he emphasized the importance of each of the three basic components of his triangle of higher educational support, Shaw was able to gain the tacit agreement of state government leaders that the UW System would not complain about the state's fluctuating financial support for the System's instructional costs—there would be no more "whining"—as long as state funding losses could be balanced by either modest increases in tuition or limits on enrollment.[31] While state government's contribution to the three-legged student support stool would never provide funding fully adequate to meet the needs identified in *Planning the Future*, this informal understanding provided critical financial stability for the support of UW System operations and the means of preserving educational quality throughout the System. Through the 1990s and early

2000s, the System made steady progress on reaching national averages of per-student support, adjusting taxpayer support, tuition, and enrollments to sustain educational quality.

Other Strategic Efforts

While improving the System's finances was *Planning the Future*'s major goal, the plan included other important strategic initiatives actively pursued by Shaw and System institutional leaders. The plan called for actions to ease college credit transfers between and among UW institutions, as well as between UW institutions and the state's Vocational, Technical, and Adult Education System (VTAE). In addition, it allowed for the designation of "Centers of Excellence" at individual UW institutions, to clarify their specific missions, highlight local strengths, and give individual campuses both a brand and a focus for improving quality. At UW–Milwaukee, Centers of Excellence included the School of Architecture and Urban Planning, the Center for Great Lakes Studies, and a Center for Business Competitiveness.[32] UW–Eau Claire established a Center of Excellence for Faculty and Undergraduate Student Research Collaborations, while UW–River Falls developed a Center for Undergraduate Physics and Chemistry and UW–La Crosse, a Center for Microbiology.

Consistent with the Wisconsin idea, *Planning the Future* continued to emphasize the importance of sharing System and institutional expertise broadly through UW–Extension's Cooperative Extension Division, with its direct services to state citizens at the county level, while supporting the ongoing work of integrating UW–Extension and campus continuing education programs, as well as applied research in economic development, social issues, and environmental concerns. In other outreach efforts, the plan also encouraged partnerships between System institutions and the private sector to pursue state economic development goals and supported collaborations with the Wisconsin Strategic Development Commission on technology transfer and business outreach issues.

In addition to the initiatives specifically outlined in *Planning the Future*, Shaw worked to strengthen and improve System effectiveness in other areas. Despite the evident hostility of the WMC to financial support for state higher education, Shaw continued the System's participation in roundtables with state business leaders, promoting ties to and assistance for state business and industry.[33] Like O'Neil, he also sought to build a case for greater management flexibilities for the System, appointing a task force to identify state-imposed restrictions that, if lifted, would improve administrative efficiency and generate cost-savings.[34] As new information technologies were developed and became more widely available, Shaw encouraged the exploration of their application in the delivery of educational programs.[35] And, in the wake of the catch-up battle, he continued to seek improvements in salaries for faculty and academic staff employees of the System, as well as focusing new attention on the problem of noncompetitive pay for top System executives.[36]

Equal Opportunity, Campus Climate, and Cultural Controversy

Along with addressing the System's financial needs, *Planning the Future* focused new attention on the System's efforts to fulfill its long-standing commitments to equal opportunity in education and employment for women, minorities, and the disabled. The civil rights era of the 1960s had brought new awareness of past inequities, new legal requirements, and new demands to address discrimination. The UW System and its institutions, like colleges and universities nationally, responded with affirmative action plans, equal opportunity and nondiscrimination policies, and curricular changes designed to educate students about a more diverse array of cultures. *Planning the Future* acknowledged these efforts, describing the System's equity policies and its groundbreaking work on such issues as sexual harassment, minority student graduation goals, and the status of women. By the late 1980s, though, it was clear that the System was not achieving the degree of access and representation of these groups in either the work force or the student body that it had sought. As *Planning the Future* noted, "much more needs to be done before true equity in education can be attained."[37]

The shortcomings of the System's previous efforts were particularly acute in the area of minority student recruitment and retention. While the number of women admitted to both undergraduate and graduate programs had grown steadily in the wake of new prohibitions on sex discrimination and while women's representation in the faculty and academic staff ranks had improved, the picture was much bleaker for minorities. Even the board's relatively modest 1984 goal[38] of enrolling a proportion of minority students at UW System institutions that reflected their representation in the population of state high school graduates as a whole had not been achieved.

Shaw had recognized the need to address these problems even before completion of *Planning the Future*. In June 1986 he engaged a consultant to review the System's minority and diversity efforts,[39] anticipating that the consultant's recommendations would eventually be incorporated in the implementation of the larger strategic plan. Events, however, soon made work on equity and diversity issues a more immediate priority as racist incidents in May 1987 at UW–Madison dramatically highlighted one of the major obstacles faced by the System as it sought to attract and retain minority students: the hostile campus climate for minorities. In one of the UW–Madison episodes, a fraternity placed a large cardboard caricature of a black man with a bone through his nose on its lawn to announce a "Fiji Island" party; another involved a campus fraternity party featuring a "Harlem room" at which watermelon punch and fried chicken were served and guests wore blackface.[40] These incidents prompted calls for immediate action to address racist conduct on all UW campuses and gave added urgency to the need to address inadequacies in the System's existing affirmative action and equal opportunity policies.

At its May 8, 1987, meeting, the Board of Regents adopted a resolution condemning racism and endorsing efforts to hold System administrators accountable for eliminating racist conduct at their institutions. Despite these actions, however, there was another incident the following semester, when racist name-calling led to an altercation at a third fraternity house on the Madison campus in October 1987.[41] At its November 6, 1987, meeting, the Board of Regents reaffirmed its May resolution, reiterating its commitment to ending campus racism. Responding, Madison's acting chancellor, Bernard Cohen, described in detail the steps his campus was taking to investigate the altercation and announced efforts to develop disciplinary policies and procedures for student organizations involved in such misconduct.[42]

At the same board meeting, Shaw presented his annual report on the status of minority students, faculty, and staff in the System. Describing the vital importance of improving minority enrollment and participation at System institutions, Shaw's report, titled "A Shared Commitment," outlined a range of measures to address the problem. Among other recommendations, the report proposed that a combination of improved financial aid and more flexible admissions criteria—for example, consideration of factors in addition to grade-point averages and test scores—be used to attract, enroll, and retain more minority students.[43] Also identified as important to the effort were setting realistic goals for expanding minority participation and working with the Department of Public Instruction, the VTAE, other state educational agencies, and the private sector to develop support for the System's activities. And, given the recent spate of racist incidents at Madison, the report emphasized the importance of taking steps to provide a more inclusive, less hostile campus environment for minorities.

While Shaw's report highlighted the critical need to improve the System's efforts to achieve equity and diversity, the means he proposed raised sensitive legal and policy concerns. By suggesting changes in admissions requirements and financial aid policies, Shaw had touched on two issues that had produced backlash and litigation at other higher education institutions. The affirmative action and nondiscrimination plans of colleges and universities, though often criticized as halfhearted or ineffective, also met with resistance and claims that they constituted illegal "reverse" discrimination against nonminorities and men. Although the US Supreme Court had determined in the 1978 case *University of California Regents v. Bakke*[44] that achieving student body diversity was a constitutionally permissible goal and that some consideration of race was therefore allowable in making admissions decisions, it had held that the quota plan used by the university there was illegal, leading to subsequent litigation over the specific elements of race-based affirmative action plans and their application to individuals denied admission at other colleges and universities.[45] Race-based financial aid faced similar legal attacks,[46] while efforts to protect women and minority groups from sexual and racial harassment were targeted for forcing "politically correct" thinking and for unconstitutionally suppressing free speech.

Aware of the potential legal pitfalls and policy implications of Shaw's recommendations, the board held public hearings on his report, receiving comments and further fine-tuning Shaw's proposals for easing admissions criteria and providing financial aid directed to minorities to ensure compliance with relevant legal precedents to avoid illegal discrimination. The result was a new plan, approved by the board in April 1988, called *Design for Diversity*. Its aim was to increase student access and retention Systemwide, enhance the multicultural environment, and provide the necessary financial resources, estimated at $6 million, to support financial aid and other programs. It set an ambitious goal of increasing minority enrollments by 50 percent over current levels within five years and by 100 percent within ten years, using consideration of race as one factor among many in admissions decisions but without relying on quotas. *Design for Diversity* also proposed the expansion of existing financial aid programs and the addition of new grants that were not race restricted but rather were need based—an approach that avoided legal constraints while also advancing racial diversity goals.[47] Recognizing the different needs and characteristics of different UW institutions, the plan further authorized the development of institution-based equity and diversity programs that would be reinforced with System funding.

Shaw worked hard to build internal support for the plan, and, as he later acknowledged, UW campuses and board members "really stepped up for this."[48] UW–Madison, responding to its local incidents of racism, had by this time developed its "Madison Plan" to improve diversity. Begun under the leadership of acting chancellor Cohen, it was continued by Donna Shalala, who had been appointed chancellor in June 1987 and who formally took office in January 1988. Shalala, although frustrated at being thrust into the racism issues, supported Shaw's Systemwide plan, participating in *Design for Diversity* through flagship-specific initiatives, including out-of-state recruitment of minority students, and providing additional funding for work-study programs redirected from the university's own resources and private grants.[49] Other UW institutions, too, united behind the plan and established their individual campus proposals consistent with *Design for Diversity*. The board requested an additional $6 million for System diversity initiatives in its state budget request, eventually gaining legislative approval of this new taxpayer funding. Externally, there was also approval of these efforts, as reflected in favorable reactions from the press.[50]

Despite these indications of support for the broad goals of *Design for Diversity*, one element of the plan became an immediate flashpoint for conflict and controversy. To deter the kinds of racist incidents seen at UW–Madison in 1987 and to address other problems associated with a hostile campus environment for minorities, the plan called for strengthening UW System codes of student and employee conduct to prohibit racial and discriminatory harassment, including hateful racist or discriminatory speech. To this end, in early 1989 the System initiated the process for amending its student conduct rules—codified in the Wisconsin Administrative Code[51]—to define discriminatory hate speech and make it subject to disciplinary action, up to and including expulsion. Prepared with the assistance of three UW Law School professors, Gordon Baldwin, Richard Delgado, and Ted Finman, the proposed amendment provided that UW students could be disciplined for racist or discriminatory speech that intentionally demeaned an individual on the basis of race, sex, or other protected status and that created a hostile environment for education.

This proposal immediately came under fire as a threat to First Amendment speech rights and academic freedom, generating intense debate both within and outside the System. Similar policies at other universities, including the University of Michigan,[52] had faced these criticisms and had been successfully challenged in litigation. UW System faculty members and others raised concerns about the constitutionality of the rule,[53] and the Board of Regents was itself sharply divided on the issue. Those supporting the rule argued that it was an important deterrent to discriminatory harassment of students and another means of achieving a positive campus climate for minorities. Those opposed saw it as an improper restriction on free speech, inappropriate in a university setting and especially at Wisconsin institutions, where the commitment to free speech and academic freedom articulated in the 1894 Ely trial is prominently commemorated on Bascom Hall's "sifting and winnowing" plaque. However deplorable hate speech might be, said regent Ody Fish, "free expression protects stupidity and crassness and distasteful comments." His view was echoed by regents Albert Nicholas and Frank Nikolay, both of whom argued that the System should err on the side of more rather than less expression and refuse to adopt the rule. The three law professors, however, contended that the rule would likely withstand a First Amendment challenge, and board president Weinstein advocated forcefully for its approval, emphasizing its importance in sending the "right signals" to both minority and majority students about the System's commitment to *Design for Diversity* and to avoiding a repetition of the racist incidents of the previous year. After a contentious hearing on the rule at its June 8, 1989, meeting, the board approved the measure by a 12–5 vote, sending it to the legislature for action. Following legislative review, the rule became effective in September 1989.[54]

Not surprisingly, adoption of the rule quickly led to litigation. Despite the care with which it had been crafted and the few instances in which it was invoked to discipline students,[55] the rule, like others, failed to withstand the legal challenge to its constitutionality. In *UW–M Post v. Board of Regents*,[56] the court, emphasizing that the First Amendment is central to our nation's concept of freedom and that the right of free speech is almost absolute, concluded that the board's rule as written was unconstitutionally vague and overbroad and did not satisfy applicable standards for restricting speech. The board responded by amending the rule to address the constitutional defects noted by the court, but the effort was eventually abandoned in 1992, following a US Supreme Court ruling that suggested that, even with amendments, the rule was unlikely to withstand a First Amendment–based lawsuit.[57] The board instead adopted a more general policy statement condemning discriminatory harassment, without specifically penalizing it as student misconduct.[58]

Although the System's defense of the rule demonstrated its firm commitment to the *Design for Diversity* goal of improving minority participation at UW institutions, the litigation loss was a disappointment, and the effort proved costly in other ways. The adoption of the rule had brought not only the legal challenge based on First Amendment speech rights but also more general charges that the board's rule reflected a nationwide trend at universities toward thought control, enforced "political correctness," and similar repressive evils.[59] Some critics saw even the weakened replacement policy statement as evidence of this kind of pressure, feeding a narrative, being aggressively advanced by groups such as Accuracy in Academia, that universities are bastions of liberal bias, dominated by "left-leaning" professors.[60] The controversy surrounding the rule also encouraged greater skepticism about other affirmative action efforts that were part of *Design for Diversity*. There were new doubts about the plan's use of race in System admissions programs, which, although consistent with the *Bakke* holding, continued to raise concerns based on new lawsuits brought against other universities and new pressures from anti-affirmative action leaders such as California's Ward Connerly who sought to ban the practice through legislative action.[61] At the same time, however, advocates of more aggressive affirmative action efforts, pressing to improve the climate on campus as a means to prevent racial harassment, were frustrated by the board's withdrawal of the rule and by the slow progress in achieving better representation of minorities in the university's student body and workforce.

The System's efforts to implement and defend *Design for Diversity* had other consequences, as well. The plan's focus on issues of affirmative action and equal opportunities for minorities increased pressure to undertake similar efforts to support other groups that had suffered past discrimination. Women demanded affirmative action efforts to address gender inequity in employment and education, including equal participation in athletics programs and protection from sexual harassment and stalking. Disabled students and employees sought access and academic accommodations to allow their full participation in university life. Growing concerns about discriminatory treatment of gays and lesbians fueled demands for their inclusion in antidiscrimination policies, along with pressure for the UW System to cut ties to ROTC and to ban military recruiters on campus because of the military's policies prohibiting homosexuals from serving in the military. As the System worked to address these issues and to respond to new demands and concerns, its efforts would continue to prompt dissatisfaction from the groups the new measures sought to help, while generating negative reactions from others. Although *Design for Diversity* was a comprehensive plan that unified the System around shared goals, the contentious debate and the ensuing litigation over the speech rule had plunged the

System into the complex divisions of the culture wars, sparking new controversies and social conflicts that would recur repeatedly in the years after the plan's adoption.

Completing Merger

Shaw's early success with the 1987–89 budget, followed by the improving internal unity reflected in support for *Planning the Future* and *Design for Diversity*, led regent president Weinstein to declare that merger was, as of 1988, finally "complete."[62] It was a widely shared sentiment, and Shaw was credited with bringing unity and stability to Lucey's shotgun marriage of the two state higher education systems. After attending a national conference on multicampus systems, student regent Robin Vos, later to become a legislator and speaker of the state Assembly, reported that the UW System had built the best governance structure for a university system in the nation and was considered a world leader in multicampus governance.[63] A special report in the *Wisconsin State Journal* of January 28, 1990, credited Shaw with solidifying the System, noting that "no one seems to be calling [him] a[n academic] wimp anymore" and citing praise from lawmakers, regents, and UW campus leaders. Pointing out that Shaw was not a "tweedy type," the report emphasized his political skills and his ability to work with state officials as essential to his successful leadership.[64]

Shaw's achievements in cementing the System's operational and organizational effectiveness were, however, clouded by looming problems. The admiration for Shaw's successful efforts to bring the System together did not result in better pay and benefits for him personally, for other System executives, or for System employees more broadly, as the state remained stubbornly tight-fisted in setting and limiting the salaries of all state employees. Although the legislature continued to provide pay increases for faculty and academic staff employees, including ongoing "catch-up" funds, the increases were never quite enough to keep up with peer institutions, and salaries remained less than competitive. Pay for executives also lagged that enjoyed by their peers, but board efforts to secure statutory authority to provide a regent salary structure separate from other state executive pay plans were consistently rebuffed by the legislature.[65]

In addition, despite Shaw's legislative work, state funding had not grown after his initial 1987–89 budget. While the number and severity of state cuts had slowed, the System continued to face decreases in real taxpayer support, and by 1991 it was clear that another budget freeze was on the horizon. There were also early signs of weakness in the other two elements—tuition and enrollment management—of Shaw's three-legged stool of System finances, as students began to resist regularly rising tuition and complained of restricted access to the flagship and other popular System institutions.[66]

Meanwhile, the improved unity within the System had done little to dampen state government's enthusiasm for audits and scrutiny of the UW and its institutions. Shaw's success in gaining a favorable budget in the 1987–89 biennium was followed by a particularly damaging 1991 LAB audit of the System's use of the new funding it had received for that period. As part of its overall request, the System had requested additional funding to address access problems, and the legislature had responded by authorizing some $18 million to be used to create new class sections to expand access to high-demand disciplines. In 1989, the System reported to the legislature that it had used these funds to add 328 new staff, who were teaching 990 new class sections in high-demand areas such as business and mathematics. State auditor Dale Cattanach and his team, however, concluded that the System had created fewer total course sections than expected and fewer sections in high-demand disciplines or in other specific disciplines with access problems, such as engineering. In a scathing critique issued April 18, 1991, the LAB determined that the System had seen a net gain of only 302 new sections in high-demand areas because previously existing courses had been reduced by 688 sections. The audit went on to suggest that the System had overestimated the severity of its access problems and questioned whether the System could justify further enrollment reductions or further budget increases to support priorities such as higher faculty salaries. The report recommended that the legislature carefully monitor student demand, assess the availability of existing System resources to meet demand, and review the need for future enrollment reductions.[67]

Shaw replied, strongly disagreeing with the premises and conclusions of the LAB report. He challenged LAB's simple net section-count methodology and countered that the legislature was fully aware that the new positions authorized in the 1987–89 budget would be used in various ways to achieve the System's broad and multidimensional access and quality improvement goals. He also emphasized that the System had reported to the legislature in detail on how the new positions were being used and noted that for each new position added, the System had added three new class sections. The damage had been done, however, and Shaw and the System were criticized for what appeared to be improper use of the new positions and for misleading the legislature.[68] The episode was another blow to UW System–state government relations and undermined Shaw's own credibility with legislators. In the midst of the controversy, Shaw resigned as System president, announcing in late April 1991 that he would leave to accept the presidency of Syracuse University.

Passing the Torch

Despite the sour note of the audit crisis and the criticisms of his role in the matter, Shaw had retained support from his board and had largely achieved the goals he had set for himself on assuming the presidency.[69] He had succeeded in repairing relations with UW–Madison, enforcing internal System unity, and improving state government relations, in effect completing the System merger. He had also developed and overseen implementation of the System's first comprehensive strategic plan for maintaining academic quality, as well as a major initiative improving equity and diversity. These achievements would continue to earn kudos from both state and UW leaders who saw him as one of the System's most politically effective presidents.[70] His work helped provide the foundation for a lengthy period of relative stability in which the UW System and its institutions would see major academic, research, and extracurricular achievements. Lyall, who succeeded him as president in 1992, would build on his efforts to lead the System to full maturity as an organization.

First meeting of the combined University of Wisconsin System Board of Regents after merger, 1971
(UW System Archive/Board of Regents)

Protests at Bascom Hill, circa 1970 (UW System Archive/Board of Regents)

Pail and Shovel Party's Lady Liberty on Lake Mendota, February 1979 (UW System Archive/Board of Regents)

Pail and Shovel Party's flamingos on Bascom Hill, September 1979 (UW System Archive/Board of Regents)

UW–Madison antiracism protest, 1987 (UW System Archive/Board of Regents)

Anti-ROTC sit-in at Bascom Hall, April 1990 (UW System Archive/Board of Regents)

Above: John Weaver, president of the University of Wisconsin System, 1971–77 (UW System Archive/Board of Regents)

H. Edwin Young, president of the University of Wisconsin System, 1977–80 (UW System Archive/Board of Regents)

Robert O'Neil, president of
the University of Wisconsin
System, 1980–85 (UW System
Archive/Board of Regents)

Kenneth Shaw, president of
the University of Wisconsin
System, 1985–91 (UW System
Archive/Board of Regents)

Katharine Lyall, president of the University of Wisconsin System, 1992–2004 (UW System Archive/Board of Regents)

Tommy Thompson, governor of Wisconsin, 1987–2001 (UW System Archive/Board of Regents)

Kevin Reilly, president of the University of Wisconsin System, 2004–13 (UW System Archive/Board of Regents)

Ray Cross, president of the University of Wisconsin System, 2014–20 (UW System Archive/Board of Regents)

7

The Mature System

Named UW System president April 1, 1992, Katharine C. Lyall brought familiarity with the System and her own strong record of internal leadership to the position. An important presence in the UW System since her appointment as vice president for academic affairs in 1982, Lyall, who had served as acting president after O'Neil's resignation in 1985 and again after Shaw's departure in 1991, was a natural choice. She would become the longest-serving System president, solidifying the unification efforts begun by Shaw, providing administrative continuity and stability, and leading the mature System through a period in which all UW institutions saw significant accomplishments. Despite these successes, however, the UW System continued to face the headwinds of declining or unstable state government support, the ongoing shift of state policy priorities away from higher education, and the small-government antitax attitudes that together foreclosed state revenue growth or the possibility of additional funding for the UW System. While the System's organizational cohesion provided a stable base for institutional achievements, this foundation continued to be undermined by budget crises and the struggle to maintain quality with steadily diminishing state resources. Although the System's achievements obscured the cracks in the foundation, the underlying problems were growing, requiring the System to search constantly for new strategies to offset the loss of state financial support, including a growing focus on gaining management flexibilities and efforts to re-examine the relationship between the UW System and the state.

Stability and Continuity

Although the transition to Lyall was largely free of the public bickering over preferred candidates that had dominated earlier presidential searches, the process did produce some controversy. The search was led by Edward Penson, a former UW–Oshkosh chancellor, who began the process by conducting an environmental scan that outlined the difficulties the System would face in attracting candidates. The scan concluded that the System was overregulated and underappreciated but also characterized it as arrogant, unfocused, bureaucratic, and declining in quality.[1] This critical assessment suggested that recruitment might be a challenge and led some regents to suggest that the board should be more open to considering business or other nontraditional, nonacademic executives for the presidency. In the end, though, the board, now led by regent president Tom Lyon, agreed on a position description that listed the traditional academic credentials— appropriate scholarly activity, commitment to shared governance, and significant higher education leadership experience—as the preferred qualifications,[2] and the search yielded a large number of nominees and applicants. Media requests for the identities of those in this pool led to further controversy when Penson sought to prevent their names from being released publicly. Penson was convinced that keeping the names of candidates confidential was essential to attracting strong applicants who might be deterred from applying if their current employers were aware they were seeking another position, and he denied the newspaper requests for the names.[3] The denial led the *Wisconsin State Journal* to file a lawsuit against the Board of Regents, claiming a violation of the state's open records law. This matter was promptly resolved with a legal settlement under whose terms the full list of all nominees and applicants for the position, as well as the names of the finalists, were released.[4] Despite these procedural hiccups, the finalist group consisted of well-qualified higher education leaders, among them Lyall, who was selected for the permanent position in April 1992.[5]

Her appointment was broadly supported both within and outside the UW System. Lyall had the scholarly credentials—a PhD
in economics from Cornell, faculty positions at Syracuse and
Johns Hopkins, and teaching experience in the UW–Madison
Department of Economics—that gave her credibility with academics,[6] while her familiarity with System operations and the
strong leadership she had provided throughout the O'Neil and
Shaw administrations and in her two stints as acting president
had earned her the respect of board members and state political
leaders. She was also popular with System staff, combining a
low-key management style with a self-deprecating sense of
humor that included the occasional surprise appearance at the
office disguised as a cartoon character, Santa Claus, or the Easter
Bunny. Her selection maintained management continuity and
internal stability as the System grappled with new financial and
public relations problems that surfaced toward the end of Shaw's
term. A sailor in her spare time, Lyall was welcomed as a capable
captain of the System. George Steil, on his election as regent
president shortly after Lyall's appointment, noted that the board
had shown its confidence in Lyall by electing her to guide the
System ship in a stormy sea and urged members to support her
leadership and avoid micromanagement.[7]

Like Shaw, Lyall recognized the importance of maintaining a
unified System voice with state government partners, and, like
Shaw, she made it clear to System chancellors that if she caught
them lobbying for themselves at the expense of others, their institutional budgets would suffer.[8] At the same time, however,
she fostered collegiality among the chancellors, preparing System budgets with their input and building internal consensus
for the System's proposals before sending them to the legislature
and governor. Lyall also worked to recruit strong leaders for all
System institutions, building on the work Shaw had begun to
attract a talented chancellor corps. In her capacity as Shaw's
executive vice president, she had supported Shalala's move to
Wisconsin and her work as Madison's chancellor, establishing an
effective relationship with the flagship. Following Shalala's 1993
departure to become US Secretary of Health and Human Services
under President Bill Clinton, Lyall continued to partner coopera-
tively with Shalala's successors David Ward and John Wiley.
She also recruited new leaders at other institutions, including

UW–Milwaukee's Nancy Zimpher, who would later head the State University of New York system; her own successor as president, Kevin Reilly, who was named vice chancellor and later chancellor of UW–Extension; and strong leaders of comprehensive institutions such as David Markee at UW–Platteville, Julius Erlenbach at UW–Superior, Thomas George at UW–Stevens Point, Douglas Hastad at UW–La Crosse, and Don Mash at UW–Eau Claire.[9] Within the System administration, she chose capable vice presidents for her management team, often drawing on the ranks of UW chancellors. Steven Portch from the UW Colleges, Keith Sanders of Stevens Point, and David J. Ward of Oshkosh were successive senior vice presidents during her term. These and similarly strong internal executive appointments maintained an effective System leadership cohort and helped enhance the UW System's national reputation as a good place to work.

Further strengthening internal System cohesion, Lyall finally put to rest the AAU representation conflict with UW–Madison. Although Shaw had served as the AAU representative—without complaint from either Shain or Shalala, who felt that she did not need the position to maintain Madison's national leadership reputation[10]—and although Lyall initially took the seat, she soon concluded that AAU activities were more relevant to the concerns of research universities than to those of university systems. A year into her term as UW president, following a discussion at the AAU as to whether participation in the organization was more appropriate for System heads or for campus leaders, Lyall made the decision to shift Wisconsin's representation to the Madison campus, by that time headed by Chancellor David Ward.[11] Her action brought closure to an old controversy and further cemented cooperation between the System and the flagship. Diminishing internal conflicts, transparent and collegial internal budgeting processes, and the recruitment of talented institutional leaders and effective System leadership provided essential internal stability. The end of the distracting family feuds allowed UW institutions to concentrate on fulfilling their individual missions and on working with Lyall and System leaders to address shared System goals, issues, and problems.

Lyall also took steps early in her presidency to restore the System's external credibility. The class-section audit at the end of Shaw's term had strained relations with state political leaders, and the 1992 Governor's Task Force on UW Accountability Measures had produced a report emphasizing the need for the UW System to better demonstrate its efficiency and effectiveness.[12] Lyall welcomed the report, embracing it as an opportunity to prove to state government, regents, and the public that the System was fully accountable for all funds, from the state and from other sources, that it administered and that it was managed in an efficient and cost-effective manner. Responding to the Task Force recommendations, she provided a progress report to the legislature in December 1993,[13] describing the System's development of Systemwide accountability standards against which UW institutions would be measured annually. She initiated a formal accountability reporting process the following year, quickly demonstrating that the System was operated with lean administrative costs and overhead expenses substantially lower than those at comparable higher education institutions, but with superior educational effectiveness by relevant measures. By 1995, the System had become a nationally recognized leader in higher education accountability efforts.[14]

But while the accountability reports established the System's efficiency and bolstered public confidence in System management, they did not insulate the System from recurring state budget problems. Lyall, like her predecessors, had to contend with the lapses and cuts caused by shifting state policy priorities, politics, and general economic swings that produced uncertain, often declining state fiscal support for the UW System. Her background as an economist and her familiarity with the UW System gave her a firm grasp of these issues. An admirer of the work of Percy and Smith in establishing the System's postmerger organizational structure,[15] she also appreciated the critical importance of the System's unified budget in maintaining equitable internal resource allocation and protecting individual System institutions from external pressures and attacks. She viewed the budget as the major driver of UW System policy and as president worked to build the case for renewed state investment in the System by tailoring budget requests to specific policy priorities.

On taking office, Lyall continued to pursue the goals set out in *Planning the Future* and *Design for Diversity*. She would later build on a study led by regent Michael Grebe that analyzed the challenges facing the System in the twenty-first century. Following closely on the heels of substantial state budget cuts in 1994 and a difficult 1995–97 biennial budget, the *Twenty-First Century Study*[16] identified actions essential to maintaining System success into the next millennium. Conducted over a period of ten months in 1995–96, the study affirmed the System's commitments to its existing policies, including the goals laid out in *Design for Diversity* and *Planning the Future*, and to the Wisconsin Idea, while emphasizing the System's critical role in state economic development. The report listed four major priorities for the System— preserving quality and access, keeping college affordable, creating new knowledge, and restructuring and improving the System's efficiency—and stressed that where fiscal limitations force a choice between quality and access, quality should be the priority. The report called for moderate and predictable tuition increases to maintain quality; utilization of new technology to support distance education and other instructional innovation; implementation of new efficiency measures; and new management flexibilities to free the System from what regent Sheldon Lubar called "outdated bureaucratic burdens" imposed by the state and by the System administration itself. Above all, however, was the crucial need to gain better state taxpayer support. As regent Daniel Gelatt noted, "We found no source of outside revenue other than state dollars or tuition that was of the scale of [our projected budget needs]. . . . I would hope that members of the board would recognize the importance in this biennium and succeeding biennia in outlining . . . the consequences of the State's not maintaining its prior commitments and its prior history of support the for the University System."[17]

Lyall used the *Twenty-First Century Study* recommendations as the basis for the System's biennial budget requests in 1997–99 and 1999–2001. By late 1996, as the System's 1997–99 budget request was being developed, the economy was robust and state revenues were growing, prompting Lyall to propose a 3 percent increase in state support for the System to advance new initiatives in areas reflecting the *Twenty-First Century Study* recommendations, such as instructional technology and distance education, diversity, and financial aid. In addition, she proposed seeking new management flexibilities as suggested in the study.[18] These requests were partially successful, as the 1997–99 biennium came with new funding for technology enhancements and training, tuition expenditure flexibilities, and pay increases for faculty and staff. The System's 1999–2001 budget, similarly based on the *Twenty-First Century Study,* brought even better results, as the System saw one of its best budgets since merger, including some $90 million in new funding, additional expenditure flexibility, and salary and benefits increases for staff.[19]

In addition to her efforts to improve the overall budget, Lyall oversaw ongoing work on other System policies and initiatives. Further pursuing the *Twenty-First Century Study* recommendations, she supported the creation of a distance education division called the Center for Learning Innovations, later simply Learning Innovations (LI). Authorized by the board in 1997 and headed by System vice president David J. Ward and Michael Offerman of UW–Extension, the purpose of LI was to involve all UW System institutions in efforts to use newly emerging technologies for distance education and other innovative instructional approaches, with special focus on reaching students for whom access to traditional physical campuses was difficult or impossible. It was also given an entrepreneurial, revenue-producing charter, receiving specific authorization from the board to enter into arrangements with other nonprofit entities that would generate income from the distance education programs it created.[20]

Continuing efforts to improve diversity and representation of minorities within the System under *Design for Diversity,* a ten-year plan that ended in 1998, Lyall initiated a successor diversity initiative, *Plan 2008,* that was approved by the board in 1998. In other areas, Lyall emphasized stronger ties with PK–12 schools and the VTAE System, supporting seamless transitions from PK–12 to higher education and easing credit transfers from VTAE schools to UW institutions.

Focusing on the UW System's pivotal role in supporting the state's economy, Lyall, with the support of board president Jay Smith, convened a series of state economic summits beginning in 2000 that brought together state leaders from the public and the private sectors to exchange ideas about how best to combine their efforts to improve the state economic conditions. The summits produced commitments from business leaders, state legislators and the governor, and the System to partner on a range of critical activities to spur economic growth. The summits affirmed the importance of the Wisconsin Idea and forged general agreement among participants on the need for joint efforts to move Wisconsin's economy forward in a new era of rapid technological change, innovation, and entrepreneurship, while continuing to build on the state's more traditional manufacturing and agricultural business base.[21] Lyall would later count the economic summits among her proudest accomplishments as System president.[22] By continuing to advance the System's long-standing policy goals, Lyall maintained a steady course for the System, while at the same time developing new programs to ensure management accountability, support technological advances, and build stronger ties to the business community.

A Fortuitous Alignment of Leaders

Lyall's efforts in pursuing these planning goals and other initiatives benefited from a fortuitous alignment of System, board, and state leaders. Lyall maintained the strong internal administrative cohesion begun under Shaw, and her administration further benefited from the support of a unified Board of Regents and from state leadership that, despite Thompson's lengthy tenure as governor, was usually bipartisan, with control of the legislature shifting between the two major parties.[23] The absence of single-party control required the sharing of power between and among the executive and legislative branches of state government, tending produce compromise and what political leaders of the time would later describe as a politically moderate, centrist state government, at some times "center right" or at others "center left," but not extreme in either direction.[24]

During Lyall's years as president, this kind of moderation was reflected in System governance as regent leaders from both parties emphasized the board's role as a nonpartisan steward of the System. With Thompson's election, in 1986, the composition of the board gradually changed, as Democratic appointees of the Earl years were replaced by Republicans chosen by Thompson. The kind of board "activism" that Young and Smith had observed in the early postmerger years under leaders like Grover and Lavine[25] gave way to a less interventionist approach to System governance, with board members less interested in micromanagement and more concerned with putting the interests of the System and the public over partisanship. Elected board president in 1990, Tom Lyon, an appointee of Governor Earl who was well regarded by both parties in the state legislature, noted that, in his experience as a regent, "the board is nonpartisan in its deliberations and advocates what it collectively believes to be in the best interest of its shareholders—the citizens of Wisconsin and the users of its services—160,000 students."[26] Two years later, when George Steil, a Thompson appointee, became board president, he described the administration of university resources as a "sacred trust,"[27] declaring that the System is the most valuable asset of the state, emphasizing the importance of maintaining its quality and avoiding micromanagement. Steil's own successor as board president, Michael Grebe—another Republican—concluded his term as board president by saying that he considered that being a regent was a stewardship and encouraging board members to take the broad view that their constituency consisted of all the people of the state, rather than "narrow political or philosophical interests."[28]

Lyall herself was steadfastly nonpartisan in her leadership of the System. Despite her past service in the Democratic administration of President Jimmy Carter, she avoided becoming closely identified with either political party, earning the respect of both Democrats and Republicans in state government, and continuing to maintain effective working relationships with board members even as the board was increasingly dominated by Republicans. The board's commitment to nonpartisanship in System governance was reflected in its advocacy of UW System interests, even when they conflicted with the governor's agenda. Thompson, sometimes frustrated when his proposals for the university were opposed or criticized by his own board appointees, often joked that they all seemed to "go native" when they became regents, putting loyalty to the UW System and its institutions above partisan allegiance to his office. The focus on trusteeship over partisanship provided strong support for internal System leadership and also improved external relations with state government.

Thompson's support for initiatives that benefited the System and particularly UW–Madison further strengthened the alignment of state and UW System leaders around common goals. A native of the small town of Elroy, Wisconsin, and a proud alumnus of UW–Madison, where he had earned both undergraduate and law degrees, Thompson understood the value of public higher education to state citizens and its importance to the economy, and, like Lyon, Steil, and Grebe, he believed that state higher education should remain nonpartisan. In the Assembly he had been a supporter of the catch-up pay plan approved under Earl, and he continued its implementation after he became governor. He had also worked across the aisle with Democrat Tom Loftus on the Assembly Select Committee on the UW System, becoming convinced that no System campuses should be closed because they all made important contributions to their communities and to the state. After the 1986 gubernatorial election, he promised not to reduce the System's budgets during his term in office, and, while he did not fulfill this pledge, he did endorse other measures that helped the System weather the recurrent fiscal crises. He backed modest tuition increases, agreeing that UW institutional tuitions should come to the midpoint of the ranges for their respective peer groups, and supported salary increases for faculty and academic staff[29]—both measures that helped the System to maintain quality and access in times when state budgets were strained. Thompson also appreciated the critical importance of public higher education for the state's economic success—the key connection that had led the state's founders to provide for a state university in the state's constitution. As governor, he encouraged the System's efforts to provide greater assistance to state businesses and to develop university–business collaboration that could in turn spur economic growth.

Like Lucey, Thompson also recognized that the success of the flagship UW–Madison was critical to the success of the entire System, and he worked to protect and enhance the flagship's national reputation. Bridging what might have become a partisan divide, he developed a particularly productive relationship with Shalala, who, like Lyall, was a former Carter administration official. On meeting Thompson, Shalala had impressed him with her political savvy, pointing out that as head of the UW–Madison she, too, had important constituents and allies in every county in the state and her own sources of popular support for flagship interests. The two quickly established a solid rapport, teaming on a highly successful and innovative approach to funding of UW capital projects. Stymied by the limitations of the slow, inflexible, and financially constrained state building program that the UW

System was required to follow, they pursued public–private partnerships that made it easier to leverage state monies and private funds to jump-start major building projects. With the support of former regent president David Beckwith and other state leaders, they proposed the Wisconsin Initiative for State Technology and Applied Research (WISTAR), under which the state used $150 million of its bonding authority to finance a $225 million research facility, with the $75 million difference to be supplied by private gifts and grants. Approved by the Board of Regents in 1991,[30] the program quickly became a success, making it a model for later public–private collaborations at the flagship.

After Shalala's departure to lead the US Department of Health and Human Services, in early 1993, Thompson continued to work with her successors at UW–Madison, David Ward and John Wiley, to advance similar large-scale projects. Shalala, Ward, and Wiley formed what was in effect a single continuous administration at the flagship as it built strategically on its strengths as a national research power. WISTAR was followed by Healthstar, launched in 1996, which leveraged $50 million from the state with $100 million from other sources for medical research,[31] and in 2000 by Biostar, a partnership that for the first time involved WARF in providing direct support for a building project. In 2004, plans were announced for an even larger public–private partnership project, the Wisconsin Institutes for Discovery/Morgridge Institute for Research, which relied on the pioneering stem cell research of Professor James Thomson, with additional support from WARF and generous donations from alumni John and Tasha Morgridge. The result of the Thompson-Shalala public–private approach to capital funding was a multiyear building boom at UW–Madison that sped construction of the physical facilities essential to sustain and grow the campus's research infrastructure.

Access to private gifts and grants and the support of WARF and the UW–Foundation made UW–Madison better able than other UW institutions to take advantage of such public–private partnerships. The struggles of other campuses to move important projects through the state building process continued to be problematic, leading the board and the System to seek legislative approval of more flexible bonding approaches in budget proposals beginning in 1997-99. The public–private opportunities successfully pioneered at UW–Madison, though, did offer a new path forward for building efforts at other System institutions that could take advantage of similar leveraging opportunities. Even more significant, these successes at the flagship helped maintain overall System stability, lending the strength and prestige of the flagship's reputation to the entire UW brand.

With cohesive executive and board leadership, well aligned with state government in support of shared goals, the System, in Lyall's words, "really began to gel."[32] On the twenty-fifth anniversary of merger, in September 1996, Lyall reported that the System was a mature and successful organization. She confirmed that merger was fully achieved, and the System was on the cutting edge nationally of advances in a range of areas—enrollment management, public accountability reporting, access, quality, private fundraising, research, affordable tuition, and low administrative costs—while System institutions, faculty, staff, and students continued to compile an impressive record of major new achievements to add to their historic record of successes in academics, research, and service to the state and their communities.[33]

Name and Fame

The original UW and, later, the UW System were a consistent source of important contributions to academics, research, and the state's civic life. On the occasion of Wisconsin's state sesquicentennial anniversary, in 1998, Lyall listed just a few of the UW's achievements: the Wisconsin Idea, the social security and worker's compensation systems, the invention of thermostats, and the Babcock milk-grading system—an impressive, if far from complete, survey.[34] The UW had continued to produce research breakthroughs following merger, including the Nobel Prize–winning cancer research of Howard Temin in 1975, and Lyall's term as president would see numerous additions to the list of historic organizational and individual accomplishments, marking an especially productive period for the UW System. As the System came together organizationally, the national visibility and stature of its institutions continued to grow, bringing widening recognition of the impressive achievements of all UW campuses. The UW–Madison under Shalala, Ward, and Wiley burnished its reputation as a vibrant research institution with dramatic advances in letters and sciences, technology transfer, facilities expansion, extramural support, and athletics. The successes of the flagship strengthened the prestige of the entire System, while other UW institutions came into their own, expanding their individual academic mission activities and building distinct individual reputations. Meanwhile, all System campuses and UW–Extension continued to provide direct economic and civic impact to their communities, driving growth for the entire state through innovation, business activity, and cultural enrichment.

Lyall enjoyed providing "good news" stories at board meetings as a way of highlighting the accomplishments of System institutions, faculty, staff, and students, but her reports could not begin to include all the achievements of what was an exceptionally productive period. There were scientific accomplishments such as the work of UW–Madison professors Thomas "Roc" Mackie and Paul Reckwerdt in using precisely targeted radiation to treat tumors without harming surrounding tissue; the trailblazing work of James Thomson in deriving induced pluripotent stem cells from adult skin cells; the improvements in flu vaccine development made by Yoshi Kawaoka; the ongoing work of Hector DeLuca on Vitamin D compounds; and the work of John Wiley and John Perepezko on integrated circuit manufacturing that improved computer processing speeds. In the arts and letters, UW–Madison's Department of English continued its work on the *Dictionary of American Regional English* (DARE), recording and defining terms used in spoken US English. The first volume of the DARE, edited by Frederic G. Cassidy, had been published in 1985 and was followed by additional volumes in 1991, 1996, and 2002 and finally completed in 2013 under the leadership of Joan Houston Hall. The work of Wisconsin Public Television was recognized with an Emmy Award in 1999.[35]

The flagship Madison campus, long a research powerhouse, remained a leader in securing federal research grants, ranking among the top five institutions nationally, continuing a run that extended from the time of merger until 2015, when it dropped to sixth place.[36] This funding spurred innovation and new inventions that advanced scientific knowledge, generated new practical and business applications, and returned financial benefits to the campus. The enactment of the Bayh-Dole Act in 1980 allowed universities to retain the benefits of federally funded research by encouraging patent development and technology transfer efforts. WARF, a pioneer in technology transfer since its creation and a moving force behind the enactment of Bayh-Dole, took advantage of the new law, and by 1993, as the result of WARF's work, UW–Madison was receiving more patent income than any other university in the United States.[37] WARF's efforts not only returned significant resources to support more research at UW–Madison but also drove economic gains for the state as new businesses were created that were based on the inventions of Madison faculty and staff. Among others, Mackie and Reckwerdt's research led to the establishment of tomotherapy, Thomson's stem cell work resulted in Cellular Dynamics, Lynn Allen-Hoffmann's development of skin cells for burn treatment led to Stratech, and Kawaoka's vaccine research supported FluGen. From 1993 on, WARF's work led to the creation of some 125 startup companies, and it was awarded the National Medal of Technology by President George W. Bush in 2005.

WARF's activities, originally limited to the flagship, were, during Lyall's term, also extended to other System campuses. In 2000, WARF, in cooperation with UW System administration, created a subsidiary corporation, the WiSys Technology Foundation, to support technology transfer at UW institutions other than UW–Madison.[38] UW–Milwaukee, with its doctoral programs, had a growing research base and, as the smaller, comprehensive UW institutions matured, their faculty members, too, had begun to engage in research that held the potential for patenting and commercial viability. WiSys made it possible for investigators throughout the UW System to take advantage of WARF's patenting and technology transfer expertise to develop their own inventions, as a result generating new campus funding and bringing their innovations to market.[39]

Meanwhile, Shain's research park on the west side of Madison entered a newly expansive phase, as more businesses, often led by UW–Madison inventors, located there. The original lands dedicated to the park filled with new buildings, and the park expanded, acquiring more land, again from former UW farms. Commercial activities were not just limited to UW–Madison, as UW–Stout, drawing on its industrial engineering and manufacturing specialities, added its own research incubators, and

UW-Milwaukee continued to increase its research activities, establishing its own techology transfer organization, the UWM Research Foundation, in 2006.

With these technology transfer and business-industry collaborations and the other activities of its institutions, the System's contributions to the state's economy—always significant—were rapidly expanding and demonstrating the value of the state's investment in higher education. UW-Madison professor William Strang's report, *The Economic Impact of the University of Wisconsin System*, presented to the Board of Regents in 1997, showed that the System was returning $10 of economic impact for every $1 invested by the state—at that time some $8 billion of impact for $800 million in state support.[40] Strang's work—later updated by System vice president David J. Ward—confirmed the System's critical role in the economic health of the state.[41]

In this same period, individual faculty and staff members continued to receive prestigious awards and garner national recognition for their work. In 1998, five UW-Madison faculty members—William Brock, Elizabeth Craig, William Dove, Perry Frey, and Paul Rabinowitz—were elected fellows of the National Academy of Science, while two—Gerda Lerner and Crawford Young—were chosen to join the National Academy of Arts and Letters. UW-Milwaukee professor Arthur Brooks was elected to the American Association for the Advancement of Science, and Margo Anderson of UW-Milwaukee received a Woodrow Wilson Fellowship.[42] History scholar William Cronon, of UW-Madison, was named to the American Philosophical Society, the oldest learned society in the country, in 1999.[43] Other UW-Madison researchers, including law and sociology professor Joel Rogers, in 1995, and geologist Jillian Banfield and biochemist Laura Kiessling, in 1999, received prestigious MacArthur Foundation "genius grants" to support their work.[44]

UW System students, too, were recognized for academic achievement, scoring well on academic skills tests such as the ACT and the national CPA examination. In 1997 Robert Kampstra, a UW-Whitewater student, earned the highest score in the nation on the Accounting examination.[45] UW-Madison continued to produce the most Peace Corps volunteers of any university in the nation, along with Rhodes Scholars Aaron Olver (1997), who would later return to Madison to become managing director of the University Research Park, and Rob Yablon (2000), who would return to the UW Law School as a faculty member.[46]

Extracurricular activities were also a source of excellence during Lyall's term, as strong and successful sports programs emerged throughout the System. At UW–Madison, Shalala led a successful revival of the athletic department. On her arrival, in 1988, the department, which was close to insolvency, could claim few winning teams, apart from men's hockey. Poor showings by the football team had been a particular problem, causing steep revenue losses and creating pressure on the university's academic budget. Understanding that a successful athletics program could bring enhanced public and alumni support, Shalala moved quickly to change the department's leadership. She named Pat Richter, a star Badger football, basketball, and baseball player of the early 1960s, as athletic director on December 15, 1989, and Richter hired Barry Alvarez as head football coach just two weeks later, on December 31.[47] In a dramatic turnaround, by late 1993, the department had addressed its financial problems, and in January 1994 the football team achieved its first Rose Bowl appearance since 1963 and its first-ever Rose Bowl victory. The successes of the football team not only kept the stadium full and self-supporting but attracted new gift resources from fans and alumni. The financial stability of football also lifted the entire athletic department, providing a base of support for women's athletics and nonrevenue sports. Other UW–Madison teams, from men's basketball to women's hockey, track and field, and volleyball, began to see their own share of successes, confirming UW–Madison's reputation as both an academic and an athletic powerhouse.

Meanwhile, other UW institutions compiled winning records as members of their athletic conferences. Lyall reported at the May 10, 1996, regent meeting that, for the past eight years, no other conference had won as many NCAA Division III team championships as the Wisconsin State University Conference, composed of the System's eleven comprehensive campuses. UW–Green Bay, which also participated in NCAA Division I men's basketball, had further earned a national reputation in that sport, with frequent appearances at the NCAA tournament and success in advancing deep into the finals.

In popular rankings of colleges and universities, too, the UW System and its institutions were doing well. In 1997, UW–Madison was listed among the top ten public universities in the country by *U.S. News and World Report*, while four of the comprehensives were among the top ten in the Midwest, and UW Hospital was among the best nationally in ten specialties. Although noting that such rankings should be taken with "a large grain of salt," Lyall said they did offer public recognition for institutional achievements.

Headwinds

The System's many accomplishments, both institutional and individual, did not shelter it from the powerful headwinds of declining state taxpayer support, shifting governmental priorities, deepening political partisanship, and changing public attitudes toward higher education. Achievements were not enough to alter these stubborn adverse trends. Success was, in fact, often taken for granted, obscuring the UW System's vulnerability to the long-term damage inflicted by the state's faltering financial commitment to the UW System and an increasingly hostile public and political environment for higher education. The UW System was not alone in facing these kinds of conditions. Wisconsin shared with many other state universities the funding problems resulting from general swings in the national economy, a twenty-year decline in state taxpayer support for higher education, and competition from prisons and health care for state resources. These broad trends were affecting state universities and university systems around the country,[48] but each unhappy university is unhappy in its own way, and the UW System continued to grapple with uniquely Wisconsin challenges.

The State Budget:
Changing Priorities, Diminishing Support

Lyall would later ruefully note that, even with a supportive Board of Regents and a generally sympathetic governor, the long slide in state financial funding for the System could not be stopped.[49] Although Shaw had won a favorable budget for the 1987–89 biennium, it would be more than ten years before this success was repeated. In the interim, even modestly positive or stable budgets were soon followed by lapses and cuts that diminished any real gains. The 1999–2001 budget—considered the best in over a decade—was followed by substantial cuts in 2002, and 2003 brought what was then the largest cut ever, a $250 million reduction that would leave the System especially vulnerable to the far deeper cuts that would come with the Great Recession of 2007–9 and continue throughout the 2010s.

At the beginning of her presidency, in 1991, Lyall immediately faced budget lapses requiring the System to return $7.7 million to the state that year and an additional $10.2 million in 1992—the largest total cuts since 1987.[50] Newly elected board president Steil declared in June 1992 that higher education in Wisconsin was in a state of crisis because of its restricted financial resources. He observed that the UW System had become a "state-assisted"—rather than state-supported—university, noting further that "state appropriations for higher education declined in the academic year 1991–92 for the first time in the 33 years that records have been kept."[51]

The situation continued to worsen over the next several years, as changing state priorities brought further reductions in the funding available for public higher education. In 1994, Governor Thompson announced a property tax freeze and a plan for the state to assume two-thirds of the cost of funding K–12 public schools. These changes effectively shifted a major share of the cost of K–12 public education from unpopular—and high—local property taxes to the broader state tax base. This additional charge on the state's general revenues, however, in the absence of any other state revenue growth, inevitably diminished the state dollars available for other purposes, including higher education. At the same time, the state's Medicaid expenses were rising, and Thompson had undertaken an aggressive expansion of the Department of Corrections,[52] building prisons and expanding related correctional programs, all further reducing the funds available for other purposes, including the UW System.

Reporting on the situation at the April 1994 board meeting, Lyall, invoking the triangulated approach to funding developed in the Shaw era, warned that tuitions would have to rise or access would need to be limited in order to maintain quality in the face of the anticipated decline in state funding.[53] As expected, by the end of 1994, the System was required to absorb a lapse of $8.7

million, and the 1995–97 biennial budget brought further sharp reductions, including a $62 million cut in state tax support for the System as a whole, a $7.7 million cut targeted to UW–Extension, and the loss of forty-six positions from the capital budget staffs of UW System Administration and UW–Madison.[54] Although the System was authorized to increase tuition by some $15 million to help compensate for these cuts, this level of tuition growth was insufficient to offset the significant losses in general tax revenues.

Describing the System's plan for how the cuts would be taken and their effects on students, Lyall at the August 1995 board meeting pointed out that for the first time since merger, the System's base budget had declined in absolute, inflation-adjusted terms. It was against this grim fiscal background that the board undertook its *Twenty-First Century Study*. Although the stated purpose of the study was to focus on policy and practices that could be changed or fine-tuned to improve the System's performance in the new century, given the bleak financial outlook, much of the focus was on changes that would improve the System's finances. When completed, in 1996, the *Twenty-First Century Study* provided a set of recommendations that became the framework for the System's budget requests for the 1997–99 and 1999–2001 biennia.

In a rare bright spot for System finances, as preparations for the 1997–99 budget began, improving economic conditions brought stronger state revenues, leading Lyall to propose that the UW System seek a budget increase to include requests for funding to implement the *Twenty-First Century Study* recommendations. The result for that biennium was modestly stronger state financial support for the System, with new funding for instructional technology and the granting of some management flexibilities in the use of System revenues. With strong continuing state revenue growth, the System also saw a successful 1999–2001 budget, a budget that was, in Lyall's view, the best in a decade, providing new funding to support libraries and additional funds for instructional technology, study abroad opportunities, and diversity efforts, along with management flexibilities and employee pay and benefit improvements. The budget was praised by board members and Lyall, all of whom expressed their appreciation to Governor Thompson and to legislative leaders Assembly Speaker Scott Jensen and Senator Chuck Chvala.[55]

These successes, however, were painfully short lived. A recession in 2001 brought another round of steep cuts driven by

generally declining economic conditions and falling state revenues. By this time, the election of George W. Bush to the US presidency in 2000 had produced a major change in state leadership.
Thompson was named by Bush to become the Secretary of Health
and Human Services, succeeding his old friend Shalala in that
post, and he himself was succeeded by Lieutenant Governor Scott
McCallum in early 2001. The following year, McCallum faced
revenues shortfalls that prompted him to call for major reductions in the System's 2003–5 budget, and a current-year reduction
of $20 million in the UW System budget—a cut that the legisla-
ture's Joint Finance Committee threatened to make even deeper,
while prohibiting any offsetting tuition increases.[56]

The situation posed an immediate threat to the System's ability to accept more students. Regent president Jay Smith advised
the board in March 2002 that if these proposals were adopted,
the university would have no choice but to reduce enrollments
by two thousand students in the next academic year, 2002–3.
Taking an action called "regrettable but necessary" by regent
James Klauser, the board directed Lyall to suspend admissions
effective March 9 until further notice.[57] This dramatic action led
to negotiations with the governor and state Senate leaders that
produced assurances that the System's cut would be limited to
$20 million and spread over the course of the next biennium.
These events, however, stimulated renewed concerns about the
System's long-term financial picture and the steady decline in
state support. Urging the state to recommit to public higher education and make it a priority again, Smith explained the trajectory of diminishing state support and revised priorities. He noted
that over the previous ten years, the state budget had increased
by 74 percent, while the UW System's budget had increased by
37 percent, with the largest growth in state spending for the Department of Corrections, K–12 education, and local government
aid. Meanwhile, the System's base budget had been reduced by
some $55 million, and these cuts had been made even in times
when state revenues were growing. The state's contribution to
UW System's operating costs had declined from one-half of the
total at the time of the merger to one-third as of 2002.[58] While
the System might have been spared the worst-case scenario of the
2002 budget problems, the trends were apparent, and the need to
address the chronic underfunding of state higher education was
more pressing than ever.

Throughout 2002, the Board of Regents reviewed options for strengthening the System's resource base, but by early 2003, as the 2003–5 biennial budget was being developed, it had become clear that continuing economic problems and low state revenues made improvements in the System's finances unlikely. Former attorney general Jim Doyle had been elected governor in the 2002 elections, defeating McCallum. Doyle appeared at the board's February 6, 2003, meeting to discuss the state's fiscal problems, emphasizing the importance of achieving a fair and balanced state budget with no tax increases. One month later, he announced that the System would be required to cut $250 million in the 2003–5 biennium. While a substantial part of this amount—$150 million—could be offset by tuition increases, it was the largest cut in the history of the System, producing a net shortfall of $100 million that dwarfed previous cuts.[59]

The size of this cut gave fresh urgency to the need for solutions to the UW System's financial woes, and in August 2003 the board initiated another study to examine these issues. The study, *Charting a New Course for the UW System*, described the national higher education context and Wisconsin's own situation, providing a new set of recommendations for improving System finances. Reiterating earlier System studies, *Charting a New Course* warned that there are no substitutes—no alternative revenue streams or internal savings—that can replace adequate, stable state support for the System's instructional mission and goals, and it urged the state to renew its commitment to providing support for higher education.[60] Along with its other recommendations, *Charting a New Course* focused attention on the importance of management flexibilities to produce savings that would help offset declining state taxpayer support. The study pointed out that the loss of state funds around the country was motivating many public universities to seek flexibilities in such areas as building and purchasing, cash and investment management, and personnel matters, as well as to consider structural changes in their relations with state governments, such as charter status.[61] The System had long sought similar kinds of management flexibilities based on proposals from work such as the *Twenty-First Century Study*, but it had met with little success. *Charting a New Course* concluded, however, that flexibilities should continue to be pursued, in view of the System's deepening financial problems. While presented as one strategy within the study's extensive set of recommendations, the pursuit of management flexibilities, already a recurring theme in System budget and legislative requests, took on growing importance and began to emerge not as just one solution among many to the System's budget problems but as an essential solution.

Political Shifts and Other Changes

Beyond the financial challenges, the early 2000s brought a series of state leadership transitions and an abrupt shift in the composition of the Board of Regents that fueled partisan tensions. Bush's election, Thompson's departure, and McCallum's defeat brought an end to sixteen years of Republican gubernatorial leadership. Doyle's victory in 2002 returned Democrats to control of the executive branch, giving the new governor the power to appoint members of the Board of Regents. In the ordinary course of events, governors appoint three new regents every year, and the composition of the board changes gradually as staggered terms expire each spring and the governor fills the vacancies that these departures create. Doyle, however, had an unusual opportunity to appoint four new board members immediately on becoming governor. Before he resigned to go to Washington, Thompson had nominated four individuals to serve as regents: Lolita Schneiders, Phyllis Krutsch, Al De Simone, and James Klauser. As was customary, this group began serving on the board before being officially confirmed by the Senate, but, because then Democratic Senate majority leader Chvala refused to bring their nominations to a vote, they continued to serve without confirmation throughout 2002 and remained unconfirmed when Doyle became governor in January 2003. On taking office, Doyle withdrew their nominations and substituted his own appointees, who then replaced the unconfirmed Thompson appointees. At the February 6, 2003, meeting of the Board of Regents, Doyle appointees Danae Davis, Peggy Rosenzweig, Jesus Salas, and David Walsh took the seats of the Thompson group.[62] It was a change that not only disrupted the normal process of board turnover and replacement but injected an overtly political element into System governance. These February appointments, with the addition of three more Doyle appointees later in the year, when the normal expiration of terms created new vacancies, gave the governor's appointees effective control of the sixteen-member board very early in his term. While System operations and management had always been affected by and intertwined with state politics and political leadership, the more gradual turnover in board membership resulting from the natural expiration of staggered terms tended to encourage bipartisanship in board governance. Board leaders from both parties had traditionally reiterated the importance of putting the interests of the UW System above politics in their roles as trustees. The abrupt transitions in board composition at the very beginning of Doyle's term in 2003, followed by the rapid shift in control to Doyle's appointees later in that year, reinforced the board's identification with the governor's political party and political agenda and would bring partisan reaction and an increasingly partisan approach to System governance in the years ahead.

As Lyall's presidential term continued, the state's overall political climate, too, became increasingly polarized. Wisconsin's 1970s shift to a full-time state legislature had by the late 1990s and early 2000s produced a permanent political class and heightened partisanship. The influence of legislative staff grew, and a kind of "promotional" career path developed, leading from staff position to state Assembly to state Senate. It was a system that rewarded party loyalty and concentrated power in the hands of legislative party leaders, widening the ideological divides between the parties, according to observers.[63] It also made the UW System more vulnerable to politically motivated attacks. Always the subject of numerous legislative audits and reporting requirements, over time the System found itself increasingly likely to be criticized over the details of its policies and actions as politicians sought controversy and publicity to enhance their careers. Thompson attributed much of the change in the state's relations with public higher education to the full-time legislature, noting that before the legislature became a full-time body, the UW System and its predecessor systems really "ran things," but afterward legislators were more likely to interfere directly in the management of the System.[64] Even as many regents and Lyall sought to emphasize their nonpartisan stewardship of the UW System, state legislators were increasingly willing to attack the System to make headlines and score political points. Legislators like Steve Nass of Whitewater and Rob Kreibich of Eau Claire became frequent critics, and it was rumored—apocryphally—that Kreibich boasted that every time he attacked his local UW institution, UW–Eau Claire, his poll numbers rose.

Public attitudes toward higher education were also evolving in ways that threatened to undermine UW System success. While opinion surveys consistently showed strong in-state public approval of the UW System,[65] higher education had more generally come to be viewed as a private rather than public benefit, making it a less attractive object of taxpayer support and helping to justify steeper tuition increases to replace tax support.[66] In addition, the Reagan era's emphasis on small government and low taxes continued to squeeze state resources available to support higher education. State leaders from Lucey on had sought to avoid tax increases, but the Reagan years made it much more difficult politically to seek increases. The resistance to expanding the state's tax base and the insistence on downsizing government created a kind of zero-sum game in which, absent revenue growth from general economic conditions, any investment or reinvestment was effectively constrained by the need to meet existing state government commitments or changed priorities. Reliance on revenue growth from general economic conditions as the basis for new program investment, however, was inherently unstable, leaving the state vulnerable to economic swings. These uncertainties had contributed to the state's repeated pattern of cutting approved biennial budgets when revenues failed to meet predictions. The situation harmed all state programs but was especially damaging to the UW System, which was routinely required to bear a disproportionate share of total state budget cuts. As Lyall pointed out in the wake of Doyle's 2003 cut, reductions to the UW System's allocation accounted for 38 percent of the total state budget cut, even though the System received only 9 percent of the state budget.[67]

The availability of tuition as an alternative source of income for the UW System helped justify the disproportionate application of statewide budget reductions to the System, in effect shifting what had once been seen as taxpayer responsibilities to students. Tuition revenues had, however, become crucial in maintaining educational quality. As the reliance on tuition to offset decreasing taxpayer support accelerated throughout Shaw's and Lyall's presidencies, concerns about steady tuition increases began to mount. Student leaders had rarely complained about tuition in the System's early days, but from the 1987–89 budget on, as tuition was increased and the shift in financial aid from grants to loans forced students to borrow more for their college educations,[68] there was increasing resistance to further increases. Students and their parents worried about the costs of college and student debt argued for keeping tuition affordable, creating political pressure to restrict tuition growth through legislative caps—limits that further squeezed System resources and threatened quality.

Enrollment limits created another type of pressure, forcing System institutions, especially the flagship Madison campus, to become more selective in admissions. The System's historical tradition of broad access was jeopardized, stirring public anger about the inability of some students to attend the UW institution of their choice and generating resentment of affirmative action efforts that were frequently attacked for encouraging the admission of allegedly less-qualified individuals.[69] Shaw's three-legged stool had become less stable, as the System's continued ability to rely on tuition and enrollment management to compensate for losses in taxpayer revenues became more vulnerable to these pressures.

The New Millennium

The year 2000 ushered in a turbulent new millennium that generated more challenges for the System. The year was bookended by widespread fears of crashing computer systems caused by the so-called Y2K programming problem and the controversial election of President George W. Bush after a bitter dispute over vote counting in Florida, which had to be resolved by the US Supreme Court.[70] While Y2K fears proved to be overblown, Bush's election and his choice of Thompson to head the Department of Health and Human Services brought dramatic changes to state political leadership. Within another year, the nation came under attack as Al Qaeda terrorists flew airplanes into the twin towers of the World Trade Center in New York and the Pentagon in the Washington, DC, suburb of Arlington, Virginia, on September 11, 2001; a third hijacked plane crashed near Shanksville, Pennsylvania. By 2003, the country was at war in Iraq, beginning the longest military conflict in the nation's history. The 9/11 attacks and the Iraq War brought new organizational challenges for the UW System. Fears of more attacks drove new security measures and emergency preparations. The war years saw UW students enlist for military service and return as veterans in need of new and different kinds of support to complete their academic careers. These upheavals intensified the headwinds the System already faced.

The Problems with Solutions

Throughout Lyall's tenure as System president, she and other board and System leaders continued to seek creative solutions to the System's complex problems, particularly its financial challenges. Both the *Twenty-First Century Study*, in 1996, and *Charting a New Course for the UW System*, in 2004, were undertaken after major state budget cuts and provided extensive sets of recommendations to address both the immediate and the long-term fiscal issues stemming from declining state taxpayer support. Pursuing these recommendations, Lyall and UW System chancellors sought new revenues from a variety of external, nonstate sources of funds—federal and extramural grants, gifts and foundation endowments, and university–industry partnerships—to offset diminishing state funding. Internally, the UW System continued to manage enrollments to maintain quality and to cut costs through administrative efficiencies while pressing for greater management flexibility from state government to maximize available resources.

These efforts brought some important successes, increasing extramural financial support, improving administrative effectiveness, and providing a margin of excellence that sustained the remarkable institutional and individual achievements that occurred throughout Lyall's tenure as president. The growing reliance on nonstate sources of funds, however, came with concerns of its own. As UW institutions increasingly looked to affiliated charitable foundations for financial support, the constant pressure to raise money began to work a fundamental change in the responsibilities of campus leaders. Growing endowments occupied an ever-larger proportion of their time, transforming the chancellor's role from academic leader to chief fundraiser. When John

Wiley, who succeeded David Ward as Madison's chancellor, was assigned to lead a major capital campaign for the UW Foundation, he was compensated through a separate contract with the UW Foundation for the "above and beyond" nature of the additional work. For his successors, however, heading such a campaign would be just one more expectation of the chancellor's position. The smaller UW institutions would see similar changes. While most of the comprehensive campuses had small foundations that served mainly as "pass-through" accounts for relatively modest gifts, by the late 1990s and early 2000s—following the example of Eau Claire's Don Mash—they had begun to conduct their own capital campaigns, working to build larger, permanent endowments of their own. The growing institutional dependence on major private giving and the need to grow endowments changed the nature of the chancellor's role and expanded the influence of wealthy donors on campus affairs.

While strengthening university–industry relations and commercializing research bolstered campus revenues, these efforts came with concerns about conflicts of interest, the integrity and independence of corporate-sponsored research, and restrictions on the free exchange of research results. The UW Research Park in Madison and the impressive technology transfer successes of WARF added critical support for UW–Madison and provided a model for other UW institutions, but issues of ethics and transparency remained.[71]

Internally, the board and Lyall's administration continued to improve administrative efficiencies and to advocate for management flexibilities to better control costs. Lyall's successes in lean administration and accountability, however, did not generate savings large enough to significantly enhance System funds or persuade state government that the System deserved more support. Lyall would later observe that her accountability reports went largely unappreciated and that few in the legislature even read them. Management flexibilities held more promise as a source of internal savings, but state government remained unwilling to cede significant authority to the System or System institutions or to loosen state regulatory controls.

While pursuing implementation of the recommendations of the *Twenty-First Century Study* and *Charting a New Course* yielded some important and notable successes, the hard truth of the studies remained: none of this activity could replace adequate, stable taxpayer support for the UW System.

Changing Course

With the turmoil of the early 2000s in the background, Lyall continued to pursue her major goals for the System, while responding to the challenges of the new millennium. In 2004, after some twenty-two years with the UW System, twelve as president, she announced her retirement. She had played a crucial role in bringing the System through the stormy years of family dysfunction and feuds, helping lead it to the organizational maturity that provided the foundation for a prolonged period of success and achievement. With support from political leaders and UW System executives, she presided over an organization that was well regarded nationally, and justly noted for the outstanding achievements of its faculty, staff, and students. The strong record of UW System accomplishment during her term, however, had not translated to any meaningful change in the downward spiral in state taxpayer support. The long, steady shift of state policy priorities away from higher education was, if anything, accelerating. The System as she left it remained vulnerable to the erosion in quality stemming from lack of funds.

System leaders—regents, presidents, chancellors, and others— had long warned of the dangers to the state of diminishing taxpayer support for the UW System. Completing his term on the board in 1991, Weinstein had urged board members to nurture the UW System—the state's most important asset—cautioning that the UW System is a fragile institution, too easily diminished.[72] In 2004, *Charting a New Course* quoted Wiley's warning that "unless we act now to protect funding for education, the state's future will be bleak." These kinds of statements, however, did not fully convey the growing urgency of the System's financial situation. Lyall would remain frustrated by her inability to convince state government of the value of the UW System or the state's need to reinvest in it. Outstanding academic and research achievements and demonstrable efficiency were not enough to bring change and even undermined the case for better support. As she and her coauthor Kathleen Sell would note in their 2006

book, *The True Genius of America at Risk*,[73] "the remarkable ingenuity and adaptability of higher education institutions seems to
have persuaded public leaders that somehow these institutions
and the values they foster will survive on their own" without new
government support.[74] Describing in detail the national economic
and political forces responsible for the erosion of public higher
education budgets beginning in the 1970s, they went on to argue
against this kind of complacency. While highlighting the need to
develop a new, twenty-first-century model for a more flexible,
entrepreneurial "public purpose university," they also warned
forcefully of the peril to democracy of failing to provide sustainable levels of public support for public higher education: loss of
educational opportunity, de facto privatization and return to a
system of higher education for wealthy elites only, and loss of
global competitiveness in a knowledge-driven economy.[75] The
truth of their words would continue to resonate as the UW System dealt with the even more painful economic and political turmoil of the later 2000s and 2010s.

8

Challenges of the New Century

Lyall had furthered administrative cohesion and organizational maturity, supporting a sustained period of academic and research accomplishment at all UW institutions and managing effectively in the face of declining state taxpayer funding for higher education. The stable foundation of the mature System was shaken toward the close of her presidency, however, as the nation entered a more turbulent time marked by deepening social and cultural divisions, war, security crises, economic distress, and political upheavals—problems that would extend into the administrations of her successors, Kevin Reilly and Ray Cross. The continuing conflicts of the culture wars, the 9/11 attacks in 2001, the ensuing US invasions of Iraq and Afghanistan, and campus shootings at Virginia Tech and increasing gun violence across the US all brought complex new problems for the UW System. The economic recession of 2001 and the Great Recession of 2007–9 would have damaging long-term budgetary effects on UW campuses and cause personal hardship for students that heightened concerns about rising college costs and raised questions about the value of a college education. As the System responded to these events, new generations of students—the millennials, or echo-boomers, and later Generation "Z"—arrived on UW campuses with new expectations about technology and campus diversity, new demands for better protection from sexual assault and harassment, and new concerns about their future educational and

196

employment prospects. These twenty-first-century issues, together with increasingly divided, rancorous state politics, presented challenges that would persist and confront the UW System throughout the 2000s and the 2010s.

Culture Wars, Continued

The culture wars—conflicts that pitted conservatives against liberals and traditionalists against progressives on a range of issues including feminism, race relations, secularism, and political correctness—had intensified following the 1980 election of Ronald Reagan, posing problems for colleges and universities nationwide, including UW System campuses. As institutions of higher education sought to expand educational and employment opportunities for minorities and women from the 1970s through the 1990s, their policies on affirmative action, sexual and racial harassment, and equal employment opportunities were met with reaction and resistance. Conservative opponents of these programs complained of reverse discrimination against whites and men, improper restrictions on free speech, enforced political correctness, and liberal bias in the academy. UW System institutions, like others, had been drawn into these conflicts, as System affirmative action programs and related policies sparked intense internal debates on UW campuses and before the Board of Regents, as well as external criticism and, sometimes, litigation. The 1981 Board of Regents policy[1] prohibiting sexual harassment in employment and in the classroom was initially attacked as undermining academic freedom and free speech and was approved only following protracted arguments at the board level and a lengthy internal review process. The board's 1989 administrative rule banning racial harassment and hate speech produced even more heated debate over possible violation of First Amendment free speech rights and led to litigation and the eventual withdrawal of the rule in 1992.[2]

The System's comprehensive affirmative action admissions plans developed in 1988 and 1998 were also challenged by conservatives as unfair and possibly illegal. Although the US Supreme Court's decision in the *Bakke* case[3] indicated that public universities had a compelling interest in educational diversity that could justify consideration of race in admissions, the specific quota system at issue in the case had been found unconstitutional, leading to additional litigation in the late 1990s and early 2000s over the details of public university admissions programs. Two cases challenging the University of Michigan's admissions policies, *Grutter v. Bollinger*[4] and *Gratz v. Bollinger*,[5] raised fresh concerns about the legality of the UW System's admissions policies, which were similar to those at issue in the *Grutter* case. Although the Board of Regents had adopted a resolution confirming its continued support for its policies at the March 2001 meeting,[6] three regents objected, prompting a further review in September 2001 of the legal bases for the System's affirmative action admissions plans and the university's compelling interest in achieving the educational benefits of a diverse student body.[7] Following this discussion, the board again affirmed its commitment to its policies. In 2003 the US Supreme Court approved the admissions plan involved in the *Grutter* case,[8] clarifying the *Bakke* decision and indicating that the UW System's policies, too, would withstand constitutional challenge and could continue to be implemented.

The result in *Grutter*, however, did not put an end to lawsuits or controversies related to university affirmative action efforts and did not deter other conflicts in the campus culture wars. Opponents of affirmative action continued their legal attacks on other college admissions programs even after *Grutter*, while also advocating for state constitutional amendments and ballot initiatives aimed at banning any consideration of race in public university admissions. In 1995, Ward Connerly, a former University of California regent, had led a successful drive to pass California's Proposition 209, which prohibited consideration of race in admissions decisions at public universities in California. Following the *Grutter* decision, Connerly and the organization he had founded, the American Civil Rights Institute, launched similar initiatives in other states, including Michigan, where a 2006 state referendum approved the Michigan Civil Rights Initiative, also banning affirmative action in state university admissions and effectively revoking the admissions plan sustained in *Grutter*.

While the UW System avoided these kinds of direct attacks on its affirmative action plans and policies, it faced recurring questions about their legality from conservative board members and critics of affirmative action even after *Grutter*. Meanwhile, as the twenty-first century approached, the UW System became embroiled in a different culture wars controversy, this one involving its mandatory student fees program. The conflict, a seemingly minor dispute about very small amounts of money, would eventually make the System party to a First Amendment free speech controversy before the US Supreme Court.

In addition to their challenges to affirmative action, conservative groups had long fought other university policies and practices seen as biased toward liberal views or contrary to conservative values, including policies involving the uses of mandatory student activities fees at public universities.[9] In the late 1970s and early 1980s, these groups filed a number of lawsuits complaining that their fees were used to support liberal student newspapers and other liberal causes with which they disagreed. They argued that this violated their First Amendment rights to free speech and association because they were being forced, through their dues, to express views contrary to their own.[10] While these arguments met with little success in early cases,[11] developing law in the late 1980s produced more favorable results for the objecting students,[12] encouraging new legal challenges to mandatory fees programs.

While not directly affected by the earlier student fees cases, the UW System, like most colleges and universities, had long required students to pay special fees, in addition to tuition, to fund student government and the extracurricular activities of student organizations. The System's 1974 merger statute had effectively codified the practice and gave students, through their student government, a direct role in determining how the fees for student organizations would be distributed.[13] In the years following merger, student governments throughout the System developed their own campus procedures and criteria for setting the amounts to be charged for student activities fees and for distributing the fees to eligible groups. Initially these processes functioned quietly, receiving little attention from students. By the mid-1980s, though, problems with the fees system were developing. Lack of participation in student government elections had contributed to cynicism about the value of student government and questions about why students should be required to pay fees for activities like the Pail and Shovel Party's Statue of Liberty in Lake Mendota.

If there was some skepticism, however, there was also growing pressure on student governments at UW–Madison and other UW campuses to allocate student fee funds not only for traditional campus-based groups but also for larger outside and inter-campus organizations that were eligible for funding because they provided specified services for students. Among these latter groups were a number of liberal organizations, including the Wisconsin Public Interest Research Group (WisPIRG), a branch of Ralph Nader's national PIRG organization.[14] For such groups, student fees were an important source of revenue. Although relatively low on a per-student basis, activities fees generated a substantial pool of funds each year. At UW–Madison in the 1990s, for example, activities fees of around $12 per student per semester generated $1.1 million annually, available for distribution to student organizations and providers of student services, largely at the discretion of student government. The mid-1980s and early 1990s saw increasing efforts, particularly by outside providers of student services, to gain access to student fees funding throughout the UW System. Although rebuffed in its effort to gain a Systemwide fee for its operations, by 1991 WisPIRG, with the support of Chancellor Donna Shalala, was receiving student fees funding at the UW–Madison campus,[15] and other outside organizations claiming to serve students were soon being funded as well.[16]

Support for WisPIRG and similar affiliated student service organizations at UW–Madison, many of them liberal, viewed against the backdrop of cynicism about the purposes and value of student government, set the stage for a conservative rebellion against all of student government and all student activities fees at UW–Madison. The leader of this insurrection was Scott Southworth, a conservative prelaw major from New Lisbon, Wisconsin. In 1993–94, Southworth campaigned for election to student government on an anti–student government platform. Charging that student government was ineffective and that the fees it used for its own operations and distributed to mostly liberal student organizations were excessive, he pledged to eliminate student government altogether. Ironically, in view of his characterization of UW–Madison's student body as a liberal monolith, Southworth's party won, and, on taking office, he and his supporters voted to disband the venerable Wisconsin Students

Association (WSA), which had served as UW–Madison's student government since 1938.[17]

Because some form of student government is required under the statutes, however, the dissolution of student government was short-lived. A new student organization, Associated Students of Madison (ASM), was formed and recognized by the university as constituting UW–Madison's student government.[18] ASM adopted a constitution and bylaws and assumed the student government roles previously fulfilled by the WSA, including operating the mandatory activities fees program, and mandatory fees to support student organizations continued to be collected by the university and distributed.

With the failure of their broad assault on student government, Southworth and his supporters focused more narrowly on mounting a legal attack on the mandatory student activities fee. In the fall of 1995 Southworth, now enrolled in the UW Law School, and two other law students launched their effort to be excused from paying student fees for UW–Madison organizations whose views they opposed.[19] They wrote to the president of the UW System Board of Regents, Michael Grebe, requesting a refund of the part of their fees that went to groups they found objectionable. Describing themselves as conservatives and Christians, they specifically identified the organizations holding political and religious views with which they disagreed; they included WisPIRG; the UW Greens; the Campus Women's Center; the Lesbian, Gay, Bisexual Campus Center; the Madison AIDS Support Network; and Amnesty International. The objecting students calculated that roughly $3 per semester of their fees went to these groups and asked for a refund of that amount and future exemption from paying that part of their fees.

The initial UW reaction to the request was underwhelming: Grebe simply ignored it. When the letter to Grebe went unanswered, Southworth and his colleagues—now backed by a national litigation organization, the Arizona-based Alliance Defense Fund (ADF)[20]—filed suit against the members of the Board of Regents, claiming that being forced to pay to support activities and organizations to which they objected violated their constitutional rights to free speech and association and asking that the university be prohibited from collecting that part of their fees. In a dramatic move to bring attention to their cause, they appeared at the Board of Regents meeting on April 12, 1996, and personally served each board member with their summons and complaint.

At the outset, it seemed likely that the case would be resolved quickly, since the students were asking for the kind of accommodation that had been provided at other universities, either as a result of litigation or voluntarily. The Board of Regents, UW System and UW–Madison leaders, and UW–Madison's student government, however, were unified in their opposition to altering the mandatory fees program or refunding any portion of the fees as requested. Although the board was by this time dominated by Republicans appointed by Governor Tommy Thompson, board members had little sympathy for the conservative position taken by Southworth and his co-plaintiffs. Without regard to political or partisan affiliations, the board believed it was important to defend the case, rather than settle, both because the fees program was enshrined in state law and closely tied to the state's commitment to giving students a voice in campus governance and because it provided important extracurricular educational opportunities for student participation in campus organizations and direct student involvement in the democratic processes of student government.[21] As regent and former Republican governor Lee Dreyfus put it, "My personal support of student govt [sic] control of student program fees dating back to the late sixties has *always* been based on the academic learning and experience value of such participation."[22]

Although faced with some unfavorable US Supreme Court case law[23] and precedents from the more recent PIRG cases suggesting that student requests to avoid mandatory fees should be accommodated, the System based the defense of its program on a legal theory suggested by the US Supreme Court decision in *Rosenberger v. Rector and Visitors of Univ. of Virginia*.[24] There, the Court had declared that the university's mandatory fees fund was a *forum* for free expression and had held that, in such a forum, fees funding could not be denied to an organization on the basis of its viewpoint—even if, as in that case, the viewpoint was religious. Extending this logic, the UW System argued that it could constitutionally require all students to pay fees to support a forum of funds for free expression, so long as the forum operated in a viewpoint-neutral manner, not discriminating against any viewpoints in the distribution of funds. Because the UW–Madison provided funds for many different student organizations, representing a range of viewpoints, not only liberal but also conservative and religious, the university alleged—and the plaintiffs conceded, initially—that the funding forum was, in fact, viewpoint-neutral and accordingly should be upheld.

While this legal theory was unsuccessful in the lower courts, it prevailed on appeal to the US Supreme Court. In its opinion issued in March 2000, the Supreme Court reversed the lower courts and unanimously sustained the university's mandatory fees program, holding in *Southworth v. Board of Regents*[25] that students could be required to pay fees for the support of a forum for free expression so long as the forum was operated in a viewpoint-neutral manner.

The Supreme Court's decision provided guidance and affirmation for student fees programs at public universities throughout the country, highlighting the UW System's role in successfully defending mandatory fees programs. But, as with other battles in the culture wars, the legal victory carried a high price, leading to more litigation and attracting national attention that made Wisconsin a regular battleground in the campus culture wars. Despite the Supreme Court ruling, the plaintiffs vowed to continue the fight. Their attorney, Jordan Lorance, told the *Daily Cardinal*, "We are going to persevere and litigate, on the issue of viewpoint neutrality, that the current system results in skewed funding for liberal and left-wing groups." Southworth, too, was determined to continue the litigation, saying, "They have a victory, and they have every right to be happy about that. If they're saying that, 'This is it; it's over,' they're not correct."[26] Although they had previously stipulated that UW–Madison's program was viewpoint neutral, the plaintiffs immediately asked the trial court to go to hearing on the issues of how to define "viewpoint neutrality" and to determine whether the UW–Madison fees program satisfied that definition. The ensuing litigation on these issues would continue until 2004 and would later give rise to more lawsuits, as student religious organizations pressed to gain fees funding for religious activities. The *Southworth* case and its progeny— like other culture wars conflicts—ultimately failed to resolve the underlying issues. If anything, the conflicts seemed to harden the

opposing positions, encouraging the involvement of ideologi-
cally driven and politically motivated national organizations in
fighting the culture wars on college campuses in general and at
UW System institutions in particular.

The culture wars would continue well after *Southworth* and
the debates over the System's admissions policies, extending
from Lyall's administration through the terms of her successors.
Although in the early 2000s the System's admissions plans were
approved and implemented, its nondiscrimination policies preserved, its mandatory student fees system sustained, the defense
of these policies came at a cost and without closure. Internally,
the heated debates among faculty, students, and administrators
over culture wars issues left polarizing divisions. Externally, the
controversies and legal cases undermined support for the System among conservatives in state government who believed
that their view of the university as a bastion of left-wing, liberal
bias had been confirmed. In an era in which the university was
already subject to increased legislative criticism, its involvement
in the culture wars invited closer scrutiny and more active intervention in its policy decisions, as even the System's legal vic-
tories only sparked more litigation and often undermined the
original programs that it had successfully defended. Funding for
campus student organizations became more complex and controversial. Conservative anger over the use of student fees to fund
outside or multicampus groups would later lead to the 2013 de-
funding of the United Council of Student Governments by the
state legislature. These and other conflicts in the culture wars
would continue to flare throughout the 2000s and 2010s, raising
new issues and constitutional questions about free speech, equal
treatment, and due process protections.

Millennial Problems

While the culture wars continued, real wars came to the nation,
along with security threats and economic crises that would shape
the experiences and attitudes of the next generations of college
students. The upheavals of the new millennium, from the 9/11
attacks on the World Trade Center and the Pentagon to the US
wars in Afghanistan and Iraq and the recessions of 2001 and
2007–9, left the so-called millennial generation—those born between 1982 and 1996[27]—and its "Generation Z" successors facing

a range of new problems involving national and campus security, the effects of war on the home front, and financial hardships. College and university leaders, too, grappled with these problems, as the nation's challenges touched campus life.

Terror, Foreign and Domestic

The devastating 9/11 attacks on the World Trade Center in New York and the Pentagon in a suburb of Washington, DC, in 2001 shocked the country, stoking fears of more terrorism and driving major efforts to improve national security. The United States immediately responded by invading Afghanistan in October 2001 in pursuit of the perpetrators, Osama Bin Laden and his Al-Qaeda organization. At home, the need for heightened vigilance to prevent other attacks affected everything from air travel to public gatherings in public spaces and forced institutions of all kinds to reevaluate the adequacy of their security measures. The Aviation and Transportation Security Act, creating the Transportation Security Administration (TSA), was signed into law in November 2001. The Department of Homeland Security was created in 2003, and the TSA was later incorporated into that new department. Colleges and universities, including UW System institutions, although not directly covered by these acts, also took steps to improve campus safety.

Meanwhile, as the conflict in Afghanistan continued, the United States invaded Iraq in March 2003, and System campuses saw faculty, staff, and student military reservists called up to active duty and later return as veterans to pursue their educations or resume their careers. At its April 2003 meeting, the Board of Regents adopted a resolution of support for members of the UW community who had been called up or volunteered to serve. What had been projected to be a brief and decisive engagement in Iraq, with early boasts of a "shock and awe" victory, gave way to a prolonged struggle costing thousands of lives and causing great suffering, while the war in Afghanistan would become the longest in US history.[28] With the wars in Iraq and Afghanistan dragging on and veterans returning to UW campuses, the board supported their postwar needs, providing a range of resources to help them to resume their careers and complete their educations. For student veterans, the UW System provided key financial aid, funding tuition remissions for eligible veterans and their families under section 36.37(3p), Wisconsin Statutes (2005), the Wisconsin "GI Bill."

In addition to wars abroad, the 2000s saw increasing violence at home. Domestic terrorism had emerged as a major security threat with the bombing of the Murrah Federal Building in Oklahoma City in 1993, while the shootings at Columbine High School in 1999 marked the beginning of an epidemic of gun violence at educational institutions. With these events in the background, the violence spread to college campuses in 2007, when a shooting rampage at Virginia Tech University took thirty-two lives and injured twenty-eight. Similar incidents at Northern Illinois and other campuses followed. The Virginia Tech episode prompted immediate reactions by colleges and universities around the nation. UW System president Kevin Reilly appointed a UW Commission on Campus Security to review existing policies and to suggest necessary changes, based on an assessment of events in Virginia. Led by UW–Madison police chief Sue Riseling, Reilly's Commission recommended improving communications to alert students to the possible presence of an active shooter on campus and disseminating information about what to do in an active shooter situation. In addition, the creation of campus threat assessment teams to help prevent attacks was encouraged. Rapidly changing technology and the emerging dominance of cell phones required a shift in the means used for providing security alerts, from e-mail to text messaging and Facebook alerts—tools that were both used in a September 2007 incident at UW–Madison. In addition, informational programs and videos were developed to demonstrate how to survive an active shooter attack. By 2008, UW–Whitewater was showing a program titled "Shots Fired" to educate the campus community about actions that could improve chances of survival in an active shooter situation.[29] While some individuals called for legal changes that would allow concealed weapons to be carried on campuses as a defensive measure, this approach was not favored by college administrators and was not consistent with UW System rules banning weapons from university lands and buildings.[30] Still, the System's response to the Virginia Tech shootings, including the stepped-up security and educational efforts, brought attention and new anxiety about issues of violence in a setting where it was relatively rare. As UW–Madison dean of students Lauri Berquam noted, "there is more fear, a heightened level of awareness," among students.[31]

Economic Distress and the Costs of College

Against this background of foreign wars and domestic violence, economic problems grew throughout the 2000s, creating additional challenges for colleges and universities and causing financial hardship for students and their families. The recession of 2001 translated to losses in state revenues, leading to Governor Doyle's deep cut to the UW System's budget in 2003, toward the end of Lyall's tenure as System president. The effects of this reduction were mitigated to some degree by tuition increases, enabling the UW System to manage through that crisis. The Great Recession of 2007–9, however, led to even steeper state budget cuts in an environment where students and their families, also suffering from the general economic decline, were less willing to support tuition hikes and more skeptical about assuming more debt for an education that might not lead to employment in a poor economy.

Although the UW System had traditionally kept tuition for resident undergraduates at a relatively low level, the long post-merger years of diminishing state taxpayer support had brought growing reliance on tuition funds to ensure quality at UW institutions. Shaw had made a clear and convincing case for the need to balance state taxpayer funding, tuition, and enrollments to maintain educational quality, and, with the tacit agreement of state leaders, tuition had increased in small but steady increments to offset falling state support. As long as UW tuition remained low in comparison to charges at similar institutions and financial aid kept pace with tuition growth, this balance worked effectively and raised few concerns. The hard times of the 2000s, however, put new financial pressures on students and their families, causing growing resistance to tuition increases and worries about student debt. Student opposition to raising tuition hardened through the 2000s, as student leaders consistently argued against further increases at meetings of the Board of Regents,[32] complaining about the shift in higher education costs from state government to students and the corresponding need to assume more debt to pay for college.[33] Financial aid, mostly in the form of loans, had grown since the 1980s, helping students pay for increasing tuitions, but the difficult economic times and poor employment prospects for graduates following the Great Recession heightened concerns about taking on new financial obligations. Adding to this problem, even the available financial aid was often inadequate to meet the educational expenses of students from low-income families, adding to the fears of incurring debt.[34] While student debt levels for UW graduates remained relatively modest and the System's tuition and fees were relatively low in comparison to those of peer institutions and UW graduates repaid their loans successfully, the opposition to tuition increases mounted in the hard economic times, making it more difficult for institutions to continue raising tuitions to offset falling state revenues.

In addition to concerns about tuition and financial aid on the part of students and their families, the general economic conditions and the very slow recovery from the Great Recession contributed to a lingering sense of uncertainty that would shadow the students entering college in the 2000s. Their lives shaped by 9/11, the Iraq and Afghanistan wars, Columbine and other campus shootings, and the Great Recession,[35] this millennial generation faced more significant obstacles to beginning their careers and family lives than had their predecessors. The cumulative effects of war, violence, and economic distress reduced employment opportunities and slowed their entry into the workforce, making it difficult for them to settle into committed relationships or take on obligations such as home ownership. The weak economy and the long, slow recovery also fueled questions about the value of a college education as the path to a secure middle-class life. Although it later became clear that baccalaureate degree holders fared better than those less educated in the wake of the downturn,[36] the Great Recession had badly damaged job prospects and slowed career progress. For many, the 2000s were what American Council on Educations leader Terry Hartle described as a "lost" decade,[37] and it led to a "slow start" for the millennial generation, the consequences of which remain unclear.[38]

The Politics of Division

The turmoil influenced the attitudes and the politics of the students entering college in the 2000s, both millennials and their successors in the next generation. Technology had changed not only the means they used to communicate but also the frequency of contacts with others, including their parents—often mocked for their "helicopter" oversight of their children's college careers[39]—as well as their instructors. Inspired by the election of Barack Obama in 2008 and much more diverse than their predecessors, this large cohort[40] arrived on college campuses with expectations of greater sensitivity to issues of discrimination and offensive speech,[41] more active and effective enforcement of prohibitions on discriminatory harassment and sexual assault, and protection from exposure to potentially distressing or trauma-inducing materials in university classes. UW System institutions responded to these expectations with initiatives such as sexual assault prevention programs and policies for providing so-called trigger warnings in advance of the use of possibly upsetting information.

These shifting expectations and the more liberal attitudes they reflected, however, were emerging along with deepening political divisions that had also developed following the Iraq and Afghanistan wars, Obama's election, and the Great Recession. Not surprisingly, the long-standing culture wars continued. Conservatives reacted to campus efforts to improve sensitivity and to protect against various forms of harassment and assault with counterpressures for stronger protection of free speech rights and more due process protections for those accused of harassment, assault, and other misconduct on campus. Organizations such as the conservative Goldwater Institute urged states to enact legislation that would eliminate campus "safe space" protections and punish campus speech disruptors with suspension or expulsion.

The UW System had entered the twenty-first century burdened with what had become the familiar problems associated with declining state taxpayer support and changing state priorities, but the 2000s brought complex new challenges. The wars, economic problems, and political and cultural conflicts would have far-reaching consequences for UW institutions. The stable and successful UW System of the Lyall era would confront much more severe fiscal problems in the 2000s and 2010s, along with these newer problems. Lyall's successors, Reilly and Cross, would face the disruptions and damaging fallout from the nation's wars and economic crises and other cultural and political divides while seeking to meet the needs of new generations of college students, whose lives had been shaped by adversity and who were reaching adulthood with new attitudes and expectations. As in the 1960s and 1970s, an old order was rapidly fading, and the times were indeed changing.

9

The Going Gets Much Tougher

The UW System reached its thirtieth anniversary in 2001 as the upheavals of the new millennium were beginning. By Lyall's retirement, in 2004, with merger fully completed, the mature System could claim numerous achievements, both organizational and individual. The successes, however, had not reversed the long decline in state taxpayer support. Like public higher education institutions nationally, the System continued to face serious financial challenges and unstable state funding. The older solutions to these problems—regular tuition increases, enrollment limits—were becoming less effective as concerns about educational costs grew, pressure on admission continued, and economic conditions deteriorated. Lyall retired following the recession that brought Doyle's massive 2003 budget cut to the UW System, and her successor, Kevin Reilly, immediately confronted the ongoing consequences of this reduction. Reilly would develop a plan for dramatic enrollment growth as a means of addressing the System's continuing fiscal woes, but before this plan could be fully implemented, the Great Recession of 2007–9 intervened. The Great Recession and transitions in university and state leadership would bring daunting new budget challenges and unforeseen destabilizing pressures on the System's organizational structure as the System neared its fortieth anniversary, in 2011.

A New President and a New Agenda for Growth

Reilly, the chancellor of UW–Extension, succeeded Lyall as UW
System president, taking office on September 1, 2004.[1] A New
York City native, Reilly had previously served as associate provost for academic programs and secretary of the State University
of New York (SUNY). He joined UW–Extension in 1996 as provost and vice chancellor and was appointed chancellor in 2000.
His UW–Extension background had given him familiarity with
all UW System institutions through Extension's campus-based
continuing education programs and with Wisconsin's seventy-
two counties through the Cooperative Extension service and its
county agents throughout the state. His Extension portfolio also
included the statewide public broadcasting service, making him
the leader of what was in many ways a small "system" itself, consisting of geographically dispersed offices that were engaged in a
wide range of different activities. Harrington's organization of
these outreach and service functions as a separate institution led
by a chancellor had been unique nationally and was controversial at the time,[2] but it had also underscored Extension's critical
role in fulfilling the Wisconsin Idea of sharing the benefits of UW
expertise with citizens throughout the state. Reilly admired the
passion UW–Extension faculty and staff members brought to their
work, reinforcing his own commitment to advancing the Wisconsin Idea. These career experiences led him to consider seeking the System presidency on Lyall's retirement. He recognized
that it was a tough job, describing it as second only to the governorship in exposure to public scrutiny in the state, but felt he
understood the nature of the office and that it was a good fit for
him, given his career at SUNY and UW–Extension.[3] When it was
offered to him, he was prepared to accept the job.

Reilly was a popular internal choice, well liked by his UW System chancellor colleagues and within the System Administration.
He shared with Lyall a low-key management style enlivened by
humor. The holder of a PhD in English literature, he was always
ready with a quip or quote and frequently opened board meetings
with poetry.[4] Internally, he maintained an organizational structure of the System administration similar to that in place under
his predecessors, even as he began to assemble his own executive
team. Recognizing the need to build effective relationships with

the state legislature and governor, he focused on media and external relations, while adding administrative depth with the appointment, in January 2005, of UW–Eau Claire chancellor Don Mash as his executive senior vice president. Mash, like Reilly, was a familiar figure within the UW System, having served as chancellor of UW–Eau Claire since 1998. Although reluctant to give up campus leadership and hesitant, from a chancellor's perspective, to join a System administration often maligned as overly bureaucratic, Mash had been encouraged by Lyall to accept Reilly's offer. Mash's administrative experiences and knowledge of the UW System allowed him to support Reilly on new initiatives and to help resolve a major problem with cost overruns on a project to replace the System's aging payroll and staff benefits operating software. In 2006, Reilly chose David Giroux, then UW–Extension director of communications, to lead his external relations effort. On Cora Marrett's appointment as an assistant director of the National Science Foundation, in 2007, Mash was joined by Rebecca Martin, provost and vice chancellor at UW–Parkside, as leader of the System's office of academic affairs.

Reilly's approach to relations between the System administration and System institutions reflected his own experiences as an institutional leader. Sympathetic to the calls of his chancellor colleagues for greater latitude in institutional program development, Reilly was less assertive of central leadership authority than his predecessors and more willing to cede control to chancellors—an approach that was also consistent with the *Twenty-First Century Study*'s encouragement of institutional autonomy and the emphasis in *Charting a New Course* on the need for management flexibilities for all System units.

On assuming the presidency, Reilly inherited the System's ongoing fiscal problems. While the System was structurally stable and organizationally cohesive, it continued to be plagued by declining state taxpayer support, making financial issues an urgent priority for his new administration. The small positive budgets of the late 1990s had effectively been reversed following the 2001–3 recession and Doyle's $250 million budget cut for the 2003–5 biennium, then the largest in the history of the System. Taking office toward the end of that budget cycle, Reilly signaled his intention to be fiscally responsible by combining the administrations of UW–Extension and UW Colleges under one chancellor as a means of holding down administrative costs. Beyond just belt-tightening, however, he hoped to find ways of expanding System resources. Convinced that increasing the number of baccalaureate degree holders in Wisconsin would benefit individuals and bolster the state's economy, he believed that adding students presented an opportunity for the UW System to grow its way out of declining state revenues. At his first board meeting as president, he announced that his priorities would be student success and "brain gain" for Wisconsin. His focus on these areas would become the basis for the major policy initiative of his administration, the *Growth Agenda for Wisconsin*.

The problem of diminishing state support for higher education intensified as Reilly came to office. Despite years of repeated warnings from UW System leaders about the negative effects of inadequate support on educational quality, access for students, and state economic success, the erosion had been steady. While the UW System was not alone in facing this problem, its state support was declining more rapidly than that of other state universities. A study by the Wisconsin Technology Council presented to the Board of Regents at its November 2004 meeting described the twenty-five-year trend to weaker public financial support for higher education everywhere, emphasizing that Wisconsin's decline was occurring at a faster rate than the national average. The report showed a drop of 47.6 percent in state funding over the preceding twenty-five-year period and projected that if the decline continued at that rate, state funding would stop altogether by 2040. At the same time, low salaries—a by-product of poor budgets—put UW institutions at risk of losing top faculty and administrators, along with the research funds that they generated for the campuses. UW–Madison was particularly vulnerable, as demonstrated when the recruitment of several of its leading Psychology Department faculty by other institutions threatened the Department's national standing as a top departmental recipient of research funding.[5]

Inadequate funding also led to plunging per-student taxpayer support. In 1986—early in Shaw's term—the annual per-student funding in the UW System had sunk to $1,222 below the national average. With the combination of enrollment management efforts and modest tuition increases begun in the Shaw era, by 1994–95 it had climbed to $161 above the average. In the wake of the 2002 cuts and the even larger Doyle cuts of 2003–5, however, per-student support had fallen again, sinking back to $1,200 below the national benchmark in 2003–4. The 2005–7 budget provided little relief from this situation. The System had sought an increase of some $300 million in state funds and tuition expenditures for the biennium but received what was, in effect, a $125 million decrease as the result of legislative actions.[6] Although tuition was allowed to rise by 6.9 percent to cover some of the losses in state funding, per-student support remained low relative to national benchmarks. State support as a proportion of the System's total budget had dropped again, to 26 percent, while the proportion funded by tuition grew to 21 percent. As students and their families were forced to shoulder an ever larger share of their educational costs, complaints about affordability and access to System institutions grew.[7]

Concerned with the 2005–7 budget results, in June 2005 the board adopted a resolution, recommended by Reilly, proposing the formation of a bipartisan statewide commission to study "what the people of the state want their university to be" and to address questions such as appropriate levels of higher education access and cost. Although a formal commission was not created, board members, led by regent president David Walsh, began a series of statewide listening sessions to get input from the public on the System's activities and priorities. At the same time, Reilly, with the help of his newly appointed executive senior vice president, Don Mash, began to focus on his "brain gain" priority and a plan to grow the number of college graduates in the state.

Reilly's pursuit of this plan flowed naturally from other System efforts to increase the number of state degree holders. In 2004, the board had established a Committee on Baccalaureate Degree Expansion (COBE) to explore means of achieving this goal, reporting in December 2004 on strategies for expanding degree completion among underserved populations such as low-income, minority, and working adult students.[8] The focus on "brain-gain" was also consistent with the work of national education support organizations, such as Lumina and the Bill and Melinda Gates Foundation, that stressed the need for stronger baccalaureate degree production to support economic growth and civic benefits, as well as to ensure US competitiveness with other nations.

Reilly's argument for increasing UW System degree production was straightforward. Higher percentages of degree holders within a given area are closely correlated with higher average incomes, demonstrating the economic value of degree attainment for both the individual and the community. In a knowledge-based economy, highly educated citizens are essential to maintaining the technological and innovative competitiveness needed to sustain broader state and national economic growth. Falling behind in the production of degree holders in a state brings the risk of stagnating economic opportunity—especially as the high school diploma becomes a less reliable path to the kind of comfortable life once made possible by abundant manufacturing jobs paying middle-class wages. Improving statewide baccalaureate-degree attainment is an economic win for individuals and for a state.[9]

Although in 2004 the fiscal environment for higher education was expected to remain difficult, both in the state and nationally,[10] Reilly was convinced that degree growth—and the benefits from degree growth—would lead to stronger state taxpayer support for the UW System. Reilly also believed that System institutions had the capacity for growth and were well positioned to attract more students. As he took office, in September 2004, UW–Madison was ranked seventh among public research universities in the *U.S. News and World Report* rankings and continued to maintain its place as one of the top five recipients of federal research grants in the country. The UW–Eau Claire, La Crosse, Stevens Point, and River Falls campuses were also highly ranked among their peer Midwest comprehensive institutions by *U.S. News and World Report*. In addition, Wisconsin had added 48,400 jobs in the previous year, the highest number in the Upper Midwest. Reflecting the connection between an educated workforce and job creation, of these, some 19,500 were in highly educated Dane County.[11] There, Epic Systems, the nation's leading developer of electronic medical record software, and other businesses resulting from WARF and UW–Madison technology transfer efforts were seeing dramatic growth. These state and System strengths demonstrated that Wisconsin had the necessary foundation for growth and the capacity to compete successfully with neighboring states, including its demographically similar rival, Minnesota, in the number of citizens holding college degrees.[12]

Mash shared Reilly's views and encouraged him to develop a clear executive agenda for the System centered around improving baccalaureate-degree production. In February 2006, Reilly announced his signature initiative, the *Growth Agenda* for the UW System. He described the goals for his growth program in sweeping and ambitious terms. The UW System, he asserted, "should be the state's premier developer of advanced human potential, of the jobs that employ that potential, and of the communities that sustain it." His plan called for the development and implementation of campus-specific programs to increase the number of baccalaureate graduates, with the long-term goal of closing the gap in per capita income between Wisconsin and Minnesota and bringing state support per student to within 95 percent of the national average.[13] With backing from Walsh, Reilly worked to gain regents' support for his proposal. As preparations for the System's 2007–9 budget request got under way in the spring of 2006, the *Growth Agenda* became the System's top priority and the basis for seeking both the restoration of state funding lost in the two previous biennia and additional new funds to support the proposed growth.

To help individual institutions design their local plans for expanding baccalaureate-degree production, Reilly engaged the Educational Delivery Institute, a Washington, DC–based consulting group. UW institutions were expected to choose an appropriate focus—for example, enrolling more students, addressing barriers to degree completion, attracting more transfer students—to serve as a basis for their own institution-specific plans. Chancellors were charged with securing community support for their institutional efforts, which, it was hoped, would persuade legislators to provide more state funding for the *Growth Agenda*. The near-term goal was to add some 2,800 new students Systemwide over the course of the 2007–9 biennium, with as many as 7,700 more in the two succeeding budget cycles. The long-term goal was to produce 80,000 more System graduates by 2025.[14]

It was an ambitious effort, and some concerns were expressed about the idea of growing the System as a means of improving state financial support and boosting the state economy. Tom Loftus, who joined the Board of Regents in 2005, cautioned that increasing the number of college graduates produced by the

System would not necessarily increase the number of degree holders who stayed in the state. Loftus, whose interest in Wisconsin higher education extended from his days in the state Assembly and his role on the 1985 Select Committee on the UW System, noted that the number of college graduates leaving the state was not currently being offset by the numbers entering.[15] A similar point was made by regent Michael Falbo, who argued that, without adequate employment opportunities to attract college graduates, educating more students would not necessarily make the state successful. This issue was also explored in a presentation to the board by Dennis Jones, of the National Center for Higher Education Management Systems (NCHEMS), in which he explained that, largely as a result of the state's heavy reliance on a manufacturing economy, Wisconsin educates many college students who go elsewhere for employment, making the state a net importer of high school graduates and an exporter of bachelor's degree holders.[16] The crux of the problem was whether producing more baccalaureate degrees from UW System institutions would bring benefits to the state or simply more brain drain.

In addition to these concerns, conservative state legislators were hostile to the idea, noting that technical college graduates make good incomes and do not leave the state.[17] Moreover, the desire for growth was not consistent within the System itself. While it was attractive to some campus leaders as a means of building enrollments and thus improving tuition income, others were worried about the impact of growth on educational quality and concerned about neglecting important needs in areas such as faculty salaries and research support. UW–Madison, sensitive to the existing size of its undergraduate student body, chose not to make any request for funds to be used for growing enrollments.[18]

Overall, though, the potential benefits of improving statewide educational attainment outweighed these concerns, and Reilly, with board approval, was able to generate widespread support for the *Growth Agenda*. Throughout 2006 and 2007, he worked to persuade legislators and the public that investing in efforts to grow the number of baccalaureate-degree holders would yield both economic and civic benefits. Governor Doyle was also receptive to the growth plan. He had himself proposed a program, the Wisconsin Covenant, to encourage more high school students to pursue a college education. The Covenant promised low-income seventh and eighth graders who achieved a "B" average in high school that they would be admitted to a UW institution and guaranteed financial aid to meet their expenses. In addition, Doyle had proposed that veterans of the Iraq War be provided tuition remissions at UW institutions to support their efforts to complete degrees. Both the Covenant program and the veterans' remissions plan fit well within the larger *Growth Agenda* plan[19] and were discussed at hearings on campus growth plans as consideration of the System's 2007–9 budget proposal and the larger *Growth Agenda* goals across the System continued throughout 2006. Meanwhile, individual campus plans for achieving growth were developed and gained strong support from community leaders hoping to see local gains from such growth. All of these efforts brought success in the governor's 2007–9 budget proposal. In early 2007, Doyle announced in his State of the State address a plan to invest an additional $225 million in funding for the UW System, financial aid, and the Wisconsin Covenant. His biennial budget proposed a significant $180 million increase to the System's budget for basic operating costs, as well as $20 million for *Growth Agenda* programs.

With the introduction of the governor's budget proposal in March 2007, the outlook for *Growth Agenda* funding seemed positive. The governor's budget encountered strong resistance in the legislature, however, as lawmakers in the Republican-controlled Assembly reacted initially by demanding a reduction of $120 million from Doyle's proposal for the System and a 4 percent cap on tuition increases. These demands set off protracted negotiations and arguments that delayed final approval of the 2007–9 budget until November 2007. The result was a considerably smaller increase in the overall budget for the System and for the *Growth Agenda*—an additional $29 million targeted to the *Growth Agenda* and a $10 million fund for the recruitment and retention of high-demand faculty. In addition, the legislature and the governor allowed tuition to rise by 5.5 percent at all institutions except the UW Colleges. Though the funding was less than Reilly and System leaders had hoped for, it was a beginning for his *Growth Agenda* plan and provided support for a variety of campus-based initiatives to graduate more students.

Growth Agenda Implementation and
Other Policy Initiatives

Detailed implementation of the *Growth Agenda* began in 2008 through a set of strategic initiatives designed to support the overarching goal of increasing baccalaureate-degree attainment and collectively known as Advantage Wisconsin. These initiatives, led by vice presidents Martin and Mash, addressed academic matters such as the need to establish clear learning outcomes and new pathways to degrees for underserved adults, along with practical matters such as the provision of information on financial aid to students and the creation of high-paying jobs through technology transfer. Among other items, a "KnowHow2Go" program was developed to educate middle and high school students about academic requirements, college affordability, and the availability of financial aid, including through support from new sources.[20] Related efforts included fostering collaboration with PK–12 schools to support college preparatory offerings and smoothing the transfer pipeline of students from the two-year UW Colleges to baccalaureate-granting campuses and from the System's four-year institutions to UW–Madison. UW institutions were also encouraged to build on existing programs that supported *Growth Agenda* goals, such as the Liberal Education and America's Promise (LEAP) initiative, which addressed core baccalaureate curricular requirements, and Doyle's Wisconsin Covenant program. It was a wide-ranging effort, but implementation of the *Growth Agenda* and the Advantage Wisconsin initiatives were central to the board's 2009–11 budget priorities. Throughout 2008, as budget preparation got under way, Reilly, Mash, Martin, and board leaders worked to gain legislative support for these initiatives.

Although efforts related to the *Growth Agenda* remained Reilly's major policy focus, he continued work in other areas of long-standing importance to the System. Lyall had presented her annual *Achieving Excellence* reports to demonstrate the System's accountability and administrative efficiency. Continuing to emphasize the System's effectiveness, Reilly and the board agreed to join a new national program, the Voluntary System of Accountability (VSA), which measured individual institutional effectiveness on a range of factors and offered a mechanism for comparing

System institutions with their peers across the nation.[21] The need to improve the campus climate for diversity was an ongoing concern, and the System's previous ten-year strategic plans to recruit and retain underrepresented minorities, *Design for Diversity* and *Plan 2008*, were followed by a new plan, called *Inclusive Excellence*, to be incorporated as part of the *Growth Agenda*.[22] To help provide quality educational experiences at System institutions, Reilly also encouraged the use of "differential tuitions" as a more flexible source of funding for campus-specific needs. These additional charges were to be targeted to clearly identified campus objectives and needs and required the approval of student and campus administrators, as well as the Board of Regents.[23] Addressing the long-standing issue of noncompetitive pay for System executives, Reilly also helped develop a new process for granting raises to individual institutional leaders to take advantage of board-approved increases in their salary ranges.[24]

Problems, Old and New

While the *Growth Agenda* initiative attracted public and political support and work continued on related policy efforts, these activities did little to shield the System from state governmental probes, audits, and overregulation—or public criticism—on other matters. Responding to these probes had become a regular feature of System management. As Reilly would later say, his true "welcome to the presidency" moment came at 1:00 p.m. on the afternoon of his first day in office, when he was presented by the LAB with a new plan to audit System administrative costs.[25] This audit came on the heels of a critical LAB review of the costs of implementing a new software program for UW System human resources and payroll functions. That project, inherited by Reilly, had already drawn legislative anger over cost overruns—a problem that he would soon ask Mash to help resolve—and the fallout from that audit would continue, while the newer audit brought further scrutiny of System operations.

Exacerbating these problems, more audits and criticism followed. First, an embarrassing series of personnel cases exposed problems with the System's employee discipline and job security policies. In an unusual convergence of events, in 2005

UW–Madison had discovered that three of its faculty members had been criminally charged with serious felonies, including assault and battery, sexual assault, and possession of pornographic materials. Although the university had initiated internal proceedings to dismiss these three individuals, UW rules required a showing of just cause, a full hearing before a faculty committee, and the approval of the chancellor and Board of Regents before they could be dismissed. Throughout this slow and cumbersome process, the faculty members had a right to be paid their salaries, which were to be continued until the final decision to terminate had been made by the board.[26] As the university opened its dismissal cases against the three, information about their arrests became public, prompting demands for their immediate terminations—without pay—and scathing criticism of the university's inability to act quickly in the face of egregious employee misconduct.

Amid the outcry over the inadequacy of the System's process for dealing with these situations, concerns about other personnel practices and policies emerged. The System faced criticism over its practice of using "back-up" appointments for certain administrators serving on an at-will basis who were terminated from their administrative posts.[27] These back-up appointments allowed administrative employees to return to their former faculty or academic staff positions when terminated from the at-will job, while being paid at the salary level they had earned as administrators. There were also complaints about litigation settlements that provided for reassignment of employees to positions requiring little or no work in exchange for the resolution of legal claims. These arrangements were sharply criticized as wasteful and inappropriate uses of state resources. Faculty sick-leave policies also came under fire, drawing complaints of inaccurate or incomplete reporting of sick-leave use when an absent faculty member's classes were taught by faculty colleagues. The failure to fully record sick-leave use produced large accumulated sick-leave balances for some individuals—balances that were applied as health insurance premium payments upon the faculty member's retirement under the current system, resulting in a large financial liability for the System.

Following a review of the System's employment policies and practices at its September 2005 meeting, the board initiated a series of actions to address these issues. In October 2005 regent president Walsh, after meeting with legislators, appointed an internal ad hoc committee to review and streamline the System's dismissal rules.[28] Led by regent Michael Spector, the committee, with input from faculty, university attorneys, and board members, proposed revisions establishing an expedited termination process in cases of serious criminal misconduct. By the end of 2006, the three notorious faculty felons had been dismissed and the System had prepared and approved new administrative rules governing dismissal of faculty members in cases involving serious criminal misconduct.[29] Meanwhile, the use of back-up appointments was suspended while clarifying policies on at-will appointments and sick-leave reporting were developed.

Despite these proactive internal steps, the LAB announced in November 2005 that it would audit the System's personnel policies and procedures, an effort that continued into 2006. By March of that year, the auditors had developed a report on the employment of felons within the System, which was followed in late fall of 2006 by the completed audit and LAB recommendations regarding UW System sick-leave policies, limited and concurrent appointments, the use of the consultant title, and faculty sabbaticals. The LAB report renewed the old criticisms of System policies but, with the board and System efforts to reform System policies and practices well under way and nearing completion, the LAB audit process and recommendations added little to the System's own actions. As Walsh and Reilly advised the board following a meeting with legislators in November 2006 and a hearing on November 29, 2006, before the legislature's Joint Audit Committee, the System's actions had largely defused legislative complaints and satisfied Audit Committee members.[30]

While the System contended with the ongoing scrutiny of its management and administrative practices, other challenges reflecting political polarization and the culture wars arose in the early years of Reilly's presidency. The state's widening political divide encouraged the pursuit of more extreme legislative agendas, including some measures that jeopardized the System's research and teaching missions. In 2005, social conservatives introduced Assembly Bill 499, making it illegal to clone stem cells and threatening UW–Madison professor James Thomson's work to develop life-saving stem cell therapies. In 2006, conservatives renewed their efforts to pass the Taxpayer Protection Act (TPA), a measure to restrict state revenue growth under a formula based on the rate of inflation and state population—in effect precluding any expansion of taxpayer support for urgent state needs, including higher education, or for new programs such as the *Growth Agenda*. Governor Doyle, who had come to office promising a major investment in biomedical research support,[31] vetoed AB 499, and the TPA failed in the legislature. Still, the System's need to respond to such initiatives was a growing problem, adding to tensions between the higher education community and state government.

Clashes related to the culture wars also contributed to conflicts between conservative groups and the System and its institutions. The System's successful defense of its segregated fee policies in the 2000 *Southworth* decision was a defeat for conservative students angry about having their student fees used to support liberal student organizations. The decision, however, also presented an opportunity for conservative organizations. The *Southworth* court had approved the UW's fee policy largely because funding was distributed in a viewpoint-neutral manner—that is, made available to all recognized student organizations, without regard to the viewpoints they expressed.[32] Conservative as well as liberal student organizations were eligible for funds, and, in the wake of the decision, conservatives—including conservative student religious organizations—were quick to use the ruling to seek funding for their own causes.

Requests from student religious groups, however, posed complex new legal problems. Although under *Southworth* fee funding could not be denied on the basis of the religious views expressed by a student organization, to be eligible for funding in the first place, the organization was required to be officially recognized. Recognition in turn required that a student organization not discriminate in membership or eligibility to hold leadership positions on any legally protected basis, including religion. In 2006, two UW System campuses, UW–Madison and UW–Superior, denied funding to student religious organizations—the Roman Catholic Foundation (RCF) at Madison and the Intervarsity Christian Fellowship at Superior—on the ground that they failed to meet the nondiscrimination requirements for recognition, and the UW System found itself in another round of litigation involving student fees.

The two student groups, aided by two conservative national litigation organizations, the Alliance Defense Fund and the Christian Legal Society, brought separate lawsuits against UW–Madison and UW–Superior. The student groups asserted that the nondiscrimination requirement violated the *Southworth* viewpoint-neutrality standard, because it effectively deprived religious groups of access to funding on the basis of their religious views. Similar suits had been filed by the same conservative litigation organizations against the University of North Carolina, the Southern Illinois University School of Law, and Hastings Law School, all of which had nondiscrimination requirements like those in place at UW–Madison and UW–Superior. To avoid further litigation, North Carolina had settled its case under an agreement that maintained the ban on discrimination as a requirement for organizational recognition but allowed student organizations to require their members to affirm their commitment to the religious organization's beliefs and goals—in effect a distinction between status-based discrimination against an individual seeking to join a religious organization and viewpoint discrimination in the allocation of student fee funds to the organization.[33] The UW System adopted that approach and settled its cases, as well, concluding litigation on the nondiscrimination aspect of its official recognition policies. More litigation ensued, however, when the RCF was denied funding to pay for religious observances and to support the costs of maintaining its facilities located in a church near the UW–Madison campus. Despite litigation fatigue, the System contested the case vigorously, but unsuccessfully, with lower federal courts concluding that the Establishment Clause did not prohibit the university from funding RCF (by then renamed Badger Catholic) and that the *Southworth* precedent required it to fund the organization's religious activities.[34] The loss brought an end to the litigation, but the protracted legal struggles, even if principled, had brought negative publicity and fed a larger political narrative casting the UW System and its institutions as bastions of liberalism at war with conservative and religious groups.

The Great Recession

While responding to these and other challenges, Reilly pressed ahead with the *Growth Agenda*, working toward the goal of adding as many as eighty thousand new students by 2025.[35] Funding, however, remained crucial to the success of the initiative. Although the 2007–9 budget had provided some support for the *Growth Agenda* along with pay increases for System employees of 2 percent in each year of the biennium, by early 2008 there were signs of looming fiscal troubles. In February, the state projected that tax revenues would be lower than expected for the year, increasing the state's structural deficit.[36] Nevertheless, as the board and Reilly began developing the 2009–11 budget request, they remained committed to seeking funds for the *Growth Agenda*. Early plans called for requesting taxpayer support for the addition of seven thousand more students in the coming biennium, along with modest tuition increases. To address the System's problems with persistently noncompetitive faculty salaries—highlighted by the recent departure of prominent UW–Madison history professor Jon Pevehouse for the University of Chicago at a salary double what he was making in Wisconsin—at the June 2008 board meeting Reilly called for the creation of a Commission on Competitiveness and Compensation to be included with the upcoming 2009–11 budget request. With the support of the board, Reilly also began building a case for long-term state reinvestment in the UW System. An invited presentation from the Wisconsin Taxpayer's Alliance at the October 2008 board meeting emphasized that Wisconsin was behind all other states but one in increases for public higher education over the previous five-year period. Similar concerns with the long-term decline in taxpayer support had been expressed by the *Wisconsin State Journal*, which, in an editorial also discussed at that meeting, urged the state not to skimp on higher education.[37] At the November 2008 board meeting, regents and System leaders engaged in an extensive discussion of the need to address faculty recruitment and retention challenges, including low salaries, and heard another presentation from the Carnegie Corporation warning that the financing system for public higher education in the United States is broken and inadequate to get 50 percent of the population educated to international standards.[38]

All these plans, proposals, and arguments for the importance of reinvesting in the UW System were, however, swiftly overtaken by the series of disastrous economic events beginning in 2007 that became the Great Recession, the worst economic downturn since the Great Depression of the 1930s. There were various complex, interrelated causes of the recession. By late 2007, a housing bubble fueled by lax lending practices finally burst. Homeowners and many who had engaged in profitable house flipping were suddenly left owing more on their property than it was worth, spurring defaults and leaving major commercial lenders with substantial liabilities. At the same time, the nation's "shadow banking" system crashed. Led by the dramatic collapse of Lehman Brothers, in September 2008, other largely unregulated private investment banks that had been engaged in high-risk transactions faced similar failure or forced sales to more stable institutions. Problems quickly spread to the major housing lenders Fannie Mae and Freddie Mac, as well as the insurance giant American International Group (AIG). The rapidly declining economy eventually affected other nonfinancial industries, including automakers, which sought bail-out assistance from the federal government to stay in business. The consequences were devastating for the nation. The economy ground to a halt, millions of jobs were lost, unemployment rose sharply, and the net worth of individuals and nonprofit organizations plummeted. Although economists would declare that the Great Recession ended officially in 2009, its effects continued to be felt for years into the future.[39]

For the UW System and its institutions, the Great Recession meant even greater state funding cuts as the deteriorating national economic situation triggered substantial declines in tax revenues in Wisconsin and throughout the rest of the country. By December 2008, Wisconsin faced a $5.4 billion revenue shortfall for the 2009–11 biennium, including some $346 million for the remaining six months of the 2008–9 fiscal year. Given the depth of this financial crisis, the board, though still attempting to address the System's academic salary problems, immediately trimmed its pay plan request from an initial goal of 5.23 percent per year for four years beginning in 2009 to a 2.5 percent increase for fiscal years 2010 and 2011. The fiscal picture darkened further in 2009, however, and by May the state budget shortfall had

grown to $6.5 billion. Raises of any kind were off the table, re-
placed by plans for eight-day furloughs for all state employees,
equaling in effect a 3 percent pay cut. In addition, the System
faced a 5.2 percent reduction in tax support, translating to another
$250 million budget cut. Describing the major reductions needed
in the 2009–10 operating budget at the July 2009 board meeting
and elaborating on the bleak economic outlook, Reilly emphasized that the System had no choice but to suffer along with every-
one else. While tuition would have to increase modestly to preserve quality and offset the cuts, he advised, the goal would be to
hold the most economically disadvantaged students harmless
from the increases.[40]

Despite these hardships, however, the System responded to
the recession effectively in several key areas and managed to
maintain some forward momentum on the *Growth Agenda*. The
agreement of Doyle and the legislature to allow the System to
make up part of the budget cuts with tuition increases eased
some of the pain and helped contain the damage to educational
quality. System chancellors were permitted to decide how to
take the necessary institutional reductions, but, reflecting the
benefits of belonging to a large System of universities, Reilly's
administration took steps to ensure that services and programs
proposed for elimination at one campus remained available elsewhere in the System, so that students and others would have
continued access to courses and instructional services needed for
degree completion. The System's capital budget continued to be
solid, as work proceeded on buildings already in the construction pipeline, and new buildings funded in whole or in part with
private gifts were approved. The building boom, notably at UW–
Madison, provided an important economic stimulus during the
downturn. Privately supported need-based financial aid also
grew by nearly 124 percent in the period, helping students to
continue their educations in spite of the challenging economic
times. Sponsored research, too, rose, providing another critical
source of funding for institutional research activities. Meanwhile, *Growth Agenda* efforts shifted to emphasize work force development, and Reilly appointed a Research-to-Jobs Task Force
chaired by WARF managing director Carl Gulbrandsen to spur
technology transfer opportunities and job creation based on UW
research. Reilly also worked to ensure the System's cooperation

with federal economic stimulus measures adopted to deal with the recession. With the enactment of the federal American Recovery and Reinvestment Act of 2009, Doyle established a state office to allow Wisconsin to participate in federally supported stimulus projects, while Reilly appointed a System task force to connect with the state efforts. As Reilly would later note, the UW System's internal management efforts and its ability to generate private funding sources to sustain programs enabled it to step up in a time of great need, contributing financial support when the state and federal governments could not provide much help.[41] Reilly would count his role in guiding the System through the crisis among his greatest accomplishments as president.[42]

The lingering effects of the Great Recession brought major across-the-board reductions in 2009. As preparations began in 2010 for the 2011–13 biennial budget, though, Reilly returned the major focus of planning to the *Growth Agenda* and its goals. In a discussion of budget issues in June 2010, the board adopted a resolution asking for legislative approval to raise tuition 5.5 percent for the 2010–11 academic year in order to compensate for the losses resulting from the previous year's substantial budget cuts. Addressing the upcoming 2011–13 biennial budget, Reilly highlighted the need to resume work on the *Growth Agenda*, with continued focus on job creation and more financial aid support to help students complete their degrees. He appointed an implementation committee to follow up on the recommendations of the Research-to-Jobs Task Force and received board support for a resolution calling on the legislature to provide automatic increases in the state's Wisconsin Higher Education Grants (WHEG) financial aid program to match the System's tuition increases.[43]

To bolster the case for reinvestment in the UW System and its institutions, newly elected board president Charles Pruitt collaborated with former board president Jay Smith on a document titled "Principles for Progress and Prosperity," which was intended to serve as the basis for a statewide conversation about the priority given funding for public higher education in Wisconsin. Returning to the *Growth Agenda* theme that Wisconsin needs more college graduates and better jobs to remain competitive, Pruitt and Smith barnstormed the state calling for a new compact between the state and the UW System that would stabilize System funding and help achieve the *Growth Agenda* goal of eighty thousand more graduates for the state by 2025.[44] The board's biennial budget request, approved in August 2010, sought new funding of $83.6 million for *Growth Agenda*-related items, including financial aid, research initiatives, libraries, technology centers, and the restoration of a 2 percent pay plan increase for faculty and staff. As the Great Recession wound down, Reilly and regent and System leaders geared up to resume work on these long-range goals.

Transitions, 2008–10

Along with the upheavals of the Great Recession and the UW System's efforts to manage the economic pain, the 2008–10 period came with state and university leadership transitions that would have similarly far-reaching consequences for the state and the System. In 2008, UW–Madison leadership changed hands with the selection of a new chancellor. In early 2008, John Wiley had announced his retirement, and he was succeeded by Carolyn A. "Biddy" Martin, who took office September 1, 2008. Martin arrived from Cornell, where she had been a faculty member in the German Department and had held several administrative positions, most recently as provost. As a newcomer to UW–Madison administration, Martin interrupted the continuous chain of campus leadership that had extended from Shalala through Ward and Wiley, a situation which, she conceded, meant she would have a steeper learning curve as chancellor.[45] Still, she had a Madison connection, having received her PhD in German there in 1985, and she was welcomed as an alumna. Her appointment as the campus's first openly lesbian chancellor was also greeted as a milestone, drawing praise from LGBTQ groups, as well as the larger campus community.[46] Seen as warm and personable, she was expected to bring a fresh approach to building trust with state government leaders, and her appointment was viewed with optimism.[47]

The initial enthusiasm surrounding Martin's selection seemed well placed, as she reached out to legislative antagonists such as Representative Steve Nass in an effort to improve relations between UW–Madison and state legislators. She also sought to mend fences with Wisconsin Manufacturers and Commerce (WMC), which Wiley had denounced as dominated by politically conservative extremists in an opinion piece for *Madison Magazine* earlier in 2008.[48] On campus, she successfully persuaded students and student government leaders to support a substantial differential tuition increase to fund improved instructional support, student services, and financial aid, even while the full impact of the Great Recession was still being felt and despite their general opposition to tuition increases. Her Madison Initiative for Undergraduates called for a four-year phase-in of these tuition increases, beginning with a $250-per-year increase for resident undergraduates in 2009–10, rising to $1,000 per year in 2012–13. For nonresident students, the increases were set at $750 per year in 2009–10, rising to $3,000 per year in 2012–13. Undergraduate students from families with adjusted gross incomes of $80,000 or less were held harmless from these increases, and the program was to be reviewed annually by an oversight board consisting of students, faculty, and staff. The funds generated by the initiative were to be used to add faculty and instructional support, as well as to provide need-based financial aid. The plan was received enthusiastically by the Board of Regents and approved at its May 8, 2009, meeting.[49] It was a positive step that helped maintainthe flagship's quality in a time of great financial difficulty and an impressive start to Martin's chancellorship that appeared to bode well for her administration.

Changes also came to state government leadership in 2008. The 2008 US presidential election swept Barack Obama to office, and in Wisconsin, Democrats took control of both houses of the state legislature, bringing single-party control to the executive and the legislative branches of state government for the first time in Doyle's governorship. With the severe fiscal constraints of the Great Recession still dominating, this state leadership shift came with few major policy changes. State Democrats, always supportive of labor unions, did pass legislation granting the System's unclassified staff members collective bargaining rights. This change would be short-lived, however. Before implementation could occur, the 2010 election would reverse the single-party control of state government from Democrats to Republicans, and the change would be followed by new legislation that effectively ended collective bargaining rights for all state employees. Pressure from environmental agencies and Democrats also led to plans requiring UW–Madison to use "biomass" material— basically, organic waste from the paper-making process—as fuel for its campus power plant. This effort, too, produced no change as it became apparent that biomass production was grossly insufficient to supply the campus's fuel needs.[50] Coping with the ongoing fallout from the recession remained the primary focus of System and state leaders. Although Doyle's September 2009 announcement that he would not seek re-election in 2010 opened the door to new state executive leadership, there was little to suggest that any major upheaval in the direction of state government was imminent.

Throughout 2010, as the state's gubernatorial contest got under way, the System worked on preparations for the 2011–13 biennial budget, hopeful of seeing some renewed state reinvestment in the System. Pruitt continued to promote the "Principles for Progress and Prosperity," while Reilly worked on new efforts to close the academic achievement gap between minorities and other students. The board endorsed continued funding of human embryonic stem cell research by the National Institutes of Health. Doyle attended the August board meeting and was honored for helping defeat the Taxpayer Protection Act, for his support of domestic partner benefits for state employees, and for allowing "Dreamers"—immigrant young people whose parents had brought them to the United States as children—to pay resident tuition to attend UW System institutions.[51] Meanwhile, in the gubernatorial campaign, public higher education was not a major issue. The economy and solutions to the state's specific economic woes were the main issues in the race between Republican Scott Walker and Democrat Tom Barrett. Neither candidate proposed sweeping change to the structure of state higher education or to the UW System, and System leaders planned the usual efforts to reach out to the new governor immediately after the election.

The results of the 2010 elections, however, would be more dramatic than the campaign suggested. Walker defeated Barrett by a substantial 56–42 percent margin, and his victory was accompanied by a complete reversal of Democratic state legislative control, returning control of both houses of the legislature to the Republicans. In one election, single-party control of state government flipped from one party to the other. The state results mirrored the national midterm elections, a "wave" election that saw leadership of the US House of Representatives shift to Republicans and left Democrats with only a small majority in the Senate.

With the coming change in state leadership, the board invited Walker to attend its November 4, 2010, meeting, just two days after the election. Welcomed with a standing ovation, Walker spoke briefly, expressing his interest in working with the System on finding ways it could help him fulfill his campaign promise to create 250,000 new jobs in the state in his first term. He warned, however, that another $3 billion state revenue deficit made it unlikely that the System would receive any additional funds in the new biennium.[52]

Walker's November caution about the poor prospects for state funding was followed in December by a more ominous warning about the future of higher education nationally from Terry Hartle, of the American Council on Education. Hartle appeared at that month's board meeting to provide an overview of the election results and federal policies affecting higher education. Describing the growing public distrust of elites, including postsecondary education institutions, he observed that, while educational institutions see themselves as a gateway to opportunity, they also establish and validate privilege. He went on to point out that for many citizens the 2000s had been a "lost" decade in terms of economic advancement and urged higher education institutions to be sensitive to the level of fear and discontent that remained.[53]

Reilly, however, remained upbeat about the System's future. At the December board meeting, he reviewed a list of recent achievements by System institutions, ranging from Professor William Cronon's election as president of the American Historical Association to Wisconsin Public Television's receipt of three Midwest Emmy awards to the Badger men's football team's coming appearance at the Rose Bowl. He noted the growth in the number of students enrolled in the System—at that time 181,782, an increase of 2,900 over the previous decade—and emphasized the value of the System to the state's economy. Reiterating the themes of "Principles for Progress and Prosperity," he urged development of a new compact with the state to sustain and strengthen System support and affirmed his commitment to working with the new governor to that end. These were goals apparently shared by Chancellor Martin, who, through her chief financial officer, Darrell Bazzell, described a proposal for a "New Badger Partnership," details of which would be unveiled, according to Bazzell, "as more is learned about possible legislative and gubernatorial interest."[54] Although not immediately apparent, the stage had been set for what would become the most consequential year since the merger that created the UW System forty years earlier. As the System's fortieth anniversary approached, the winds of change for higher education in Wisconsin were again blowing.

10

De-Merger, Division, and Distrust

On becoming president of the UW System in 2004, Reilly assumed leadership of a mature, successful, and unified System. He began his presidency by building on this solid organizational foundation, seeking to attract state reinvestment in public higher education with ambitious plans for growth. Although the Great Recession of 2007–9 stalled progress on his *Growth Agenda* initiative, Reilly provided steady management through the economic crisis and hoped to resume his programmatic efforts as the economy recovered. Scott Walker's election in 2010 as governor and the return of total Republican control of the state legislature, however, brought intensifying political partisanship that made it especially difficult for Reilly and the Democratic-dominated Board of Regents that had appointed him to work effectively with the new Republican administration. As communications between System leaders and the new administration faltered, Walker and UW–Madison chancellor Carolyn Martin developed a plan for a new governance structure for UW–Madison that would separate the flagship from the UW System as an independent public authority with its own governing board. The bruising conflict over this plan and its eventual failure would set the stage for a series of renewed restructuring efforts, punitive state budget cuts, and attacks on the System's educational mission that would continue through the 2010s.

Innovative Ideas, Old and Bold

Although he had attended Marquette University, Walker was not a college graduate and had no direct relationship with the UW System or UW institutions. Like his predecessors, however, he came to the governorship affirming his general support for the System, and—though warning that because of what he described as a $3.6 billion deficit in the state budget there would likely be no additional funding for the System in his first biennial budget[1]—expressing his interest in working with UW leaders on bold, innovative ideas for higher education. Confronting the prospect of no new funds or even further UW System budget reductions in the 2011–13 biennium, regent president Charles Pruitt, Reilly, and former System president Katharine Lyall met with members of Walker's transition team on December 6, 2010, to share their thoughts on moving the System forward in a time of continuing economic stress and reduced state revenues. Their conversation focused on cost-cutting measures and the importance of gaining money-saving management flexibilities that could help the UW System deal with the anticipated continuing financial adversity.

Requests for management flexibilities—freedom from certain state regulations that would allow the UW System to operate more like a private business—had become by this time a kind of UW System mantra. System leaders had long sought changes in state rules and requirements that would improve the System's administrative efficiency, reduce costs, and generate some additional revenues from improved cash management practices and interest earnings. Over the years, the System's strategic planning documents had identified a variety of areas in which relaxation of state regulations would improve its operations. In 1986, *Planning the Future* had advocated, among other items, giving the System greater freedom from state purchasing requirements and bidding procedures, removing university staff from state civil service rules, eliminating state controls on the number of employees the System could hire, relaxing state restrictions on expenditures of program revenues, and granting the System full authority over the use of auxiliary reserve balances. Ten years later, the *Twenty-First Century Study* again urged freedom from state position controls, along with greater authority over faculty, staff, and executive compensation and conditions of employment. That study also suggested streamlining the capital budget process and expanding System authority to set and expend tuition. Similar recommendations were repeated in *Charting a New Course*, in 2004, which asked for specific changes in capital project financing, the ability to manage cash, retention of investment earnings and the interest on tuition and other program revenue balances held by the System, and—again—authority over personnel matters, including compensation and position controls.

These planning studies did not, for the most part, attempt to quantify precisely the amounts that might be generated from regulatory changes, emphasizing that, while they could provide important added support, the relatively modest savings and revenue enhancements they would produce would not be sufficient to compensate for major cuts in state funding. The *Charting* study, for example, identified savings of approximately $500,000 per year if certain procurement flexibilities were provided and projected interest income of as much as $15 million annually if the System could retain interest on program revenue balances— significant amounts, but inadequate to offset reductions such as the $250 million cuts imposed in the hard economic times of 2003–5 and during the Great Recession.[2] Still, as taxpayer support for the System continued to decline and the state's fiscal picture worsened, System leaders pressed for various management flexibilities they argued would make the System more efficient and would help it manage through economic adversity.

Walker's warning at the November 2010 board meeting that there would be no new funds and that there likely would in fact be reductions in funding for the System in his first biennial budget gave heightened urgency to the need to gain management flexibilities that could help mitigate the pain from state revenue losses. At their December 6, 2010, meeting with Walker administration officials, Pruitt, Reilly, and Lyall reiterated the importance of these management tools in maintaining educational quality in hard financial times. In addition, responding to Walker's call for "bold, innovative ideas" for public higher education, Reilly suggested consideration of a more sweeping organizational change—the creation of a "public authority" to govern the UW System. The public authority structure offered the possibility of gaining not only the kinds of management flexibilities long requested by the

System but also significantly greater autonomy and independence from state regulation. The public authority framework had
been successfully employed to operate the University of Wisconsin Hospital and Clinics since 1996. Established at the urging of
Chancellor David Ward and with Governor Thompson's support, the University of Wisconsin Hospitals and Clinics Authority (UWHCA), had been granted, among other items, statutory
powers to acquire property, borrow money, devise its own personnel and compensation system, and set hospital rates, in effect
allowing it to operate as an independent, self-supporting business
enterprise that did not receive any direct state taxpayer funding.[3]
The public authority structure had freed the hospital from state
regulations that prevented it from expanding its business operations and acquiring other health care organizations needed to remain competitive and financially stable in the rapidly changing
health care industry. In the years since its creation, UWHCA had
developed as an effective, financially sound, and commercially
competitive quasi-public corporation.

The success of the UWHCA, familiar to Reilly and other UW
System leaders, and the freedom from state regulation that the
public authority framework promised made it an attractive
governance model for a UW System seeking the flexibilities, autonomy, and independence that would help UW institutions
maintain crucial educational services and manage efficiently in
hard times. State public authorities are, however, creatures of
state law, with their specific powers and areas of autonomy defined and limited by state statutes consistent with the public
purposes for which they are established and always subject to
change by state lawmakers. While UWHCA's statutory powers
gave it wide latitude to make business decisions, it was governed by a board of state government officials, regents, and UW–
Madison leaders, and its authority was constrained by defined
state regulations and bonding requirements. The public authority
model had not been studied in the context of public higher education or the UW System's extensive, complex statewide operations, and neither the kinds of powers and duties appropriate for
a UW System authority nor the role of state government in funding such an organization had been analyzed. The effectiveness of
the UWHCA, however, and the System's long-standing quest for
flexibilities made the idea seem worth exploring, leading Reilly
to suggest it at the December 2010 meeting.[4]

While the public authority model was Wisconsin-specific, Reilly's suggestion that a major change in the state's higher education governance structure be considered was also consistent with broader national trends and the System's own calls for a new understanding or compact with the state. Public universities in other states were struggling with fiscal challenges similar to those facing the UW System, as state taxpayer support for public higher education—diminishing since the 1970s—entered a much steeper trajectory of decline following the 2001 economic downturn and the Great Recession of 2007-9. Higher education leaders nationally agreed that the funding system for public higher education in the United States—crucially dependent on state government support—was broken,[5] and these leaders were pursuing new organizational structures or seeking to develop new understandings or compacts with state government that would give management autonomy to operate more like private businesses, as well as the revenue-generating authority to maintain high-quality education programs. Throughout the 2000s, models such as partial privatization, voucher programs, constitutional[6] or charter status, or hybrids such as Cornell University's public-private structure were promoted as alternatives to the traditional highly regulated, state government-controlled management of public higher education.[7]

Virginia's Higher Education Restructuring Act of 2005 reflected this trend. Under the act, the state's public universities were offered the opportunity enter into a contractual arrangement with the state government that allowed them to negotiate agreements for full authority over tuition setting, capital projects, leases of real property, information technology, procurement, and human resources—all in exchange for meeting state-established performance standards. Meeting these standards, as determined by a state council, made institutions eligible for state financial incentives.[8]

The Virginia model had the appeal of giving public universities more control over their budgets through the ability to set tuition, as well as greater management latitude in areas such as building programs and purchasing and personnel matters, while giving state government the means of ensuring accountability and cost containment by holding institutions to established performance standards. The approach had drawbacks, though. It raised institutional concerns about how to determine reasonable and appropriate measures of success and whether the state's role in setting performance standards came with a loss of university control over academic activities.[9] In addition, the model's heavy reliance on tuition to offset state funding reductions led to worries about rapidly escalating college costs and the resulting burdens on students and their families, as the shift in higher education costs from state taxpayers to students was a barrier to access for lower-income students. Despite these problems, however, the Virginia model generated interest among higher education leaders attracted by its promise of management flexibility — including Chancellor Martin, a Virginia native and a graduate of the College of William and Mary. There was interest from others, too, including the Wisconsin Public Research Institute (WPRI, later renamed the Badger Institute), a Milwaukee-based conservative think tank, which in a December 2010 report discussed the Virginia model approvingly, arguing that a similar restructuring of Wisconsin higher education that gave the UW System more autonomy could also make it more accountable to state government.[10]

Although the UW System had not pressed for the kind of sweeping structural changes provided under the Virginia model, strategic planning documents like *Charting a New Course* had urged establishing a new kind of relationship or compact with the state in support of their calls for greater management and financial autonomy. Reilly's suggestion at the December 6 meeting with Walker's transition team that public authority status for the System be explored was consistent not only with the kind of restructuring effort undertaken by Virginia but also with the System's own calls for a new understanding between the state and its institutions of higher education. Against this background and facing continued state funding challenges, Reilly felt the time was right to consider whether the UWHCA's public authority structure might be adapted to suit the UW System and to provide it with greater operational independence and autonomy, as well as long-sought management flexibilities. The idea had never been analyzed in detail or subjected to the kind of careful vetting that had preceded approval of the UWHCA, however, and Reilly had not developed and did not propose a specific public authority plan at the December 6 meeting. He suggested the idea to gauge interest on the part of the Walker administration in starting a conversation about a new kind of governance model for the UW System.[11]

There was no immediate reaction to the suggestion from the governor-elect's office, but the idea was discussed again at a January 7, 2011, meeting attended by Michael Huebsch, the governor's appointee as secretary of the state Department of Administration (DOA), and Reilly, Pruitt, and board vice president Michael Spector from the UW System.[12] As in December, though, the System representatives received no request for additional information or signal of interest in the concept from the governor's administrative team. Assuming that further consideration of the idea was at an end as of the January 7 meeting, Reilly and System leaders did not further pursue development of a public authority plan for the UW System. While apparently not interested in Reilly's suggestion of public authority status for the UW System, however, Walker and his team had in fact begun to work with UW–Madison's chancellor Martin on a very different public authority proposal. This plan, based on the New Badger Partnership that had been announced, without details, by Madison vice chancellor for finance Darrell Bazzell at the December 2010 meeting of the Board of Regents, created a public authority to govern UW–Madison only, separating the flagship from the rest of the UW System under its own board of trustees. Intended for inclusion in Walker's first biennial budget, the plan effectively divorced the flagship from the System, dissolving the union created by the 1971 merger of the UW and WSU.

A Tale of Two Budget Bills

As Reilly and board leaders attempted to connect with the Walker administration on UW System issues following the November election, the new governor and his staff were also working on broader state budget issues. Relying on his estimate of a budget deficit of $137 million for the current 2010–11 fiscal year and a projected $3.6 billion deficit for the 2011–13 biennium,[13] Walker was planning for an immediate short-term "budget repair" bill to address the current-year deficit and developing a comprehensive biennial budget proposal expected to contain deep cuts for all state agencies. When introduced, however, both budget measures went far beyond standard budget reductions and adjustments, proposing major policy changes that sent shock waves throughout the state. The budget repair bill proposed the repeal of collective bargaining rights for thousands of state employees and unleashed a firestorm of criticism and protest. The biennial budget, introduced just a few weeks later, included the UW–Madison public authority plan Walker had been developing with Chancellor Martin. Although the two proposals were not directly linked, public anger and demonstrations over the budget repair bill fueled an increasingly toxic political environment that would spread to the public authority proposal.

Act 10—The Budget Repair Bill

The first of the two budget measures to be announced, legislation to address the current-year shortfall, drew an immediate and furious reaction. More than a straightforward fix to a short-term problem, the Wisconsin Budget Repair Bill of 2011, later known simply as "Act 10," proposed requiring public employees to pay a significantly larger share of the cost of their health insurance and other benefits, along with a much more radical change: the elimination of collective bargaining rights for most public employees. In 1959, Wisconsin had been the first state in the nation to grant public employees these rights, permitting public school teachers and most employees of the state's classified civil service to join unions and to bargain with management on compensation, benefits, and other terms and conditions of employment. In the years since then, well-financed public-sector unions had emerged as a strong voice for represented public employees and wielded significant political influence in the state. It was no secret that public-sector unions—like unions in general—tended to be politically allied with Democrats, but governors and legislative leaders from both parties had worked effectively with the unions for years.[14] Although Walker had a history of union conflicts from his tenure as Milwaukee county executive and was associated with conservative organizations, including the Bradley Foundation and the American Legislative Exchange Council (ALEC),[15] that promoted limiting the influence of public-employee unions by curtailing their collective bargaining rights, he had not campaigned on these issues.[16] His sudden proposal to eliminate public-employee collective bargaining in Wisconsin came as a stunning surprise[17] that infuriated those protected by public-sector union contracts—most of them public school teachers and state civil service employees—and many other supporters of collective bargaining rights. Anger at the abrupt reversal of long-standing state policy brought protesters from around the state and the country to the state capitol in Madison. Following the bill's introduction, on February 11, 2011, and continuing to mid-June 2011, thousands—including many UW System faculty and academic staff members sympathetic to the protesters[18]—marched in opposition to Act 10 in the largest protests seen since the Vietnam War era.[19] Although not represented by unions themselves, UW–Madison's faculty senate adopted a statement supporting collective bargaining rights for all workers,[20] as did the faculty senate of UW–Milwaukee.

Democrats in the state Senate, now in the minority, attempted to prevent passage of Act 10 by leaving the state for Illinois in a move to deprive the Republicans of the quorum necessary under Senate rules to bring the measure to a vote. Democratic leaders hoped that by withholding the quorum, they might be able to negotiate to preserve at least some collective bargaining rights, but the governor refused to make concessions, and negotiations collapsed on March 7.[21] Meanwhile, Senate majority leader Scott Fitzgerald separated the collective bargaining provisions from the budget provisions in the bill, which allowed the Senate to take action on the collective bargaining measure with a smaller quorum of only seventeen members.[22] Act 10 was passed in the Senate by an 18–1 margin on March 10, 2011, and by the Assembly on the same day. Walker signed the legislation on March 11, and the Democrats returned to Madison on March 12.[23]

While the efforts of the Democratic senators to prevent the vote were unsuccessful, the senators were greeted as heroes on their return, cheered by a crowd of some 100,000 opponents of Act 10 gathered outside the state capitol. Protests over the passage of Act 10 continued to attract demonstrators to the capitol on a daily basis throughout much of the rest of the year. As the furor continued, Act 10 was challenged in both state and federal courts, litigation that would continue until 2014.[24] The anger over the change also prompted an effort to recall the governor in 2012. Although the law was eventually upheld in federal court and the Wisconsin Supreme Court[25] and the recall effort later failed, the continuing unrest in 2011 fed powerful anti-Walker sentiment and brought heightened scrutiny of his other legislative proposals, including his "de-merger" plan for public higher education and the UW System.

Act 32—The Biennial Budget: De-Merging the UW System

With the turmoil around Act 10 unfolding in the background, Walker pressed ahead with preparations for his first biennial budget, including the plan he was developing with Chancellor Martin for UW–Madison's separation from the UW System as an independent public authority. Whether because of the failure of System leaders to press more aggressively for their own version of a Systemwide public authority model or because of simple unwillingness on the part of the governor's office to accept any ideas associated with a Board of Regents dominated by Democrats, Reilly's suggestion that public authority status be considered for the UW System as a whole had elicited dead silence.[26]

While ignoring System leaders, however, Walker's team was in confidential talks with Martin and her staff about granting public authority status to UW–Madison and separating the flagship from the rest of the UW System. Martin met with DOA secretary Huebsch on December 28, 2010, to discuss the New Badger Partnership (NBP), the plan her vice chancellor for finance, Darrell Bazzell, had referenced—without details—at the December 10, 2010, regent meeting. At the December 28 meeting, Huebsch confirmed that Walker intended to propose public authority status for UW–Madison in the biennial budget. Martin was eager to support the plan and began developing the organizational framework for a UW–Madison public authority. Responding to questions raised by Huebsch at their December 28 meeting, Martin prepared a draft memo dated January 7, 2011—ironically, the same day Huebsch was discussing the public authority idea with Reilly, Pruitt, and Spector—outlining the powers that she believed should be granted to a UW–Madison authority. Her list included not only the System's routinely requested personnel, purchasing, cash management, and building flexibilities but also full tuition-setting authority to be vested in a new governing board of trustees. This new board—in contrast to the UW System Board of Regents, which was composed of sixteen state residents appointed by the governor and subject to confirmation by the state Senate and two ex officio members, the Superintendent of Public Instruction and a representative of the Technical College System board system[27]—was to be composed of individuals representing UW–Madison "constituencies"—obliquely described as those with an understanding of the university's research mission and sensitive to the importance of private fundraising—whose members would be selected by UW–Madison and the governor without legislative approval. It was a structural change that would effectively transfer direct control of flagship operations to Martin and Walker, removing the Board of Regents from governance and the legislature from the selection process for trustees.[28]

In the same memo, Martin explained that—with the new board, added flexibilities, private fundraising, and tuition increases on the order of 10 percent per year—her campus could accommodate a $50 million budget reduction in each year of the coming biennium. Although providing few details, she suggested that tuition increases would produce $17.5 million per year, private fundraising would generate $7.5 million, and the remaining $25 million would come from unspecified internal reductions and increased flexibilities and efficiencies. Noting the importance of continuing to work with key internal constituencies and alumni on other items to be addressed under the new structure, she promised to work with these groups to garner their support for the separation plan.[29]

Martin's January 7 memo was followed by meetings between her staff and the governor's team throughout the month. Martin did not, though, advise Reilly, Pruitt, Spector, other regents, or System leaders of these meetings and communications with the governor's staff or of the proposed UW–Madison public authority plan. As she later explained in an e-mail message to the UW–Madison campus community, during these meetings Martin and her staff "continued working with the governor's staff on their suggested approach to UW–Madison"—meaning public authority status[30]—but she did not believe it was her prerogative to speak with the board or the System president about the governor's plan.[31] As a result, Reilly and System leaders remained uninformed of Martin's dealings with the governor's staff through much of January, even as she and her staff were at work with the governor's office preparing statutory language and other details of the separate public authority structure for UW–Madison as a part of the NBP plan.[32]

The secrecy surrounding the Walker-Martin efforts, however, began to unravel in late January and early February 2011. By this time, it was clear that Walker's biennial budget would include a major cut to the UW System, expected to be on the order of Doyle's $250 million reduction of 2003, and rumors that a bargain had been struck between Martin and the governor in which the governor promised to secure UW–Madison separation and public authority status in exchange for UW–Madison's agreeing to accept the steep anticipated budget cuts were widely circulating. On February 8, 2011, ahead of the regular February regent meeting, Pruitt and Reilly met with the governor, and Reilly followed up with a letter to him attaching his own plan for granting the flexibilities necessary for all UW System institutions, including UW–Madison, to manage effectively and maintain quality in hard financial times. Emphasizing the importance of flexibilities for the entire System, Reilly committed to working with UW–Madison and the governor's office to pursue common goals.[33] At the Board of Regents regular meeting on February 11, 2011, Reilly discussed his letter to the governor, prompting an expression of concern from regent Edmund Manydeeds that the flexibilities he understood were being proposed under Martin's NBP might mean separation and differential treatment of UW–Madison, marking a return to the premerger days of competing university systems. Referring to Reilly's February 8 letter, Martin responded to Manydeeds's concern, stating that, while the NBP didn't "aim" to treat Madison separately, "this might happen, given the lateness of the System proposal."[34]

Martin's comment confirmed the rumors that separation of the flagship from the System was under serious consideration. Angered by her failure to advise them of her communications and work with the governor's office on the issue, Reilly, Pruitt, and Spector met with her after the February regent meeting, taking her to task for her failure to keep them informed of her activities.[35] On February 15, Reilly prepared another letter to the governor, again urging that all System institutions be granted the flexibilities outlined in Reilly's letter of the previous week but arguing against any separation of UW–Madison under a new governing board.

Meanwhile, the contents of Martin's January 7 draft memo to Huebsch had been leaked to the media, revealing Martin's early support for separate public authority status for an independently governed UW-Madison, her behind-the-scenes work with the governor, the flexibilities—including full tuition-setting authority—she proposed, and her projection of a 10 percent per year tuition increase over the course of the biennium to offset cuts of $50 million in each year.[36] On February 18, the details of the separation proposal became public when the final draft bill prepared by the Legislative Reference Bureau (LRB) that would create the UW-Madison authority was released.

Prepared for incorporation in the governor's biennial budget, the draft, which drew heavily on concepts, terms, and provisions of the UWHCA statutes and the Virginia Restructuring Act of 2005, proposed creating a new public authority to operate UW-Madison, separating the flagship from the UW System and governance by the Board of Regents, and in effect undoing the 1971 merger that established the UW System. Under the proposal, all UW-Madison assets and liabilities were to be transferred from the Board of Regents to the new public authority board. Reflecting Martin's suggestion in the January 7 draft memorandum to Huebsch, this new board of trustees was to consist of twenty-one members, eleven appointed by the governor and ten appointed by UW-Madison governance groups and affiliated organizations, including faculty (2), nonfaculty staff (1), students (1), WARF (2), the Wisconsin Alumni Association (2), and the UW Foundation (2). All trustees would serve terms of three years, except the student, who would have a two-year term. Appointments to the new board would not require confirmation by the state Senate.

The proposal also included significant management flexibilities. The UW-Madison authority would receive state funds in the form of a block grant, allowing it to expend monies for any necessary institutional purposes without regard to rigid appropriation lines that had historically restricted shifting funds between programs. Other sources of university revenue, including tuition, student fees, program revenues, gifts, and grants, would be treated as "nonstate" funds and could be held in university accounts administered directly by the university, rather than state accounts, a change that would allow the university, rather than the state, to retain interest earnings on these funds. While the draft bill retained state controls of purchasing—with some exceptions for procurement of goods and services related to higher education—and capital building projects, it gave the new entity greater authority to manage the construction of buildings funded with nonstate funds. The measure also permitted the new public authority to develop and implement its own personnel system and determine its own salary structure, subject to maintaining categories of employment similar to those already in place for the UW System. The proposal also provided the new governing board with the crucial authority to set and manage tuition rates, freeing it from restrictions dictated by state budget negotiations.

On the same day that the LRB's final draft bill became public, February 18, Martin sent her e-mail to the "Campus Community," explaining how the NBP proposal had been advanced, offering her rationale for not informing the Board of Regents or Reilly of her work with the governor's office on the plan, and urging the importance of management flexibility for the flagship. Describing her contacts with Governor Walker and his staff, she expressed confidence that Governor Walker would propose public authority status for UW–Madison in his forthcoming budget bill.[37]

The following week, before his budget was to be unveiled, the governor invited Reilly and UW System chancellors other than Martin to his office to discuss the Madison separation plan. The capitol building was still under siege by Act 10 protesters, and Reilly and the chancellors, jeered by demonstrators who assumed that the members of this business-attired group were allies of the governor, needed a police escort to reach the governor's office. Once there, they were informed by Walker of his plans for the UW–Madison separation. The governor also suggested that he would eventually take similar action for their campuses, effectively dismantling the UW System. Leaving the meeting, Reilly recognized that it was "game on": public and vigorous resistance to the Walker-Martin plan would be essential if flagship separation and the ultimate dissolution of the System were to be stopped.[38]

A System Divided

The prospects for successful opposition to the separation plan were grim. With the proposal slated for inclusion in the budget and with Martin actively working to gain campus support for it, the plan appeared to have the momentum needed for approval.

Unchastened by her meeting with Pruitt, Spector, and Reilly, Martin had made it clear that she was committed to pursuing the separation idea for Madison alone and would not support modifications that would include Madison with the other UW institutions as part of a UW System public authority. Along with the governor, Martin had strong backing from DOA secretary Huebsch, who reiterated the administration's determination to proceed with the plan. When news of Martin's failure to inform the board and Reilly of her independent negotiations with the governor led to speculation that the board might dismiss her for insubordination, Huebsch warned Reilly that these rumors were "disturbing," telling him that the budget was written and would go out with the "Madison spinoff" provisions.[39] The regents, however, were firmly opposed to the separation plan, and Pruitt, having spoken with each of them individually, concluded that the best chance of preventing the split was to force a public discussion of the plan's merits and its impact on the System as a whole. To that end, Pruitt called a special session of the Board of Regents for February 25, 2011, and by letter of February 22, Reilly invited Martin to attend and address these issues.[40]

In advance of the meeting, Martin stepped up her efforts to rally support for the separation proposal, meeting with the *Milwaukee Journal Sentinel* editorial board to defend the plan and securing the endorsement of former UW–Madison chancellor Donna Shalala, who promoted the public authority idea in a guest editorial in the *Wisconsin State Journal* on February 23, 2011. Although former System president Robert M. O'Neil and former UW–Madison chancellor John Wiley raised concerns about the plan,[41] Martin had additional backing from alumni, UW–Madison officials, and members of the boards of WARF, the UW Foundation, and the Wisconsin Alumni Association who affirmed their support for her leadership in a well-coordinated February 24 letter-writing campaign directed to the Board of Regents and to Reilly.

This flurry of activity was followed by the special regent meeting on February 25 to discuss UW–Madison's potential separation. The atmosphere was tense. The location had been moved to the UW–Extension's Pyle Center rather than the board's usual Van Hise Hall meeting room to accommodate more attendees, and there was an overflow crowd, most there to support Martin, who received a standing ovation on her arrival.[42] The protests over Act 10 were continuing less than a mile away at the state capitol, and concerns about the effects of the collective bargaining legislation—not yet passed at that point, with the Democratic state senators still in Illinois—on UW employees in general and on UW–Madison employees in particular if the flagship were to be separated from the System were also in the background. Looming over all was the threat of the possible $250 million budget cut to the System. The uncertainty and anxiety in the room were palpable.

Opening the meeting, Pruitt emphasized that its purpose was not to have a political debate or to conduct a hearing but to begin a much deeper conversation about the separation of UW–Madison and the creation of a public authority and the impact of such a change on the citizens of the state. No official action or resolutions would be considered, he said, and he asked that the meeting remain focused on the separation issue, calling on Martin to begin the discussion. Reviewing her consistent support of management flexibilities for all UW System institutions, Martin argued that, in the urgent budget circumstances, flexibilities were more critical than ever and that public authority status as provided under the LRB draft legislation offered the tools essential for UW–Madison to manage the cuts that were likely to be included in the governor's biennial budget. She further maintained that separating UW–Madison from the System would not harm other System institutions, describing public authority status as an "extraordinary opportunity" for UW–Madison that should not be missed.

Board members then posed a series of questions and comments, pressing Martin on both the chronology of her interactions with the governor in developing the public authority structure and the substance of the proposal. Martin again acknowledged, as she had in her February 18 e-mail message to the campus, that she had withheld information about her dealings with the governor from board and System leaders, saying that she thought the governor's office had been keeping System leaders informed and reiterating that she felt it was not her prerogative to share the governor's proposals with them. Professor Judith Burstyn, chair of the UW–Madison University Committee, confirmed that Martin had told her committee in early January that public authority status for UW–Madison was under consideration and that Martin's legal staff was drafting statutory language for the governor to include in the budget bill. Martin had asked the University Committee's advice regarding the essential governance principles that should be included in a public authority structure but told them that, at that stage, confidentiality about the proposal was crucial and that they were not to tell anyone. UW–Madison provost Paul DeLuca went on to maintain during the course of the board meeting that UW–Madison still could not release details about the proposed statutory language to the board and System leaders because it did not "own" the draft legislation.

As the discussion continued, however, the focus shifted from the secrecy surrounding development of the proposal and Martin's lack of candor about her dealings with the governor to the merits of UW–Madison's separation from the System as a public authority. Although the exact details of the proposal would not be known until the governor's budget was introduced—at this point it was scheduled for release the next week—its broad outlines were understood from the LRB's draft bill, Martin's own description of the NBP, and the information provided by Walker at his recent meeting with System chancellors. As a result, board members and other speakers at the meeting directed their comments to the implications of the "split" for public higher education in the state, the public authority governance structure that had been suggested, and the more general need for flexibilities.

Many board members and others who spoke at the meeting, echoing comments in news reports about the proposal,[43] worried about the consequences of removing the flagship from the UW System and risking a return to the problems of premerger days. The 1971 merger had been driven in large part by concerns about competition for resources and program duplication between two separate state higher education organizations. The merged UW System had successfully dealt with these problems, protecting UW–Madison, with its small legislative delegation, against competition for resources from other campuses and their more numerous state representatives, limiting undergraduate program duplication and the proliferation of graduate programs at nondoctoral UW institutions, and providing a unified budget allocation process that recognized the differing needs of different types of institutions. Separation of UW–Madison from the System, they warned, could bring a reprise of these old problems, with renewed competition that could damage Madison along with all the other UW institutions.

Other speakers worried about the reputational damage to UW System institutions that might occur if, as UW–Oshkosh chancellor Richard Wells put it, the flagship "sailed away." At the time of the 1971 merger, Lucey had recognized the value of extending the UW brand to all state universities, and the importance of including "UW" in their names. Regent Tom Loftus alluded facetiously to the problems UW–Madison's separation might create for institutional names, but the larger threat was the loss of reputation that could result from severing the ties between the flagship and the other System institutions.

In addition to these problems, as several UW System chancellors noted, the separation raised the issue of differential treatment. The need for management flexibilities to deal with budget cuts was not limited to UW–Madison but, as the UW System and regents had repeatedly argued, extended to all UW institutions. As these speakers noted, there was no substantive reason why, if all institutions needed flexibilities, they shouldn't all move forward together with the kind of Systemwide flexibilities plan advanced by Reilly in his February letters to the governor or even public authority status for the entire UW System. There seemed to be no compelling rationale for separating UW–Madison if essential flexibilities could be made available to all UW System institutions.

Other commentators questioned whether the public authority structure had been adequately studied in the context of either the UW System or UW–Madison. The Walker-Martin plan as reflected in the LRB's final draft legislation was an amalgam of the UWHCA and Virginia Restructuring Act governance models, but it had been proposed without the lengthy, multiyear public vetting that had preceded the creation of the UWHCA. Although the UWHCA had been successful, simply grafting the UWHCA structure onto UW–Madison or the UW System would not necessarily produce a governance structure appropriate for a university or a university system, given the fundamentally different missions of these enterprises and the fact—pointed out by regent Walsh—that the UWHCA, unlike UW–Madison and UW System institutions, receives no direct state funding. As Walsh also observed, any public authority is a creature of state law, with its powers defined and limited by state statutes to reflect the unique purposes and needs of that entity. Care in developing the elements included in any authority's proposed statutory charter is therefore essential.

The application of the Virginia model to the Wisconsin situation also raised questions. Virginia's public higher education structure differs from Wisconsin's in crucial ways, including its larger size and the historical independence of its more numerous institutions, which had long been governed by separate boards of trustees. The 2005 Virginia Restructuring Act relied heavily on the ability of these independent boards to gain full tuition-setting authority as the means of balancing losses in state funding. The Virginia model did not appear to fit well in the context of Wisconsin's historic higher education organizational structures and, more important, gave rise to concerns about major tuition hikes that could drive the de facto privatization of the state's public universities.[44] As the discussion at the board meeting revealed, full tuition-setting authority was the essential ingredient of the public authority structure being proposed by Walker and Martin. Asked by regent Walsh if she would support the proposal without this authority, Martin said that she would not, because "this would not be a public authority."[45] Full tuition-setting authority was the sine qua non of the UW–Madison public authority proposal because, in the end, only full tuition authority could give the university sufficient revenue-generating capacity to offset major cuts in state funds. While private giving and donations from supporting foundations might provide critical added support, especially at UW–Madison, amounts from such sources fluctuate and gifts are often restricted to donor-directed purposes, leaving tuition as the primary source of funds to balance state funding cuts. No other management flexibility or combination of management flexibilities could produce as much income as tuition, a fact that had been pointed out in all the System studies, from *Planning the Future* to *Charting a New Course*, that had argued the importance of management flexibilities.[46] Martin herself, in her January 7 memorandum to Huebsch, had not been able to identify any specific set of flexibilities that would produce as much in savings as tuition increases would generate in revenue.

Granting full tuition-setting power to the proposed UW–Madison public authority, however, virtually ensured that there would be steep hikes in tuition to offset the state's declining contributions to university support. As Martin had indicated in her January memo to Huebsch, tuition increases of around 10 percent in each year of the biennium would be needed to deal with a $50 million annual cut to UW–Madison, and, with the power to continue raising tuition in the hands of an independent authority, those increases might only be expected to grow. Students and others at the meeting worried about the financial burdens of an immediate tuition increase, as well as the long-term threat of constant increases that could eventually turn the flagship into a semiprivate institution accessible only to the affluent few. These were the kinds of problems also pointed out by Lyall and Sell in their 2006 book warning of the dangers of replacing state funds with tuition[47] and echoed by former UW–Madison chancellor John Wiley, who had warned just a week before the board meeting that UW–Madison could become an elitist institution for the rich if tuition were to rise dramatically to make up for major losses in state support.[48]

Saving the Union

The lengthy February 25 meeting and discussion concluded, as Pruitt had promised, without formal action. The questions, comments, and concerns that had emerged, however, framed the arguments for and against the separation and the public authority plan. With the release and formal introduction of the governor's budget, 2011 Senate Bill 27 (later, 2011 Wisconsin Act 32), the week after the meeting, battle lines were clearly drawn. As anticipated, when introduced, Walker's budget proposed a $250 million cut to the UW System, with some $125 million to come from UW–Madison and the rest to be absorbed by the other System institutions. The bill included the public authority provisions essentially as set out in the LRB draft legislation, providing for the creation of a separate UW–Madison, governed by its own board of trustees and having full tuition-setting authority and other flexibilities. Following introduction of the budget, Martin resumed her active campaign for the separation, again calling on faculty, staff, students, alumni, and supporting foundation for support and enlisting the additional help of a group of powerful— mainly Republican—lobbyists led by Brandon Scholz, organized as the "Badger Advocates."[49]

Meanwhile, at its March 10, 2011, meeting, the Board of Regents discussed the budget and Reilly presented the Wisconsin Idea Partnership, an alternative plan that extended the Walker-Martin management flexibilities to all System institutions under delegated authority from the board and UW System administration, while keeping UW–Madison in the UW System. Martin attended the meeting and again defended the UW–Madison separation proposal, but the conversation was becoming much less polite. Martin complained about the disrespectful tone—"smug snottiness," in her words—that she believed had been directed at her since the unveiling of the separation proposal.[50] Reilly objected to the characterization, and the discussion proceeded, but the growing antagonism between Martin and UW System leadership was obvious. Equally plain were the worries of Martin's chancellor colleagues as they described the problems the separation plan would cause for their institutions in dealing with the proposed budget cuts. After hearing comments on Reilly's Wisconsin Idea Partnership, the board adopted a resolution urging amendment of Walker's budget bill to provide all UW institutions the management flexibilities proposed for UW–Madison but within the board's current governance and statutory framework. The resolution also recommended further study of alternative governance structures, including public authority status for the entire System, and concluded by warning of the risks of splitting up a UW System that had served the state well for the past forty years.[51]

Despite this action and the concerns expressed by the chancellors at the March board meeting, there continued to be rumors that some UW chancellors supported Martin's split plan. With Reilly's approval, UW–Stout's Charles Sorenson organized a dinner meeting of all UW chancellors except Martin to discuss the separation proposal and Reilly's alternative, the Wisconsin Idea Partnership. At this dinner, also attended by Pruitt and Reilly, Sorenson reminded the group of the board's resolution opposing the Walker-Martin proposal. Pruitt, pointing out the dangers posed by the Madison separation, emphasized the need to unite if they were to prevent passage of the measure. Speaking bluntly, he told the group that it was time to choose one side or the other in the debate, saying, "There are two jerseys here— Madison versus System—pick your jersey."[52] It proved to be a clarifying moment. By the time of the board's April 2011 meeting, thirteen of fourteen UW System chancellors had endorsed the Wisconsin Idea Partnership, signing a letter supporting the plan and opposing the Walker-Martin split. With support from the UW chancellors secured, the board and the UW System began their own lobbying efforts to convince legislators to stop the UW–Madison separation, emphasizing the damaging impact it might have on the smaller System schools and the potential for rapidly rising tuition at the flagship.

As the board, System leaders, and chancellors united behind the Wisconsin Idea Partnership alternative, political support for the Walker-Martin separation proposal began to collapse. Signs of legislative opposition had appeared in late February, with Representative Steve Nass's vow to "oppose the legislation vigorously." Nass, chair of the Assembly Colleges and Universities Committee and a frequent critic of the UW System, echoed the concerns expressed by regents and others that separation would lead to higher tuition, preventing low- and middle-income students from attending the flagship.[53] Reservations from other legislators emerged in late March, as the Joint Finance Committee began its deliberations on the budget. Following appearances before the committee by Reilly, as well as Martin and other System chancellors, Republican Senator Luther Olsen urged System and UW–Madison leaders to work together on a flexibilities plan.

Although there were meetings in late March and early April between Reilly's staff and Martin's concerning how the NBP and Wisconsin Idea Partnership proposals could be melded in a unified plan for flexibilities to help manage the governor's proposed $250 million budget cuts, Martin continued to insist on the need for UW–Madison's immediate separation. Around April 1, she contacted other UW System chancellors, inviting them to discuss amendments to the budget that would add flexibilities for their campuses, but without any change to the budget's plan for separating UW–Madison as a public authority. Martin's unwillingness to compromise on this issue and her continued advocacy for the separation plan were further confirmed when, on April 6, 2011, she issued a "call for action" to her faculty, staff, and students, arguing that public authority status and separation were essential for UW–Madison and urging them to communicate their support for the NBP and the split proposal directly to the Joint Finance Committee.[54] The next day, in advance of the board's April meeting, she informed Reilly, Pruitt, and Spector via e-mail of her intent to persevere in seeking adoption of the separation proposal presented in Walker's budget.[55] As Martin's communications made plain, there would be no compromise on the separation proposal, and further attempts to modify the plan on the part of System officials would be futile. Meeting in Platteville on April 7, the board affirmed its support for Reilly's plan, emphasizing the need for the System to speak with one voice on the issue and criticizing Martin's attempts to convince the chancellors to support her.[56]

With Martin's growing isolation from the rest of the System's leadership, it was becoming clear that the separation proposal was likely to fail. Legislative support for the idea faded as concerns about the Walker-Martin proposal grew. Neither the governor nor Martin had articulated a compelling reason for separating UW–Madison from the System or for proceeding with a public authority structure that had not been thoroughly studied. They had responded to the concerns raised about the proposal by insisting that it would benefit the flagship but without fully explaining how. In the end, their failure to make a persuasive case for the plan confirmed what skeptics had long suggested: that it was a Faustian bargain giving the governor UW–Madison's agreement to accept a $125 million budget cut, the chancellor independence from the System and the "freedom" to raise tuition, and allowing them together to name a new board of trustees that they would control. With full tuition-setting authority the essential ingredient of the deal, however, it was unacceptable to legislators like Nass, who worried about its impact on their constituents, and to others who had not been consulted or informed about the separation proposal. It was also unpopular with citizens concerned about a semiprivate, more exclusive, more expensive UW–Madison that was less likely to admit their children. Although the plan was bold, it had arrived without the benefit of thorough analysis and with little consideration of the risks to students and families from spiraling tuition costs or of the potential harm to UW system institutions other than the flagship. The poor preparation reflected the inexperience and hubris of its proponents, while the emphasis on management flexibility as the principal solution to the System's funding problems distracted from the more serious issue of the long-term decline in taxpayer support for public higher education.

As the *Capital Times* noted in May 2011, "the Walker-Martin plan is apparently going nowhere, slowly and with great fanfare."[57] In early June, during budget deliberations in the legislature, the separation–public authority proposal was deleted from the bill, without a single vote in favor of retaining it in the measure. On June 14, just days after this defeat, Martin announced her resignation to accept the presidency of Amherst College. The budget, now 2011 Wisconsin Act 32, was officially completed and signed into law by the governor on June 26, 2011.

Although the UW System had survived intact, the battle over the separation and public authority idea brought longer-term damage to the System. The biennial budget approved by the legislature included the governor's requested cut of $125,125,000 to the UW System for each year of the biennium, for a total of $250,250,000 over the two-year period, forcing all UW institutions to manage major reductions. The System administration budget, too, was slashed—by 25 percent—greatly diminishing its capacity to provide Systemwide services. The bill also created a Special Task Force on UW Restructuring and Operational Flexibilities, leaving the door open to a renewal of efforts to de-merge the System. The Act did provide some of the management flexibilities that had been sought for all UW institutions: state appropriations to the System would be in the form of "block grants," and the System was given greater control of program revenues; undergraduate resident tuition was allowed to rise 5.5 percent in each year of the biennium; the UW–Madison chancellor received authorization to develop a new personnel system for UW–Madison employees, while the Board of Regents was granted similar authority to establish a personnel system for other UW System employees, both subject to approval by the legislature's Joint Committee on Employment Relations; and some additional relaxation of construction and purchasing requirements was also granted. The stubborn underlying problem remained, though. The flexibilities granted were not adequate to offset continuing losses in state taxpayer funding, quality remained threatened, and the state's contribution to the support of its public universities continued its steady decline.

The divisive struggle between Martin and the rest of the System over separation and the public authority brought other problems, too. Martin's insistence on UW–Madison's separation revived old tensions over the 1971 merger and created painful internal divisions within the System and within UW–Madison itself. Her secret dealings with the governor on the proposal damaged her own credibility, undermined Reilly's leadership, and fostered distrust on the part of state government toward the System and System institutions. Martin would depart, leaving a troubled legacy. The erosion of System leadership and cohesion resulting from the failed separation plan jeopardized the stability and future success of an organization that, despite its achievements, faced continuing struggles in the increasingly hostile environment for state higher education.

Following Martin's resignation, the board and Reilly asked former UW–Madison chancellor David Ward to return as interim chancellor, while a search for the permanent chancellor could be conducted. His return would do much to restore calm and heal divisions within the flagship and to repair relations with the Board of Regents and other System leaders. The winds of change that came with the Walker administration and the flagship separation plan, though, would continue to blow.

11

Punitive Damage

The defeat of Walker's budget proposal to separate UW–Madison from the UW System as an independent public authority came at a high cost both financially and politically. The System had been preserved but faced an immediate $250 million budget cut, while alternative forms of System governance, including the public authority status, remained under consideration by the Special Task Force on UW Restructuring and Operations Flexibilities created in the biennial budget bill. Throughout 2011 and 2012, as Reilly and System leaders dealt with the System's punishing budget cuts, they worked to redefine the governance roles of the Board of Regents and System administration and to evaluate other potential structural changes in System organization. These efforts, however, occurred against the background of the state's deepening political divisions. Anger over the passage of Act 10 led to an attempt, in 2012, to recall Walker, heightening partisanship in an already poisonous political environment and making it even more difficult for Reilly and the remaining Doyle appointees on the Board of Regents to work effectively with the state's Republican leadership. Managing in the face of these problems left little capacity for developing new education programs or building on older efforts. Although in late 2102 Reilly launched an innovative new "Flexible Option" degree program allowing individuals to earn baccalaureate degrees on the basis of a combination of life experiences and formal college credits, this success was quickly overshadowed by a controversy over the System's reserve balances that brought a punitive $200 million cut to the System budget and a tuition freeze that inflicted even deeper damage on the state's struggling public higher education enterprise.

Budget Fallout, 2011–13

Restructuring Redux

The approval of the 2011–13 biennial budget, 2011 Wisconsin Act 32 ("Act 32"), in June 2011 left the UW System and its institutions to deal with massive cuts and the lingering internal tensions from the UW–Madison separation battle. The grim financial situation worsened later in the year, as the System was forced to lapse an additional $174 million to the state treasury in October 2011. Although former chancellor David Ward's return to head UW–Madison on an interim basis restored confidence in leadership at the flagship and began to repair some of the internal divisions left in the wake of Martin's departure, the flagship, like all other UW institutions, confronted major budget challenges. Throughout the year, chancellors and other institutional leaders reported regularly to the board on steps they were forced to take to manage the budget cuts.

In addition to the serious and immediate financial problems left by Act 32, the bill posed longer-term threats to the System's organizational effectiveness. The legislation included a direct attack on central leadership, slashing the System administration budget by 25 percent and requiring staff cuts of fifty-one full-time equivalent positions out of two hundred, while it kept alive ongoing efforts to restructure the System through the work of the Special Task Force. The magnitude of the System administration cuts and the loss of staff significantly impaired the System's capacity to maintain previous levels of policy support to the board or to provide services to UW institutions, forcing an immediate assessment of what functions central leadership could or should continue going forward. Reacting to the cuts, the board approved the appointment of an Advisory Committee on Roles of System Administration to advise Reilly on potential changes in the structure, functions, and support of System administration, given the System administration's mission, as well as the funding reductions and new flexibilities provided in the biennial budget. Chaired by Pruitt, whose term as board president ended in June, the committee included several current regents, former board president Jay Smith, chancellors, and System administration staff and was facilitated by an experienced higher education leader, consultant and former UW–Superior chancellor Terrence MacTaggart.[1]

The advisory committee's report, presented at the September 2011 board meeting, proposed what Pruitt described as a new model for leadership throughout the System. Describing the approach, Pruitt emphasized that it was based on the assumption that governance of all institutions in the UW System would remain with the Board of Regents, maintaining the established leadership roles of the regents, the System president, and System administration, while honoring historic commitments to quality, affordable access, and the Wisconsin Idea and continuing to advance newer policy initiatives such as the *Growth Agenda* and *Inclusive Excellence*. Given the budget-imposed financial constraints and pressures to shift management authority from central administrative authority to institutions, however, the Pruitt committee model significantly narrowed the roles and activities of central leaders, delegating greater operational authority to UW institutions and chancellors. The plan envisioned a role for the Board of Regents focused on what the committee identified as the board's critical functions: advocating for strong state investment in the UW System and Systemwide initiatives like the *Growth Agenda*; providing for the effective transfer of students within the UW System; incentivizing collaboration among UW institutions; ensuring accountability; and setting tuition rates to ensure access to high-quality education. The System administration itself, the committee recommended, should concentrate its efforts on providing services to UW institutions that involve interpreting, training, monitoring, advocating, and consulting, while streamlining or abandoning academic program regulation. Although the report endorsed the Wisconsin Idea Partnership plan developed in response to the UW–Madison separation proposal and urged Reilly to continue advocating for more independence from state regulations and more management flexibilities for the UW System, it recommended that most new authorities and flexibilities granted to the System be delegated from that level directly to individual UW institutions. The report also recommended that Reilly explore the benefits and drawbacks of creating institutional-level governing boards—a controversial element of the UW–Madison public authority proposal that was based on Virginia's higher education structure—as a means of improving advocacy for individual UW campuses. Although the Pruitt committee affirmed the importance of single-board governance of the entire UW System and the values of quality, access, and the Wisconsin Idea, the decentralized structure it proposed was a distinct departure from the unified, cohesive central leadership model that had characterized the mature System.

Despite the diminished role for his administration proposed by the Pruitt committee report, Reilly had little choice but to adopt its recommendations as he implemented the budget cuts and sought to address preemptively organizational issues that were slated to be considered by the state's Special Task Force on System restructuring. At the September 2011 board meeting, Reilly requested board approval of his plans, developed in response to the committee report, to manage internal staff changes in the System administration, involve UW chancellors more actively in Systemwide policy development, and delegate or "devolve" administrative authority to UW institutions. Outlining his plans, Reilly described a national trend, reported by the National Center for Higher Education Management Systems (NCHEMS) but also manifested in Wisconsin's own 2011–13 biennial budget, of states asking their public higher education systems to shift central administrative activities away from institutional management and control and toward a focus on connecting public higher education to the needs of the states. Reilly's proposal sought to respond to this newer approach, involving chancellors directly in communications with the board between meetings and adding several chancellors to his own System administration "cabinet" of senior executive staff members. He also committed to study the idea of establishing institutional-level advisory boards for UW campuses and outlined his plans for restructuring the System administration's academic program review process, changes in internal operations audits, and a more targeted approach to the UW System's investment in economic development.

The Pruitt committee's recommendations and Reilly's plans prompted a lengthy discussion at the September 2011 board meeting that elicited various concerns about the devolution of central System authority. Board members expressed reservations about what some saw as a too rapid or too radical move to decentralize. Regent Walsh commented that the System must be centralized, not balkanized, to enable it to respond quickly to new, unforeseen challenges. Regent Tony Evers, State Superintendent of Public Instruction, urged care in implementing Reilly's plan, warning, on the basis of his K–12 experiences, that decentralization can lead to poor results, including inconsistent quality and duplication of services. Interim UW–Madison chancellor David Ward, who had recently served as president of the American Council on Education (ACE), observed that, while many systems across the nation were thinking about how to create a more "federated," campus-based structure, there was still a need for overall coordination and interinstitutional collaboration on key Systemwide issues such as student transfers. Faced with fiscal realities and the policy direction suggested in the budget bill, however, the board endorsed the Pruitt committee's approach and Reilly's implementation plan.[2]

As the board and Reilly proceeded with implementing these internal plans, the Special Task Force created under the budget bill began its work. This group, created in response to the collapse of Walker's plan to separate the flagship from the UW System, was charged, under the budget legislation, with considering a range of questions that had been discussed in the debate over the separation plan. Among the issues to be reviewed were whether there was a need to restructure the UW System and, if so, how the new structure should be organized; how UW–Madison and UW System employees would transition to the nonstate personnel systems to be established under Act 32; whether tuition-setting authority could be extended to the UW System and what role the legislature should have in tuition-setting; how compensation plans for UW System employees should be set; additional operational flexibilities that could be provided to UW System institutions; and how credit transfer could be improved.[3] Chaired by regent Michael Falbo and advised by Dr. Aims McGuinness, an expert in higher education management systems from NCHEMS, the Special Task Force included legislators, former regents, current and past UW System chancellors and administrators, and other UW System stakeholders.[4] Originally required to report to the legislature on its work by January 1, 2012—a deadline later extended to January 1, 2013—the Special Task Force began meeting on December 7, 2011.

Anticipating that System leaders would be actively engaged in the deliberations of the Special Task Force, regent Michael Spector, who had succeeded Pruitt as board president, at the October 2011 board meeting appointed several ad hoc committees to elaborate on structural and governance matters likely to come before the Special Task Force. He named committees to "commit to writing" the board's key functions and responsibilities going forward and to examine how best to meet them; to evaluate internal board organization and consider whether new board standing committees might be needed; and to review governance structures at other university systems, including the idea of establishing institutional-level boards.[5]

The work of Spector's committees and Reilly's own related restructuring plans were well under way as the Special Task Force held its first meeting, on December 7, 2011. The following day, at the board's regular December meeting, Falbo reported that the Special Task Force would emphasize maintaining accessibility in terms of cost while controlling the System's need for state revenues as it addressed the issues within its charge.[6] At the Task Force's 2012 meetings, UW System leaders kept the group fully apprised of their own internal postbudget restructuring efforts, as well as the work of Spector's ad hoc committees. By early 2012, the Spector committees had produced reports on several key governance questions also slated for consideration by the Special Task Force. Reviewing the benefits of institution-level boards, Spector's committee on System governance recommended that the Board of Regents retain primary governance authority but supported the creation of institutional advisory boards at all UW campuses. The ad hoc committee on board responsibilities proposed establishing a new standing board committee, the Research, Economic Development, and Innovation (REDI) committee, to focus new attention on the System's role in improving the state's economy. Details on the management of the System administration budget cuts and implementation of the recommendations of the Pruitt committee, including Reilly's planned devolution of greater management authority to System institutions, were also provided to the Special Task Force. In addition, System officials reported on the support services offered by System administration to UW institutions, made suggestions for additional management flexibilities needed to improve System effectiveness in the areas of building projects and procurement, and proposed further work on cost containment and the development of the new UW–Madison and UW System personnel systems authorized under the 2011–13 biennial budget.[7]

The Special Task Force report, completed in August 2012,[8] recognized and incorporated much of the proactive work completed by the board and System administration. Resolving the crucial governance question raised by the Walker plan to separate UW–Madison from the System, the Special Task Force affirmed that the UW System established by the 1971 merger should remain intact, under the governance of a single Board of Regents. While recommending that chancellors be given discretion to establish institution-level boards, the Special Task Force stipulated that these groups would be advisory, not governing, bodies. The Special Task Force also endorsed granting some of the additional management flexibilities sought by the board and System and made other specific recommendations regarding personnel matters and transfer issues consistent with board and System requests. Although it did not make a recommendation on the issue of tuition-setting authority, the report contained a detailed description of the Special Task Force's deliberations on the issue, noting the legislature's ultimate power to limit board authority in this area and encouraging the System to work on a tuition-setting plan with the legislature.[9]

The conclusions of the Special Task Force provided important support for keeping the merged UW System intact and for retaining the Board of Regents as its governing body. The changes in management structure and the devolution of authority to UW institutions approved by the board and the System in the immediate aftermath of the 2011–13 budget and encouraged by the Special Task Force, however, were a clear departure from the organizational framework that had evolved following the 1971 merger and that had supported the successes of the mature System of the early 2000s. The dramatic shift to decentralization and delegation of management authority to UW institutions undermined central coordination and oversight of Systemwide initiatives, while the board's own narrower focus further limited its role in the development of statewide higher education programs and its ability to respond to state higher education needs. These internal changes, along with the encouragement of institution-level advisory boards and a new statutory requirement that the board include at least one representative from each of the state's congressional districts,[10] suggested a return to the kind of loosely coordinated System organizational structure preferred by the former WSU institutions at the time of merger. While the pressure for restructuring in the aftermath of the failed UW–Madison separation plan and the need to adapt in a time of severe budget challenges had driven these changes, the board's new leadership model risked a recurrence of the old, premerger problems of poor coordination, competition, and program duplication. It also threatened the loss of key benefits of "systemness":[11] System-wide policy cohesion, a unified voice in dealing with state government leadership, the capacity to ensure the provision of core programs and services throughout the System in times of financial need,[12] and the board's ability to fulfill its critical mission in planning and advocating for the future needs of state public higher education. While the UW System had survived the 2011 de-merger effort, the weakening of its central leadership authority that followed began a more insidious piecemeal dissolution of the union.

Politics and Partisanship

As the board and System efforts to respond to the 2011–13 biennial budget cuts and the related budget-driven governance and restructuring continued through 2011 and 2012, the state's political conflicts continued to churn in the background. Anger over the passage of Act 10 and its assault on collective bargaining rights prompted an effort to recall the governor in 2012. Organizers began circulating the required petitions in late 2011, and the recall process was officially initiated on November 15, 2011.[13] Following a May 8, 2012, Democratic primary, Milwaukee mayor Tom Barrett was nominated to face Walker in the recall election, which took place June 5, 2012. Barrett, who had lost to Walker in the 2010 general election, was again defeated, making Walker the first governor in the nation to beat back a recall attempt and solidifying his political strength in the state. The victory, achieved in the midst of a presidential contest that saw the reelection of

Barack Obama in November, raised Walker's national profile, fueling speculation about his own prospects as a presidential candidate in 2016. Buoyed by his new prominence, Walker, in a speech at the Reagan Presidential Library in November 2012, touted his previous efforts to reduce benefits for public workers and outlined an even more conservative legislative agenda for Wisconsin, including implementing deep tax cuts and tying UW System funding to UW's success in meeting state-imposed performance measures.[14]

The passage of Act 10 and the recall election had fractured the state along partisan lines, however, and Walker's emphasis on pressing ahead with this conservative agenda further deepened these divisions. Walker had successfully mined a vein of public anger at institutions—including state government and the UW System—perceived to be elitist or disconnected from the lives of ordinary citizens to build support for Act 10 and, later, to withstand the recall bid. Although in the 2010 gubernatorial election he had not campaigned on a program of cutting state employee benefits or eliminating collective bargaining rights for state employees, he had characterized state workers as "haves" and others as "have nots" in talking about the importance of reducing health insurance benefits for teachers and other public employees to balance the state budget.[15] In doing so, he had struck a chord of antigovernment, antistate-employee resentment, fully documented and analyzed by UW–Madison professor Katherine Cramer in research papers and in her subsequent book *The Politics of Resentment*,[16] that drew approval for his agenda from those viewing Act 10 as a reasonable check on state government and overpaid government employees.[17] Walker's successful exploitation[18] of these attitudes and his embrace of an aggressively conservative legislative agenda following the 2012 recall election fueled the steadily growing political polarization in the state's political environment.

As former state senator Cullen observed, partisanship in state politics had been growing gradually since the 1970s, but the state's political leaders had largely adhered to a kind of "containment" policy, governing from either a center-right or center-left philosophy that kept party extremes under control and emphasized compromise and collaboration.[19] His assessment was widely shared by state leaders from both parties, including

Doyle, Thompson, and Loftus.[20] This centrist approach, however, essentially ended with Walker's introduction of Act 10
and its subsequent passage by the Republican-controlled legislature. Approval of that act, which was based on the legislative
agenda of the American Legislative Exchange Council (ALEC),[21]
a corporate-funded national conservative group that Walker had
frequently supported during his time in the state legislature,[22]
upended not only long-standing state labor laws and practices
but also the kind of pragmatic, middle-of-the-road containment
philosophy described by Cullen. Legislative compromise had
become virtually impossible, as policy modeled on partisan out-
of-state organizations was imposed on Wisconsin in a top-down,
nonparticipatory manner. Supported by a Republican-controlled
legislature and pursuing his own presidential ambitions, Walker
appeared to have little interest in bridging the state's widening
political divide. His November 2012 speech in California gave a
clear indication of his intention to continue a more partisan, ideo-
logically driven approach to state leadership.

For the UW System, the speech had direct policy implications. While Walker had been vague about UW System policy
during the 2010 gubernatorial campaign, the 2012 California
speech signaled his intention to pursue further changes to Wisconsin higher education operations and funding derived from the
agendas of national conservative organizations. His reference to
performance-based funding suggested his interest in tying public
higher education funding to state-dictated performance measures as a means of tightening state control. The idea of requiring
public universities to meet state-approved accountability standards in exchange for greater institutional autonomy had been
discussed approvingly in WPRI's December 2010 report on re-
making the UW System's structure and by Aims McGuinness in
connection with the work of the Special Task Force.[23] It was also
a feature of the Virginia Restructuring Act, a model for the failed
UW–Madison public authority proposal, and had been recommended in ALEC model legislation for K–12 public education
and state two-year postsecondary institutions.[24] Walker's California speech hinted at performance-based funding as the direction
of changes that might be in store for the UW System.

Change was also coming to the Board of Regents, as Walker
appointees began to replace Doyle members and contests for

board leadership offices in 2011 and 2012 took on a more overtly partisan tone. Signs of internal conflict surfaced with the board's June 2011 meeting. Under the board's bylaws, the June meeting is the annual session at which board officers are elected for the following year.[25] Officer terms last one year, but the usual practice is for board presidents to have two such terms, after which they are succeeded by the board vice president. In keeping with this tradition, in June 2011 Spector, Pruitt's vice president, had been elected board president, leaving a vacancy for the vice presidency. Falbo, though a Doyle appointee, was a Republican, and he expected that, with his ability to offer a stronger connection between the board and the Republican governor and legislature, he was the logical choice to become board vice president and then Spector's successor as president. Although he was nominated for the position, however, he was challenged by regent Brent Smith, a Doyle appointee who had been nominated by regent Edmund Manydeeds. With Doyle Democrats still retaining a board majority, Smith defeated Falbo on a 12–5 vote that put Smith, as the new vice president, in the traditional line to succeed Spector as board president.[26]

When Spector's term as a regent ended in 2012, making him ineligible for the usual second term as board president, the conflict between Falbo and Smith was renewed in the context of the election for the board presidency. Although custom suggested that Smith would be chosen to follow Spector as president at the June 2012 board meeting, when Smith was nominated for the presidency, he was challenged by Falbo. By this time, new Walker appointees had replaced several of the Doyle Democrats,[27] opening the door to a departure from the usual succession practice. The vote, by secret ballot,[28] resulted in a 9–9 tie, forcing a second ballot and then a third, all producing the same 9–9 deadlock. The impasse was not resolved until regent Gerald Whitburn, one of the recent Walker appointees, a former DOA secretary, and a long-time Republican party leader, moved the election of a "slate" of officers consisting of Smith for president and Falbo as vice president, with the tacit agreement that Falbo would succeed Smith the following year.[29] While this action resolved the immediate conflict, the two leadership elections were politically charged contests that strained collegiality. While board membership inevitably changes as one governor's appointees are rather quickly

replaced by his or her successor's, the turnover in board leadership is normally slower—Doyle's use of the opportunity to replace four regents immediately on coming to office in 2003 being
a notable exception—allowing for smoother, more gradual leadership transitions. The pressure for more rapid leadership turnover in the contested elections of 2011 and 2012, however, was
undisguisedly partisan and, against the background of the state's
painful political turmoil, heightened the politicization of System
governance.

Some Hopeful Signs

Despite the lingering fallout from the budget and political upheavals of 2011, there were, by the end of 2012, some hopeful signs
for the future of the UW System, on both the policy and the financial fronts. Not surprisingly, the System's distracting and
damaging fight over the UW–Madison separation proposal, the
ensuing loss of funds, and the weakening of central policy leadership had brought new program development to a virtual standstill. With central leadership focusing primarily on managing
cuts and responding to the pressure to reconsider System structure and governance, there was a dearth of new program activity,
while further work on older programs such as the *Growth Agenda*
slowed through most of 2011 and early 2012.

There was, however, one important exception. In late 2012,
Reilly unveiled what he would later count as one of the most
important developments of his presidency[30]—a new "flexible
degree" program, designed to afford working adults and other
nontraditional students a pathway to earning a college degree on
the basis of an assessment of their formal educational attainments
and the competencies they had gained in their career and life
experiences. Demonstrating the value of a unified system in fostering collaborative endeavors, the program was intended to involve all UW System institutions. It was led initially by Dr. Aaron
Brower, vice provost for teaching and learning at UW–Madison,
who was serving in a second role as interim provost at UW–
Extension, and by Dr. John Koker, dean of the College of Letters
and Sciences at UW–Oshkosh. The idea was to create what Brower
described as a "portfolio" degree program centered around essential degree competencies, strong student advising, assessment

measures, and innovative, faculty-developed curricula.[31] By December 2012, Brower reported that the program, renamed the
UW Flexible Degree Option, or "UW Flex," had begun operating,
with its first student cohorts entering UW–Milwaukee and UW
Colleges. The program was praised as "visionary and evolution-
ary" by Molly Broad, ACE president and former president of the
University of North Carolina,[32] and in January 2013 the program
also received favorable notice in an article in the *Wall Street
Journal*.[33]

Governor Walker, too, seemed enthusiastic about the program, traveling the state with Reilly to promote the plan.[34] The
successful launch of UW Flex sounded a hopeful note for the
UW System's continued role as a national leader in innovative
academic programming, along with cautious optimism that the
2013–15 budget might bring a restoration of some of the funding
lost by the System in the previous two-year cycle and possibly
even support for new programs supported by the governor, including UW Flex.

Late 2012 also brought reasons for cautious optimism about
improved state support for the UW System in the coming 2013–
15 budget cycle. As the national economy slowly recovered from
the Great Recession and other states began to increase spending
on higher education,[35] Wisconsin's tax revenues were projected
to rise, suggesting that there would be more funds available for
the System and its institutions in the next biennial budget, for
2013–15. The cyclical work of developing the System's budget
request got under way at the board's June 2012 meeting, with a
presentation by Michael Morgan, Reilly's senior vice president
for administration. Morgan recommended that the System's
budget request focus on salary improvements for faculty and
staff, continued efforts to gain management flexibilities, and
support for the new UW Flex program. At the August 23, 2012,
meeting, the board approved a modest request, consistent with
preliminary discussions with DOA, for $21 million to fund new
initiatives, including $18 million for quality, access, and economic
support efforts and $3 million for UW Flex. The board suggested
that compensation issues be addressed separately, in connection
with discussions before the legislature's Joint Committee on Employment Relations[36] related to the new personnel systems being
developed for UW–Madison and the other System institutions.

With budget matters proceeding along routine lines, as 2012 drew to a close, Reilly and the board looked forward to resuming work on the *Growth Agenda* and pursuing UW Flex, while continuing to implement the organizational and structural changes that had followed from Act 32, the work of the internal System restructuring committees, and the recommendations of the Special Task Force.

Reserves and Reverses

The announcement of the governor's 2013–15 biennial budget proposal, in March 2013, seemed to encourage the modestly hopeful outlook of System leaders. The budget, discussed by the board at its March 7 and April 4 meetings, contained, for the first time in several years, no cuts or lapses and provided some $181.4 million in new state support over the two-year period. The proposal allowed the System to keep tuition low, while appearing to set the stage for some movement on employee compensation issues, a critical need. UW faculty and staff had suffered through the furloughs that followed the Great Recession, the loss of employee benefits from Act 10, and years without pay raises, and their compensation, always low, had fallen even further behind that offered at peer institutions. Improving salaries and benefits was essential to retaining and attracting talented employees, and UW System leaders were hopeful that the 2013–15 budget and the flexibility to develop UW–Madison and UW System personnel systems provided under the previous biennial budget would allow them to move ahead with compensation improvements.[37] This positive outlook, however, was sharply reversed by late April, when legislators seized on the existence of large accumulated balances in UW System program revenue accounts to impose punitive cuts to the proposed 2013–15 UW System budget, delay implementation of the personnel flexibilities gained in the 2011–13 budget, and freeze tuition for two years.

The System's program revenues consist of funds received from nontaxpayer sources,[38] such as tuition, fees, certain federal indirect cost reimbursements, and other revenue-generating operations. These fund balances, held in numerous separate accounts across the System and its institutions, are accumulated and maintained for designated purposes, including academic programs, salaries and instructional costs, infrastructure needs, and auxiliary activities such as residence halls and student unions. UW institutions typically end each fiscal year with some unexpended program revenues. These unexpended funds are carried over to the following year as a reserve that ensures the uninterrupted delivery of program services and protects against fluctuations in funding resulting from variables such as changes in enrollment numbers. Program revenue balances at the end of each fiscal year represent the accumulated difference between revenues and expenses for that prior period.

The existence of the System's program revenue balances was and is a matter of public record. They are included in the annual financial audits of the System conducted by the Legislative Audit Bureau (LAB) and are reported to and discussed by the Board of Regents each year in conjunction with the System's annual financial report. In 2013, as in previous years, the LAB's audit for the previous fiscal year, 2012, was presented to the board at its February meeting. At that time, the LAB issued an unqualified opinion regarding the System's finances, and the System's program revenue balances, included as unrestricted assets in the financial report[39] and used to calculate the System's primary reserve ratio (a standard measure of an institution's financial strength)[40] raised no comments or concerns.[41] If anything, the System reserves, representing less than 25 percent of the annual operating budget at that time, were low by industry standards.[42] In April 2013, however, the LAB and the Legislative Fiscal Bureau (LFB) prepared information for a memorandum specifically focused on program revenue balances for fiscal year 2012. The memorandum indicated that as of June 30, 2012, the System had program revenue balances totaling $1 billion across multiple UW institutional accounts; UW–Madison, as the largest institution, held roughly half of the total. Although more than 60 percent of these balances were committed for specific capital projects, technology purchases, and program initiatives, much of the remainder was for what were categorized as "undesignated" purposes.[43]

Legislators, professing shock and anger that these program revenue balances existed and that large amounts of the balances were not obligated for specific line item expenditures, accused UW leaders of "hiding" the funds. In addition, because tuition payments account for the largest proportion of program revenue balances, System leaders were criticized for building up reserves as they raised tuition. Reilly and UW–Madison interim chancellor Ward, appearing at a hearing of the legislature's Joint Committee on Employment Relations on April 23, 2013, to testify about their proposed new personnel systems, were instead subjected to a ninety-minute grilling on program revenue balances. Attacked for embarrassing the state and for "squirreling away" tuition funds, Reilly defended the balances as a necessary reserve to protect against volatile state funding and an uncertain enrollment picture. He also argued that the amounts of the balances were consistent with the levels recommended by the National Association of College and University Business Officers for universities with similar-size operating budgets. Legislators, unsatisfied, railed against the size of the balances. Senator Michael Ellis declared he was disgusted by the situation, while Representative John Nygren said he felt "played." Assembly Speaker Robin Vos, saying Reilly had lost credibility, suggested the System's legislative priorities were in jeopardy and threatened to defer action on personnel and management flexibilities until the System provided a better response on the reserve question. Other legislators proposed a two-year tuition freeze.[44] The bruising confrontation also led some to speculate that Reilly would be fired.

Following the hearing, Reilly and board leaders provided Senator Ellis and others with answers to specific questions they had raised about the program revenue balances, along with details about the planned uses for these funds. They also committed to taking steps to be more transparent and explicit about the balances going forward. It was, however, a case of too little, too late to avert political wrath. The System had been unable to present a timely or satisfactory explanation for the size of the balances as a prudent level of reserves or to justify the rapid rate at which they had been accumulated in the period since 2009 when tuition had been rising. It was a disastrous communications failure that brought disastrous consequences, as the poor handling of the crisis brought a retaliatory attack on the System's budget. David J. Ward, who had served as senior vice president for academic affairs in Lyall's administration and would return in 2014 to join the System administration in the same position, believed that the fund balances issue caused more damage than any other problem the System had faced in his experience.[45]

With public attention focused on the headline-grabbing legislative outrage over the reserves, legislators working on the 2013–15 budget saw in the reserve balances a source of funds for the System that would allow them to shift state taxpayer dollars to support other governmental priorities, from K–12 funding to income tax cuts for agriculture and business. The "discovery" of the System's reserve balances—always hidden in plain sight—provided an opportunity to create a political controversy, fill other budget needs, and excuse an attack on the UW System.[46] Echoing the maneuver used in the 1986 "raid" on the System auxiliary reserve balances, the ploy again proved effective as a means of diverting monies collected from nontaxpayer sources—primarily students and their parents in the form of tuition and fees—and intended for the support of UW programs to more general state government priorities.[47] The result was another punishing budget cut for the System.

On May 15, the governor, seizing the opportunity to take credit for addressing the reserves situation, amended his budget proposal to impose a two-year tuition freeze, reduced UW System support, and required the System to "self-fund" new initiatives and other expenses. By June, the Joint Finance Committee had added more cuts, bringing the total reductions to some $200 million for the biennium and effectively forcing the System to draw down its program revenue balances to meet the obligations for other System initiatives and expenses now mandated by the budget bill. By 2013, the System had suffered back-to-back biennial budget reductions totaling nearly $500 million, and this 2013–15 budget added another $200 million cut—a cut whose impact was exacerbated by the legislatively imposed two-year tuition freeze that deprived the System of revenues to offset the reductions. Making matters worse, approval of the new personnel systems promised in the previous 2011–13 biennial budget was postponed to the end of 2015. This delay, combined with the budget reductions and tuition freeze, left UW–Madison and the rest of the System without either adequate funds or the authority to provide faculty and staff—who had absorbed furloughs and benefit reductions and gone without raises for three biennia—with long overdue compensation improvements. In a year that had begun with some hope for state reinvestment, the System had suffered a major reversal of fortune.

There were personal consequences, as well. Reilly had always been closely identified with the Democratic board that had hired him. His selection, in 2010, of Michael Morgan, Doyle's DOA secretary, as his senior vice president for administration and the revelation that David Giroux, his communications director and another key member of his administrative team, had signed the petition to recall Walker, heightened these perceptions of Reilly as a Democratic partisan, leaving him especially vulnerable to the shifting political winds that came with a Republican governor and an increasingly Republican Board of Regents. The harsh criticisms from Republican legislators for his handling of the program revenue issues damaged his effectiveness with state government and further undermined his ability to work with a board now dominated by Walker appointees. Frustrated with the diminishing internal support and the increasing partisanship and feeling the pressure to let the Republican board appoint its own president, he announced his resignation in July, to be effective at the end of 2013.[48]

Ward, who with Reilly had been criticized for the growth of the program revenue balances, was also preparing to depart. His term as interim chancellor ended in July 2013, and his successor, Rebecca Blank, was scheduled to take office at the end of that month. While Ward had done much to heal the internal campus divisions left behind by Martin, the storm caused by the program revenue balances issue and the resulting budget reductions added to the challenges facing Blank. On leaving, Ward, seeking to smooth Blank's transition and move beyond the controversy, urged the university to present a more positive agenda for the university—to be the "city on the hill"—rather than to constantly talk about money and cuts. He also warned, however, that such a change would not matter if the political agenda was uncompromisingly focused on minimal taxation, minimal public investment, and efforts to keep as much money as possible in the private sector. Pointing out the challenges of the increasingly divisive partisan atmosphere, he went on to note: "I mean if you were to compare my first chancellor term [1993–2001] with this one, this has been politically much tougher. The alliances you can build among the parties, it is just much harder now."[49]

Like Ward, Reilly saw that, in the aftermath of the 2011–13 budget, the defeat of the UW–Madison separation plan, and the efforts to restructure System governance, the board and the UW System were increasingly captive to a partisan political agenda. In the months following the announcement of his resignation, Reilly continued to work on budget matters and the UW Flex program. On leaving the presidency, he was credited with getting results on the *Growth Agenda* despite the hard times following the Great Recession and for his success in keeping the UW System together. He also won praise for his intelligence, hard work, and knowledge of Wisconsin.[50]

The System he left, however, was fragile, embattled, and more vulnerable than ever to political pressure. The System's ongoing quest for flexibilities had ended not with a bang but a whimper. The tuition and personnel flexibilities gained in the 2011–13 budget were rendered effectively meaningless by the 2013–15 tuition freezes and the budget-mandated postponement of the implementation of new personnel systems for UW–Madison and the UW–System. The failure of the poorly conceived UW–Madison separation plan had seriously undermined central board leadership and System cohesion, while inviting ongoing attempts to alter System governance and organization. The deep budget cuts to the entire System threatened educational quality at all institutions, while the System administration cuts had resulted in the loss of staff capacity to fulfill important Systemwide functions. Forced to define new leadership roles, the board and System leaders approved a much more limited set of activities for central administration, delegating authority to institutions and abandoning broader Systemwide functions, including assessing the higher education needs of the entire state and coordinating UW institutional efforts to ensure the availability of essential educational services throughout the System. What had begun with Walker's election in 2010 as an effort to provide the UW System with the management tools to be more efficient, cut costs, and deal with hard times had by 2013 produced only illusory flexibilities, diminished board and System leadership capacity, and continuing budget reductions, threatening the System with the slow death of a thousand cuts.

12

The UW System on the Defensive

Following Reilly's resignation, the Board of Regents selected another UW–Extension leader, Chancellor Ray Cross, as UW System president. Cross inherited the 2013–15 budget that had resulted from the crisis over program revenue balances and a financial picture that would darken further in the budget for the 2015–17 biennium. As Governor Walker took the first steps in a campaign for the US presidency in early 2015, he introduced a budget bill that proposed not only another major funding cut to UW System institutions but also policy changes that threatened the UW System's commitment to the Wisconsin Idea and undermined legal protections for faculty governance and tenure. While Cross took office hoping to improve the System's relations with the governor and legislature and to restore the funds lost as a result of the reserve balances controversy, the UW System he led was an organization on the defensive. Cross would quickly face the policy and fiscal challenges presented by the 2015–17 biennial budget, renewed attempts to create a UW System public authority in exchange for deeper budget reductions, and efforts to tie higher education funding to performance measures based on workforce development efforts. Walker's budget proposals and anger at the seemingly weak opposition offered by the regents and Cross led to a series of no-confidence votes against them by UW institutional faculties, damaging Cross's internal credibility. As his presidency continued, he confronted continued budget crises, new policy pressures, free-speech controversies, and demographic challenges that affected the UW Colleges and Extension and that would bring the most sweeping change to the structure of the UW System since merger.

A Presidential Transition

Cross was named to succeed Reilly on January 10, 2014, and took office on March 1 of that year.[1] Cross had become chancellor of UW Colleges and UW–Extension in 2011, having previously served in other academic leadership positions, including the presidencies of SUNY Morrisville and Northwest Technical College in Bemidji, Minnesota. As the leader of UW Colleges and UW–Extension, Cross, like Reilly, had gained familiarity with all UW System institutions and had earned praise from Governor Walker and legislators for his work as a champion of UW Flex, the flexible degree program launched by Reilly and operated through UW–Extension. Widely believed to have strong connections to Republicans in state government, Cross came to office promising to mend political fences and to restore confidence in System financial reporting lost in the wake of the controversy over the program revenue balances.

At his first regent meeting, on March 6, 2014, Cross outlined his plans for addressing the fund balances issue, making the System's financial and reporting processes more transparent, and redesigning the annual budget.[2] He went on to highlight what he saw as the System's key roles: improving the state's economic landscape; cooperating with K–12 colleagues to support the pipeline from elementary school to higher education; leveraging "system-ness" through intra–UW System collaborations and focus on urban challenges; and encouraging innovation and experimentation with new programs like UW Flex.

Cross presented his plans for financial reporting and annual budget improvements at the April 2014 board meeting, as the board adopted amendments to its policy on program revenue balances. The changes were meant to provide greater clarity in System reports about the balances, to set limits on their accumulation, and to establish requirements for their expenditure.[3] As promised, Cross incorporated all of these changes in preparing the System's 2014–15 annual budget, which he presented to the board at the June 2014 board meeting.[4] His efforts were praised by board members, who endorsed his approach in connection with their approval of the annual budget.

With work to repair the damage from the fund balances issues under way, Cross moved forward on preparations for the System's 2015–17 biennial budget request, providing at the August 21–22, 2014, board meeting a preview of the process and his recommendations for items to be included. The focus of the System's request, he announced, would be on seeking new funds for what he described as "talent development." Emphasizing the UW System's crucial role in developing the intellectual talent essential to support state economic growth, he recommended that the System request some $95.2 million in new funding for programs to develop a talent pipeline. The goal of these programs was to improve the "talent path" to college by strengthening remedial education, to enhance the "talent infrastructure" by increasing capacity in high-demand degree areas, and to provide additional incentive grants to spur economic development. Although the board adopted Cross's recommended budget request as presented, regent John Behling cautioned that other state agencies had been advised that their budget requests should remain "flat"—an early signal that requests for new funding might not be seriously entertained by the governor or legislature.[5]

Determinedly optimistic, however, at board meetings during the fall of 2014 Cross and System institutions began to make the case for the board's new funding requests and argued for the restoration of the funds that had been cut from the System's budget as a result of the fund balances controversy. At the October board meeting, Cross described the System's success with the UW Flex program and the continued solid performance of UW System institutions in *U.S. News and World Report* rankings of colleges and universities.[6] Again addressing the fund balances issue as a key first step in repairing state government relations and gaining legislative support for a better System budget in the 2015–17 cycle, Cross also presented a detailed report to the board on the System's fund balances for the 2013–14 fiscal year. It was the first report prepared in accordance with the board's revised policies, and, as Cross explained, it described in clear terms each UW institution's individual fund balances and their spending plans for drawing down the balances to required levels. UW–Madison chancellor Rebecca Blank also spoke to the issue, seeking to clarify misconceptions about the balances and their purposes and reviewing her own campus's actions to draw down the balances. At the same meeting, Blank went on to underscore the need for state reinvestment in the System, warning that continuing budget cuts prevented the campus from offering competitive faculty salaries, which in turn undermined its ability to recruit and retain faculty members—the critical individual talent essential for winning federal research grants.

Continuing his efforts to bolster the System's case for its budget request at the November board meeting, Cross highlighted the System's strong performance on accountability measures. David J. Ward, who had recently rejoined the System as Cross's interim vice president for academic affairs, presented accountability reports for all institutions except UW–Madison, while Vice Chancellor Sarah Mangelsdorf presented the flagship's reports. As had been the case consistently since the presidency of Katharine Lyall, the reports presented by Ward and Mangelsdorf demonstrated the efficiency and effectiveness of all UW System institutions against all measures. Their reports were followed by an in-depth discussion of state demographic trends and workforce needs and the role of the UW System in supporting state economic development. Governor Walker, just re-elected for a second term on November 4, was unable to attend the meeting but sent a brief note applauding the board's emphasis on workforce development, high-impact talent, and the UW Flex option program. Echoing Behling's comment in October, however, board members at the November meeting warned that support for Cross's talent initiative programs—approved in their own budget request— might not translate to additional funding for the System's budget. Regent Drew Peterson observed that the System's budget would be challenged by policymakers seeking to freeze tuition and to restrict university research on social issues, while regent Whitburn pointed out that the growing costs of Medicaid would limit the availability of state funds for other purposes, including the UW System and its institutions.[7] By the December board meeting, it was clear that prospects for the success of the System's 2015–17 budget requests—for the talent initiatives or otherwise—were dim, and Cross began backing away from advocacy for funding increases, instead focusing internal budget discussions on the System's need to reform its business practices, assess academic priorities, and redesign segregated fees policies.[8]

Things Fall Apart

This gloomy outlook for the System's 2015–17 biennial budget was further complicated by Governor Walker's presidential ambitions. His success in surviving the 2012 recall effort had brought him national attention, winning him the admiration of conservatives around the country for his attacks on collective bargaining rights and unions. He had burnished his reputation as a courageous champion of conservative causes with the publication, in 2013, of his autobiography, *Unintimidated: A Governor's Story and a Nation's Challenge*,[9] in which he described his perseverance through the protests that followed the passage of Act 10 and the ensuing recall election. Walker's solid victory over Democrat Mary Burke in the November 2014 gubernatorial election further cemented his reputation as a rising Republican star, and he was widely regarded as a serious 2016 presidential contender. In January 2015, he took the first steps toward a campaign for the presidency, forming an exploratory committee that would allow fundraising on his behalf to begin.

Now in the national spotlight and reaching out for political support, Walker prepared a 2015–17 state biennial budget that was directed not only to state needs and policy goals but also to a wider national conservative audience, incorporating policy ideas drawn from ALEC and other conservative think tanks. Introduced in late January 2015, the proposal brought not only fiscal shock but also an effort to radically alter the UW System's mission. The governor's 2015–17 budget bill proposed cutting the System by $300 million, another stunning blow that exacerbated the pain of the $250 million cut imposed following the defeat of the UW–Madison separation plan in 2011–13 and the further $200 million cut resulting from the fund balances reserves controversy in 2013–15. Making the situation worse, the plan included another freeze on tuition for resident undergraduates, preventing System institutions from generating revenue to offset the proposed cuts, even as the required drawdown of the System's program revenue balances left UW institutions with no carry-over reserves

to smooth the impact of the cuts on instructional support needs
in the next biennium.

Beyond the financial damage to the UW System, the governor's
budget proposal attacked policies and principles that had guided
Wisconsin public higher education—and supported its success—
for more than a century. The budget bill, 2015 Senate Bill 21, as
introduced, amended the UW System's statutory mission to delete
the Wisconsin Idea and the commitment to the search for truth,
substituting instead the goal of meeting state workforce development needs. The Wisconsin Idea, that the knowledge of UW
institutions should be shared widely for the benefit of the public
and to improve the human condition, had been a bedrock principle of the University of Wisconsin since the administration of
President Charles Van Hise in the early twentieth century. The
university's dedication to the search for truth had been articulated by the Board of Regents in the 1894 trial of Richard Ely and
was memorialized on the "sifting and winnowing" plaque in
UW–Madison's Bascom Hall. Both principles had been affirmed
and incorporated in the UW System's mission in the merger implementation legislation of 1974. Walker's proposal erased these
principles from the statutes in favor of the much narrower function of supplying workforce needs. The language of the proposed changes in the System's mission, as shown by strikeovers
and italics, was as follows:

> 36.01(2) The mission of the system is to develop human
> resources *to meet the state's workforce needs,* to discover and
> disseminate knowledge, ~~to extend knowledge and its
> application beyond the boundaries of its campuses~~ and to
> ~~serve and stimulate society by developing~~ *develop* in
> students heightened intellectual, cultural, and humane
> sensitivities, scientific, professional and technological
> expertise, and a sense of purpose. ~~Inherent in this broad
> mission are methods of instruction, research, extended
> training and public service designed to educate people
> and improve the human condition. Basic to every purpose
> of the system is the search for truth.~~[10]

Going further, the Walker budget sought to repeal faculty
tenure and governance rights that had been in place since

merger, removing statutory tenure protections, restricting the faculty's direct participatory role in institutional governance, and making it easier for campus administrators to close academic programs and lay off faculty members. Taken together, these proposals reflected a dramatically constricted vision of public higher education in Wisconsin and a retreat from the goals of the framers of Wisconsin's constitution, who had established a state university not simply to prepare workers for jobs but also to educate students for citizenship and to create and share knowledge for the public good. The proposal also undermined the critical role of faculty in academic and curricular decisions, shifting greater control in these areas to administrators, who were given more latitude to eliminate academic programs, along with their faculty and staff.

Although the governor's budget contained some provisions supported by Cross—revival of a public authority plan for the System, some added management flexibilities, and a plan to establish a formula-based mechanism for regularly adjusting the state funding provided to the System according to changes in the Consumer Price Index (the so-called dedicated funding stream intended to replace the System's biennially determined block grant funding)—overall, the plan was another punishing blow to the UW System's financial stability and a direct assault on the core values that had historically supported its success. As media reports noted, it was also a plan that, by incorporating policies endorsed by ALEC and other conservative organizations, appeared calculated to court a conservative Republican base of supporters for Walker's presidential campaign.[11] The UW System, already caught up in deepening state political partisanship, was now vulnerable to the governor's presidential ambitions and national political divisions.

Whatever its appeal to a potential conservative constituency, however, Walker's budget encountered stiff resistance following its release. His effort to remove the Wisconsin Idea and the search for truth from the System's mission statement brought an immediate public outcry—in Wisconsin and nationally—that eventually forced him to withdraw the proposal. Although Walker had apparently instructed the bill's drafters to remove the Wisconsin Idea language from the statute over the objections of UW System leaders and legal counsel, he initially claimed that these changes were a "drafting error."[12] Later acknowledging that it had been a mistake to replace the UW System's historically broad academic and service missions with a workforce development goal, he amended his proposal to restore the Wisconsin Idea and the search for truth to the System's mission.

The major budget cut and the remaining key policy elements of Walker's budget also drew criticism and concern as the proposal was discussed at the February 5, 2015, regent meeting. The session began with a presentation by UW–Madison chancellor Rebecca Blank, who described the many achievements of the flagship in the previous year but offered a grim appraisal of the fiscal problems that would occur if Walker's budget were to be enacted. Reviewing the recent history of budget cuts and tuition freezes, she noted that the System had been required by the legislature to draw down its program revenue fund balances in the preceding biennium with the tacit understanding that once the reserves were gone, they would be replaced by taxpayer funding in the state budget. Having used up its reserves, she emphasized, UW–Madison now confronted the largest decline in state taxpayer support in its history, and the governor's proposed budget would reduce the state's share of support for the flagship's educational mission even further, to a mere 7 percent of its budget. The extent of the proposed reductions would have a direct impact on the quality of education, erasing the modest, hard-won gains of the previous ten years. In addition, she explained, the flagship was losing its competitive edge, facing state funding decreases at a time when forty-one of the fifty United States were increasing their support for public higher education. Asked by regent Pruitt if she was aware of any peer institution facing the same combination of budget cuts and four-year tuition freezes, Blank said she was not aware of any. She concluded by reiterating that "the cuts are too large. They are too large for our university, and they are too large for the state." Her comments brought a standing ovation from many of those present.[13]

Despite the alarms raised by the chancellor, however, board president Falbo sought to dampen criticism of the governor's proposal, suggesting it would be counterproductive to speculate on the final impact of the proposed cuts. Falbo noted that more details about the budget would be known by the March board meeting, when there would be further opportunity for discussion.

He then addressed the major policy changes proposed in the budget, seeking to assure faculty of the board's continued commitment to tenure and faculty governance. Cross provided his own overview of the budget, which, he indicated, offered new opportunity, as well as significant challenges. Cross described what he identified as the three broad components of the proposal: the public authority, the budget cuts, and the dedicated funding stream for the System going forward. While supportive of the public authority idea and the potential for gaining a dedicated funding stream, Cross expressed concern about the size of the cuts, pointing out that the $150 million reduction in each of the two years of the biennium was the equivalent of all the operational taxpayer funding for seven of the fourteen UW institutions. He also emphasized that the proposed cuts to the state's support to the System would return state funding to its 1998 level and that the tuition freeze would substantially limit the System's ability to manage the cuts.[14]

Cross's presentation was followed by a relatively brief discussion in which most board members followed Falbo's cautious lead, expressing the need to understand the state's overall budget circumstances and the importance of avoiding an emotional response to the governor's plan. While a few members argued that the board needed to speak out more forcefully and publicly about the damage that would result if the budget were enacted as proposed, they were a distinct minority. Regent Bradley, a former board president, emphasized that the board has a duty to advocate for the best interests of public higher education, including "speaking truth to power" and honestly communicating the issues to the public. Regent Evers agreed, stating that the current circumstances demanded a strong response, not quietly holding back. With Walker appointees now in the majority, however, the board's reaction to the governor's budget proposal was subdued and opposition muted.

Concerned about the board's seemingly quiescent attitude to the budget at this meeting, regent Walsh pressed Cross in late February for a more detailed briefing and analysis of the budget proposal, arguing that the board and the System should use their platform to begin a public discussion of the budget and its consequences.[15] By the time of the board's March 5 meeting, though Cross had provided some additional information and the implications of the budget proposal were better understood, the dismal picture was unaltered and System leaders had not initiated the broader public conversation urged by Walsh. Cross had appeared before the legislature's Joint Finance Committee earlier in that week, making just three requests: the creation of the UW System public authority; approval of a dedicated, predictable funding stream; and reductions in the size of the proposed budget cut. Gone from the conversation were Cross's and the board's earlier budget request for $95 million in new funds for the talent improvement initiatives or mention of the need to restore the program revenue reserves that had been virtually wiped out by the cuts of the 2013–15 biennium. Instead, Cross confirmed his support for the public authority structure and the management flexibilities promised, along with proposing a dedicated funding stream. Reporting on his legislative appearance at the board meeting, Cross presented the details on these items, providing a list of flexibilities and explaining that the dedicated funding stream was to be fixed at an initial amount and then adjusted annually for changes in the Consumer Price Index.

In the lengthy discussion that followed, critical information about the actual size of the proposed reductions and possible means of paying for them emerged. Legislators and the Walker administration had suggested to the press and others that the $300 million cut was a "modest" 2.5 percent of the UW System's total budget.[16] The facts presented at the board meeting, however, did not support that assertion. The claimed 2.5 percent reduction was based on the System's total $6 billion operating budget—an amount that includes the revenues from research grants, gifts, auxiliary operations, athletic revenues, and similar nonstate-taxpayer sources. The actual amount of the taxpayer contribution to the System, however, was at the time $1.142 billion, making the governor's proposed reduction of $300 million equal to a 13 percent cut in the System's budget, a significant decrease in the state's contribution to System support and a loss further magnified by the tuition freeze.[17] The board discussion also confirmed, once again, that the proposed flexibilities—with or without public authority status—would not be enough to offset the proposed cut. As Cross explained, savings from the flexibilities proposed were estimated to total only $15 million, hardly adequate to compensate for the $300 million cut.

The severity of the governor's proposed 2015–17 cut, added to the cumulative effects of the massive cuts of the two preceding biennia and the ongoing tuition freeze, had driven funding for the System to new lows, and the discussion about how the board should respond was heated. Several regents expressed distrust of the "dedicated funding stream" proposal and cast doubt on the need for the proposed public authority. Regent Walsh characterized the funding stream as "fairy dust" and not something the System could rely upon if the legislature was intent on imposing budget cuts. Regent Pruitt pointed out—again—that public authority status and related flexibilities would never provide cost savings adequate to offset major funding cuts, while Walsh noted that the long-requested flexibilities could be provided through simple statutory amendments, without the need to create a public authority, which is a creature of the statutes and always subject to legislative amendment. The sense of the meeting that emerged, however, was that a major budget cut was a fait accompli and would not be reversed. The discussion concluded with the approval of a resolution that effectively supported Cross's restrained approach to the Joint Finance Committee the week before, requesting that the legislature "substantially reduce the base funding cuts recommended" by the governor and asking for the flexibilities sought by the System, either through an "agreed-upon" public authority or amendments to existing statutes.[18]

Board reaction to the major tenure and governance changes proposed by the governor was similarly quiet. As he had in February, Falbo tried to assure faculty, staff, and students of the board's commitment to faculty tenure and governance. NCHEMS consultant Aims McGuinness, who in 2012 had worked with Falbo's Special Task Force, advised that the inclusion of faculty tenure and governance provisions in the UW System's statutory charter is unique in the United States and suggested that these matters could be addressed in university policies, as they commonly were at other universities. Falbo, with the support of board vice president Regina Millner, promised that, if the governor's proposal to repeal the statutes on tenure and governance was adopted, they would work to replace the statutory provisions with board policies continuing the same protections. Reminding board members that the proposed repeal of the tenure and governance sections would not be effective until July 1, 2016, Falbo indicated that he would appoint task forces to develop these new board policies over the course of the next year. Should the legislature make the repeal of the tenure and governance statutes effective sooner than July 1, 2016, Millner recommended that the board adopt the exact language of the current statutes as board policy, to be in force until the work of Falbo's task forces could be completed.[19] Her proposal, offered as a resolution, was also approved by the board. Again, however, there was little support for active opposition to the governance changes in the budget.

With the board majority offering little resistance to Walker's budget plan and continuing single-party Republican control of the state legislature, the proposal faced few obstacles to passage. Although there was speculation in the media that Walker was using the reductions in System funding to pay for a costly 2011 agriculture and manufacturers income tax credit or to support construction of a new arena for the Milwaukee Bucks basketball team, these concerns did not generate significant opposition to the bill or slow its progress to passage. Republican legislators endorsed the proposed cuts to the System, contending they were needed to help balance the state budget,[20] and for those board members continuing to argue against the cuts, Assembly Speaker Robin Vos[21] had a warning, telling the Board of Regents that "you can either be cheerleaders for the university or advocates for the taxpayers."[22]

In the end, Walker's budget bill survived largely intact. While the public authority idea again failed and the formula-based funding stream was not approved, the massive System budget cut—reduced from the originally proposed $300 million by $50 million—remained, and a few additional flexibilities were granted. Tuition, however, remained frozen; the faculty tenure statute, Section 36.13, Wisconsin Statutes (1973) was repealed immediately; the governance role of faculty, staff, and students shrank from active participation to an advisory role; and campus administrators gained greater authority to close programs and lay off staff. The day before officially announcing his presidential candidacy, on July 12, 2015, Walker signed the state's 2015–17 budget, leaving the System and its institutions to face yet another multimillion-dollar cut, weakened revenue-generating capacity, battered internal morale resulting from the tenure and governance changes,[23] and threats to its national reputation and competitiveness lingering from the unsuccessful assault on the Wisconsin Idea.

The responses of the board and Cross to Walker's budget were criticized as weak and ineffective, but the one-party control of state government offered few choices but to try to mitigate the damage imposed by a legislature whose general hostility to public higher education was increasingly open. With few champions and many antagonists in the legislature and an ambitious governor courting a national partisan audience in the presidential campaign, the Board of Regents and the UW System were on the defensive and intimidated.

Trying to Hold the Center

Throughout the remainder of 2015 and into 2016, System institutions struggled to manage the budget fallout. Faculty, staff, and students were still achieving research successes, such as UW–Madison professor John Hawks's identification of a new human species, *homo naledi*, and winning academic awards, including a Rhodes Scholarship for UW–Madison student Colin Higgins.[24] Researchers at UW–Milwaukee were developing a simple test for the Ebola virus, while students at UW–Whitewater were engaged in projects with the Hubble telescope, and UW–Stevens Point won the NCAA Division III men's basketball championship.[25] The lack of adequate funding, however, remained a serious, persistent problem that threatened continued success. As Chancellor Blank reported in February 2016, her campus was effectively in a deficit position, still "owing" an additional $86 million due to requirements associated with drawing down the reserve balances. Low salaries—with no compensation increases planned—and sinking morale made retention of faculty increasingly difficult.

The tenure and governance changes forced through as part of the budget added to these underlying problems. Because the budget act repealed the tenure statute immediately, the former statutory provisions were automatically adopted as board policy, in accordance with regent Millner's proposal at the March 2015 board meeting. Falbo's task force on tenure policy, however, was charged with reviewing this change, along with other governance issues raised in connection with the budget legislation. The task force began meeting in August 2015 and in December presented a set of three proposed tenure policies for adoption at the March 2016 board meeting. The first of these codified the former statutory tenure protections as board policy, essentially confirming the board's earlier action, while the second dealt with periodic post-tenure performance reviews. Both were approved with little discussion. The third proposal, however, established procedures for laying off faculty for reasons of financial emergency or program discontinuance that significantly curtailed faculty input on program closures and layoffs, shifting the authority to chancellors and encouraging consideration of the cost-effectiveness of programs in making program closure decisions. As task force chair regent John Behling made clear, the goal of the policy changes was to "empower chancellors and give them the flexibility" to deal with hard times, but the shift to administrative control and away from academic considerations was concerning. The emphasis on cost-cutting and diminished faculty input stoked the fear—initially raised by Walker's failed effort to delete the Wisconsin Idea from the System's mission and replace it with a goal of serving workforce needs—that its purpose was to eliminate from the curriculum the liberal studies or any field not leading to an "in-demand" degree. Although the few remaining Doyle appointees on the board introduced several amendments designed to give faculty a greater voice in program closure decisions, they failed on a series of essentially party-line votes, and the proposed policy was approved as recommended by Behling and his task force. Anger remained among faculty, however, leading to votes of "no confidence" in Cross and the board by faculty members at UW–Madison, UW–Milwaukee, UW–La Crosse, UW–River Falls, and other institutions in May 2016, putting the Board of Regents at odds with key internal constituencies.[26]

The board's relatively passive acceptance of the 2015 budget cuts and the subsequent tenure and governance changes also raised concerns about whether it was fulfilling its responsibilities for stewardship of the System. Since the 1971 merger, board members, both Republicans and Democrats, had consistently affirmed that they served as independent, nonpartisan trustees responsible for acting in the best interests of the System and state higher education and pushing back when necessary against legislative and gubernatorial actions damaging to the System and its institutions. Responding to the 2015–17 biennial budget, however, the board appeared to have abandoned its traditional independence, offering little resistance to a measure that came with damaging financial and policy consequences. Concluding his term on the board in June 2015, regent Walsh decried the cuts, pointing out that state taxpayers' contribution to the System's budget had fallen below levels that prevailed in both Thompson's and Doyle's last years as governors. He went on to urge the board to take a more active role in advocating for System needs, suggesting that they take the System's case directly to the people through statewide listening sessions and by seeking the support of business organizations such as Wisconsin Manufacturers and Commerce.[27] In 2016, on his own departure from the board, regent Pruitt shared a similar sentiment. Recalling Assembly Speaker Vos's suggestion that regents could either be advocates of the taxpayers or cheerleaders for the UW System a false choice, Pruitt argued that it is the special responsibility of the regents to defend and protect the Wisconsin Idea and that being cheerleaders for the System is their highest calling.[28]

These appeals, however, could not undo the damage from the 2015–17 budget or relieve the budget and political pressures on the UW System. If anything, Governor Walker seemed intent on pursuing his attacks on the System's budget, even as the UW System continued to suffer the cumulative effects of decades of declining state taxpayer support followed by the even steeper cuts and intensifying partisan hostility of the 2010s. Many public university systems nationally had faced similar problems in the long, post-1970s period of sagging state support, increasingly seen by some as an era of neglect of public higher education.[29] Unlike Wisconsin, though, other states, as Chancellor Blank had reminded the regents, had by 2015 begun to reinvest in their state universities, leaving the UW System and its institutions at a competitive disadvantage, behind their peers, and struggling in a hostile state environment.

Controlling the Higher Education Agenda

In the aftermath of the 2015–17 biennial budget process, President Cross and the board in August 2015 began a new strategic planning effort. The result, *2020FWD*, built on themes Cross had articulated on taking office, such as his emphasis on improving the educational pipeline and the university experience and the need to develop stronger connections with business and industry. Presenting the plan to the board in August 2016, Cross described the System's challenges to success, emphasizing the demographic problems associated with an aging population and outflow of college graduates and the System's limited financial resources. He expressed confidence, however, that the plan he proposed would allow the System to address these challenges, while fulfilling its statutory mission. *2020FWD* was unanimously approved, and Cross was delegated the authority to begin developing specific implementing actions.[30]

Meanwhile, Walker's presidential campaign, announced July 13, 2015, had proved to be one of the briefest in history, ending September 21, 2015, shortly after approval of his 2015–17 state budget. While no longer seeking the presidency, however, Walker continued to pursue his conservative public higher education agenda. As the board and Cross began their preparations for the System's 2017–19 budget request based on the *2020FWD* plan, Walker was developing his own proposal for the next biennium, including several higher education policy changes inspired by ALEC and other conservative groups. Reflecting the extent to which Wisconsin's public higher education agenda was now being shaped not so much by the Board of Regents with the support of System leaders but by the governor and legislature with the strong influence of outside organizations, Walker's plan called for creating a performance-based funding process for UW institutions, in which institutional funding would be allocated on the basis of each institution's success in meeting statutorily defined performance metrics, such as workforce development efforts. He further proposed the creation of an "Innovation Fund" available to UW institutions for increasing access to high-demand programs.[31] Other proposals required the Board of Regents to develop policies for monitoring the teaching workloads of faculty and academic staff and for rewarding those who showed extra effort.[32] The plan also established an educational opportunity office to authorize and oversee state-supported charter schools at the K–12 level.[33] While this budget contained some modest funding improvements for the UW System, it continued the freeze on resident undergraduate tuition for a fifth year.

As in the previous biennium, the governor's budget plan met with little opposition from the board and was praised by regent president Behling as the System's best budget in more than a decade.[34] With the budget another fait accompli and forced to maintain a defensive posture to secure even modest fiscal gains, the board in late 2017 deliberated plans for implementing the new statutory requirements in late 2017. The lone voice expressing concern with the policy results of the 2017–19 state budget was that of regent—soon to become governor—Tony Evers. From his experience as State Superintendent of Public Instruction, Evers warned that there was no place in the country where performance-based funding or outcomes-based accountability systems had been shown to work—skepticism that was shared by higher education experts, including UW–Madison's Nicholas Hillman.[35] Evers also cautioned that the proposed workload monitoring diminished the work of System staff, forcing them to defend its value.[36] As required by law, however, the board approved the necessary implementation policies at its December 6, 2017, meeting.[37]

Culture Wars, Continued

Further confirming the increasing influence of national conservative organizations on UW System policy, the board's response to a culture wars controversy over free speech ended with the adoption of a board policy derived from a model offered by the Goldwater Institute, a conservative think tank. The controversy involved the collision of competing free-speech interests. In November 2016, a conservative guest speaker, Ben Shapiro, appeared at UW–Madison and was shouted down by students. Similar incidents involving conservative speakers at other college campuses around the country had prompted calls to punish students who disrupted speech, along with pressure for the adoption of so-called campus free speech legislation requiring that universities remain officially neutral on current public policy controversies by not taking action in a way that would require students or faculty to publicly express a given view of social policy and further providing for disciplinary action to be imposed on those who disrupt free expression on campus.[38]

Responding to the Shapiro incident, Walker introduced a neutrality provision similar to the Goldwater Institute model in his 2017–19 budget, seeking to protect conservative voices and punish those who disrupted speakers. The bill raised concerns about academic freedom, however, and the possible intrusion on the rights of faculty members and students to speak freely in the classroom.[39] Although the proposal received support in the state Assembly, it did not survive the budget process. The issue was, however, taken up by the Board of Regents at its July 2017 meeting, when regent president Behling asked Cross to analyze the System's existing policies on freedom of expression and recommend any necessary changes to address the neutrality and disruption issues.

After several months of study, Cross recommended board adoption of a policy document incorporating key elements of the Goldwater Institute model. Cross's proposed policy affirmed the UW System's historic support for academic freedom and freedom of expression and its commitment to providing all members of the university community the opportunity to speak but added institutional "neutrality" language and a statement, based on the Goldwater model, that it is not the university's role to shield individuals from offensive ideas, while committing the board to amend its student disciplinary code to allow the suspension or expulsion of students found to have been responsible for disrupting the expressive rights of others on two or more occasions. Regent Evers objected to the proposed policy, observing that policies already existed to deal with these issues and characterizing the policy as a "solution seeking a problem," but again he was a lonely voice, and Cross's recommended policy was approved and codified as Regent Policy Document 4–21.[40] While the board's action relieved the immediate pressure for legislation on the issue, it was a further demonstration of the growing influence of outside organizations on UW System policy.

Back to the Future:
The New UW System

While the financial and policy issues associated with the 2017–19 biennial budget commanded most of the board's attention throughout 2017, there was also growing concern about the impact of state demographic trends on enrollments at UW System institutions, particularly the two-year UW Colleges. In presenting the *2020FWD* strategic plan in 2016, Cross had pointed to Wisconsin's aging population and the loss of college-educated individuals as challenges to the System's efforts to improve the higher education pipeline. Reporting on his *2020FWD* strategic plan at the October 6, 2017, board meeting, Cross warned that the changing demographic environment now posed an urgent threat to the viability of the UW Colleges and that it required immediate actions with implications for the entire UW System. He noted that the population between the ages of eighteen and sixty-four in the state was projected to remain flat or decline over the next thirty years, while growth in the over-sixty-five group would continue, accounting for some 95 percent of all state population growth. He went on to explain that the state population is also increasingly moving from rural to urban areas and that fewer students in rural areas are pursuing college degrees, shrinking enrollments at smaller, rural campuses and accounting for a 32 percent decline in the number of full-time equivalent students attending UW Colleges—often the most accessible higher education option for rural students—since 2010. The combination of rapidly decreasing enrollments and the cumulative impact of years of budget reductions were jeopardizing the capacity of some campuses to continue operations and undermining the entire UW Colleges organization. In response to this troubling information, Cross proposed a plan to restructure UW Colleges and UW–Extension that would affect all UW System institutions.

Unveiled just one month later, at the board's November 2017 meeting, Cross's plan called for integrating each of the thirteen two-year Colleges into a four-year comprehensive or doctoral UW institution, effective July 2018. In addition, he recommended moving the UW–Extension's Cooperative Extension division and UW–Extension Conference Centers to UW–Madison, while moving other UW–Extension units, including Continuing Education, Business and Entrepreneurship, and Public Broadcasting, to UW System administration.[41] Cross described other options that he had considered to maintain the UW Colleges' ongoing viability but had concluded that reorganization was the best solution to the crisis. Outlining alternatives he had considered, he explained that the status quo could not be maintained financially, while a merger with the state's technical college would be impractical and individual campus closures would be contrary to the System's commitment to making higher education geographically accessible. As a result, he had concluded that restructuring along the lines he proposed offered the most effective means of addressing the UW Colleges' immediate problems, while preserving access and affordability.

As the plan was proposed and presented to the board, it was not altogether clear why it was urgent to address demographic and financial problems that had been unfolding for some time or why it was necessary to dismantle UW–Extension to solve the Colleges' enrollment problem. Cross argued, however, that further study would not change the underlying demographic trends and that he was proposing an approach to implementation that would include broader internal consultation and participation of the affected institutions, faculty, staff, and students.[42] Opening the discussion of the proposal at the board's November 2017 meeting, regent president Behling described Cross's plan as the next step in taking the UW System into the twenty-first century, a reform that would make the System more efficient and accessible without "closing any doors." Although concerns about the rapid implementation of such a sweeping plan were expressed by regent Janice Mueller, who suggested that some additional time should be taken to analyze the financial implications of the plan, and by regent Evers, who objected to approving the plan without further study, the majority of board members were persuaded that immediate action was needed and approved the plan, with implementation to begin in January 2018.[43]

The long-term impacts of this reorganization remain to be seen, but in an extraordinarily short time frame Cross had achieved what he described as the most consequential restructuring since merger. It was a redesign that produced a UW System structure eerily similar to that of the premerger period, with the two-year Colleges linked as satellites to four-year institutions and Extension's important outreach and broadcast functions returned to UW–Madison, reversing the Fred Harvey Harrington organizational scheme that had been confirmed at the time of merger. It was a restructuring effort that seemed to take the UW System back to its future.

Conclusion

The State of a Union

The UW System has proved to be a durable institution. Nearly fifty years after Lucey's shotgun marriage of the former University of Wisconsin and the Wisconsin State University systems, the merged UW System remains unified organizationally and committed to the fundamental principles of the Wisconsin Idea, academic freedom, and the search for truth. Overcoming initial organizational and leadership struggles, the System matured as an effective administrative structure supporting a remarkable range of academic, research, and service achievements at all UW institutions and providing high-quality educational opportunities for its students. At the same time, however, the System has experienced a steady erosion in state taxpayer funding, economic crises, and mounting attacks on its mission and purposes. While the union created by Lucey has shown its resilience and value to the state and beyond, its capacity for continued success remains vulnerable to these persistent challenges.

Lucey saw merger as a solution to a number of problems, from long-standing concerns about program duplication and costly competition for resources between the two older university systems to the need to protect the flagship University of Wisconsin at Madison from political and public anger over violent, disruptive anti–Vietnam War and civil rights protests. It was a difficult merger, forcing poorly matched organizations into a union that was, in the beginning, uncomfortable and sometimes dysfunctional. Following merger, however, state and System leaders, including System president Weaver's team of Don Percy and Don Smith, developed and implemented a coherent organizational structure for the newly combined entity. The legal framework for the UW System, codified in state statutes in 1974 and modeled generally on former president Fred Harvey Harrington's structure for the University of Wisconsin, affirmed the state's historic commitments to the Wisconsin Idea and the search for truth and provided for strong central governance and administrative leadership, a unified budget, and well-defined institutional missions. Despite lingering internal resistance to the merger, the System proved to be an effective structure for stabilizing resource allocation, promoting cohesion around shared goals, and encouraging collaboration, while insulating individual institutions from political and public criticism.

As the System matured, UW institutions achieved numerous outstanding academic, research, and service successes, from groundbreaking scientific research and medical advances to scholarly projects and productive partnerships with businesses and industry. UW campuses and extension offices contributed directly to the economic success and civic vitality of their communities, fulfilling the Wisconsin Idea goal of sharing academic knowledge and expertise for the benefit of the entire state. With well-aligned internal leadership from a talented group of UW chancellors, dynamic flagship leadership, and solid support from the administrations of governors Tommy Thompson and Jim Doyle, the System during the administration of Katharine C. Lyall enjoyed an especially productive period of institutional growth and progress in the 1990s and early 2000s. The mature System's effectiveness in supporting the successes of a diverse group of academic institutions earned it recognition as one of the best state university systems in the nation.

From its earliest days, however, the UW System was forced to deal with budget cuts and diminishing state taxpayer support, as the post–World War II "golden age" for higher education came to an end, hard economic times decreased state tax revenues, and the aging of the baby boom generation raised concerns that college enrollments would decline. Merger came with immediate state budget cutbacks and pressure to downsize. Later, although enrollments continued to grow, other state programs became higher budget priorities than public higher education. Health care costs, state commitments to support public K–12 education, and an ambitious and expensive prison-building program consumed a growing share of the state budget, reducing the state funds available to support the UW System. The shift in state priorities, the ups and downs in state revenues arising from general economic conditions, and a nearly absolute refusal to raise state taxes for any purpose all translated into steadily diminishing state taxpayer support for the System.

Although System leaders—regents, System presidents, chancellors, and others—consistently argued for improved state government support, they made little headway. State government leaders, dealing with competing constituent demands and state needs, tended to see UW alarms about the consequences of budget cuts as whining or crying wolf and to view UW accomplishments as evidence that more state support was not really needed. System presidents John Weaver, Robert M. O'Neil, and Kenneth Shaw made the case for increased state support based on the need to maintain educational quality and to provide competitive faculty salaries. President Lyall promoted the value of the System as an economic engine for the state and touted the System's record of efficiency and accountable stewardship of state resources as grounds for improving state support. President Kevin Reilly pressed for System growth by highlighting the benefits of increased baccalaureate production to the state's economy. These arguments, however, met with only occasional modest success in improving state taxpayer contributions to the System's budget. Over time, the System became increasingly reliant on nontaxpayer sources of funding from research grants, gifts, and tuition revenues to maintain adequate financial support. With gift and grant funds typically restricted to specific purposes, tuition—particularly the large pool of resident undergraduate tuition—became increasingly critical, and resident undergraduate tuition increases, negotiated between the System and state leaders during the state budget development process, became central to the System's ability to manage and offset declines in state taxpayer support for its budget.

This trade-off between tuition and budget cuts worked well enough until the economic crises of the 2000s, when state tax-payer support began to fall at a much faster rate and concerns about rising tuition grew, stoking fears that some students would be priced out of higher education or that public institutions would be effectively privatized. A major state budget reduction to the UW System in the 2003-5 biennium was followed by even deeper cuts in the wake of the Great Recession of 2007-9, but there was continuing pressure to keep tuition affordable, and tuition increases only partially offset these reductions. Facing limits on their ability to increase tuition, System leaders sought management flexibilities—freedom from state regulations that would allow them to operate more like businesses—as an alternative source of cost savings and potential revenue generation that would help them manage through hard fiscal times.

The growing emphasis on management flexibilities as the solution to the chronic underfunding problems, however, proved to be a two-edged sword that nearly brought the dissolution of the System. Following the election of Governor Scott Walker in 2010, President Reilly and regent leaders approached the new governor with suggestions for management flexibilities and cost-saving or revenue-generating measures that would help the System deal with widely anticipated budget reductions. They also suggested study of a more extensive organizational change, the creation of a public authority to govern the UW System. While not pursuing such a governance structure for the System as a whole, however, Walker worked with UW–Madison chancellor Carolyn Martin to develop a much more radical flexibility proposal: a public authority for UW–Madison that would separate the flagship from the rest of the System, giving it greater autonomy, management flexibility, and full tuition-setting authority under a new and separate governing board chosen by the governor and the chancellor. It was, in effect, a plan to de-merge Lucey's unified UW System.

Introduced as part of Walker's 2011-13 biennial budget against the background of the public outcry over Walker's controversial proposal to repeal collective bargaining rights for public employees, the UW–Madison separation plan was opposed by the Board of Regents, Reilly, and other UW System institutions. Not fully analyzed or vetted, the separation plan failed in the legislature due to concerns about the risks to students from spiraling tuition costs and the impact on UW institutions other than the flagship. Still, the defeat of the proposal did significant damage. While the System remained intact, the budget legislation kept in place a $250 million cut to the System, imposed an additional 25 percent reduction to the System administration's staff and budget, and created a task force to study further System restructuring. The flagship was painfully divided, while System leadership, weakened by the loss of staff and funds, faced continuing pressure to devolve administrative authority to institutions.

The political turmoil stemming from the 2011 biennial budget clashes continued long after approval of the budget, bringing an unsuccessful attempt to recall the governor in 2012. Partisanship, deepening in the state throughout the 2000s, intensified and began to affect the operations of the Board of Regents. The System confronted punitive budget cuts in 2013–15, the result of the legislative ire over discovery of the System's sizable program revenue balances. Adding to the pain, tuition was frozen, preventing the System from offsetting the cuts and forcing a drawdown of reserves that left some UW campuses with budget deficits. Meanwhile, the governor—courting support for a 2016 presidential bid—pursued an agenda for public higher education in Wisconsin designed to appeal to a national conservative base. His 2015–17 biennial budget proposed language that deleted the Wisconsin Idea and the search for truth from the System's mission and replaced it with the goal of meeting state workforce needs. The same budget proposal repealed statutory tenure and faculty governance protections, made another $250 million cut to the System's budget, and imposed another tuition freeze. Although the proposed change to the System's mission was later withdrawn from the budget, the repeal of the tenure statute, the revisions to shared governance provisions, and the budget cut and tuition freeze were approved. This series of bruising financial and policy attacks kept the UW System on the defensive, undermining its capacity to plan for the future needs of state higher education and its ability to manage new challenges and the pressures arising in connection with new state demographic trends, population shifts, and the slower enrollment growth at some UW institutions and

UW Colleges that produced the hastily devised 2018 plan to re-organize UW–Extension and integrate the UW Colleges with four-year and doctoral campuses.

Throughout this history, however, even in times of great adversity, the System and its institutions have continued to demonstrate their resilience and their ability to achieve academic, research, and outreach excellence. They have repeatedly proved their vital importance to the civic and economic life of the state, stimulating and supporting new businesses, contributing directly to local economies, and sustaining vibrant communities. These accomplishments are a testament to the foresight of the state's founders in providing for a state university and state colleges in the Wisconsin constitution and to the continuing vitality and power of the Wisconsin Idea and the System's central purpose, the search for truth. They also reflect the value of the merged and united UW System in providing an organizational framework that supports the achievements of all state public higher education institutions. The winds of change that brought the 1971 merger creating the System have shifted many times in the years since then and will continue to blow, bringing new state leadership, new priorities, and new challenges. The election in 2018 of Democrat Tony Evers as governor has brought a shift away from single-party control of state government that will bring new policy directions and a different agenda for state higher education. Whatever the changes, though, preserving the System's legacy of achievement and the promise it holds for future generations will remain crucial to the success of the state. Fulfilling the promise of higher education opportunity provided in the state constitution is essential to the state's forward progress, but it requires sustained public and political support, financial reinvestment, and a recommitment to the state's public higher education enterprise, the UW System.

Acknowledgments

In writing this book, I have had the support and assistance of many wonderful colleagues, friends, and family. Particular thanks are due to Kevin Reilly, who encouraged the project from the beginning and has been a helpful reader and sounding board along the way; to Katharine Lyall, who generously shared her perspectives and insights; to Ray Cross, who continued the System administration's support for and involvement with the effort; and to my research assistant, Kathleen Oliver, who tracked down details, contributed background information, and provided important feedback and editing help with the text. Sincere thanks, as well, go to all the individuals mentioned in the list of interviewees for taking the time to talk with me about the UW System. Their comments and viewpoints were invaluable in informing my own approach to the System's history. I am particularly grateful, too, for the assistance of David Null and Troy Reeves, of the UW–Madison's University Archive and Records Management Office, who provided essential research help and access to a trove of documents and reference materials, and to their extensive and excellent collection of oral interviews. Jane Radue, former Board of Regents secretary, also provided much-appreciated assistance in locating relevant System administration records and reports. The UW Press and editor Gwen Walker have also given me expert guidance and editorial suggestions to improve the manuscript, for which I am very grateful.

Finally, I owe thanks and gratitude to my friends and family for their understanding and support as I worked on the book. My daughters, Sarah and Jennifer Hodulik; Jennifer's husband, Andrew Jurkowski; and their sons Jack, Teddy and Bobby Jurkowski have been there for me throughout the process. Sarah also pitched in with some timely research help, and my brother Tim Brady—a real writer—offered encouraging advice and sympathy. The very most special thanks go to my husband, Bob Smith, my best reader, editor, critic, and mainstay. I truly could not have done it without him.

Appendix

All UW System institutions have achieved important academic and research successes, while making vital civic contributions to their communities and the state. As noted in the preface, this volume is "Madison-centric" for a number of reasons and as a result it contains numerous references to the achievements of the flagship and its faculty, staff, and students. This appendix offers a brief overview of the unique histories, special strengths, and exceptional offerings of other UW System institutions. Additional resources for the stories of each System institution can be found in the bibliography.

UW–Eau Claire

The Eau Claire campus opened as a normal school in 1916 and began offering four-year bachelor of education degrees in 1927 as Eau Claire State Teachers College. Consistently ranked by *U.S. News & World Report* as one of the top regional universities in the Midwest, UW–Eau Claire offers rigorous undergraduate programs and degrees in the arts, the humanities, the social sciences, health sciences, select engineering fields, education, nursing, and business. The campus is a UW System Center of Excellence for Faculty and Undergraduate Student Research Collaboration. It has also partnered with Marshfield Medical Center for more than three decades, providing hands-on learning opportunities to nursing students. As of fall 2017, it enrolled 9,483 full-time students.

UW–Green Bay

Opening for classes in the fall of 1969, UW–Green Bay was originally a part of the former University of Wisconsin, established to meet the higher educational needs of northeastern Wisconsin. Initially offering an unconventional interdisciplinary curriculum organized around "theme" colleges, the curriculum today includes a broad range of degrees in the arts and humanities; business, management, and communication; science and technology; education; the environment; health science; the social and behavioral sciences; and social justice. UW–Green Bay's NCAA Division I men's basketball team, the Phoenix, has been a consistent top performer, making its first NCAA tournament appearance in the early 1990s under coach Dick Bennett (later coach of the UW–Madison Badgers). Bennett's son, Tony (now the University of Virginia's coach), was also a star for the team.

UW–La Crosse

UW–La Crosse was founded in 1909 with an academic focus that reflected the values of Fassett Cotton, its founding president. Summed up in its motto, *mens corpusque*, meaning "mind and body," the campus emphasized the importance of physical as well as academic education. Fittingly, the oldest club on campus is the Physical Education Club, established in 1912, and the school's reputation for excellence in preparing teachers of physical education continues. Building on this traditional focus, UW–La Crosse has expanded its offerings to include highly regarded physical therapy and physician assistant programs in partnerships with Gundersen Medical Foundation, the Mayo Clinic School of Health Sciences, and Marshfield Clinic Health Systems. The campus also offers undergraduate degrees in the arts and humanities, health and sciences, education, and business administration, as well as graduate degrees in business administration, education, and health sciences. It is consistently ranked by *U.S. News & World Report* as one of the top regional universities in the Midwest and for sixteen consecutive years was ranked the number one regional university in the state.[1] It currently enrolls more than nine thousand full-time students.

UW–Milwaukee

Now the second-largest university in the state, with nearly twenty thousand students, UW–Milwaukee is an urban doctoral institution serving the state's largest metropolitan area. Established as a normal school in 1880, it later became the Milwaukee State Teachers College and, still later, Wisconsin State College: Milwaukee. In 1956, it merged with the original University of Wisconsin at Madison and was known as UW–M until the 1971 merger creating the UW System, when it became UW–Milwaukee. The campus, located on Lake Michigan, is home to a number of distinguished graduate programs, including the only graduate school of freshwater science in the United States; the School of

Architecture and Urban Planning, the state's only school of architecture; and the Peck School of the Arts. The institution's expanding research efforts earned it a "Research I" designation in the Carnegie Classification of Institutions of Higher Education in 2016. Its technology transfer efforts have expanded rapidly with the support of the UW–Milwaukee Research Foundation, established in 2006. In addition to its academic programs, UW–Milwaukee supports community service programs such as the Institute for Urban Health Partnerships, which provides health services to underserved populations in the Milwaukee area, and the Community Designs Solutions program, which provides architectural and planning help. The main campus library is the Golda Meir Library, which also houses the American Geographical Society Library. Fifteen UWM Panthers athletic teams compete in the NCAA Division I.

UW–Oshkosh

Established as Oshkosh State Normal School, UW–Oshkosh has grown to become the third-largest campus in the UW System, offering programs in nursing, education, business, the social sciences, the natural sciences, the humanities, the fine and performing arts, engineering technology, information technology, health sciences, and applied and liberal studies that lead to undergraduate and graduate degrees. It has the largest graduate school among the System's comprehensive institutions and is a frequent recipient of the Regents' Teaching Excellence Awards. Consecutively winning twenty-five international Outstanding Delegation awards, UW–Oshkosh is among the most successful model UN programs in the world. The campus also boasts the historic distinction of being the first American institution of its type to establish a program to train kindergarten teachers, beginning in 1880 by enrolling children ages four to seven in an experimental campus laboratory school. Its strong NCAA Division III athletic program has won forty-two national championships.[2] As of fall 2017, it enrolled 8,208 full-time students.

UW–Parkside

UW–Parkside was created under 1965 legislation combining two-year centers at Racine and Kenosha. Located near both cities in the village of Somers, the university was officially founded on July 1, 1968, as a part of the former University of Wisconsin. Academic programs at UW–Parkside focus on custom-tailored degrees with small class sizes and one-on-one instruction. Now enrolling some three thousand students, the campus has the lowest tuition of any four-year accredited university in Wisconsin; 100 percent of courses are taught by professors, and the student/faculty ratio is 19:1.[3] The campus library was named Library of the Year by the Wisconsin Library Association in 2017.

UW–Platteville

The second-oldest public university in Wisconsin, UW–Platteville was founded as the state's first teacher preparation institution in 1866. The Platteville Normal School later combined with the nearby Wisconsin Mining Trade School (later the Wisconsin Institute of Technology), established in 1907, to provide training in mining engineering.[4] In 1959 the two institutions became the Wisconsin State College and Institute of Technology at Platteville, and the institution was renamed in 1966 as the Wisconsin State University–Platteville. Known since merger as UW–Platteville, the university is the fastest-growing campus in the System, with nearly seven thousand students. UW–Platteville continues to focus on offering exceptional engineering education. Students throughout the state of Wisconsin can complete an engineering degree through UW–Platteville Engineering Partnerships, a distance education program that does not require relocation to Platteville in order to complete the degree.[5] The university also offers associate, baccalaureate, and master's degrees in science, technology, engineering, and mathematics; criminal justice; education; business; agriculture; and the liberal arts. The campus also boasts a strong basketball tradition, with nine consecutive playoff appearances and four national NCAA Division III men's basketball titles under coach Bo Ryan, who would later lead UW–Madison's Badgers. A visible reminder of its roots as the Wisconsin Mining School, one of the university's oldest traditions began in 1936 when mining school students constructed the world's largest "M" from limestone found on Platte Mound, a large hill a few miles east of Platteville. The lighting of the "M" continues to be the featured ceremony at the school's homecoming each year.

UW–River Falls

Beginning as a normal school in 1873, UW–River Falls, located in the Minneapolis-St. Paul metropolitan area, saw dramatic enrollment growth following the end of World War II, leading to an expansion of its curriculum and a construction boom on campus. Now with some five thousand students, it is home to the second-largest undergraduate dairy science program in the country and to the St. Croix Institute, which works to foster sustainable communities. The campus also offers robust study-abroad opportunities, including the Experience China program, offering students a full semester of study in China and language immersion opportunities. In addition, the campus has developed a strong international partnership with Heilongjong Province in China to attract Chinese students to UW–River Falls and to foster economic cooperation between the province and Wisconsin businesses. River Falls students and faculty members are actively involved in civic affairs, including performing with the St. Croix Valley Symphony Orchestra, which presents five public concerts a year and performs for and with local elementary school students.

UW–Stevens Point

Now well known for its forestry program, UW–Stevens Point had its origins as a normal school, established in 1893. Growing rapidly in the post–World War II era, the campus built a strong foundation for lasting success under the leadership of future governor Lee Sherman Dreyfus, who served as chancellor from 1967 to 1977. The campus has the highest percentage of undergraduate courses taught by full-time faculty of any UW System institution and encourages strong student engagement in outside activities as home to more than two hundred student organizations. The university ranks highly for its postgraduation job placement rates. As of fall 2017, it enrolled 7,312 full-time students.

UW–Stout

Inspired by the industrial arts movement, lumber baron James Huff Stout in 1891 founded the Stout Manual Training School in his hometown of Menomonie. Today, UW–Stout is "Wisconsin's Polytechnic University" as designated by the Board of Regents in 2007 and offers a broad polytechnic education focusing on applied learning and liberal arts. Equipped with three times as many lab spaces as classrooms, UW–Stout emphasizes learning and partnerships with corporate and industry leaders. In 2001, it became the first higher education institution ever to receive the Malcolm Baldrige National Quality Award for excellence, presented by President George W. Bush. A leader in polytechnic education, in June 2019 the campus hosted the Polytechnic Summit, a conference that brought together national and international academic professionals and community leaders engaged in the field. As of fall 2017, it enrolled 6,851 full-time students.

UW–Superior

Established by the state legislature in 1893, UW–Superior opened its doors in 1896 as Superior Normal School. First accredited in 1916, it is one of the oldest continuously accredited institutions in the state.[6] In

1923, it became the first state normal school to offer a four-year high school teacher training program; renamed Superior State Teachers College, in 1926 it began granting bachelor's degrees in education. The campus continued its focus on the field of education, introducing a graduate program in school administration in 1950; an education specialist degree for principals, superintendents, and business managers in 1965; and degrees in instruction and special education in the late 1980s. The campus has maintained a deep commitment to its long-standing liberal arts mission, but it also emphasizes the ecology and management of local water resources through three entities: the Lake Superior Research Institute, created in 1967, which researches and teaches about the Great Lakes Region; the Great Lakes Maritime Research Institute, established in 2004; and the Lake Superior National Estuarine Research Reserve, designated in 2010. As of fall 2017, it enrolled 1,898 full-time students.

UW–Whitewater

UW–Whitewater developed its focus on business education essentially by default. According to its first director of curriculum, James C. Reed, "The other normal schools in Wisconsin had a chance to choose the subject they would select as their special work before Whitewater got a chance, and we had to take what was left. . . . No one at that time seemed to realize the importance of commercial work to forsee [sic] its future popularity."[7] The emphasis on "commercial" education proved to be a fortunate choice as the field grew in importance and "put Whitewater on the map."[8] For more than twenty years, the accounting program at the UW–Whitewater School of Business has consistently produced graduates who achieve among the highest scores nationally on Certified Public Accounting examinations. The Whitewater Warhawks athletic teams have seen major athletic success. The football team has won six NCAA Division III national championships since 2007, and in 2014 the school won NCAA Division III national championships in football, men's basketball, and baseball.[9]

UW Colleges

The thirteen two-year campuses organized as UW Colleges had their beginnings as satellites of larger four-year institutions, established in cooperation with counties to improve access to higher education for rural and place-bound, nontraditional adult and working students. Located throughout the state, these campuses provide two-year associate degree programs, preparing students to transfer to four-year UW

System campuses to complete their baccalaureate degrees. The colleges together serve more first-generation college students, more part-time students, and more adult undergrads than any other institution in the UW System,[10] making them a vital part of accomplishing the Wisconsin Idea.

Structurally, the UW Colleges were organized as a separate institution of the UW System at the time of the 1971 merger and operated under a central administration that oversaw all the campuses. In 2006, the administrations of UW Colleges and UW–Extension were combined under the leadership of a single chancellor. Faced with fiscal challenges, declining enrollments, and new demographic trends, the UW Colleges were again restructured in late 2017 and are now affiliated with nearby four-year UW System institutions. Under the new structure, UW Barron County is joined with UW–Eau Claire; UW–Manitowoc, UW–Marinette, and UW–Sheboygan are joined with UW–Green Bay; UW–Washington County and UW–Waukesha are joined with UW–Milwaukee; UW–Fond du Lac and UW–Fox Valley are joined with UW–Oshkosh; UW–Baraboo Sauk County and UW–Richland are joined with UW–Platteville; UW–Marathon County and UW–Marshfield/Wood County are joined with UW–Stevens Point; and UW–Rock County is joined with UW–Whitewater.

UW–Extension

UW–Extension has long been the embodiment of the Wisconsin Idea, disseminating the knowledge of the UW System campuses broadly throughout the state. Originally part of UW–Madison, UW–Extension functions were combined as a separate administrative unit of the flagship under President Fred Harvey Harrington and recognized as a separate UW institution following the 1971 merger. The postmerger UW–Extension included Cooperative Extension, providing county services through local educators and agents, nondegree programs, and 4-H youth programs; Wisconsin Public Television and Wisconsin Public Radio; the Division of Continuing Education, Outreach, and E-Learning and the UW Flexible Option degree program; and business and entrepreneurship divisions that provide assistance to small business owners throughout the state.

The UW–Extension administration was combined with that of the UW Colleges in 2006 and has also been reorganized in connection with the 2017 restructuring of the Colleges. The new structure moves the cooperative extension and public broadcasting functions to UW–Madison, while shifting other divisions to UW System administration.

Notes

Chapter 1. Merger

1. For a regent's description of the board's efforts to force Harrington's resignation, see, e.g., Walter Renk, interviewed by Donna Taylor, compact disc, University Archives and Records Management Services, Madison, Wisconsin (hereafter UARM) (1970).

2. "Olson Blames Democrats for Campus Trouble," *Capital Times* (Madison, WI), April 4, 1970.

3. "Lucey Terms Olson's Campus Stand 'Cheap,'" *Capital Times*, April 17, 1970.

4. Lucey, News Conference, June 11, 1970, cited in E. David Cronon and John W. Jenkins, *The University of Wisconsin: A History 1945–1971*, vol. 4, *Renewal to Revolution 1945–1971* (Madison: University of Wisconsin Press, 1999), 544; and Dave Zweifel, "Lucey Asks Delay in Choice of U. System Chiefs; Says Next Governor and Legislature May Want to Combine Regents," *Capital Times*, June 12, 1970.

5. Lucey, "Statement on Campus Unrest," September 3, 1970, cited in Cronon and Jenkins, *The University of Wisconsin*, 556, from typed manuscript, on file with UW Clip Sheet, Series 40/00/3 Box 15, UARM.

6. David Adamany, interviewed by Laura Smail, UARM (1985).

7. See, e.g., John R. Thelin, *A History of American Higher Education*, 2nd ed. (Baltimore, MD: Johns Hopkins University Press, 2011).

8. See Cronon and Jenkins, *The University of Wisconsin*, 598–99.

9. Before merger, the UW had established its UW Center System, with two-year campuses at Wausau, Sheboygan, Waukesha, Janesville, Marshfield, West Bend, and Baraboo, while UW–Green Bay administered centers at Manitowoc, Marinette, and Fox Valley/Menasha; in the late 1960s, WSU campuses opened branches at Barron, Richland Center, Fond du Lac, and Medford.

10. For fuller accounts of these early struggles, see J. Rost, "The Merger of the University of Wisconsin and the Wisconsin State University Systems: A Case

Study in the Politics of Education" (PhD dissertation, University of Wisconsin–Madison, 1973), 47–57; and Cronon and Jenkins, *The University of Wisconsin*, 521–36.

11. Renamed the Coordinating Council on Higher Education in 1968.

12. Lucey was born in La Crosse, grew up in Ferryville, and was educated at nearby Campion High School, a Jesuit institution in Prairie du Chien. He later attended St. Thomas College in St. Paul and UW–Madison, where he received a degree in philosophy in 1945. He went on to develop a successful real estate business in Madison.

13. He had initially supported the development of the Green Bay campus and its addition to the UW but had become increasingly worried about the creation of doctoral programs there and at the Parkside campus. He believed these efforts were redundant and unnecessary, in view of what was then a glut of PhD graduates. Patrick Lucey, interviewed by Martin Dowling, UARM (1985).

14. Lucey was especially offended by the kind of expensive program duplication reflected in actions such as the construction of an Olympic swimming pool at a WSU campus to "balance" one being built at Madison and the decision of the CCHE to allow the construction of two schools of veterinary medicine. Patrick Lucey, interviewed by Martin Dowling, UARM (1985); David Adamany, interviewed by Laura Smail, UARM (1985).

15. Patrick Lucey, interviewed by Martin Dowling, UARM (1985).

16. Assemblyman John Shabaz attacked the CCHE for the appointment, saying that hiring Percy "is like the fox watching the chickens." Donald Percy, interviewed by Martin Dowling, UARM (1985); Cronon and Jenkins, *The University of Wisconsin*, 553.

17. See, e.g., "CCHE Snubs Its Staff on U Budget Cuts," *Wisconsin State Journal* (Madison, WI), October 3, 1970; "Function of CCHE Staff Is Put in Doubt as Regents' Budget Figures Are OK'd," *Capital Times*, October 3, 1970.

18. Lucey had early in the summer urged delay in the selection of Harrington's successor. The UW Board, however, continued with its search process and at its October 1970 meeting selected John Weaver, then president of the University of Missouri System, to lead the UW. The Republican-dominated board seems to have been more focused on the need for securing strong leadership following the Sterling Hall bombing than on the larger issues being raised by candidate Lucey, but its action in proceeding with Weaver's appointment would continue to irritate Lucey. Patrick Lucey, interviewed by Martin Dowling, UARM (1985).

19. Lucey would later say that if Harrington had remained UW's president, merger would not have succeeded. As it was, however, with Weaver as president during the push for merger, Lucey ultimately "welcomed the fact that he [Weaver] wasn't very strong" in opposing it. Patrick Lucey, interviewed by Martin Dowling, UARM (1985).

20. Patrick Lucey, interviewed by Martin Dowling, UARM (1985).

21. The creation of the campuses at Green Bay and Parkside had been controversial from the beginning. Both the UW and the WSU had fought to make the schools part of their own systems. When they became part of the UW, campus leaders within the WSU were angered by the higher pay and more generous resources the two new campuses received. Even some UW supporters were concerned about the development of the Green Bay and Parkside campuses. At a meeting of the regents in 1968, UW regent president Charles Gelatt raised the question whether the state had adequate resources to support the new institutions and suggested they might more appropriately be included in the WSU. See Cronon and Jenkins, *The University of Wisconsin*, 208; Minutes of the October 5, 1968, Regular Meeting of the Board of Regents of the University of Wisconsin (hereafter BOR).

22. See Gerald H. Gaither, *The Multicampus System: Perspectives on Practice and Prospects* (Sterling, VA: Stylus, 1999).

23. See Aims McGuinness, "History and Evolution of Higher Education Systems," in *Higher Education Systems 3.0: Harnessing Systemness, Delivering Performance*, ed. Jason E. Lane and D. Bruce Johnstone (Albany: SUNY Press, 2013). As McGuinness notes, some of these systems were the result of consolidations of existing independent institutions, while others developed from the growth and expansion of flagship universities as they added new campuses.

24. See "A Forward Look: The Final Report of the Governor's Commission on Higher Education," Educational Resources Information Center, US Department of Education (November 1970).

25. The Kellett Commission's sweeping consolidation proposals failed to attract enough political support to be adopted, and Kellett would eventually endorse Lucey's proposal. See, e.g., Jim Hougan, "Kellett Endorses U. Merger Plan," *Capital Times*, August 31, 1971.

26. Patrick Lucey, interviewed by Martin Dowling, UARM (1985); David Adamany, interviewed by Laura Smail, UARM (1985). Focused on UW and WSU issues, neither Lucey nor Adamany appears to have considered the inclusion of the technical colleges in a merger.

27. Wisconsin state budgets are prepared on a biennial basis, beginning in odd-numbered years on a July 1–June 30 fiscal year cycle. As a result, a newly elected governor chosen in an even-numbered year has an immediate opportunity to develop the budget for his or her first two years in office.

28. Dreyfus would later claim credit for the idea of merger, describing a conversation with his old friend Lucey shortly after the 1970 election in which he impressed on the new governor that it was time to go forward. Lucey, however, disputed his influence. Lee Dreyfus interviewed by Robert Lang, UARM (2006); Patrick Lucey, interviewed by Martin Dowling, UARM (1985).

29. Rost, "Merger of the University of Wisconsin and the Wisconsin State University Systems," 45.

30. Ibid., 217–19; Cronon and Jenkins, *The University of Wisconsin*, 559–62.

31. David Adamany, interviewed by Laura Smail, UARM (1985); Donald Percy, interviewed by Martin Dowling, UARM (1985).

32. Rost, "Merger of the University of Wisconsin and the Wisconsin State University Systems," 42–47, 170–72.

33. Cronon and Jenkins, *The University of Wisconsin*, 562.

34. Rost, "Merger of the University of Wisconsin and the Wisconsin State University Systems," 232–35.

35. Donald Percy, interviewed by Martin Dowling, UARM (1984); Rost, "Merger of the University of Wisconsin and the Wisconsin State University Systems," 96–98.

36. Rost, "Merger of the University of Wisconsin and the Wisconsin State University Systems," 221–22.

37. John C. Weaver, interviewed by Donna Taylor, UARM (1977). Weaver recalled that he "had his hands full" with just the budget and merger seemed a less important issue at the time, especially in view of the many failed previous efforts to pass such a consolidation.

38. Minutes of the May 21, 1971, Regular Meeting of the BOR; John Weaver, interviewed by Donna Taylor, UARM (1977).

39. See Minutes of the March 12, 1971, Regular Meeting of the BOR.

40. Although Weaver later asserted that the UW board was immediately opposed to merger, the public comments at the March 12, 1971, board meeting gave little public indication of opposition. See John Weaver, interviewed Donna Taylor, UARM (1977); Rost, "Merger of the University of Wisconsin and the Wisconsin State University Systems," 226–28.

41. Rost, "Merger of the University of Wisconsin and the Wisconsin State University Systems," 234.

42. Minutes of the March 12, 1971, Regular Meeting of the BOR, 8–14. Some of the discussion at the WSU meeting suggested that the WSU board was in favor of merger, but WSU board president Roy Kopp had by this time con-tacted the UW board to clarify that the WSU had not endorsed the proposal.

43. Rost, "Merger of the University of Wisconsin and the Wisconsin State University Systems," 261–63.

44. See Robert J. Gough and James W. Oberly, *Building Excellence: The University of Wisconsin–Eau Claire: 1916–2016* (Virginia Beach, VA: University of Eau Claire Foundation, 2016), 165–67.

45. See Rost, "Merger of the University of Wisconsin and the Wisconsin State University Systems," 264, describing Dreyfus's failed efforts to secure support for merger from WSU presidents.

46. Rost, "Merger of the University of Wisconsin and the Wisconsin State University Systems," 222–25, 265–68, citing editorial support for merger from the *Capital Times*, *Green Bay Press Gazette*, and *Milwaukee Journal*.

47. Rost, "Merger of the University of Wisconsin and the Wisconsin State University Systems," 280; Matt Pommer, "Weaver Still Lucey's Choice for Merged University Chief," *Capital Times*, May 3, 1971.

48. Rost, "Merger of the University of Wisconsin and the Wisconsin State University Systems," 234. The "wrinkle committee" included Madison chancellor H. Edwin Young and Percy from the UW, River Falls president George Field and Eau Claire president Leonard Haas from the WSU, and DOA secretary Joseph Nusbaum.

49. Rost, "Merger of the University of Wisconsin and the Wisconsin State University Systems," 265–68.

50. Ibid., 102.

51. Ibid., 99–100.

52. Ibid., 239.

53. Ibid., 261–65; Cronon and Jenkins, *The University of Wisconsin*, 567–68.

54. See, e.g., Rost, "Merger of the University of Wisconsin and the Wisconsin State University Systems," 282, describing Nusbaum's trip to the Parkside campus.

55. See, e.g., Percy's "third alternative to merger," undated but apparently prepared during this time frame, in which he laid out a possible structure for merging the systems and their administrations. See Series 40/1/2/3-2, Boxes 4 and 5, UARM, and Cronon and Jenkins, *The University of Wisconsin*, 559, 586. Percy, always more open to the idea of merger than others in the UW's central administration, believed the UW's interests could best be served by working to improve the merger legislation rather than hoping it would fail. Donald Percy, interviewed by Martin Dowling, UARM (1984).

56. Rost, "Merger of the University of Wisconsin and the Wisconsin State University Systems," 261, 279–83.

57. Ibid., 283–84.

58. Substitute Amendment 3 to SB 213.

59. Rost, "Merger of the University of Wisconsin and the Wisconsin State University Systems," 298–300.

60. Ibid., 313; Minutes of the June 18, 1971, Regular Meeting of the BOR.

61. See, e.g., Rost, "Merger of the University of Wisconsin and the Wisconsin State University Systems," 332; Cronon and Jenkins, *The University of Wisconsin*, 572.

62. Rost, "Merger of the University of Wisconsin and the Wisconsin State University Systems," 332–44.

63. Ibid., 332–44; Cronon and Jenkins, *The University of Wisconsin*, 580–90.

64. John Weaver, interviewed by Donna Taylor, UARM (1977).

65. Rost, "Merger of the University of Wisconsin and the Wisconsin State University Systems," 365–66; Cronon and Jenkins, *The University of Wisconsin*, 587–90.

66. Senator Fred Risser, Democrat of Madison and representative of many UW faculty and staff, was opposed.

67. Lee Dreyfus, interviewed by Robert Lang, UARM (2006).

68. §990.05, Wisconsin Statutes, provides that laws go into effect the day after they are published; in the case of the merger bill, publication occurred on October 11, 1971, so the law became effective the following day.

Chapter 2. A Shotgun Wedding and Its Problems

1. See, e.g., Cronon and Jenkins, *The University of Wisconsin*, 329, citing UW publications office; Eugene McPhee, March 5, 1971, materials in 40/1/2/3-2, Box 6, UARM.

2. These included items such as making employees of the UW and the WSU employees of the new System while maintaining their existing employment rights; transferring the powers, functions, appropriations, records, and property from the former systems to the new Board of Regents. Sections 19–24, Chapter 100, Wisconsin Laws of 1971.

3. Indeed, Adamany seems not to have anticipated the creation of a statutory charter for the new system, apparently believing that the System's organizational structure would be developed as internal policies. David Adamany, interviewed by Laura Smail, UARM (1985).

4. Specifically, Section 26, Chapter 100, Wisconsin Laws of 1971, required the MISC to "study and make recommendations to the board of regents and the legislature by January 31, 1973, on merging chapters 36 and 37 of the statutes and on such areas as a) faculty tenure and retirement; b) faculty government and campus autonomy; bm) the practicability, feasibility and wisdom of merger; c) graduate and undergraduate credit transfer policies; d) student participation in government of the system; e) comparable funding for comparable programs and comparable teaching loads and comparable salaries for faculty based on comparable experience and qualifications; f) relevant criteria for research programs; g) uniform system-wide standards for utilization of classroom and other facilities; h) the role, efficiencies and economies contemplated by educational television in the system; i) year-round and evening utilization of facilities; j) collegiate transfer course standards employed by the state's vocational technical educational system; k) admissions and tuition policies; l) the role of teaching assistants and instructors throughout the merged system; and m) a complete review of saving and efficiencies effected by or contemplated by merger, so that such recommendations and studies may with practicability be applied to university of Wisconsin system budget determinations by the legislature."

5. John C. Weaver, interviewed by Donna Taylor, UARM (1977).

6. Minutes of the October 8, 1971, Regular Meeting of the BOR, Exhibit I.

7. Clara Penniman, interviewed by Laura Smail, UARM (1981).

8. At the time, the merger made the UW System the fourth largest public system in the country. See "UW Facts" (UW–Madison, 1970–75); Larry Van Dyne, "A Crucial Test in Wisconsin," *Chronicle of Higher Education*, April 2, 1973.

9. Weaver had no stomach for politics generally, either small "p" or large, according to Percy. Donald Percy, interviewed by the author, May 2, 2014.

10. Patrick Lucey, interviewed by Martin Dowling, UARM (1985).

11. Donald Percy, interviewed by Martin Dowling, UARM (1985).

12. See Percy drafts and notes on organizational possibilities (1971), Series 40/1/2/3-2, Boxes 4 and 5, UARM.

13. See, e.g., Memorandum, Percy to Central Policy Group and Van Hise central staff, October 25, 1971, Series 41/1/2/3-2, Boxes 4 and 5, UARM.

14. In keeping with the transitional provisions in the merger law, this number was to be gradually reduced to sixteen. Section 24, Chapter 100, Wisconsin Laws of 1971.

15. Donald Percy, interviewed by the author, May 2, 2014.

16. Fish later recalled that once merger passed, there was a genuine desire on the part of board members to make it work, saying that "you can't unscramble an omelet." Ody Fish, interviewed by Joel Skornicka and Art Hove, UARM (2005).

17. John Weaver, interviewed by Donna Taylor, UARM (1977).

18. Donald Percy, interviewed by Martin Dowling, UARM (1985).

19. See Percy drafts and notes on organizational possibilities (1971), Series 40/1/2/3-2, Boxes 4 and 5, UARM (includes Percy's "third alternative to merger").

20. Clara Penniman, interviewed by Laura Smail, UARM (1981).

21. Donald K. Smith was selected for the position in September 1972 and assumed the office in January 1973.

22. Minutes of the January 7, 1972, Regular Meeting of the BOR. In the WSU system, campus leaders had held the title "president," while in the UW, the president was the system head and campus executives were "chancellors." Although there had been initial resistance to changing the titles on the part of WSU leaders, at this meeting they expressed their agreement with the proposal.

23. Minutes of the December 17, 1971, Regular Meeting of the BOR.

24. See "Retrospect and Prospect: A Sense of Direction," May 11, 1973, a special report to the Board of Regents by Weaver, Percy, and Smith describing progress on merger implementation and goals for the future.

25. See Minutes of the January 7 and February 11, 1972, Regular Meetings of the BOR.

26. Although these equity issues were also assigned to the MISC for review under Section 26(e), Chapter 100, Wisconsin Laws of 1971, the board's actions preempted the MISC work.

27. See, e.g., Minutes of the May 5, 1972, Regular Meeting of the BOR; see also, Report of the MISC (January 29, 1973); "Retrospect and Prospect: A Sense of Direction," presented at the May 11, 1973, Regular Meeting of the BOR.

28. See Minutes of the January 11, 1974, Regular Meeting of the BOR. With limited exceptions, doctoral programs would not be offered at comprehensives until pressure to provide "professional" doctorates led to change in the 2000s.

29. Edwin Young and Donald K. Smith, interviewed by Laura Smail, UARM (1987).

30. At the time of merger, the laws establishing and governing the former UW were set forth in Chapter 36 of the Wisconsin Statutes, while the provisions governing the WSU were in Chapter 37.

31. Section 26, Chapter 100, Wisconsin Laws of 1971.

32. The legislation provided that the MISC would include three citizens appointed by the governor; the current president of the WSU Board or a designee and two other WSU regents appointed by him; the current president of the UW Board or a designee and two other regents appointed by him; the co-chairs of the legislature's Joint Finance Committee; the chairs of the Assembly and Senate education committees; one faculty member and one student from the WSU; and one faculty member and one student from the UW. The executive head of the new UW System was to serve as secretary to the MISC and provide staff services. In addition, the MISC was required to choose two advisers from the central staffs of the WSU and UW to serve in "advisory capacities." Section 26, Chapter 100, Wisconsin Laws of 1971.

33. The members were state representative Manny S. Brown, state senator Ray F. Heinzen, state senator Walter G. Hollander, and state representative George Molinaro; regents Norman Christianson (WSU), Ody J. Fish (UW), Milton E. Neshek (WSU), Frank J. Pelisek (UW), Walter F. Renk (UW), and chair James G. Solberg (WSU); citizen members Edward Hales, John M. Lavine, and Joe E. Nusbaum; faculty members Clara Penniman (Madison) and Marshall Wick (Eau Claire); and students Robert Brabham (UW) and Randy Nilsestuen (WSU).

34. Section 26, Chapter 100, Wisconsin Laws of 1971, provided, in part: "The executive head of the university of Wisconsin system shall serve as secretary of the committee and shall be responsible for providing staff services."

35. Donald Percy Papers, 40/1/2/3-2, Box 5, UARM.

36. See, e.g., "Merger Panel Splits on Staff Advisory Unit," *Green Bay Press Gazette*, December 4, 1971, reporting that "many state officials not directly involved in higher education have been pushing for outside staff 'to prevent the UW System from complete control over the study of its own merger process.'"

37. Minutes of the December 3, 1971, MISC meeting.

38. Solberg, UW System Press Release, January 19, 1972.

39. The Legislative Council, Fiscal Bureau, and Reference Bureau were represented, assisted by UW attorneys Burton Wagner, John Tallman, and David J.

Hanson. See Report of the Merger Implementation Study Committee, January 29, 1973, to Members of the Wisconsin Legislature.

40. Although this formulation of the Wisconsin Idea cannot be traced to a specific statement or quotation, Charles Van Hise, president of the University of Wisconsin from 1903 to 1918, is generally credited with the basic notion. In his 1904 inaugural address and in later speeches he used similar language, emphasizing his commitment to ensuring, for example, that the "beneficent influences of the University reach into every home in the commonwealth, and the boundaries of the campus are coextensive with the boundaries of the state." The phrase "the boundaries of the university are the boundaries of the state" seems to have come into common usage as the result of the work of Robert Foss of the University Press Bureau. See also J. David Hoeveler, *John Bascom and the Origins of the Wisconsin Idea* (Madison: University of Wisconsin Press, 2016); Jack Stark, "The Wisconsin Idea: The University's Service to the State," in *State of Wisconsin 1995–1996 Blue Book*, ed. Lawrence S. Barish, 101–79 (Madison: Joint Committee on Legislative Organization of the Wisconsin Legislature, 1996); and Alan B. Knox and Joe Corry, "The Wisconsin Idea for the 21st Century," *State of Wisconsin 1995–1996 Blue Book*, ed. Lawrence S. Barish, 181–92 (Madison: Joint Committee on Legislative Organization of the Wisconsin Legislature, 1996).

41. Section 20(13), Chapter 100, Wisconsin Laws of 1971.

42. See Section 20(13)(a), Chapter 100, Wisconsin Laws of 1971; cf., §36.01, Wisconsin Statutes, which was adopted verbatim from the MISC's proposed statutory draft.

43. See, e.g., Clark Kerr, *The Great Transformation in Higher Education, 1960–80* (Albany: State University of New York Press, 1991).

44. See §36.12, Wisconsin Statutes (1969), and Report of the Merger Implementation Study Committee (January 29, 1973), 7.

45. See §37.31, Wisconsin Statutes (1971), which provided for the automatic achievement of tenure after six consecutive years of service at an institution.

46. There was some disagreement as to whether the statute should also provide for "periodic review of tenure status." After discussion, however, the group unanimously agreed to remove such a requirement, believing that it conflicted with the provision allowing dismissal only for just cause. See Report of the Merger Implementation Study Committee, 12.

47. See Report of the Merger Implementation Study Committee, 12–13. The academic staff included nontenure-track instructors and academic administrator positions.

48. As discussed earlier, these titles were changed to "chancellor" by the new UW System Board of Regents in early 1972.

49. Section 20(13), Chapter 100, Wisconsin Laws of 1971.

50. Ibid.

51. The sharp differences between the two former systems are reflected in

documents prepared by faculty groups from each. Compare, e.g., "Findings and Recommendations of the University Faculty Council on Problems Related to Merger," March 6, 1972 (a report of UW faculty governance), with "A Faculty Statement on Problems Related to Merger," March 7, 1972 (a report of a faculty group including both UW and WSU members), on file with Office of the Secretary, UW System Board of Regents.

52. See proposed §36.09, Wisconsin Statutes, Report of the Merger Implementation Study Committee, January 29, 1973.

53. Patrick Lucey, interviewed by Martin Dowling, UARM (May 2, 1985); Lee Dreyfus, interviewed by Robert Lange, UARM (2006).

54. See Section 26(e), Chapter 100, Wisconsin Laws of 1971.

55. Percy attributed much of the factionalism on the MISC to these faculty concerns, noting there was less conflict over the board and executive consolidations and policy work. Donald Percy, interviewed by Martin Dowling, UARM, Session 1 (1985).

56. Nusbaum had had a long career in Wisconsin state government, helping establish the state's Department of Administration in 1959 and serving as its secretary under Governor Gaylord Nelson. Following positions with Nelson in Washington, DC, and as head of Western Washington State College in the 1960s, he returned to the DOA as secretary under Lucey in 1971. See obituary of Joseph E. Nusbaum, *Wisconsin State Journal*, September 7, 2006.

57. See, e.g., Minutes of the April 20, May 10, November 11, and December 1, 1972, MISC meetings.

58. Weaver letter to Solberg, on file with the Office of the Board of Regents, Drawer 95 (December 20, 1972).

59. See Cronon and Jenkins, *The University of Wisconsin*, 295–372, for a thorough discussion of the changes in UW–Extension organization and programming under Harrington.

60. Weaver, Letter to Solberg, on file with the Office of the Board of Regents, Drawer 95 (December 20, 1972).

61. Report of the Merger Implementation Study Committee, January 29, 1973.

62. See, e.g., Eugene C. Lee and Frank M. Bowen, October 21, 1975, letter to board president Bertram N. McNamara, forwarding their book *Managing Multi-Campus Systems*, Carnegie Council on Policy Studies in Higher Education (San Francisco: Jossey-Bass, 1975).

63. Donald Percy, interviewed by Martin Dowling, UARM (1985); Clara Penniman, interviewed by Laura Smail, UARM (1981); Edwin Young and Donald Smith, interviewed by Laura Smail, UARM (1987).

64. Prior to 1968, the Wisconsin Constitution provided that the state legislature would meet no more than once in every two years unless convened in special session by the governor. In 1968, Article IV, Section 11 of the Constitution was amended to allow the legislature to meet oftener, as provided by state

law. Chapter 15, Wisconsin Laws of 1971, then created §13.02, Wisconsin Statutes, providing for the first time that the legislature would meet annually,
rather than biennially. Related legislation provided that members would receive salaries on a full-time equivalent basis tied to state civil service pay grades.
With these changes, the Wisconsin Legislature effectively became a full-time
body, as classified by the National Conference of State Legislatures (NCSL).

65. David Adamany, interviewed by Laura Smail, UARM (1985).

Chapter 3. Welcome to Hard Times

1. Kerr, *The Great Transformation*.

2. The Economic Stabilization Act of 1970, Public Law 91–379, 84 Stat. 799
(1970), authorized executive and regulatory action to stabilize the economy by
controlling wages and prices through the Cost of Living Council. Nixon implemented a wage-price freeze beginning August 15, 1971, and controls continued
for the next two years, followed by gradual decontrol and abolition of the Cost
of Living Council in April 1974.

3. Donald K. Smith, interviewed by Laura Smail, UARM (1984).

4. Irving Shain, interviewed by Barry Teicher, UARM (1995).

5. John Weaver, interviewed by Donna Taylor, UARM (1977).

6. David Adamany, interviewed by Laura Smail, UARM (1985). Adamany
denied that he supported the productivity cuts, suggesting that others in the
administration, possibly Nusbaum, were behind the idea.

7. Affidavit of Gene Arnn, 40/1/2/4–1, Box 10, Papers of Donald Smith,
UARM; Minutes of the September 21, 1972, May 11, and June 8, 1973, Regular
Meetings of the BOR.

8. See §36.31, Wisconsin Statutes (1971), providing that faculty holding
tenure at the time of merger retained their status. The statute also provided that
tenured employment was permanent and that tenured employment could not
be terminated involuntarily, except for cause.

9. See Papers of Donald K. Smith, 40/1/2/4–1, Box 10, describing the conditions forcing layoffs, layoff procedures, and efforts to reassign affected staff
to other positions in the UW System; Minutes of the September 21, 1972, and
May 11, 1973, Meetings of the BOR.

10. Sam Daleo, "University Faculty Group Doubts 'Crisis' Reason for
Layoffs," *Eau Claire Leader-Telegram* (Eau Claire, WI), March 20, 1974.

11. See *Johnson v. Board of Regents*, 377 F. Supp.22 (W.D. Wis. 1974), aff'd.
510 F. 2d 975 (7th Cir. 1975); *Graney v. Board of Regents*, 92 Wis. 2d 745, 286
N.W. 2d 138 (1979).

12. "Flintrop Is Pessimistic on UW–O Outlook," *Oshkosh Advance-Titan*
(Oshkosh, WI), October 5, 1973.

13. Letter of January 8, 1975, from Patrick Lucey to board president Frank J.
Pelisek.

14. Pelisek succeeded Roy Kopp as board president in June 1973.

15. Minutes of the April 18, 1975, Special Meeting of the BOR and Attachments.

16. Minutes of the April 18, 1975, Special Meeting of the BOR, and Attachments vii, i (emphasis in original).

17. Ibid.

18. Patrick J. Lucey, interviewed by Martin Dowling, UARM (May 2, 1985). Since merger, only one campus, the tiny two-year center at Medford in 1980, has ever been closed.

19. *Retrospect and Prospect Revisited*, Exhibit B, Minutes of the December 5, 1975, Regular Meeting of the BOR.

20. Letter of Eugene C. Lee and Frank Bowen to BOR president Bertram McNamara (October 21, 1975), forwarding their book *Managing Multi-Campus Systems*, also discussed at the December 1975 BOR meeting.

21. See, e.g., "UW's Weaver Progressing Well," *Wisconsin State Journal*, April 21, 1976.

22. Minutes of the July 16, 1976, Meeting of the BOR; "Weaver to Quit as UW President Next Year," *Capital Times*, July 16, 1976.

23. Kauffman had also served as a college president himself, at Rhode Island College, and had become an expert in university presidential selection processes. See, e.g., Joseph Kauffman, *The Selection of College and University Presidents* (Association of American Colleges, 1974).

24. See Kauffman, *Selection of College and University Presidents*.

25. Donald K. Smith, interviewed by Laura Smail, UARM (1984); Joseph Kauffman, interviewed by Laura Smail, UARM (1987).

26. Minutes of the September 8, 1976, Executive Committee Meeting of the BOR.

27. Ibid.

28. See also Gaither, *The Multicampus System*; Lee and Bowen, *Managing Multicampus Systems*.

29. At that time, the UW Board was composed of the appointees of Republican governor Warren Knowles, and Lucey presumed that Weaver, too, was a Republican. Weaver, however, did not believe that he had been hired because he was a Republican and tried to avoid associating himself with partisan views. John C. Weaver, interviewed by Donna Taylor, UARM (1977).

30. Lucey would have preferred Young for the position, but his pledge to retain Weaver as president of the new system had helped gain support for the merger. Patrick J. Lucey, interviewed by Martin Dowling, UARM (1985); H. Edwin Young and Donald K. Smith, interviewed by Laura Smail, UARM (1987).

31. Patrick J. Lucey, interviewed by Martin Dowling, UARM (1985). Similarly, Young and Smith believed that Weaver had been chosen as UW president over Young because he was a Republican. H. Edwin Young and Donald K. Smith, interviewed by Laura Smail, UARM (1987).

32. See Exhibit C, Minutes of the September 17, 1976, Regular Meeting of the BOR.

33. See Matt Pommer, "Weaver Sees Nonpolitical Successor," *Capital Times*, July 16, 1976, in which Weaver rules out successors lacking strong academic leadership qualifications such as Percy, Carley, and Adamany. Of this group, however, Adamany—who held a PhD—did pursue an academic career, later serving as president of Wayne State University in Michigan and Temple University in Philadelphia.

34. The search committee had its own difficulties in preparing the list of finalists. The committee's decision rules required the agreement of three-fourths of the group in order to forward a name for further consideration, but it proved impossible to get this level of support for any one candidate. In its post-search report on the process, the committee recommended setting a lower percentage and identified various other problems with the process. See Weaver papers, UARM, 40/1/1/2–2, Box 60.

35. Jack Peltason, of the University of Illinois, had withdrawn. See Roger Gribble, "UC-Berkeley Official Was Third Finalist for UW Post," *Wisconsin State Journal*, March 16, 1977.

36. Joseph Kauffman, interviewed by Laura Smail, UARM (1987).

37. Like Lucey, Young believed that Weaver had been chosen over him to lead the UW in 1970 because the Board of Regents wanted a Republican and a new look for Madison. H. Edwin Young and Donald K. Smith, interviewed by Laura Smail, UARM (1987); see also, Patrick J. Lucey, interviewed by Martin Dowling, UARM (1985).

38. Ben R. Lawton, interviewed by Laura Smail on written questions and answers, UARM (1987).

39. According to Kauffman, he agonized over the decision. Joseph F. Kauffmann, interviewed by Laura Smail, UARM (October 19, 1987).

40. His choice of this party affiliation apparently reflected a major shift in position and not necessarily a positive one. As Young's successor as UW–Madison chancellor Irving Shain put it, "His conversion from Democrat to Republican had convinced him he had the insights of Gandhi." Irving Shain, interviewed by Barry Teicher, UARM (1995–97).

41. Joseph Kauffman, interviewed by Laura Smail, UARM (1987).

42. H. Edwin Young, interviewed by Laura Smail, UARM (1987).

43. See §36.09(1) and (2), Wisconsin Statutes. Section 36.09(1)(a) provides: "The primary responsibility for governance of the system shall be vested in the board which shall enact policies and promulgate rules for governing the system, plan for the future needs of the state for university education, ensure the diversity of quality undergraduate programs while preserving the strength of the state's graduate training and research centers and promote the widest degree on institutional autonomy *within the controlling limits of system-wide policies and priorities established by the board*" (emphasis added). Section 36.09(2)(a) provides that the president is to be president of all the faculties, vested with the

responsibility of administering the system under board policies, directing a central administration, and establishing Systemwide policies in program planning, finances, physical development and budget.

44. While the UW System was not established as a "flagship system" in the sense that it consisted of a flagship institution and its branch campuses, its governance and central administrative structure—largely modeled on the UW under Harrington—were similar to that type of organization. For a discussion of different types of higher education systems and definitions of "flagship" and "consolidated" systems used by the National Association of System Heads (NASH), see, e.g., Aims C. McGuinness Jr., "The History and Evolution of Higher Education Systems in the United States," in Lane and Johnstone, *Higher Education Systems 3.0.*

45. See Rost, "Merger of the University of Wisconsin and the Wisconsin State University Systems," 467. On October 6, 1971, shortly before the merger became law, Young advised his Faculty Senate, "I'm not dismayed by the prospect of joining with the State Universities. I believe we can join them and still maintain our excellence."

46. As he later noted, "We [Madison] lost the battle on merger but won some back on implementation." H. Edwin Young, interviewed by Laura Smail, UARM (1987).

47. Donald Percy, interviewed by Martin Dowling, UARM (1984).

48. Percy, who had worked for Harrington and Weaver, was deemed a "centralizer" and quickly clashed with Young, leaving to become the secretary of the state's Department of Health and Social Services. Young did, however, maintain a close relationship with Smith, who continued to serve as a vice president.

49. See §36.09(1), Wisconsin Statutes.

50. H. Edwin Young and Donald K. Smith, interviewed by Laura Smail, UARM (1987).

51. Joseph F. Kauffman, interviewed by Laura Smail, UARM (1987).

52. See Minutes of the March 11, 1977, Regular Meeting of the BOR, Resolution 1410, and attached report developed by the faculty governing bodies of all UW System institutions.

53. Ben R. Lawton, interviewed on written questions and answers by Laura Smail, UARM (1987).

54. Ironically, though, Young did effectively divert one Madison resource to the UW System. As Madison's chancellor, Young had use of an official residence, the Brittingham House, located in a Madison neighborhood several miles from the campus. The System president had the use of a different home, the Olin House, located within blocks of the Madison campus. Young effected a trade of the two houses, allowing him to continue to reside at the Brittingham House after becoming System president and making Olin House the permanent official residence of the Madison chancellor.

55. The use of WARF funds had long been a source of controversy at the Madison campus. Well before merger, Fred Harvey Harrington had arranged to allocate some $500,000 in WARF funding to UW–Milwaukee, a situation that angered the UW–Madison faculty, as well as the WARF board of trustees. Post-merger, UW–Milwaukee was no longer directly tied to Madison as it had been in the former UW, and the WARF trustees declined to provide further support to Milwaukee. As chancellor, Young supported this change, and as System president he ensured that all WARF funds went to Madison, confirming that WARF support was limited to Madison and should be directed only there.

56. See Minutes of the December 17, 1976, Regular Meeting of the BOR.

57. H. Edwin Young, interviewed by Laura Smail, UARM (1987). Character-izing the AAU as "the club," Young believed the Board of Regents should adopt a formal policy requiring UW–Madison's chancellor to be the representative—a step that the board never took. In addition to the AAU, there were other orga-nizations, including the Big Ten Athletic Conference and the Committee on Institutional Cooperation (CIC—the academic counterpart of the Big Ten and now the Big Ten Academic Alliance) on which the System president served, but Young did not attempt to transfer these roles to the Madison chancellor.

58. He had served as a chemistry professor, department chair, and Young's vice chancellor.

59. Irving Shain, interviewed by Barry Teicher, UARM (1995). Shain feared that the former WSU institutions would seek equality with UW–Madison and that, since state resources were insufficient to raise all institutions to Madison's level, the result would be diversion of Madison's resources elsewhere. He blamed Lucey for encouraging "complete egalitarianism" and would decline to be considered for the System presidency in the 1979 search, later suggesting that if chosen as president he would have "dismembered" the entire System.

60. See budget discussions from the Minutes of the June 10,1977, June 8, 1978, and July 14, 1978, Regular Meetings of the BOR. In addition, although Weaver had challenged these demographic predictions in the 1975 Scope Re-duction Report, updated demographic data now predicted declining enroll-ments until at least 1992, a result of the aging of the baby boom generation. The projected loss of students indicated that the System's financial needs would likewise diminish, making budget increases unlikely. This forecast was later confirmed in a legislatively required report prepared by the System titled "Pre-paring for a Decade of Enrollment Decline" (November 30, 1979).

61. See, e.g., Roger Gribble, "13% Spending Hike Asked for Education," *Wisconsin State Journal*, February 14, 1979; Matt Pommer, "Budget Plan Gets Non-Partisan Boo but UW Placated," *Capital Times*, February 14, 1979.

62. Minutes of the February 6, 1976, Meeting of the BOR.

63. See Minutes of the October 7, 1977, Meeting of the BOR, Exhibit A, describing the discussion at the Joint Audit Committee hearing of October 5, 1977.

64. The City University of New York (CUNY) had by this time implemented collective bargaining, and it was authorized also at the State University
of New York (SUNY). In 1980, the US Supreme Court held in *NLRB v. Yeshiva
University*, 444 US 672 (1980), that most tenure-track faculty are managerial
employees and therefore do not have a right to unionize under the National
Labor Relations Act (NLRA). While the decision slowed pressure for collective
bargaining at colleges and universities, and particularly at private institutions,
it did not prevent TAUWF from its own efforts to secure the right to unionize
under state law.

65. Minutes of the April 18, 1975, Meeting of the BOR (position statement
on collective bargaining).

66. H. Edwin Young and Donald K. Smith, interviewed by Laura Smail,
UARM (1987).

67. Exhibit E to Minutes of the November 11, 1977, Regular Meeting of the
BOR. The Board of Regents would consistently decline to endorse collective
bargaining, pointing out the dangers it posed to governance and board control
of faculty and academic personnel policies and, over the next ten years, lobbying
against various collective bargaining bills on the basis of the specific problems
each posed.

68. H. Edwin Young and Donald K. Smith, interviewed by Laura Smail,
UARM (1987).

69. Irving Shain, interviewed by Barry Teicher, UARM (1995–96). Shain
suggests that Young felt forced to retire as a result of this episode, although the
applicable retirement rules that effectively forced retirement at age sixty-two
would have led to his departure in any case.

Chapter 4. Family Dysfunction

1. Minutes of the April 6, 1979, Regular Meeting of the BOR.

2. The divisions between "activists" and others and the differences over
these selection process issues were not, however, partisan, according to Kauffman. While Democrats Lavine, Grover, and Hales were considered among the
activists, McNamara and DeBardeleben, although also Democrats, were not.
Joseph Kauffman, interviewed by Laura Smail, UARM (1987); see also Donald
K. Smith, interviewed by Laura Smail, UARM (1984).

3. Minutes of the April 6, 1979, Regular Meeting of the BOR.

4. Joseph F. Kauffman, interviewed by Laura Smail, UARM (1987).

5. See Minutes of May 11, 1979, Regular Meeting of the BOR, and attached
Exhibit F.

6. Joseph F. Kauffman, interviewed by Laura Smail, UARM (1987).

7. See, e.g., Matt Pommer, "Lawmakers Want UW Chief with 'Inside' Experience," *Capital Times*, October 24, 1979.

8. Shain had withdrawn and, reflecting his distaste for the merged System

and its administrators, would later state that had he been chosen president, he would have taken the System apart. Irving Shain, interviewed by Barry Teicher, UARM (1995–97).

9. The finalists included O'Neil; Lattie Coors, then president of the University of Vermont; Juanita Kreps, US Secretary of Commerce; Thomas Ehrlich, director of the International Development Coop Agency; William Boyd, president of the University of Iowa; and David Gardner, then president of the University of Utah. See Roger Gribble, "Indiana Man to Head UW," *Wisconsin State Journal*, December 14, 1979.

10. Word of Gerrard's actions had even leaked to the finalists, forcing Kauffman to contact them to assure them that no new names had been added to the list. Robert M. O'Neil, interviewed by the author (2016).

11. Minutes of the December 14, 1979, Regular Meeting of the BOR.

12. Joseph F. Kauffman, interviewed by Laura Smail, UARM (1987).

13. Fred Risser, interviewed by Laura Smail, UARM (1985).

14. Robert M. O'Neil, interviewed by the author (2016).

15. During the interim between Young and O'Neil, with Smith still recovering, UW–Platteville chancellor Warren Carrier served in an acting capacity as System president.

16. H. Edwin Young and Donald K. Smith, interviewed by Laura Smail, UARM (1987).

17. Irving Shain, interviewed by Barry Teicher, UARM (1995 and 1996).

18. Letters from Young to Bartlett (July 3, 1979) and Bartlett to Young (July 11, 1979), Record Series 40/1/1, Box 1, UARM.

19. Joseph Kauffman, interviewed by Laura Smail, UARM (1987).

20. Letters from Bartlett to O'Neil (May 14, 1980) and O'Neil to Bartlett (May 29, 1980), Record Series 40/1/1, Box 1, UARM.

21. Irving Shain, interviewed by Barry Teicher, UARM (1997–99).

22. Karen O'Neil, interviewed by Laura Smail, UARM (1985).

23. Donald K. Smith, interviewed by Laura Smail, UARM (1984); Edwin Young, interviewed with Donald K. Smith by Laura Smail, UARM (1987).

24. Joseph F. Kauffman, interviewed by Laura Smail, UARM (1987); Donald K. Smith, interviewed by Laura Smail, UARM (1984). Smith recalled that when his advice on the AAU matter was ignored, O'Neil never sought further advice from him.

25. Joseph F. Kauffman, interviewed by Laura Smail, UARM (1987); Karen O'Neil, interviewed by Laura Smail, UARM (1985). Young did recall, however, that Mrs. Weaver sometimes sent letters to the Youngs regarding what they should and should not do socially. H. Edwin Young, interviewed with Donald K. Smith by Laura Smail, UARM (1987).

26. Harry Peterson, interviewed by Laura Smail, UARM (1987). Peterson, Shain's lobbyist, conceded that, as a group, these flagship administrators spent too much time on fighting merger.

27. Robert M. O'Neil, interviewed by the author (2016).

28. Joseph F. Kauffman, interviewed by Laura Smail, UARM (1987).

29. Letters, O'Neil to Shain and Shain to O'Neil, December 18, 1981, UARC Series 40/1/1/4–2, Box 3.

30. Exhibit A, O'Neil's report on the tenth anniversary of merger from the Minutes of the October 9, 1981, Regular Meeting of the BOR.

31. See, e.g., Gaither, *The Multicampus System*; D. J. Weerts, *State Governments and Research Universities: A Framework for a Renewed Partnership* (New York: Routledge Palmer, 2002); Mark Yudof, "Are University Systems a Good Idea?," *Chronicle of Higher Education*, February 15, 2008.

32. Katharine C. Lyall, interviewed by Phil Certain, UARM (2006).

33. Lyall and Kevin Reilly both emphasized that, as System presidents, they believed that their relations with UW–Madison were the most important of all campus relations for System success. Katharine C. Lyall, interviewed by the author (2014); Kevin P. Reilly, interviewed by the author (2016).

34. Harry Peterson, interviewed by Laura Smail, UARM (1987).

35. See Minutes of the December 10, 1982, Regular Meeting of the BOR. The board did agree to undertake administrative rulemaking in the narrow area of use of its facilities by the public but otherwise rebuffed JCRAR's proposals.

36. *Capital Times v. UW–Madison* (Dane Cty. Cir. Ct. 1983); Section UWS 8.03, Wis. Adm. Code.

37. See Minutes of the September 11, 1981, Regular Meeting of the BOR. Unlike other board and System policies, conflict-of-interest policies for faculty and academic staff employees were specifically subject to legislative approval through the administrative rule-making procedures applicable to state agencies generally.

38. See, e.g., the September 11, 1981, April 8, 1983, December 9, 1983, June 8, 1984, October 5, 1984, March 8, 1985, July 12, 1985, and November 8, 1985, Minutes of Regular Meetings of the BOR.

39. See https://www.vetmed.wisc.edu/about-the-school/history.

40. Minutes of the December 17, 1976, Regular Meeting of the BOR.

41. Minutes of the December 8, 1978, Regular Meeting of the BOR.

42. At one point, Dreyfus himself seemed willing to drop his support (see Reid Beveridge, "Dreyfus May Reevaluate Vet School," *Wisconsin State Journal*, March 3, 1979), but he signed the budget authorizing funds in July of that year (see Thomas Still and Paul Rix, "Governor Signs Budget," *Wisconsin State Journal*, July 26, 1979).

43. See, e.g., Minutes of the November 7, 1980, December 5, 1980, and February 6, 1981, Regular Meetings of the BOR.

44. See, e.g., Doug Mell, "Dreyfus Tells Dane Board Vote Won't Halt Vet School," *Wisconsin State Journal*, March 4, 1981.

45. See Kaye Schultz, "Forget about PhD Nursing, UW Vice President Says," *Capital Times*, February 9, 1984.

46. See Kaye Schultz, "UW Regents Give OK to Nursing PhD," *Capital Times*, February 10, 1984; Robert M. O'Neil, interviewed by Laura Smail, UARM (1985).

47. Donald K. Smith, interviewed with H. Edwin Young by Laura Smail, UARM (1987).

48. Fred Risser, interviewed by Laura Smail, UARM (1985).

49. See Minutes of the March 5, 1982, Regular Meeting of the BOR; Irving Shain, interviewed by Barry Teicher, UARM (1995). Shain later complained that Dreyfus, who should have been a strong supporter of the UW, became one of its most serious problems, driving some faculty members to press for unionization and others to seek work elsewhere because of this threatened salary freeze.

50. See, e.g., Deborah Rankin, "Your Money; Reagan Cuts in Student Aid," *New York Times*, October 24, 1981; Edward B. Fiske, "Reagan Record in Education: Mixed Results," *New York Times*, November 14, 1982.

51. Minutes of the March 6, 1981, Regular Meeting of the BOR.

52. See Minutes of the March 5, 1982, Regular Meeting of the BOR.

53. Minutes of the October 9, 1981, Regular Meeting of the BOR.

54. Exhibit B to the Minutes of the July 16, 1982, Regular Meeting of the BOR.

55. Ibid.

56. Ibid.

57. Minutes of the June 5, 1981, Regular Meeting of the BOR.

58. Robert M. O'Neil, interviewed by the author (2016).

59. Minutes of the July 15 and September 9, 1983, Regular and Special Meetings of the BOR.

60. Anthony Earl, interviewed by Laura Smail, UARM (1987); Robert M. O'Neil, interviewed by Laura Smail, UARM (1985);Thomas Still, "UW Raise Seems Dead," *Wisconsin State Journal*, July 14, 1983; Rob Fixmer, "UW Star Fund Aims for Young Profs," *Capital Times*, August 10, 1983.

61. See "Faculty Advertise for Jobs," *Wisconsin State Journal*, August 31, 1983; "UW Committee Labels Job Ad Self-Defeating," *Capital Times*, September 1, 1983; Anthony Earl, interviewed by Laura Smail, UARM (1987).

62. Katharine C. Lyall, interviewed by Phil Certain, UARM (2006).

63. Irving Shain, interviewed by Barry Teicher, UARM (1996); Harry Peterson, interviewed by Laura Smail, UARM (1987); Katharine C. Lyall, interviewed by Phil Certain, UARM (2006).

64. Irving Shain, interviewed by Barry Teicher, UARM (1996); Katharine C. Lyall, interviewed by the author (2014).

65. Generous salary increases also tended to obviate the need for collective bargaining, undermining TAUWF's lobbying efforts.

66. Anthony Earl, interviewed by Laura Smail, UARM (1987).

67. Ibid.

68. Ben R. Lawton, interviewed on written questions by Laura Smail, UARM (1987).

69. Anthony Earl, interviewed by Laura Smail, UARM (1987).

70. Minutes of the November 8, 1985, Meeting of the BOR.

71. Joseph Kauffman, interviewed by Laura Smail, UARM (1987).

72. Harry Peterson, interviewed by Laura Smail, UARM (1987).

73. Minutes of the September 6, 1985, Regular Meeting of the BOR.

Chapter 5. Forward Momentum, Changing Conditions

1. Robert M. O'Neil, interviewed by the author (April 2016).

2. See WARF History/Success Stories, https://warf.org.

3. See https://www.nsf.gov/od/nms/results.jsp#.

4. Frank A. Cassell, J. Martin Klotsche, and Frederick I. Olson, *The University of Wisconsin–Milwaukee: A Historical Profile, 1885–1992* (Milwaukee: UWM Foundation, 1992), 103.

5. See Minutes of the July 16, 1982, Regular Meeting of the BOR.

6. See WARF History, https://warf.org/success stories. Steenbock, with the support of Agriculture dean Harry L. Russell and Graduate School dean Charles S. Slichter, had persuaded the Board of Regents to agree to the creation of a nonprofit corporation that would return the profits from patenting and licensing university research-based products for use in support of more research.

7. Pub. L. 96–517 (December 12, 1980), 335 USCs. 200–212.

8. See WARF History.

9. Under former UW president Fred Harvey Harrington, some WARF funds had also been used to support research at UW–Milwaukee prior to merger, when UW–Milwaukee was a part of the former UW. This transfer of funding, always controversial at UW–Madison, was discontinued after merger.

10. See WARF History.

11. See, e.g., Derek Curtis Bok, *Universities in the Marketplace: The Commercialization of Higher Education* (Princeton, NJ: Princeton University Press, 2003); Jennifer Washburn, *University Inc.: The Corporate Corruption of Higher Education* (New York: Basic Books, 2005).

12. Chapter UWS 8, Wisconsin Administrative Code (1986).

13. See, e.g., UW–Madison conflict-of-interest provisions, https://research.wisc.edu (compliance and ethics); also, https://rsp.wisc.edu (November 2018).

14. See Minutes of the July 16, 1982, Regular Meeting of the BOR.

15. UW–Milwaukee's chancellor J. Martin Klotsche on May 7, 1970, had to call a state of emergency at the campus in response to protests, closing it to visitors completely. UW–Oshkosh was also a site of anti–Vietnam War protests. See "The Anti-War Movement in UW–Oshkosh," www.uwosh.edu.

16. "City Unrest Rests after Tension-Filled Week," *Wisconsin State Journal,* May 12, 1969.

17. "Wisconsin Police and Youths Clash," *New York Times*, May 4, 1969; "Madison Police Rout 1,000 Students," *New York Times*, May 5, 1969. The *Times* also ran the story a week later when a peaceful party for students was held at the home of Madison fire captain Edward Durkin ("A Party in Madison: Peace Breaks Out," May 10, 1969).

18. *Like It Is*, UW–Madison, January 26, 1972, UARM.

19. Events such as the 1976 arrest of David Fine, one of the Sterling Hall bombers, would continue to be a source of emotion and conflict, as some students remained sympathetic to the goals—if not the consequences—of the New Year's Day Gang's activities, while most students and faculty strongly disapproved. See, e.g., 1976 Badger Yearbook, "Fine's Return Sparks Campus Controversies."

20. See, e.g., 1975 Badger Yearbook, describing the return of the Homecoming Ball event at UW–Madison.

21. Students paid fees, in addition to tuition, for a variety of purposes, including support for student government and student organizations, as well as capital expenditures for student unions and student recreational facilities.

22. See §36.09(5), Wisconsin Statutes, providing that student are to be "active participants" in the governance of their institutions and giving them "primary responsibility" for "the disposition of those student fees which constitute substantial support for campus student activities."

23. See, e.g., Regent Policy Document 30–3.

24. *UW–Milwaukee Student Association v. Baum*, 74 Wis. 2d 283 (1976).

25. 90 Wis. 2d 79 (1979).

26. §15.91, Wisconsin Statutes.

27. See "Chancellors' Questions Related to United Council's Proposed Policy Statement on Student Responsibilities Under Merger: Section 36.09 (5)."

28. Not all students were happy with the process or the attitudes of Mallon and Varjian. Both campus newspapers published editorials opposing the Pail and Shovel Party, several members of WSA resigned after the election, and there were claims of election rules violations.

29. 1979 Badger Yearbook.

30. The flamingos cost some $4,000, while the Statue of Liberty cost $70,000, according to the 1979 Badger Yearbook.

31. WSA president Jim Mallon apparently wore a red and white toga to the event.

32. Gianofer Fields and Stephanie Lecci, "How Wisconsin Students Pulled Off One of the Greatest College Pranks Ever," Milwaukee Public Radio, October 1, 2015.

33. See "The History of ASM and Student Governance at UW–Madison," http://www.asm.wisc.edu/about-us/.

34. See Thelin, *A History of American Higher Education*, 322.

35. Ibid., 321.

36. Ibid., 326–27.

37. See Cassell, Klotsche, and Olson, *The University of Wisconsin–Milwaukee*, 81.

38. Of the 600 women, 366 were at Madison, 154 at Milwaukee, 51 at Extension, and 31 at Green Bay. "Raises Give 600 Women at UW Same Pay as Men," *Capital Times*, December 6, 1971.

39. See Thelin, *History of American Higher Education*, 320.

40. Sue Stein, "Task Force Defines UW–O Racism," *Advance Titan*, November 2, 1972.

41. Roger A. Gribble, "Three Women Ejected from Regent Meeting," *Wisconsin State Journal*, May 6, 1972.

42. Bruce Swain, "Women Profs Threaten to Sue U," *Capital Times*, September 22, 1972. Donald Percy responded by emphasizing that around a million dollars in equity pay adjustments had been made over the last biennium, saying, "We haven't just been sitting around."

43. Diane Sherman, "Latins Rap UW, Say It's Lax on Minority Plan," *Capital Times*, March 9, 1973.

44. Diane Sherman, "Students Question Regents on Ethnic Center Closings," *Capital Times*, September 7, 1973.

45. "Fall Registration Form Asks Students' Race," *Like It Is*, April 19, 1972 (UARM). This move was initially viewed with suspicion, as some considered the request for self-identification to be a discriminatory act in itself.

46. "Office for Women Opened in UW System: Marian Swoboda at Head," *Kenosha News*, May 11, 1972.

47. See Regent Policy Documents, Sections 14 and 17 (Board of Regents of the University of Wisconsin System 2015), codifying and updating board policies on equal opportunity, affirmative action, sexual assault (formerly codified as Regent Policy Documents 72–7, 72–9, 72–21, 75–5, 83–4 and 84–5), and sexual harassment (formerly codified as Regent Policy Document 81–2).

48. Bruce Swain, "$12,500 Pay Gap Stuns UW Women: Similar Jobs, Half the Money," *Capital Times*, December 9, 1972.

49. "Assistant to Weaver Gets $6,000 Hike to $21,000," *Wisconsin State Journal*, February 10, 1973.

50. Robin Thompson, "Hiring Data on Women, Minorities Dismays Regents," *Journal Times*, March 9, 1974. Also, William Jordan, "UW Hiring Policies Faulted: Report Says Women, Minorities Fare Poorly," *Wisconsin State Journal*, July 16, 1974.

51. Julianne Corty, "Minorities, Women Would Benefit from New UW–P Plan," *Journal Times*, November 20, 1974.

52. See, e.g., Thompson, "Hiring Data on Women."

53. Thelin, *History of American Higher Education*, 320–25.

54. See "UW System Fact Book" (University of Wisconsin System, March 2019).

55. For a chart of the numbers of women enrolled in UW Law School from

1964 to 1980, see Marian J. Swoboda and Audrey Roberts, eds., *Wisconsin Women, Graduate School and the Professions* (Madison: University of Wisconsin System, Office of Women, 1980), 70.

56. See, e.g., "UW–Madison Enrollment Data" (Office of the Registrar, UW–Madison, 2019).

57. UW–Milwaukee's Experimental Program in Higher Education (EPHE) enrolled Milwaukee-area students not otherwise admissible on the basis of an assessment of their ability to succeed in college. Although not race-restricted, the program accounted for an 85 percent increase in UWM's minority enrollment between 1970 and 1971 (Cassell, Klotsche, and Olson, *The University of Wisconsin–Milwaukee*, 80–81).

58. Executive Order 10925, March 6, 1961, establishing the President's Committee on Equal Employment Opportunity, https://www.eeoc.gov/eeoc/history/35th/thelaw/eo-10925.html.

59. 438 US 265 (1978).

60. See, e.g., *Hopwood v. Texas*, 78 F. 3d 932 (5th Cir. 1996). The issue would not be settled until *Grutter v. Bollinger*, 539 US 306 (2003), which held that student body diversity is a compelling state interest that can justify consideration of race as a plus factor in a college admissions program.

61. See, e.g., James Davison Hunter and Alan Wolfe, *Is There a Culture War?* (Washington, DC: Brookings Institution, Pew Research Center, 2006); James Davison Hunter, *Culture Wars: The Struggle to Define America* (New York: Basic Books, 1991).

62. See the Education for All Handicapped Children Act, Public Law 94–142 (1975), renamed the Individuals with Disabilities Education Act in 1990; Americans with Disabilities Act, 42 USC 126 (1990).

63. https://mcburney.wisc.edu/information/history/.

64. At UW–Madison, the ROTC program included the Departments of Naval Science, Military Science, and Air Force.

65. Minutes of the April 10, 1987, Regular Meeting of the BOR.

66. Minutes of the February 2, 1990, Regular Meeting of the BOR.

67. See "In Protest of ROTC," *On Wisconsin*, Fall 2015.

68. See Samuel J. Pfeiffer, "8,600 Miles from Cape Town: The Anti-Apartheid Movement in Madison, Wisconsin, 1969–1994" (poster, UARM).

69. "Business in South Africa," *Wall Street Journal*, August 18, 1978.

70. See, e.g., Regent Policy Document 31–13 (2015); see also §36.29, Wisconsin Statutes, prohibiting investments of university funds in companies that practice illegal discrimination.

Chapter 6. Merger 2.0

1. The state was notoriously tight-fisted, with some state leaders even insisting that a UW System president should not earn more than the governor. The pay situation, combined with knowledge of the O'Neil-Shain problems,

was a serious obstacle to the recruitment of national leaders for the position. Kauffman later said that three-quarters of the national leaders he approached about the position said that they did not want to be considered. Joseph F. Kauffman, interviewed by Laura Smail, UARM (1987).

2. See Kaye Schultz, "Earl Supports Carley; Dreyfus Says He's Interested," *Capital Times*, July 23, 1985. Despite his apparent popularity with some state politicians, however, some thought Carley arrogant, one source noting that he had a personality problem that made it difficult for him to get along with others and impossible for him to get elected to public office.

3. Katharine C. Lyall, interviewed by Phil Certain, UARM (2006).

4. See, e.g., "Are 3 State Men in Running for UW Position?," *Capital Times*, August 6, 1985; Roger A. Gribble, "Carley, Shain Remain UW Candidates," *Wisconsin State Journal*, August 7, 1985.

5. See Patricia Simms, "Carley Blasts UW Job Hunt," *Wisconsin State Journal*, September 21, 1985.

6. Brian Mattmiller, "Idea of UW Inquiry Rapped," *Wisconsin State Journal*, September 23, 1985; Opinion, "UW Presidency Hunt Suffered from Secrecy," *Wisconsin State Journal*, September 15, 1985.

7. Kenneth A. Shaw, interviewed by the author (2016).

8. See "An Evaluation of Reserve Balances in the University of Wisconsin System Auxiliary Operations," *Report 85-5*, Wisconsin Legislative Audit Bureau (February 28, 1985).

9. Minutes of the December 6, 1985, and April 11, 1986, Regular Meetings of the BOR.

10. Minutes of the March 11, 1986, Regular Meeting of the BOR.

11. "A Management Audit of the University of Wisconsin System Administration," *Report 86-5*, Wisconsin Legislative Audit Bureau (November 10, 1986). In response to the attack on System management, Shaw explained the history of System-legislative relations, noting: "The UW System has not remained static over the past 15 years, it has changed with a changing world. The Board of Regents and System Administration recognize that the current environment requires more aggressive leadership and management."

12. Minutes of the September 5, 1986, Regular Meeting of the BOR and Exhibit B (Weinstein to Haney letter).

13. Kenneth A. Shaw, interviewed by the author (2016).

14. Lucey had often complained about university whining, and Earl would later note that "it falls on deaf [legislative] ears to keep threatening imminent doom if the university doesn't get what it wants." Anthony Earl, interviewed by Laura Smail, UARM (1987).

15. Minutes of the February 7, 1986, Meeting of the BOR.

16. Tom Loftus, interviewed by the author (2016).

17. Kenneth A. Shaw, interviewed by the author (2016).

18. Katharine C. Lyall, interviewed by Phil Certain, UARM (2006).

19. Shaw took office in January 1986, and Shain retired from UW–Madison at the end of that year.

20. Irving Shain, interviewed by Barry Teicher, UARM (1995–97).

21. Kenneth A. Shaw, interviewed by the author (2016).

22. Tommy G. Thompson, interviewed by the author (2016).

23. Minutes of the July 12, 1985, Regular Meeting of the BOR, Exhibit B, Memorandum, Robert M. O'Neil to BOR.

24. *Planning the Future, Report on the Future of the University of Wisconsin System* (Board of Regents, December 1986).

25. Although the Board of Regents has the statutory authority to set tuition, as a practical matter the actual rates are determined through the biennial budget development process and are linked to student instructional costs, which are funded by tax dollars and student fees. Because the legislature and the governor control the budget on which tuition levels are based and also control the UW System's authority to expend tuition revenues, tuition levels proposed by the board must, in practice, be agreed upon by the state government. For a detailed explanation of the tuition-setting process, see, e.g., "University of Wisconsin Tuition," *Information Paper 37*, Wisconsin Legislative Fiscal Bureau (2003).

26. *Planning the Future*, 14.

27. Minutes of the December 5, 1986, Regular Meeting of the BOR. The report's endorsement of tuition increases conflicted with a recently published report of the National Commission on the Role and Future of State Colleges and Universities, which had suggested in "To Secure the Blessings of Liberty" that rising tuitions were a serious concern nationally. Tuition at Wisconsin institutions had remained so low, however, that the board—including regent Ruth Clusen, who had served as a member of the National Commission—agreed that rising tuition was not a problem in Wisconsin.

28. Earl had urged the System to agree with him on a budget before the election, but no agreement was reached. Anthony Earl, interviewed by Laura Smail, UARM (1987).

29. Minutes of the November 7, 1986, Regular Meeting of the BOR.

30. Minutes of the July 10, 1987, Regular Meeting of the BOR.

31. Katharine C. Lyall, interviewed by the author (2014).

32. See, e.g., *2007 Milwaukee Track and Field Media Guide*, https://static .mkepanthers.com.

33. Minutes of the September 5, 1986, Regular Meeting of the BOR.

34. Minutes of the July 11 and September 5, 1986, Regular Meetings of the BOR.

35. Minutes of the November 7, 1986, Regular Meeting of the BOR.

36. Minutes of the November 14, 1986, Special Meeting of the BOR.

37. *Planning the Future*, 16.

38. Described in the Minutes of the November 6, 1987, Regular Meeting of the BOR, Exhibit B ("A Shared Commitment").

39. Minutes of the June 6, 1986, Regular Meeting of the BOR.

40. See *Wisconsin State Journal*, May 5, 1987.

41. See *Wisconsin State Journal*, November 8, 1987.

42. Minutes of the May 8 and November 6, 1987, Regular Meetings of the BOR.

43. Minutes of the November 6, 1987, Regular Meeting of the BOR, Exhibit B.

44. 438 US 265 (1978).

45. See, e.g., *Hopwood v. Texas*, 78 F. 3d 932 (5th Cir. 1996). The issue of the extent to which race could constitutionally be considered in college admissions programs would not be settled until *Grutter v. Bollinger*, 539 US 306 (2003), which confirmed what had been suggested by *Bakke*, holding clearly that student body diversity is a compelling state interest that can justify the use of race as a plus factor in a university admissions program.

46. See, e.g., *Podboresky v. Kirwan*, 38 F. 3d 147 (4th Cir. 1994).

47. Schmeling, "Shaw Aid Plan Now Multicolored," *Capital Times*, April 9, 1988.

48. Kenneth A. Shaw, interviewed by the author (2016).

49. Donna Shalala, interviewed by Laura Smail, UARM (1988); Kenneth A. Shaw, interviewed by the author (2016).

50. See, e.g., "Give Design for Diversity and the Madison Plan a Chance to Succeed," Opinion, *Wisconsin State Journal*, April 19, 1988; "Shalala and Shaw Need Help," Opinion, *Capital Times*, February 14, 1989, supporting UW System's budget request for $6 million to fund the plan. There were also early signs of the plan's effectiveness in improving minority enrollments, as reported in "Shaw Claims Design for Diversity Working," *Oshkosh Advance Titan*, November 30, 1989, describing a 16.2 percent increase in minority enrollments.

51. Chapter UWS 17, Wisconsin Administrative Code, first approved after merger, described the misconduct that could lead to disciplinary action and provided accused students an opportunity to be heard before discipline was invoked. Administrative rules have the force of law and are subject to review by the legislature before they can be adopted by state agencies. See Chapter 227, Wisconsin Statutes.

52. See *Doe v. University of Michigan*, 721 F. Supp. 852 (E.D. Mich. 1989).

53. See, e.g., the collection of essays in W. Lee Hansen, *Academic Freedom on Trial: 100 Years of Sifting and Winnowing at the University of Wisconsin–Madison* (Madison: University of Wisconsin Press, 1998).

54. Minutes of the June 9, 1989, Meeting of the BOR.

55. Instances of student conduct that resulted in disciplinary proceedings under the rule included calling a woman a "f****** c*** and f****** bitch"; calling a black residence hall employee "a piece of s*** n*****"; and sending an Islamic professor an e-mail message saying "Death to all Arabs!!!! Die Islamic scumbags!" See *UW–M Post v. Board of Regents*, 774 F. Supp. 1163 (E.D. Wis. 1991); Patricia Hodulik, "Racist Speech on Campus," *The Wayne Law Review* 37, no. 3 (1991).

56. 774 F. Supp. 1163 (E.D. Wis. 1991).

57. The decision of the US Supreme Court in *R.A.V. v. City of St. Paul, Minnesota*, 505 US 377 (1992) indicated that further efforts to change the board's rule would be unlikely to pass constitutional muster. The case involved an incident in which a cross was burned on the lawn of a black family. The perpetrators were prosecuted under a city ordinance that punished bias-motivated crimes, including cross burning, and appealed their conviction on grounds that the ordinance violated their First Amendment rights. The city defended its ordinance on grounds similar to those the board had argued in support of its rule, but the Supreme Court held that the city ordinance was unconstitutional, thus making it unlikely that the board's rule, even as amended, could be sustained if challenged in further litigation.

58. Former System president O'Neil, by 1992 the director of the Thomas Jefferson Center for the Protection of Free Expression, was among those concerned about the rule's constitutionality, telling the *Washington Post* then that "Speech codes were unwise and for the most part unnecessary, even though they were adopted for the best reasons." *Washington Post*, Obituaries, October 3, 2018.

59. See, e.g., Jerry Adler, "Taking Offense: Is This the New Enlightenment on Campus or the New McCarthyism?" and "Thought Police," *Newsweek*, December 24, 1990; Ken Emerson, "Only Correct," *New Republic*, February 18, 1991; Dinesh D'Souza, "Illiberal Education," *Atlantic Monthly*, March, 1991.

60. See, e.g., Minutes of the December 6, 1985, Regular Meeting of the BOR, discussing the activities of this organization, which was devoted to monitoring classroom lectures to expose liberal bias.

61. See, e.g., *Hopwood v. Texas*, 78 F. 3d 932 (5th Cir. 1996).

62. Minutes of the June 10, 1988, Regular Meeting of the BOR.

63. Minutes of the December 8, 1989, Regular Meeting of the BOR.

64. "Shaw's Leadership 'Solidifies' System" and "He's Not One of the Tweedy Types," *Wisconsin State Journal*, January 28, 1990.

65. See, e.g., Minutes of the February 2, 1990, Regular Meeting of the BOR, discussing the need for a more competitive executive salary structure and problems with the pay plan for faculty and academic staff.

66. Kenneth A. Shaw, interviewed by the author (2016) and, see, e.g., Minutes of the October 9, 1987 (United Council request for a cap on tuition), and April 8, 1988 (reports that financial aid increased, but with more loans and fewer grants), Meetings of the BOR.

67. See Report 91-7, Wisconsin Legislative Audit Bureau (1991).

68. See, e.g., "Study Knocks UW System," *Janesville Gazette*, April 20, 1991.

69. See "Shaw Resigns as UW System Chief," *Eau Claire Leader Telegram*, April 25, 1991; Dan Holtz, "Some Not Sorry to See Shaw Go," *Eau Claire Leader Telegram*, April 25, 1991.

70. Harry Peterson, interviewed by Laura Smail, UARM (1987); Tom Loftus, interviewed by the author (2016).

Chapter 7. The Mature System

1. Phil McDade, "UW President Hunt Begins," *Wisconsin State Journal*, October 24, 1991; AP, "In-House Report Says UW Quality Dropping," *Kenosha News*, November 1991.

2. McDade, "UW President Hunt Begins."

3. Ibid.

4. The board agreed that it would release the names of all applicants and nominees who did not specifically request confidentiality, as well as the names of all candidates in the finalist group.

5. The list of all nominees and applicants—some 142 in all—was published in the *Wisconsin State Journal*, March 10, 1992. Shalala was among the nominees but declined to be considered.

6. Lyall agreed that it is important for a System president to have an academic background, noting later that it would be a mistake to have a president who had never taught and was not qualified to teach. While recognizing that it is tempting for boards to want to consider business or political leaders, she observed, it is the academic and scholarly experience that provides important leadership credibility. Katharine C. Lyall, interviewed by Phil Certain, UARM (2006).

7. Minutes of the June 5, 1992, Regular Meeting of the BOR.

8. Katharine C. Lyall, interviewed by Phil Certain, UARM (2006).

9. See Minutes of the August 23 and September 13, 1996, Regular Meetings of the BOR.

10. Donna Shalala, interviewed by Laura Smail, UARM (1988).

11. Katharine C. Lyall, interviewed by Phil Certain, UARM (2006).

12. Minutes of the July 16, 1993, Regular Meeting of the BOR.

13. See Minutes of the December 10, 1993, Regular Meeting of the BOR, discussing "Accountability for Achievement: Progress Report."

14. See Minutes of the December 8, 1995, Meeting of the BOR.

15. Katharine C. Lyall, interviewed by Phil Certain, UARM (2006).

16. See Board of Regents Study of the UW System in the 21st Century, Office of the Secretary to the Board (1996).

17. Ibid.

18. Minutes of the August 23, 1996, Regular Meeting of the BOR.

19. Minutes of the October 8, 1999, Regular Meeting of the BOR.

20. Minutes of the October 10, 1997, Regular Meeting of the BOR.

21. See, e.g., Minutes of the December 8, 2000, Regular Meeting of the BOR, describing the outcomes of the first economic summit.

22. Katharine C. Lyall, interviewed by Phil Certain, UARM (2006).

23. When Thompson took office as governor in 1987, the legislature was controlled by Democrats, a situation that continued until 1995, when Republicans took control of both legislative houses for a brief two-year period. From

1997 to 2001 the Democrats controlled the state Senate, again producing shared legislative power.

24. See Tim Cullen, *Ringside Seat: Wisconsin Politics, the 1970s to Scott Walker* (Mineral Point, WI: Little Creek Press, 2015), and Tommy G. Thompson and Doug Moe, *Tommy: My Journey of a Lifetime* (Madison: University of Wisconsin Press, 2018), describing Wisconsin's "center right"/"center left" government.

25. Other later leaders, including Weinstein, had similarly "activist" approaches to governance. Weinstein was a strong board president in Shaw's tenure and a vigorous advocate for the System and for policies such as *Design for Diversity*, but his efforts to assert control over management details had made him a difficult partner for System and campus executives. See Katharine C. Lyall, interviewed by Phil Certain, UARM (2006); Irving Shain, interviewed by Barry Teicher, UARM (1995–97). Shain was especially incensed over Weinstein's intervention in a flap over the sale of *Playboy* magazines at the Memorial Union.

26. Minutes of the July 13, 1990, Regular Meeting of the BOR.

27. Minutes of the June 5, 1992, Regular Meeting of the BOR.

28. Minutes of the June 5, 1998, Regular Meeting of the BOR.

29. Thompson also repeatedly vetoed legislation to permit collective bargaining by faculty and academic staff, ending, at least for a time, internal System debate and legislative pressure on this controversial issue.

30. Minutes of the February 8, 1991, Regular Meeting of the BOR.

31. Minutes of the August 23, 1996, Regular Meeting of the BOR.

32. Katharine C. Lyall, interviewed by Phil Certain, UARM (2006).

33. Minutes of the September 13, 1996, Regular Meeting of the BOR.

34. See Minutes of the June 5, 1998, Regular Meeting of the BOR.

35. Minutes of the September 10, 1999, Regular Meeting of the BOR.

36. See, e.g., Natasha Kassulke, "UW–Madison Dips in Research Ranking," *UW–Madison News*, November 22, 2016, and November 15, 2019. UW–Madison was among the top five nationally from 1972 through 2015, when it fell to sixth.

37. Minutes of the April 2, 1993, Regular Meeting of the BOR.

38. Minutes of the June 9, 2000, Regular Meeting of the BOR.

39. Initially, UW–Milwaukee was to serve as the host campus for WiSys and provide services throughout the System. In 2006, however, UW–Milwaukee established its own technology transfer organization, the UWM Foundation.

40. Minutes of the May 9, 1997, Regular Meeting of the BOR.

41. See, e.g., Minutes of the September 12, 2002, Regular Meeting of the BOR.

42. Minutes of the May 7, 1998, Regular Meeting of the BOR.

43. Minutes of the June 11, 1999, Regular Meeting of the BOR.

44. Minutes of the September 10, 1999, Regular Meeting of the BOR.

45. Minutes of the December 5, 1997, Regular Meeting of the BOR.

46. Minutes of the February 5 and December 10, 1999, Regular Meetings of the BOR.

47. Vince Sweeney, *Always a Badger: The Pat Richter Story* (Black Earth, WI: Trails Press, 2005).

48. Katherine C. Lyall and Kathleen R. Sell, *The True Genius of America at Risk* (Westport, CT: Praeger, 2006).

49. Katharine C. Lyall, interviewed by Phil Certain, UARM (2006).

50. Minutes of the October 9, 1992, Regular Meeting of the BOR.

51. Minutes of the June 5, 1992, Regular Meeting of the BOR.

52. Thompson later acknowledged that he had gone too far in directing state resources to the corrections expansion, saying he was not "particularly proud" of all the prison construction in the 1990s. Thompson and Moe, *Tommy*, 166.

53. Minutes of the April 8, 1994, Regular Meeting of the BOR.

54. Minutes of the March 10, 1995, Regular Meeting of the BOR.

55. Minutes of the October 8, 1999, Regular Meeting of the BOR.

56. Minutes of the March 8, 2002, Regular Meeting of the BOR.

57. Minutes of the March 8, 2002, Regular Meeting of the BOR.

58. Minutes of the April 4, 2002, Regular Meeting of the BOR.

59. Minutes of the February 6 and March 6, 2003, Regular Meetings of the BOR.

60. *Charting a New Course for the UW System*, UW System Board of Regents (2004).

61. Ibid., 8.

62. See Minutes of the February 6, 2003, Regular Meeting of the BOR.

63. See Cullen, *Ringside Seat*. The situation also set the stage for a major political scandal in 2002, when Chvala and his Republican counterpart, Assembly Speaker Scott Jensen, were charged with misconduct in public office for illegally using state employees of their respective legislative caucuses to conduct political campaigns. Both men lost their leadership posts and their political careers, and Chvala served time in jail.

64. Tommy Thompson, interviewed by the author (2016).

65. See, e.g., Minutes of the July 10, 1992, Regular Meeting of the BOR, presenting the results of a study by the Wisconsin Survey Research Lab on public perceptions of the UW System; Minutes of the December 8, 2000, Regular Meeting of the BOR, discussing a report by Chamberlain Research Associates showing that 82 percent of state citizens believe the UW System is critical to the state's economy and quality of life; and Minutes of the May 9, 2003, Regular Meeting of the BOR, presenting the result of surveys conducted by *The Chronicle of Higher Education* and the American Council on Education.

66. See, e.g., Lyall and Sell, *True Genius of America at Risk*, xv.

67. Minutes of the May 8, 2003, Regular Meeting of the BOR.

68. See, e.g., Minutes of the October 9, 1987 (United Council request for a cap on tuition), and April 8, 1988 (reports that financial aid increase, but with more loans and fewer grants), Meetings of the BOR.

69. From 1972 to 1985 the acceptance rate for all UW System institutions was close to 90 percent. This declined to about 80 percent through 1999 and to 62 percent by 2009. http://www.lafollette.wisc.edu/images/publications/workingpapers/wolfe2009-005.pdf.

70. *Bush v. Gore*, 531 US 70 (2000).

71. See, e.g., Bok, *Universities in the Marketplace*; Washburn, *University Inc.*

72. Minutes of the June 7, 1991, Regular Meeting of the BOR.

73. Lyall and Sell, *True Genius of America at Risk*.

74. Ibid., xiv.

75. Ibid., 149–57.

Chapter 8. Challenges of the New Century

1. Regent Policy Document 81-2 (now 14-2).

2. See *UW-M Post v. Board of Regents*, 774 F. Supp. 1163 (E.D. Wis. 1991).

3. See *Bakke v. Board of Regents*, 438 US 265 (1978).

4. *Grutter v. Bollinger*, 506 US 306 (2003).

5. *Gratz v. Bollinger*, 539 US 244 (2003).

6. Minutes of March 9, 2001, Regular Meeting of the BOR. Regents Fred Mohs, Greg Gracz, and Guy Gottschalk opposed the motion.

7. See Minutes of the September 7, 2001, Regular Meeting of the BOR.

8. The *Grutter* case sustained the University of Michigan Law School admissions program. The companion *Gratz* case involved a challenge to the university's undergraduate admissions policy, which the Court concluded did not meet constitutional standards. The UW System policies were similar to those of the Michigan Law School.

9. Unlike private universities, state universities are subject to the US Constitution's First Amendment ban on infringing freedom of speech. Although the First Amendment provides only that *"Congress* shall make no law . . . abridging the freedom of speech," the prohibition is applicable to states and their agencies, such as state universities, under the Fourteenth Amendment.

10. In a line of cases dating to the 1940s, the US Supreme Court had recognized that governmentally compelled speech or association could violate the Constitution. In these decisions, the Supreme Court held that various governmentally imposed requirements such as saluting the flag, affirming a belief in God, and displaying a state's "Live Free or Die" motto on automobile license plates were unconstitutional "compelled speech" or "compelled association." Opponents of student fees contended that being forced to provide financial support for groups expressing views and engaging in activities they found offensive was, likewise, compelled speech or association in violation of their First Amendment rights.

11. Some courts concluded that the fees did not violate students' constitutional rights so long as they were used to support programs and activities that

included a wide range of views, fostering free expression in general but without compelling any particular speech or association. Other courts simply found no constitutional violations or determined that any infringement of rights was adequately addressed by compliance with state restrictions on the use of fees.

12. See, e.g., *Galda v. Rutgers*, 772 F. 2d 1060 (3d Cir. 1985); *Carroll v. Blinken*, 957 F. 2d 991 (2d Cir. 1992); *Carroll v. Blinken*, 42 F. 3d 122 (2d Cir. 1994); *Smith v. Regents of the University of California*, 844 P. 2d 500 (Cal. 1993).

13. §36.09(5), Wisconsin Statutes (1974), provided: "The students of each institution or campus subject to the responsibilities and powers of the board [of regents], the president [of the UW System], the chancellor and the faculty shall be active participants in the immediate governance of and policy development for such institutions. As such, students shall have primary responsibility for the formulation and review of policies concerning student life, services and interests. Students in consultation with the chancellor and subject to the final confirmation of the board shall have the responsibility for the disposition of those student fees which constitute substantial support for campus student activities. The students of each institution or campus shall have the right to organize themselves in a manner they determine and to select their representatives to participate in institutional governance."

14. The national PIRG had throughout the 1980s pursued a successful strategy of affiliating with universities to gain student fee support for their consumer protection and other public-interest activities. The University of Minnesota was the first school to affiliate with PIRG, establishing MPIRG, and was quickly followed by the University of Oregon, with OSPIRG. Both schools relied on student fees to fund their PIRG organizations. Other schools followed suit, providing student fees funding for their own PIRG chapters. Although they characterized their activities as politically neutral, the PIRGs supported liberal causes, and many of their programs were not conducted on the campuses that supported them, instead involving broader community organizing and legislative lobbying efforts.

15. WisPIRG also secured student fees funding at UW–Milwaukee.

16. The UW System, too, faced pressure to provide student fees funding for Systemwide organizations. Student governments from most UW campuses joined in asking the Board of Regents to impose an additional fee to fund a UW Systemwide student government representing the combined student bodies of all System institutions. In addition, following the approach, taken by PIRGs nationally, of associating with universities, the Wisconsin Public Interest Research Group (WisPIRG) requested funding for its programs through a Systemwide membership fee. Aware of the lack of engagement by most students in student government matters and wary of being drawn into the kind of litigation over PIRGs brought against other schools, UW leaders were reluctant to approve Systemwide fees for student activities. Nevertheless, in 1985 the Board of Regents established a "mandatory refundable fee" for the support of the UW

System United Council of Student Governments, a membership organization composed of the elected student governments at UW campuses. Because this fee was refundable, it was not challenged by Southworth. In the 2013–15 budget, however, the legislature defunded the United Council.

17. See History of Associated Students of Madison at https://www.asm.wisc.edu.

18. Because §36.09(5), Wisconsin Statutes, required that students have a voice in campus governance, some form of student-selected organization was needed to provide that voice, and UW–Madison's associate dean of students, Roger Howard, assisted in the formation of the ASM and in obtaining recognition for it as the student government by the campus administration.

19. The others were Amy Schoepke and Keith Bannock.

20. Active in other cases involving mandatory student fees, the ADF worked to deny funding to student groups opposed to "biblical values, religious freedom and the spread of the gospel." To achieve that goal, the organization was prepared to bankroll lawsuits attacking mandatory student fees.

21. There were also practical reasons for defending the operation of the fees system. Exempting students from any part of the mandatory fees could seriously undermine the entire program. If students could pick and choose among groups to support or could avoid paying major portions of the fees, some organizations—particularly small groups without any other sources of support—might be left with no funding at all, forcing them out of existence. And, if the overall number of student organizations declined, the program would be less effective in reaching all students and achieving its educational goals. Further, because the actual mandatory fees were quite low, it was difficult to identify, calculate, and apply refunds or exemptions. Devising a system that could accommodate a large number of students seeking partial refunds would be administratively problematic, while too many exemptions from the mandatory fees could doom the program completely.

22. Personal note to the author.

23. *Abood v. Detroit Bd. of Educ.*, 431 US 209 (1977). Similarly, in *Keller v. State Bar*, 496 US 1 (1990), dealing with bar association dues and other dues cases, the Court found that the state could require that the dues be paid but that the rights of objecting individuals were entitled to protection in the form of an exemption from portions of the dues used to pay for lobbying and similar activities.

24. 515 US 819 (1995).

25. *Board of Regents v. Southworth*, 529 U.S. 217 (2000). Wisconsin assistant attorney general Susan Ullman appeared on behalf of the UW, while attorney Jordan Lorance of ADF represented the objecting students.

26. See Andrew Krueger, "Supreme Court Favors UW, 9-0," *Daily Cardinal*, March 23, 2000.

27. Michael Dimock, "Defining Generations: Where Millennials End and Post-Millennials Begin," Pew Research Center, March 1, 2018.

28. See, e.g., Adam Taylor, "These Are America's Nine Longest Foreign Wars," *Washington Post*, May 29, 2014.

29. See "Freshman 101: How to Survive—and Stop—a Campus Shooting," *Milwaukee Journal Sentinel*, August 30, 2008. Other UW institutions, including UW–Superior and UW–Parkside, had also purchased the program for use.

30. By administrative rule, the UW System prohibits anyone other than law enforcement officers from carrying or possessing dangerous weapons on university lands or in university buildings or facilities (Section 18.10[3], Wisconsin Administrative Code). The enforceability of this rule has, however, been limited in light of Wisconsin's Concealed Carry Law (2011 Wisconsin Act 35).

31. M. Alex Johnson, "College Security Tighter, but Is It Enough?" MSNBC .com (November 17, 2008).

32. Among regents, too, there was growing support for holding down tuition. See Minutes of the July 12, 2001, Regular Meeting of the BOR, where State Superintendent of Public Instruction Elizabeth Burmaster voted against tuition increases.

33. See, e.g., Linette Lopez, "America's Student Debt Nightmare Actually Started in the 1980s," *Business Insider*, October 13, 2015.

34. The Fund for Wisconsin Scholars, established by John and Tashia Morgridge in 2008, was in part an effort to address this problem of "unmet need."

35. See Dimock, "Defining Generations"; "Americans Name the 10 Most Significant Historic Events of Their Lifetimes," Pew Research Center, December 15, 2016.

36. See David Leonhardt, "Is College Worth It? Clearly, New Data Say," *New York Times*, May 27, 2014.

37. See Minutes of the December 9, 2010, Regular Meeting of the BOR.

38. Dimock, "Defining Generations."

39. See, e.g., Preston Schmitt, "One Text Away," *On Wisconsin*, Fall 2016; Patti K. See, "Confessions of a (Sometimes) Helicopter Parent," *Inside Higher Education*, July 16, 2010; Jessica Ullian, "The Really Long Good-Bye, Part 2," *BU Today*, 2007.

40. Millennials were expected to soon become the largest generation in the United States, outnumbering their baby-boomer parents by 2018. Dimock, "Defining Generations."

41. By 2015, a striking 40 percent of millennials would say they supported speech limitations. Jacob Poushter, Pew Research Center (November 20, 2015).

Chapter 9. The Going Gets Much Tougher

1. A national search had produced a small pool of finalists, including Reilly, former Wisconsin congressman Steve Gunderson, and SUNY executive vice president Elizabeth Capaldi.

2. Cronon and Jenkins, *The University of Wisconsin*.

3. Kevin Reilly, interviewed by Troy Reeves, UARM (2015).

4. He was especially fond of Irish literary references, for example his reading at the February 5, 2010, Regular Meeting of the BOR of Molly Bloom's soliloquy from James Joyce's *Ulysses*.

5. Minutes of the November 4 and December 9–10, 2004, Regular Meetings of the BOR; Report of the Wisconsin Technology Council (2004).

6. Minutes of the July 7, 2005, Regular Meeting of the BOR.

7. See, e.g., remarks of Stephanie Hilton, of the United Council of Student Governments, in the Minutes of the February 11, 2005, Regular Meeting of the BOR.

8. Minutes of the December 9, 2004, Regular Meeting of the BOR.

9. The argument has had continued vitality. See, e.g., "The Connection between Educational Attainment and Earnings, Amplified by the Four-Year College Degree/Optimizing Education," blog.masu.org, February 20, 2019.

10. See, e.g., remarks of C. Peter McGrath of the National Association of State Universities and Land Grant Colleges, in the Minutes of the December 9, 2005, Meeting of the BOR.

11. Minutes of the September 9, 2004, Regular Meeting of the BOR.

12. Lack of degree attainment was also a national problem. As the number of degree holders in other nations continued to climb, US graduation rates were stagnant or declining.

13. Minutes of the February 9, 2006, Regular Meeting of the BOR.

14. Kevin Reilly, interviewed by Troy Reeves, UARM (2015).

15. Minutes of the March 9, 2006, Regular Meeting of the BOR.

16. Minutes of the June 7, 2007, Regular Meeting of the BOR.

17. See, e.g., comments of Glenn Grothman in the Minutes of the March 10, 2006, Regular Meeting of the BOR; comments of Scott Suder reported by board president Walsh in the Minutes of the April 13, 2007, Regular Meeting of the BOR.

18. Minutes of the August 2, 2006, Special Meeting of the BOR.

19. Minutes of the February 9, 2006, Regular Meeting of the BOR.

20. The System had recently received generous gifts from the Great Lakes Higher Education Corporation and from John and Tashia Morgridge, who established the Fund for Wisconsin Scholars, a permanent endowment to award grant support to low-income students whose educational costs were not fully covered by federal or state grants or loans. Minutes of the June 5, 2008, Regular Meeting of the BOR (presentation of Mary Gulbrandsen).

21. Minutes of the November 8, 2007, Regular Meeting of the BOR.

22. Minutes of the March 5, 2009, Regular Meeting of the BOR, at which the Final Report on Plan 2008 was discussed and *Inclusive Excellence* was announced.

23. See, e.g., Minutes of the April 10–11, 2008, Regular Meeting of the BOR.

24. See Minutes of the July 1, 2008, Regular Meeting of the BOR, at which the board exercised its authority under Regent Policy Document 6-5 (2003) to

raise executive salary ranges, making chancellors and others whose pay had been effectively capped by the old ranges eligible for salary increases. Reilly himself became eligible for an increase, but to avoid the appearance of any conflict of interest, he chose to donate his raise to the UW Foundation for scholarships.

25. Kevin Reilly, interviewed by Troy Reeves, UARM (2015).

26. See Chapter UWS 4, Wisconsin Administrative Code (1975).

27. These administrative positions, or "limited" appointments, typically included executive positions such as chancellors and vice chancellors and System president and vice presidents. See Chapter UWS 15, Wisconsin Administrative Code (1975).

28. See Minutes of the October 6–7, 2005, Regular Meeting of the BOR, and the November 3, 2005, Special Committee Meeting of the Faculty and Academic Staff Disciplinary Process Committee of the BOR.

29. See Chapter UWS 7, Wisconsin Administrative Code (2007).

30. See Minutes of the November 10 and December 8, 2006, Regular Meetings of the BOR.

31. See Terry Devitt, https://news.wisc.edu/research-on-human-embryonic-stem-cells, November 6, 2008.

32. See *Board of Regents of the University of Wisconsin System v. Southworth*, 529 U.S, 217 (2000).

33. Agreed Order of Settlement, No. 06-C-0562-S (W.D. Wis. Apr. 11, 2007); No. 3-06-CV-649 (W.D. Wis. Dismissed May 3, 2007). Under the agreement, for example, a Jewish student could not be prohibited from joining the Roman Catholic student organization, as long as she affirmed her agreement with the organization's beliefs and goals; in addition, as long as the student organization did not prevent her from joining, it would retain its status as a recognized student organization eligible for student fee funding.

34. *Badger Catholic, Inc. v. Walsh*, 578 F. Supp. 2d 1121 (2008), rec. den., 590 F. Supp. 2d 1083 (2008), 620 F. 3d 775 (7th Cir. 2010), cert. den. (2011).

35. Kevin Reilly, interviewed by Troy Reeves, UARM (2015).

36. See Minutes of the February 8 and June 6, 2008, Meetings of the BOR. The "structural deficit" is, essentially, the amount by which the state's revenues are less than the amounts it has budgeted to spend on state agencies, including the UW System, in a particular year.

37. Minutes of the October 3, 2008, Regular Meeting of the BOR; Opinion, "State Money for 'U' Must Improve," *Wisconsin State Journal*, September 28, 2008.

38. Minutes of the November 6, 2008, Regular Meeting of the BOR.

39. See Robert Rich, Federal Reserve Bank of New York, Federal Reserve History (November 2013), www.federalreserve.gov.

40. Minutes of the July 9, 2009, Regular Meeting of the BOR.

41. Kevin Reilly, interviewed by Troy Reeves, UARM (2015).

42. Kevin Reilly, interviewed by Troy Reeves, UARM (2015).

43. Minutes of the June 10–11, 2010, Regular Meeting of the BOR.

44. Minutes of the July 23, 2010, Special Meeting of the BOR.

45. Biddy Martin interviewed by Todd Finkelmeyer, *Capital Times*, August 27, 2008.

46. See Foley, "Selection of Openly Gay Leader Praised," *Wisconsin State Journal*, May 30, 2008.

47. See, e.g., Opinion, "New Chancellor Offers Fresh Start," *Wisconsin State Journal*, August 24, 2008.

48. "Martin Meets with WMC Leaders," *Wisconsin State Journal*, November 18, 2008; Mark Pitsch, Jason Stein, and Deborah Ziff, "Wiley Blasts WMC's Influence," *Wisconsin State Journal*, August 22, 2008; John Wiley, "From Crossroads to Crisis," *Madison Magazine*, September 2008.

49. Minutes of the May 8, 2009, Regular Meeting of the BOR.

50. Minutes of the June 11, 2010, Regular Meeting of the BOR.

51. Minutes of the August 19–20, 2010, Regular Meeting of the BOR.

52. Minutes of the November 4, 2010, Regular Meeting of the BOR.

53. Minutes of the December 10, 2010, Regular Meeting of the BOR.

54. Minutes of the December 10, 2010, Regular Meeting of the BOR.

Chapter 10. De-Merger, Division, and Distrust

1. The $3.6 billion deficit figure was disputed by Democrats. Former state senator Tim Cullen argued that the amount was exaggerated and that the current-year deficit was minimal, noting that the $3.6 billion included not only ongoing state commitments but also some $1.2 billion in state agency requests for new funds, while the current-year shortage of $137 million was small, representing only 0.2 percent of the total state budget—not enough to require a repair bill under Legislative Fiscal Bureau guidelines. See Cullen, *Ringside Seat*, 117–18.

2. See, e.g., comments of Regent Danial Gelatt in the 1996 *Study of the UW System in the 21st Century* and *Charting a New Course*, Office of the Secretary to the University of Wisconsin Board of Regents (2004).

3. See Chapter 233, Wisconsin Statutes. Public authorities are creatures of state law, with powers defined and limited by state statutes on the basis of the specific public functions they serve but typically structured as quasi-public corporate entities with management powers similar to those of private business organizations. As of 2010, Wisconsin had established two such state authorities, the Wisconsin Housing and Economic Development Authority (WHEDA) (Chapter 234, Wisconsin Statutes) and the University of Wisconsin Hospitals and Clinics Authority (UWHCA).

4. Kevin Reilly, interviewed by the author (2015); Charles Pruitt, interviewed by the author (2015); Minutes of the February 25, 2011, Special Meeting of the BOR.

5. See, e.g., Reilly's report from a Carnegie Council meeting on the subject, Minutes of the November 6, 2008, Regular Meeting of the BOR; Lyall and Sell, *True Genius of America at Risk*, 105–24.

6. A few public universities—including Wisconsin's neighbors the University of Michigan and the University of Minnesota—enjoy state constitutional protections that afford them considerable operational autonomy. See Michigan Constitution, Article VIII, Sections 3 and 4; Minnesota Constitution, Article VIII, Section 4.

7. See Lyall and Sell, *True Genius of America at Risk*.

8. A complex piece of legislation, the Virginia Act creates a three-tier hierarchy of autonomy under which all institutions agree to meet certain statewide goals and receive Level 1 status, while the highest level of autonomy, Level III status, permits universities with demonstrated capacity to provide more complex management functions to negotiate management agreements with the state that give them full tuition-setting authority and independent management powers. Level III institutions include the University of Virginia, the College of William and Mary, Virginia Technical Institute, and Virginia Commonwealth University. See www.virginia.edu/restructuring/restrucuring.html, Rector and Visitors of the University of Virginia (2018).

9. See, e.g., David W. Leslie and Robert O. Berdahl, "The Politics of Restructuring Higher Education in Virginia: A Case Study," *Review of Higher Education* (Spring 2008) 31, no. 3, discussing the risks of gaining procedural freedom from state regulation in exchange for tighter state controls of the substantive academic purposes and activities of public universities.

10. Christian Schneider, *Wisconsin Public Research Institute Report: Making the University of Wisconsin More Accountable through Greater Autonomy*, December 2010, vol. 23, no. 3.

11. See Minutes of the February 25, 2011, Special Meeting of the BOR.

12. Ibid.; also Charles Pruitt, interviewed by the author (2015); Kevin Reilly, interviewed by Troy Reeves, UARM (2016).

13. See Cullen, *Ringside Seat*, 117–18.

14. See, e.g., Thompson and Moe, *Tommy*, 115–17, in which the former governor describes his collaborative relationship with the late Marty Beil, executive director of the Wisconsin State Employees Union, a division of the American Federation of State, County, and Municipal Employees, in negotiating state employee labor contracts.

15. See Jason Stein and Patrick Marley, *More Than They Bargained For: Scott Walker, Unions, and the Fight for Wisconsin* (Madison: University of Wisconsin Press, 2013), 36–38; see also "Scott Walker and ALEC Have Long History," *Badger Democracy*, June 10, 2011.

16. See Stein and Marley, *More Than They Bargained For*, 22–23. While not an issue in the 2010 campaign, however, Walker's longstanding intention to curtail union rights was revealed later. In a video taped during the 2010 election

but surfaced during the 2012 effort to recall him, Walker expressed sympathy for making Wisconsin a "right-to-work" state—that is, a state where union membership and dues paying could not be compelled, even in the private sector—telling one of his major financial backers, roofing supplies billionaire Diane Hendricks, that he would indeed pursue right-to-work legislation.

17. See Stein and Marley, *More Than They Bargained For*, 56–58.

18. Some UW Medical School physicians went so far as to provide medical excuses for protesters missing work to attend demonstrations, actions that brought disciplinary actions against them.

19. See, e.g., Abby Sewell, "Protesters Out in Force Nationwide to Oppose Wisconsin's Anti-union Bill," *Los Angeles Times*, February 26, 2011.

20. See e-mail message of February 18, 2011, from UW–Madison University Committee to UW–Madison faculty (Office of the UW–Madison Secretary of the Faculty).

21. Senator Tim Cullen of Janesville, Superior's Bob Jauch, and other colleagues did reach out to legislative Republicans, but to no avail. See Cullen, *Ringside Seat*, for a full description of the events surrounding the trip to Illinois and the effort to negotiate with the Republicans.

22. Ordinarily, a quorum of the thirty-three-member Senate is seventeen senators, but because Act 10 was originally a budget measure, under Senate rules the quorum requirement was twenty. By removing the budget provisions, Fitzgerald was able—with the concurrence of the Republican Assembly—to force the vote.

23. Only one Republican, Senator Dale Schultz, voted against the measure.

24. On March 18, 2011, Dane County circuit court judge Maryann Sumi stayed implementation, in a decision that was later overturned by the Wisconsin Supreme Court. Other lawsuits, based on different legal theories as to why Act 10 should not be enforced, followed.

25. *WEAC v. Walker*, Nos. 12–1854, 12–2100, and 12–2058 (Seventh Circuit Court of Appeals, 2013); *Madison Teachers, Inc., et al., v. Walker, et al.*, 2014 WI 99.

26. Charles Pruitt, interviewed by the author (2015).

27. §15.91, Wisconsin Statutes.

28. Martin memo to Huebsch, dated January 7, 2011, from the *Wayback Machine*, http://budget.wisc.edu/up-content/uploads/2011/02; see also Martin e-mail dated February 18, 2011, to Members of the Campus Community, Subject "Update on the New Badger Partnership" (Kevin Reilly files, UW System Administration), in which she explains the sequence of events leading to the governor's budget proposal to separate UW–Madison from the System.

29. Martin memo to Huebsch, January 7, 2011.

30. Martin, February 18, 2011, e-mail to Campus Community.

31. Ibid.

32. Ibid.

33. February 8, 2011, letter, Reilly to Walker (Kevin Reilly files, UW System Administration).

34. Minutes of the February 11, 2011, Regular Meeting of the BOR.

35. Charles Pruitt, interviewed by the author (2015).

36. Sharif Durhams and Alan Borsuk, "Walker to Gut MPS, Break Up UW, Education Leaders Say," *Milwaukee Journal Sentinel*, February 16, 2011; Deborah Ziff, "State of Chaos; UW–Madison: $50 Million Cut in State Aid Could Mean Splitting from System, 20% Tuition Hike," *Wisconsin State Journal*, February 18, 2011.

37. See Martin, February 18, 2011, memorandum to "Campus Community." The release of this memo, coming when it did, led to criticism of Martin for lack of transparency in communicating to the campus the details of the NBP and her dealings with the governor. See Opinion, "Transparency Key for Partnership; Chancellor Needed to Be Open Earlier," *Daily Cardinal*, February 22, 2011, suggesting Martin should have leveled with the university community earlier with regard to the details of the separation plan.

38. E-mail, Reilly to author, September 25, 2018.

39. Notes dated February 21, 2011 (Reilly files, UW System Administration).

40. Letter, Reilly to Martin, February 22, 2011 (Reilly files, UW System Administration).

41. Sharif Durhams, "UW–Madison Current, Former Heads Defend Split from UW System," *Milwaukee Journal Sentinel*, February 24, 2011; Donna Shalala, "Shalala: UW–Madison Needs New Business Model," *Wisconsin State Journal*, February 23, 2011; Sharif Durhams, "University Model for UW Autonomy," *Milwaukee Journal Sentinel*, February 20, 2011; Deborah Ziff, "Divided over UW Division," *Wisconsin State Journal*, February 21, 2011.

42. Deborah Ziff, "Leaders Debate Proposal," *Wisconsin State Journal*, February 26, 2011.

43. See, e.g., Deborah Ziff, "Divided over UW Division; Some See Splitting UW–Madison from System as Return to Bad Old Days; Martin Says It Would Bring Autonomy," *Wisconsin State Journal*, February 20, 2011, quoting former UW–Madison chancellor John Wiley and former regent president Jay Smith; Sharif Durhams, "University Model for UW Autonomy," *Milwaukee Journal Sentinel*, February 22, 2011, quoting former UW System president Robert M. O'Neil.

44. See, e.g., Sam Dillon, "At Public Universities, Warnings of Privatization," *New York Times*, October 16, 2005.

45. Minutes of the February 25, 2011, Special Meeting of the BOR.

46. See, e.g., Gelatt comments on the *Twenty-First Century Study*.

47. Lyall and Sell, *The True Genius of America at Risk*.

48. Ziff, "Divided over UW Division."

49. Jason Stein and Sharif Durhams, "Lobbyist Group Forms to Back UW–Madison Split from System," *Milwaukee Journal Sentinel*, March 3, 2011. Scholz was a former executive director of the Wisconsin Republican Party.

50. Minutes of the March 10, 2011, Regular Meeting of the BOR; Todd Finkelmeyer, "Walker Has Divided Us," *Capital Times*, March 16, 2011.

51. Minutes of the March 10, 2011, Regular Meeting of the BOR.

52. Charles Pruitt, interviewed by the author (2015).

53. Deborah Ziff, "Leaders Debate Proposal; Other System Campuses Seek Same Flexibility UW Madison Could Have," *Wisconsin State Journal*, February 26, 2011.

54. E-mail message, Martin to Faculty, Staff, and Students, April 6, 2011 (Kevin Reilly files, UW System Administration).

55. E-mail message, Martin to Reilly, Pruitt, and Spector, April 7, 2011 (Board of Regents files, Office of the Board Secretary).

56. Minutes of the April 7, 2011, Regular Meeting of the BOR.

57. Paul Fanlund, "At UW–Madison, Right Diagnosis, Wrong Remedy," *Capital Times*, May 11, 2011.

Chapter 11. Punitive Damage

1. Minutes of the June 9–10 and September 8, 2011, Regular Meetings of the BOR.

2. Minutes of the September 8, 2011, Regular Meeting of the BOR.

3. 2011 Wisconsin Act 32.

4. See Report of the Special Task Force on UW Restructuring and Operational Flexibilities, UW System Board of Regents (August 13, 2012).

5. Minutes of the October 7, 2011, Regular Meeting of the BOR. It was agreed at the meeting that this last ad hoc committee would replace a separate committee Reilly had proposed to study the benefits and drawbacks of institution-level boards.

6. Minutes of the December 8, 2011, Regular Meeting of the BOR.

7. Minutes of the February 9–10, 2012, Regular Meeting of the BOR.

8. See Report of the Special Task Force.

9. Ibid., 33–41.

10. 2011 Wisconsin Act 89; §15.91, Wisconsin Statutes.

11. See Nancy Zimpher, "Systemness: Unpacking the Value of Higher Education Systems," in Lane and Johnstone, eds., *Higher Education Systems 3.0.*

12. See §36.09(1), Wisconsin Statutes.

13. Other Wisconsin elected officials, too, were the subject of recall petitions in 2012, producing the largest number of recalls against lawmakers from one state in the nation's history. See Stein and Patrick, *More Than They Bargained For*, 264–73.

14. Dee J. Hall and Samara Kalk Derby, "Gov. Scott Walker Unveils His Agenda for Wisconsin during Speech in California," *Wisconsin State Journal*, November 19, 2012.

15. See Stein and Marley, *More Than They Bargained For*.

16. See Katherine J. Cramer, *The Politics of Resentment* (Chicago: University of Chicago Press, 2016); Katherine Cramer Walsh, "Putting Inequality in Its Place: Rural Consciousness and the Power of Perspective," *American Political Science Review* 6, no. 3 (2012); Katherine C. Walsh, "Making Sense of the Link between Anti-Government and Small Government Attitudes," American Political Science Association Annual Meeting, August 23, 2012.

17. Katherine Cramer Walsh, "Listen to the Legitimacy of Other Voters," *Wisconsin State Journal*, June 23, 2012.

18. See Paul Fanlund, "Race, Rural Identity Shape Wisconsin," *Capital Times*, August 27, 2012.

19. Cullen, *Ringside Seat*, 79–89.

20. Thompson and Moe, *Tommy*; Tom Loftus, interviewed by the author (2016); Jim Doyle, interviewed by the author (2017).

21. American Legislative Exchange Council, www.ALEC.org.

22. Doug Porter, "The ALEC Annual Meeting in San Diego: Who's Coming and Why," *San Diego Free Press*, July 17, 2015.

23. Report of the Special Task Force, 9–11; see also remarks of Dr. McGuinness, Minutes of the December 8, 2011, Regular Meeting of the BOR.

24. American Legislative Exchange Council, www.ALEC.org.

25. Bylaws of the Board of Regents of the University of Wisconsin System.

26. Minutes of the June 10, 2011, Regular Meeting of the BOR.

27. The fourteen citizen board members serve staggered seven-year terms, and the two student members serve two-year terms. See §15.91, Wisconsin Statutes. As a result, three board terms expire annually, creating normal turnover in membership that allows a new governor's appointees to gradually become the majority—usually within around three years, fewer if there are resignations—and so to control the board and its leadership positions. The shift is not immediate, though, and in 2011, despite Walker's 2010 election, Doyle appointees, mostly Democrats, remained in the majority.

28. One of the few exceptions to the Wisconsin Open Meetings Law, secret ballots are permitted for the election of the officers of a governmental body, §19.88(1), Wisconsin Statutes.

29. Minutes of the June 8, 2012, Regular Meeting of the BOR.

30. Ibid.

31. Minutes of the August 23, 2012, Regular Meeting of the BOR.

32. Minutes of the December 6, 2012, Regular Meeting of the BOR.

33. Minutes of the February 8, 2013, Regular Meeting of the BOR; Caroline Porter, "College Degree, No Class Time Required," *Wall Street Journal*, January 24, 2013.

34. Kevin Reilly, interviewed by Troy Reeves, UARM (2016).

35. See Eric Kelderman, "State Spending on Higher Education Rebounds in Most States after Years of Decline," *Chronicle of Higher Education*, January 21, 2013.

36. Minutes of the August 23, 2012, Regular Meeting of the BOR.

37. Minutes of the March 7 and April 4, 2013, Regular Meetings of the BOR.

38. Although program revenues do not come from state taxpayers, they are kept in state accounts and are, in that sense, "state" funds subject to state control.

39. See www.wisconsin.edu/financial-administration, the UW System Administration site that publishes the System's annual financial reports and related documents.

40. The primary reserve ratio is calculated by dividing expendable net assets, including program revenue balances, by total operating expenses. See Letter of April 30, 2013, from Smith, Falbo, and Reilly to Senate president Michael G. Ellis (Reilly files, UW System Administration), providing background information on System financial reports and audits and the board's process for reviewing these reports.

41. Ibid.

42. Ibid.; the National Association of College and University Business Officers (NACUBO) recommends a program revenue balance of 40 percent of an institution's annual operating budget as a best practice.

43. See Reilly files, UW System Administration; Legislative Audit Bureau, "Level of Commitment for UW System Program Revenue Balances," Report 13-17 (2013).

44. See Dan Simmons, "Legislators Hammer UW Officials," *Wisconsin State Journal*, April 24, 2013; Douglas Belkin, "School's Reserve Fund Draws Ire," *Wall Street Journal*, April 24, 2013.

45. David J. Ward, interviewed by the author (2015).

46. Kevin Reilly, interviewed by Troy Reeves, UARM (2016).

47. See Minutes of the March 7, 1986, Regular Meeting of the BOR.

48. Kevin Reilly, interviewed by Troy Reeves, UARM (2016).

49. Paul Fanlund, "Ward Tries to Clear the Decks for His Successor," *Capital Times*, June 26–July 2, 2013.

50. Editorial, *Wisconsin State Journal*, August 1, 2013.

Chapter 12. The UW System on the Defensive

1. In the two months between Reilly's departure and Cross's taking office, UW–Whitewater chancellor Richard Telfer served as interim UW System president and was thanked for his service at the March meeting. Minutes of the March 6, 2010, Regular Meeting of the BOR.

2. Ibid.

3. Minutes of the April 10–11, 2014, Regular Meeting of the BOR; Regent Policy Document 21-9.

4. Minutes of the June 5–6, 2014, Regular Meeting of the BOR.

5. Minutes of the August 21–22, 2014, Regular Meeting of the BOR.

6. Minutes of the October 9–10, 2014, Regular Meeting of the BOR. UW–Madison, he noted, had been ranked the thirteenth best public university, while nine UW comprehensive campuses had placed among the top 25 regional public universities.

7. Minutes of the November 6, 2014, Regular Meeting of the BOR.

8. Minutes of the December 5, 2014, Regular Meeting of the BOR.

9. Scott Walker and Marc Thiessen, *Unintimidated: A Governor's Story and a Nation's Challenge* (New York: Sentinel, 2013).

10. 2015 Senate Bill 21 (Wisconsin Legislature).

11. See, e.g., Julie Bosman, "2016 Ambitions Seen in Walker's Push for University Cuts in Wisconsin," *New York Times*, February 16, 2015; Matt Viser, "Scott Walker's Political Ambitions Fostered at Marquette," *Boston Globe*, February 11, 2105; Jamelle Bouie, "Conservative Warrior," *Slate*, February 17, 2015.

12. See Jason Stein, Patrick Marley, and Karen Herzog, "Walker Forced to Admit UW Objected to Wisconsin Idea Changes," *Milwaukee Journal Sentinel*, February 5, 2015; Editorial, "Governor Walker's 'Drafting Error,'" *New York Times*, February 6, 2015; Alia Wong, "The Governor Who (Maybe) Tried to Kill Liberal-Arts Education," *Atlantic*, February 11, 2015. Walker's explanation was met with skepticism, as internal memoranda leaked to media—and later released in 2016 after a public-records lawsuit—revealed Walker's instructions for removal of the Wisconsin Idea from the statutes.

13. Minutes of the February 5, 2015, Regular Meeting of the BOR.

14. Ibid.

15. See Walsh-Cross e-mail messages of February 25–28, 2015 (Walsh Board files).

16. See, e.g., Dave Zweifel, "GOP Should Stop Playing Numbers Game with UW Cut," *Capital Times*, March 18, 2015.

17. Minutes of the March 5, 2015, Regular Meeting of the BOR. The actual amounts of the cuts at each UW institution varied. As the chancellors explained in detail at the meeting, the drawdown of program revenue balances in the previous years and other differing circumstances at the institutions had created differences in the actual amounts of the reductions they would face in the 2015–17 biennium. See also, John Conley, "This Is What Wisconsin's 2.5% Budget Cut Looks Like," *Chronicle of Higher Education*, March 27, 2015.

18. Ibid.

19. Ibid.

20. See, e.g., Mike Ivey, "Factory Owner Tax Cuts Cost $275 Million More—Twice Original Projections," *Capital Times*, March 11, 2015; see also Steven Salzberg, "Scott Walker Takes $250 Million from U. Wisconsin, Gives $250 million to Billionaire Sports Team Owner," *Forbes*, August 14, 2015, proposing the theory that Walker used the System cuts to help pay for a new arena for the Milwaukee Bucks basketball team.

21. Vos, a former student regent, had also strongly supported the repeal of

the statutory protections on tenure and governance, reportedly because of his frustration with litigation involving the dismissal of tenured faculty members.

22. Charles R. Pruitt, "Politics Is Cutting the Heart Out of Public Ivies," *Washington Post*, September 2, 2016.

23. See, e.g., Peter Schmidt, "Faculty Foe: Scott Walker," *Chronicle of Higher Education*, December 18, 2015.

24. See Minutes of the September 10–11, 2015, Regular Meeting of the BOR.

25. See Minutes of the April 10, 2015, Regular Meeting of the BOR.

26. Minutes of the March 10, 2016, Regular Meeting of the BOR.

27. Minutes of the July 9, 2015, Regular Meeting of the BOR.

28. Minutes of the June 9, 2016, Regular Meeting of the BOR.

29. See, e.g., Karin Fischer and Jack Stripling, "An Era of Neglect," *Chronicle of Higher Education*, Mach 3, 2014; David Sarasohn, "The Republican War on Public Universities, *New Republic*, August 10, 2016; Jeremy Suri, "Public Universities Need Cheap Political Attacks to End," *Dallas News*, January 1, 2015; and *Starving the Beast*, documentary film, 2016.

30. Minutes of the August 18, 2016, Regular Meeting of the BOR.

31. §36.112, Wisconsin Statutes (2017).

32. §36.115, Wisconsin Statutes (2017).

33. §36.64, Wisconsin Statutes (2017).

34. Minutes of the October 6, 2017, Regular Meeting of the BOR, 3–4.

35. See, e.g., Nico Savidge, Madison.com, August 27, 2016; Nicholas Hillman, *Why Performance-Based College Funding Doesn't Work*, Century Foundation College Completion Series, Part 4 (May 25, 2016).

36. Minutes of the December 6, 2017, Regular Meeting of the BOR, 23.

37. Ibid.

38. See the model Campus Free Speech Act of the Goldwater Institute, https://goldwaterinstitute.org; compare Regent Policy Document 4–21.

39. See, e.g., Allison Geyer, "Speech Wars," *Isthmus*, March 23–29, 2017; Pat Schneider, "Gagging the UW," *Capital Times*, June 7, 2017; Tom Loftus, "UW Doesn't Need State Law to Ensure Free Speech," Madison.com, April 14, 2017.

40. Minutes of the October 6, 2017, Regular Meeting of the BOR.

41. Minutes of the November 9, 2017, Regular Meeting of the BOR. In the course of implementing the proposal, some changes were made, and, among other items, Public Broadcasting was shifted to UW–Madison.

42. Minutes of the November 9, 2017, Regular Meeting of the BOR.

43. Ibid.

Appendix

1. "U.S. News: UWL Still Top-Ranked in UW System," *Campus News*, September 12, 2016, https://news.uwlax.edu/u-s-news-uwl-still-top-ranked-in-uw-system/.

2. https://uwosh.edu/about-uw-oshkosh/points-of-pride/, accessed March 2019.

3. https://www.uwp.edu.

4. https://www.uwplatt.edu/150/uw-platteville-history.

5. https://www.uwplatt.edu/ems/uw-platteville-engineering -partnerships.

6. https://www.uwsuper.edu/about/mission-history.cfm (but this source is in conflict with this source about Madison: https://hlcaccreditation.wisc .edu/).

7. Walker D. Wyman, ed., *History of the Wisconsin State Universities* (River Falls, WI: River Falls State Press, 1968).

8. Ibid.

9. Rob Reischel, "In Southern Wisconsin, a Winner Takes All," *New York Times*, May 30, 2014.

10. https://www.uwex.uwc.edu/about.

Bibliography

Interviewees

Adamany, David (adviser to Governor Lucey; secretary of the Department of Revenue, 1973–76; higher education leader at several institutions, ending his career as president of Temple University, 2010–16), telephone interview with the author, November 6, 2014.

Blank, Rebecca (chancellor, University of Wisconsin–Madison, July 2013–), interview with the author, Madison, WI, March 27, 2017.

Bradley, Mark (regent and board president, University of Wisconsin System, 2007–9), interview with the author, Madison, WI, May 11, 2017.

Cohen, Bernard (acting chancellor, University of Wisconsin–Madison, 1987), interview with the author, Madison, WI, April 14, 2018.

Cross, Ray (chancellor, University of Wisconsin Colleges and University of Wisconsin–Extension; president, University of Wisconsin System, 2014–20), interview with the author, Madison, WI, October 20, 2016.

Doyle, James, Jr. (governor of Wisconsin, 2003–11), interview with the author, Madison, WI, December 5, 2017.

Falbo, Michael (regent and board president, University of Wisconsin System, 2013–15), telephone interview with the author, August 2, 2018.

Gulbrandsen, Carl (managing director, Wisconsin Alumni Research Foundation, 2000–2016), interview with the author, Madison, WI, June 29, 2016.

Hanson, David (attorney and former legal counsel, University of Wisconsin–Madison, 1971–76), interview with the author, Shorewood Hills, WI, October 19, 2016.

Harris, Freda (director, assistant vice president, and associate vice president of budget and planning, 2004–16, University of Wisconsin System), interview with the author, Madison, WI, May 25, 2018.

Loftus, Tom (speaker of the Wisconsin Assembly, 1983–91; US ambassador to Norway, 1993–98; regent, University of Wisconsin System, 2006–13), interviews with the author, Madison, WI, June 24 and August 30, 2016.

Lyall, Katharine (president, University of Wisconsin System, 1992–2004), interviews with the author, Madison, WI, October 4, 2014, and November 12, 2015.

Mash, Don (chancellor, University of Wisconsin–Eau Claire, 1998–2005; executive senior vice president, University of Wisconsin System, 2005–8), interview with the author, Madison, WI, September 21, 2016.

McGuinness, Aims (National Center for Higher Education Management Systems), telephone interview with the author, November 16, 2015.

Miller, David (senior vice president and vice president for administration and fiscal affairs, University of Wisconsin System, 2013–16), interview with the author, Madison, WI, November 4, 2016.

Millner, Regina (regent and board president, University of Wisconsin System, 2015–17), interview with the author, Maple Bluff, WI, May 7, 2018.

O'Neil, Robert M. (president, University of Wisconsin System, 1980–85), telephone interview with the author, April 20, 2016.

Percy, Donald (senior vice president for administration, University of Wisconsin System, 1971–77), interview with the author, Madison, WI, May 2, 2014.

Peterson, Harry (administrative assistant to Chancellor Irving Shain, University of Wisconsin–Madison, 1978–87; chief of staff to Chancellor Donna Shalala, University of Wisconsin–Madison, 1988–91), interview with the author, Madison, WI, March 11, 2015.

Pruitt, Charles (regent and board president, University of Wisconsin System, 2009–11), interview with the author, Milwaukee, WI, September 14, 2015.

Reilly, Kevin (chancellor, University of Wisconsin Extension, 2000–2004; president, University of Wisconsin System, 2004–13), interviews with the author, Madison, WI, August 4, 2015, and June 9 and July 26, 2016.

Shalala, Donna (chancellor, University of Wisconsin–Madison, 1988–92), telephone interview with the author, October 7, 2017.

Shaw, Kenneth A. (president, University of Wisconsin System, 1985–91), telephone interview with the author, June 24, 2016.

Smith, Jay (regent and board president, University of Wisconsin, 2000–2002), telephone interview with the author, July 27, 2018.

Spector, Michael J. (regent and board president, University of Wisconsin System, 2011–12), interview with the author, Whitefish Bay, WI, September 11, 2014.

Stathas, Charles (general counsel, University of Wisconsin System, 1964–98), interview with the author, Shorewood Hills, WI, September 23, 2015.

Thompson, Tommy (governor of Wisconsin, 1987–2001), interview with the author, Madison, WI, June 16, 2016.

Walsh, David (regent and board president, University of Wisconsin System, 2005–7), interview with the author, Madison, WI, September 2, 2016.

Ward, David (chancellor, University of Wisconsin–Madison, 1993–2000 and 2011–13), interview with the author, Madison, WI, December 8, 2015.

Ward, David J. (acting chancellor, University of Wisconsin–Oshkosh, 1989–90;

senior vice president for academic affairs, University of Wisconsin System, 1994–2000 and 2015–16), interview with the author, Madison, WI, November 30, 2015.

Weerts, David (associate professor, University of Minnesota), telephone interview with the author, October 22, 2014.

Wiley, John (chancellor, University of Wisconsin–Madison, 2001–8), interview with the author, Madison, WI, 2015.

Sources

Bates, Tom. *Rads: The 1970 Bombing of the Army Math Research Center at the University of Wisconsin and Its Aftermath*. New York: HarperCollins, 1992.

Bohi, Janette. *A History of the Wisconsin State University Whitewater, 1868–1968*. Whitewater: Whitewater State University Foundation, 1967.

Bok, Derek Curtis. *Universities in the Marketplace: The Commercialization of Higher Education*. Princeton, NJ: Princeton University Press, 2003.

Bower, Jerry L. *The University of Wisconsin Colleges 1919–1997: The Wisconsin Idea at Work*. Friendship, WI: New Past Press, 2002.

Buhle, Mary Jo, and Paul Buhle, eds. *It Started in Wisconsin: Dispatches from the Front Lines of the New Labor Protest*. London: Verso, 2011.

Carter, Hilda R., and John R. Jenswold. *The University of Wisconsin–Eau Claire: A History, 1916–1976*. Eau Claire: University of Wisconsin–Eau Claire Foundation, 1976.

Cassell, Frank A., J. Martin Klotsche, and Frederick I. Olson. *The University of Wisconsin–Milwaukee: A Historical Profile, 1885–1992*. Milwaukee: UWM Foundation, 1992.

Cramer, Katherine J. *The Politics of Resentment: Rural Consciousness in Wisconsin and the Rise of Scott Walker*. Chicago: University of Chicago Press, 2016.

Cronon, Edmund David, and John W. Jenkins. *The University of Wisconsin: A History*. Vol. 3, *Politics, Depression, and War, 1925–1945*. Madison: University of Wisconsin Press, 1994.

———. *The University of Wisconsin: A History*. Vol. 4, *Renewal to Revolution, 1945–1971*. Madison: University of Wisconsin Press, 1999.

Cullen, Tim. *Ringside Seat: Wisconsin Politics: The 1970s to Scott Walker*. Mineral Point, WI: Little Creek Press, 2015.

Curti, Merle, and Vernon Carstensen. *The University of Wisconsin: A History, 1848–1925*. 2 vols. Madison: University of Wisconsin Press, 1949.

Downs, Donald Alexander. *Restoring Free Speech and Liberty on Campus*. Independent Studies in Political Economy. Oakland, CA: Independent Institute; New York: Cambridge University Press, 2005.

Drury, Gwen. *The Wisconsin Idea: The Vision That Made Wisconsin Famous*. https://sohe.wisc.edu/wordpress/wp-content/uploads/wi-idea-history-intro-summary-essay.pdf.

"A Forward Look: The Final Report of the Governor's Commission on Higher Education." Educational Resources Information Center, US Department of Education (November 1970).

Gaither, Gerald H. *The Multicampus System: Perspectives on Practice and Prospect*. Sterling, VA: Stylus, 1999.

Gamble, Richard D. *From Academy to University, 1866–1966: A History of the Wisconsin State University, Platteville, Wisconsin*. Platteville: Wisconsin State University, Platteville Foundation, 1966.

Gough, Robert J., and James W. Oberly. *Building Excellence: University of Wisconsin–Eau Claire, 1916–2016*. Virginia Beach, VA: University of Wisconsin Eau Claire Foundation, 2016.

Hansen, W. Lee, ed. *Academic Freedom on Trial: 100 Years of Sifting and Winnowing at the University of Wisconsin–Madison*. Madison: University of Wisconsin Press, 1998.

Heim, Joseph Peter. "Decision-Making in the Wisconsin Legislature: A Case Study of the Merger of the University of Wisconsin and the Wisconsin State University Systems." PhD diss., University of Wisconsin–Milwaukee, 1976.

Hoeveler, J. David. *John Bascom and the Origins of the Wisconsin Idea*. Madison: University of Wisconsin Press, 2017.

Hove, Arthur. *The University of Wisconsin: A Pictorial History*. Madison: University of Wisconsin Press, 1991.

Hunter, James Davison. *Culture Wars: The Struggle to Define America*. New York: Basic Books, 1991.

Hunter, James Davison, and Alan Wolfe. *Is There a Culture War?* Washington, DC: Brookings Institution, Pew Research Center, 2006.

Kauffman, Joseph. *The Selection of College and University Presidents*. Washington, DC: Association of American Colleges, 1974.

Kaufman, Dan. *The Fall of Wisconsin: The Conservative Conquest of a Progressive Bastion and the Future of American Politics*. New York: W. W. Norton, 2018.

Kerr, Clark. *The Great Transformation in Higher Education, 1960–80*. Albany: State University of New York Press, 1991.

Klotsche, J. Martin. *The University of Wisconsin–Milwaukee: An Urban University*. Milwaukee: University of Wisconsin–Milwaukee, 1972.

Knox, Alan B., and Joe Corry. "The Wisconsin Idea for the 21st Century." In *State of Wisconsin 1995–1996 Blue Book*, edited by Lawrence S. Barish, 181–92. Madison: Joint Committee on Legislative Organization of the Wisconsin Legislature, 1996.

Lane, Jason E., and D. Bruce Johnstone. *Higher Education System 3.0: Harnessing Systemness, Delivering Performance*. Albany: State University of New York Press, 2013.

Lee, Eugene C., and Frank M. Bowen. *The Multicampus University: A Study of Academic Governance*. New York: McGraw-Hill, 1971.

———. *Managing Multicampus Systems: Effective Administration in an Unsteady*

State. Carnegie Council on Policy Studies in Higher Education. San Francisco: Jossey-Bass, 1975.

Lyall, Katherine C., and Kathleen R. Sell. *The True Genius of America at Risk: Are We Losing Our Public Universities to De Facto Privatization?* Westport, CT: Praeger, 2006.

McCarthy, Charles. *The Wisconsin Idea*. New York: Macmillan, 1912.

Newfield, Christopher. *Unmaking the Public University: The Forty-Year Assault on the Middle Class*. Cambridge, MA: Harvard University Press, 2008.

Nichols, John. *Uprising: How Wisconsin Renewed the Politics of Protest, from Madison to Wall Street*. New York: Nation Books, 2012.

Noyes, Edward. *Here to Serve: The First Hundred Years of the University of Wisconsin–Oshkosh*, edited by Tom Herzing. Oshkosh: n.p., 1997.

Oliver, Robert. *Making the Modern Medical School: The Wisconsin Stories*. Canton, MA: Science History Publications, 2002.

Paul, Justus F. *The World Is Ours: A History of the University of Wisconsin–Stevens Point, 1894–1994*. Stevens Point: University of Wisconsin Stevens Point Press, 1994.

Planning the Future: Report of the Regents on the Future of the University of Wisconsin System. Madison: University of Wisconsin System, 1986.

Rost, J. "The Merger of the University of Wisconsin and the Wisconsin State University Systems: A Case Study in the Politics of Education." PhD diss., University of Wisconsin–Madison, 1973.

Sagrans, Erica, ed. *We Are Wisconsin: The Wisconsin Uprising in the Words of the Activists, Writers, and Everyday Wisconsinites Who Made It Happen*. Minneapolis, MN: Tasora Books, 2011.

Specht, Ellen L. *History of the Wisconsin State University at Stevens Point*. Stevens Point: n.p., 1969.

Stark, Jack. "The Wisconsin Idea: The University's Service to the State." In *State of Wisconsin 1995–1996 Blue Book*, edited by Lawrence S. Barish, 101–79. Madison: Joint Committee on Legislative Organization of the Wisconsin Legislature, 1996.

Stein, Jason, and Patrick Marley. *More Than They Bargained For: Scott Walker, the Unions, and the Fight for Wisconsin*. Madison: University of Wisconsin Press, 2013.

Sweeney, Vince. *Always a Badger: The Pat Richter Story*. Black Earth, WI: Trails Books, 2005.

Swoboda, Marian J., and Audrey Roberts, eds. *Wisconsin Women, Graduate School and the Professions*. Madison: University of Wisconsin System, Office of Women, 1980.

Thelin, John R. *A History of American Higher Education*. 2nd ed. Baltimore: Johns Hopkins University Press, 2011.

Thompson, Tommy G., and Doug Moe. *Tommy: My Journey of a Lifetime*. Madison: University of Wisconsin Press, 2018.

Walker, Scott, and Marc Thiessen. *Unintimidated: A Governor's Story and a Nation's Challenge*. New York: Sentinel, 2014.

Washburn, Jennifer. *University Inc.: The Corporate Corruption of Higher Education*. New York: Basic Books, 2006.

Weerts, D. J. *State Governments and Research Universities: A Framework for a Renewed Partnership*. New York: Routledge Palmer, 2002.

Weidemann, Dennis. *Cut from Plain Cloth: The 2011 Wisconsin Workers Protest*. Fitchburg, WI: Berens House, 2012.

Wyman, Walker D., ed. *History of the Wisconsin State Universities*. River Falls, WI: River Falls State University Press, 1968.

Index